Digital Crime and Digital Terrorism

ROBERT W. TAYLOR

TORY J. CAETI

D. KALL LOPER

ERIC J. FRITSCH

JOHN LIEDERBACH

PEARSON

Prentice
Hall

Upper Saddle River, New Jersey 07458

Library of Congress Cataloging-in-Publication Data

Digital crime and digital terrorism / Robert W. Taylor . . . [et al.].

   p. cm.

  ISBN 0-13-114137-6

 1. Computer crimes. 2. Cyberterrorism. 3. Computer hackers. 4. Computer
crimes—Investigation—United States. 5. Computer crimes—United States—Prevention. I. Taylor,
Robert W.

  HV6773.D54 2006

  364.16′8—dc22

                                                   2004028224

Executive Editor: Frank Mortimer, Jr.
Assistant Editor: Mayda C. Bosco
Production Editor: Karen Berry, Pine Tree
Composition
Production Liaison: Barbara Marttine Cappuccio
Director of Manfacturing and Production: Bruce
Johnson
Managing Editor: Mary Carnis
Manufacturing Buyer: Cathleen Petersen
Creative Director: Cheryl Asherman

Cover Design Coordinator: Miguel Ortiz
Cover Artist: Joseph DePinho
Cover Image: Boden/Ledingham/Masterfile
Executive Marketing Manager: Tim Peyton
Editorial Assistant: Kelly Krug
Formatting and Interior Design: Pine Tree
Composition
Printing and Binding: Phoenix Color Book
Technology Park

Pearson Education LTD.
Pearson Education Singapore, Pte. Ltd
Pearson Education, Canada, Ltd
Pearson Education–Japan
Pearson Education Australia PTY, Limited
Pearson Education North Asia Ltd
Pearson Educación de Mexico, S.A. de C.V.
Pearson Education Malaysia, Pte. Ltd
Pearson Education, Upper Saddle River, New Jersey

10 9 8 7 6 5 4 3
ISBN 0-13-114137-6

For Mary, Matt, Scott, and Laura

For Melinda, Anthony, and Lauren

For Matthew

For Cheryl, Jerod, Jacob, Joley, and Jadyn

For Allyson

Contents

CHAPTER 8
Anarchy and Hate on the World Wide Web   221

Preface

I was teaching the lab class for a doctoral statistics course in graduate school and had a very interesting interaction with one of my fellow students. The course was quite technical and complex, covering both statistical methods and the computer applications of the methods covered in class. Many of us were quite excited since this class would be one of the first utilizing SPSS™ for Windows™ 3.1, the first release not requiring the entry of command text from the code "bible." My job was to help the class with using the computer and instructing the lab portion of the course, each week serving as both the technical consultant and the lab instructor. During the first couple weeks, I kept getting strange glances and looks from one of the students in the course, a retired detective from a large metropolitan police department. During the fourth week of the course, his looks changed from confusion to pure frustration and irritation. Finally, he blurted out, "All right. That's it! What the hell do you mean 'doubleclick'?"

His comment and clear frustration taught me a lesson that I have not forgotten to this day when I teach technical courses and Internet courses for students, cops, and student-cops—not everyone is up to speed with current technology. Each year an infamous list is circulated from Beloit College that concerns the experience (or lack thereof) of the incoming freshman class. This is termed the mindset list. The list always reports some technological invention or innovation that the current class (at the time of this writing the class of 2008) has always had access to. Recently the list noted that the incoming class has always had access to e-mail, doesn't know what a vinyl LP is, UHF hasn't existed in their lifetime, and that PCs had long been invented and available to them when they started school. The technical competency among the population varies tremendously from the "wired" generation to the retired cops returning to school only to find that computers are now the norm and technical competency is required and expected in every course of instruction.

Even the more technically savvy among us have to marvel at the fact that we can do almost all of our academic research from our office, with full-text access to most academic journals and legal search engines. Conversely, professors and instructors must also now deal with "downloading your degree" issues such as Internet plagiarism and the electronic sharing of homework and other assignments. Regardless, it is the authors shared experience that there is little in the way of introductory textbooks covering the issues of digital crime and digital terrorism. We have found numerous books covering the details of the technical side of these issues and others that cover the legal side. However, there are very few works that attempt to provide a summary introduction and overview of these issues. Our approach in writing this book was to attempt to bridge the "technical" and knowledge gap that exists with many people in learning about the material in this area. In this vein, we have tried to approach the various topics covered in this book in a non-technical and non-jargon style. Criminal justice students and practitioners will find the technical components quite readable and understandable. Computer science students and practitioners will find the criminal justice material bereft of jargon and written in a readable and understandable style as well. In sum, we specifically tried to bridge the gap between criminal justice knowledge and competence and the technical issues that arise during investigations of the crimes and terrorist acts we cover. It is our fervent hope that the "technie" will get as much out of this book as the criminal justice student. Further, we believe that this book will help students and practitioners alike prepare for additional study in these areas.

The first section of the book covers the etiology of the digital crime and digital terrorism problem. The focus in this section is on the types of crimes and acts of terrorism that are committed using computers, networks, and the Internet. Additionally, the reasons why offenders commit these types of crimes are examined in relation to current criminological theories and explanations. As the reader will find, applying criminological theory to digital crime and terrorism is a relatively recent conception. Finally, the section concludes with a chapter on digital criminals and hackers. Chapter 1 provides an introduction and overview of computer crime. In particular, a categorization of types of computer crimes is presented including 1) the computer as the target, 2) the computer as an instrument of a crime, 3) the computer as incidental to crime, and 4) crimes associated with the prevalence of computers. Chapter 2 provides a definition and overview of two key areas of concern in regards to computer crimes, specifically "information warfare" and "cyber-terrorism." Chapter 3 reviews criminological theories that can explain digital crime. Since few theories have been applied directly to digital crime, this chapter focuses on the classic criminological theories that can be applied to digital crime. In other words, the theories discussed in this chapter were developed to explain crime in general, not digital crime specifically. In particular, this chapter focuses on choice, deterrence, psychological, social structure, and social process theories. Finally, Chapter 4 presents an overview of the hacker subculture and presents a typology of hacker types based on relative levels of skill, resources, and enculturation in the values of the hacker subculture. The chapter closes with a discussion of contemporary hacker roles and terminology.

The second section of the book details the various types of crimes that are committed using digital technology. Chapter 5 describes the ways in which the computer revolution has altered the techniques used to commit some of the most common white-collar offenses, including embezzlement, corporate espionage, money laundering, and fraud. In addition to these traditional white-collar offenses, the chapter provides an overview of the newly emerging area of identity theft crimes. Chapter 6 discusses viruses and other types of malicious code. The chapter takes an etiological approach with an emphasis on description, examples, and categorical analysis of these various threats. Each of the major types of viruses and malicious code are reviewed by examining the names and categories of the viruses, how they operate and infect systems, what types of damage they cause, and what the extent of the virus is in the wild. The chapter concludes with a discussion of virus writers and the reasons and dynamics behind virus creation. Chapter 7 focuses on crimes against persons committed over the Internet, including exploitation, stalking, and obscenity. The chapter goes into detail on the etiology of these types of offenses and the offenders who commit them. The chapter attempts to provide insight into how the offenders commit these types of crimes, the mechanisms and methods they use, investigative insight and strategies, and why the offenders commit these offenses. Finally, Chapter 8 provides the reader with an introduction to the issues surrounding the growth of the Internet and the dissemination of extremist ideologies over the World Wide Web. Initially, the chapter outlines various extremists groups that have begun to use the Internet to purvey their ideologies, including groups espousing both left and right wing viewpoints. The chapter continues with an outline of domestic terrorism in cyberspace, including the dangers associated with such phenomena, the techniques and methods used by these groups, and the storage and dissemination of hate ideologies over the Internet. The latter portion of the chapter investigates the issue of intelligence gathering as it relates to cyberspace, as well as the issues arising from the enactment of the USA PATRIOT Act.

The third section of the book discusses the law, law enforcement, and investigation of digital crime and digital terrorism. Chapter 9 reviews the law and legislation as it applies to the collection of evidence and prosecution of digital crime. First, search and seizure law for digital evidence is discussed, including searches with warrants and numerous searches without warrants. Second, the major federal statutes governing the collection of digital evidence, especially electronic surveillance law, are discussed along with federal criminal statutes that forbid certain types of computer crime. Third, issues related to the admission of digital evidence at trial, including authentication and hearsay, are reviewed. Finally, significant U.S. Supreme Court cases in the area of digital crime are discussed. Chapter 10 then discusses the primary role of the many federal agencies involved in detecting and enforcing computer crimes. The chapter continues with a discussion concerning the role of local agencies, with an emphasis on detailing the myriad of limitations associated with the local agencies' response to computer crime. The chapter concludes with a discussion concerning the need for inter-agency cooperation in the fight against computer criminals. Chapter 11 highlights the role that investigators play in the enforcement of digital crime laws. Techniques for acquiring investigative information are presented in this chapter, along with conceptual tools that allow an investigator to communicate with the Internet experts. Finally, Chapter 12 reviews the collection and evidentiary issues related to digital crime and terrorism.

The final section of the book covers prevention of digital crime and terrorism and an overview of what the future might hold in these areas. Chapter 13 presents the problems associated with information security and infrastructure protection. The chapter discusses at length the problems and prospects presented by the USA PATRIOT Act as well as other laws designed to protect the information infrastructure. Chapter 14 uses research developed by Carter and Katz to present an analysis of what the future of digital crime and digital terrorism might look like. The researchers surveyed numerous experts in the computer security and academe regarding their predictions of the future and the problems they are currently encountering. The results of the research led to the development of eight predictions for the future. Each forecast is accompanied by examples, trends, and analysis of what the future may hold.

Dr. Tory J. Caeti

Acknowledgments

First and foremost, we want to thank our wives, significant others, children, and friends for their support and patience with all of us as we compiled this book. As is the case with many of these projects, we locked ourselves in our offices, missed family functions, and in general put out our loved ones while writing this book. Thank you for your support and for not divorcing us.

We want to express our sincere appreciation to our editorial staff at Prentice Hall and Pine Tree Composition. Frank Mortimer's invaluable patience and support was instrumental in getting this book to press. We also want to thank Mayda Bosco, assistant editor at Prentice Hall, and Karen Berry, our Project Coordinator at Pine Tree Composition. They epitomize patience and understanding in dealing with slow academics who take forever to return phone calls and e-mails. We would also like to thank the reviewers: Lanny Lockhart, Jr., Rochester Institute of Technology, Wilmington, DE; Tom O'Connor, North Carolina Wesleyan College, Rocky Mount, NC; Gene Stephens, The University of South Carolina, Columbia, SC; and William L. Tafoya, University of New Haven, West Haven, CT, who provided invaluable insight and suggestions for the final version of this manuscript.

Chapter 1

Introduction and Overview
of Digital Crime
and Digital Terrorism

Chapter Objectives

After completing this chapter, you should be able to:

- Describe the current issues, trends, and problems in the areas of digital crime and digital terrorism.
- Understand the intended audience, purpose, and scope of this text.
- Be able to discuss how cyber victimization has changed in the recent history of digital crime.
- Be able to describe the four primary categorizations of computer crime.

INTRODUCTION

Viruses destroying data and shutting down the Internet, computer thieves stealing credit card and social security numbers, millions of victims of identity theft, and terrorists laundering money and using the Internet to coordinate their attacks; all of these scenarios are endemic to the growing problems of digital crime and digital terrorism. Worsening this situation is the perception that law enforcement and governmental officials are ill-equipped to deal with these crimes and attacks. Digital crimes inspire fear in consumers and lead to a lack of trust in the security and safety of conducting business online. Our reliance on computers and networks for military operations, utilities, and mass transit inspires fear that an attack on our information structure would cripple our society. The images of thousands of people walking home from work due to a power problem that began in Canada and quickly spread to the United States led many to believe that terrorists had attacked the nation's power grid. In sum, the areas of digital crime and digital terrorism are marked by perhaps more misperception and fear than by actual threat. Nonetheless, these problems are real and present unique challenges to law enforcement and other governmental officials.

The first electronic computer was completed in 1945, and the first long distance electronic communication on the Internet was sent in 1969.[1] Until the creation of the personal computer, computers and the Internet were the exclusive tools of society's scientific elite and the military, housed at major university campuses, military bases and corporate research parks. In fact, the coming "information society" would become increasingly dependent on computers and networks to keep our society operational. Computers are now fixtures of everyday life and almost every form of interaction and communication between people relies on computers and network systems in some fashion. The Internet has truly made the world a smaller place. Students can register for or drop classes in real time from their homes while sitting in front of a keyboard. Individuals are able to swiftly and conveniently withdraw money from bank accounts at any time by using automated teller machines (ATM). Friends use satellite transmissions linked across vast computer networks to "instant message" one another. Stock transactions, flight schedules, reference libraries, on-line commerce, the latest news, and innumerable other resources—are all available with a few clicks of the mouse.

The advancement of computer technology and networking rapidly expanded communications and information markets, but this progress comes with costs, both social and economic. The same technology that provides useful services has also been perverted for criminal and terrorist purposes. The advancing technology provides criminals and terrorists with a variety of new tools and opportunities to conduct their activities. The Internet is, in essence, a lawless frontier where bullies, criminals, and terrorists can roam freely with reckless abandon. Computers and networks advanced so rapidly, and without adequate regulation and monitoring, that the law of the jungle prevailed. Lawmakers and police officials are still playing catch-up to this day.

New Threats in the Information Age

Now, computers are also used to perform many traditional criminal acts, most prominently the production and distribution of child pornography, financial crimes, information and corporate espionage, exploitation, stalking, and identity theft. The openness of the Internet expanded the scope of criminal opportunities and has spawned whole new categories of crimes and criminals, including "hackers" who seek to invade our computer networks, and virus writers who are most akin to Internet vandals. The opportunities to commit computer crimes and the technical competence of the criminals have expanded faster than we can control them.

Currently, there are nearly 171 million named hosts on the Internet, with each host representing a network of up to 254 million computers.[2] The expansion and sheer amount of Internet traffic has already exceeded the estimates predicted by experts and commentators a few years ago. Perhaps the most feared online crime is the interception of privileged information, such as credit card numbers or passwords, perhaps leading to identity theft. Abuses associated with the issuance of credit have reached epidemic proportions. In 1997, fraudulent VISA transactions were reported at $828 million. Theft of intellectual property ranging from trade secrets to illegal reproduction of copyrighted consumer materials such as music and movies has an incalculable cost. The Recording Industry Association of America (RIAA) has estimated its losses to music swapping on the Napster network alone in the billions. Trading and selling illicit information on the Internet is a recurring problem and instills fear in online consumers.

While identity theft is probably the most feared online crime, it is not the only threat to Internet consumers. The other category of digital crime that inspires the most fear and disdain is virus writing. Any time a person has a problem with their computer, the average user is likely to have a knee-jerk response, blaming the problem on a virus. The virus protection industry is now a multimillion dollar business, selling and proffering security online. Beyond these dangers, threats from would-be terrorists and politically motivated "hactivists" threaten the functioning of our government, commerce, and military operatoins. Recent studies indicate that many corporations, government agencies, and utility companies are highly vulnerable to computer attacks from outsiders, who in some cases may be able to seriously affect large segments of the population through a single organization's computer system. The National Infrastructure Protection Center, an interagency initiative led by the FBI, concluded that the potential exists for serious harm emanating from attempts to tamper with the information infrastructure.

Purpose and Scope of This Book

This text is primarily intended to be an introduction to the problems of digital crime and digital terrorism. A special emphasis is placed on being decidedly nontechnical in our writing and explanations; however, some technical terms and issues are inevitable in this field of study. We hope that we have described the technical jargon in sufficient detail such that the casual reader will not be lost in the shuffle. The intended audience is anyone interested in learning more about the etiology of digital crime and digital terrorism. The average criminal justice student may have a solid knowledge of the law, criminology, and criminal justice systems, yet possess little knowledge of the complexities of digital crime and victimization. Computer science students well versed in the technical aspects of computers and networks may have little knowledge of the legal aspects of their field and issues of criminality and victimization. Further, practitioners in both the criminal justice field and the computer science field typically have limited knowledge of each other's occupations. Finally, many students and casual readers may simply wish to become better educated in this area. This text is written with all of these groups in mind.

The ambition of the authors was to bring aspects of both of these fields together in a readable, nontechnical text designed to increase knowledge about the problems of digital crime and digital terrorism. Anyone with a little knowledge about computers and the criminal justice system should find merit in the topics covered in this text. We have also consciously focused on common digital crimes and common computer systems, as these will be most familiar to the neophyte. The text is decidedly focused on Microsoft-based systems, common Internet systems, and the most typical types of digital crime and digital terrorism. As such, certain types of digital crimes and certain operating systems/software are beyond our scope and intent. Again, a decided effort was made to explain the more technical parts of this book in a "user-friendly" tone; however, readers who know very little about computers might have some difficulty with some of the details and level of description.

The first section of this book covers the etiology of digital crime and digital terrorism, and includes a discussion of the criminology of these types of crimes and potential offenders. Who are the digital terrorists and digital hackers, and why do they commit their crimes and acts of aggression? The second section addresses the various types of digital crimes and covers the nature, extent, and offender groups in each of the chapters. Chapters on white collar crime, viruses and malicious code, exploitation, and hate are all covered in this section. The third section covers the law, enforcement, and investigation of digital crimes and terrorism. Included in this section are chapters on the laws and legislation covering digital crime and digital terrorism, the agencies charged with enforcing these laws, and the investigative and forensic aspects of this area. Finally, the book concludes with chapters on preventing these types of crimes and threats, and discusses what the future might hold.

DIGITAL CRIME AND DIGITAL TERRORISM[3]

Computer-related crime has increased dramatically in recent years—indeed, both the character and nature of these offenses and their frequency of occurrence has changed notably since about 1995, when the Internet experienced explosive growth.[4] One simply needs to search the phrase "computer crime" on LEXIS-NEXIS® or an Internet news site to find a plethora of incidents and commentaries on the problem. How much computer crime is occurring? It is simply unknown. Not only is there significant inconsistency in defining computer crime offenses, there is an absence of any attempt to collect offense data systematically.

Offenses vary in character from clear criminality (e.g., theft, fraud, or destruction of data files) to acts where criminal culpability is less clear, such as violations of privacy (e.g., unauthorized access to credit reports or medical records). Similarly, types of criminal behavior by computer users also varies (e.g., pornography, extortion, cyberstalking, or gambling). This situation is complicated by the global character of networking offenses—transactions and behavioral interactions can occur between people worldwide from their homes with no scrutiny by immigration, customs, or other government entity. The gravity of the problem is illustrated by the Computer Crime and Intellectual Property Section of the U.S. Department of Justice, which estimates cybercrime costs as high as $10 billion annually.[5]

Since data are not collected to document the nature, trends, and extent of computer crime, it is difficult to develop a clear image of the problem and to predict future trends. Pragmatically, the utility of having good data would be to serve as the basis of law and policy related to cybercriminality. Prevention programs, resource allocation for investigation and prosecution, as well as risk management, can all be more effectively designed and employed if data existed providing insights on the character and extent of the crime problem. Hence, perhaps the first problem is how to get an accurate picture of the crime problem and the nature and extent of digital crime and digital terrorism.

A Developmental Perspective on the Growing Problem

Since the introduction of the microcomputer on the public market, personal computing and the Internet have grown substantially. Technological development of memory capacity, processing speed, software capabilities and remote communications via computer (i.e., networking) grew geometrically. Similarly, there was rapid integration of computing, telecommunications, multimedia, and information archiving technologies. With the public's embrace of the Internet and its staggering growth since 1995—Sky Dayton, founder of the Earthlink Network has described 1995 as "pre-historic" in networking terms[6]—the need for network security became obvious. Certainly there were some early efforts in exploring the idea of computer crime and recognition of it as a criminal problem. These inquiries were groundbreaking yet limited, just as was the technology.

One of the earliest publications on computer crime was by Parker,[7] discussing the feasibility and potential of cybercriminality. Parker's foresight recognized the potential for such criminality even in systems which were, in comparison to today, archaic. Despite this, Parker noted the potential for abusing information which was in a compact, easily accessible form. In the late 1970s, the Bureau of Justice Statistics focused on the issue through a series of publications which included an overview of computer crime issues,[8] computer security,[9] and crimes related to electronic fund transfers.[10] These monographs focused on the potential for cybercriminality and considered issues of law, investigation, case development, and possible criminal strategies. This research was groundbreaking, and many of the methodologies still have applications to operational aspects of security and crime control today. Yet, the reports contain very limited documentation of actual criminality nor do they include discussion of cybercriminals, per se. In the 1980s a few more publications emerged on the topic, predominantly dealing with logistical issues associated with computer-related criminality. Several publications discussed methods to prevent computer crimes.[11] Others explored practices for effectively investigating and prosecuting a computer crime case.[12]

As research developed on the problems of computer crime, several common themes emerged. Some research offered classifications for the emerging crime problem,[13] which are now largely dated as a result of the significant changes in computing capabilities (such as digital imaging) and networking. Scholars began documenting cases of computer-related fraud which occurred in government agencies (nearly all of which were cases of trust violations)[14] and discussed the capabilities of hackers in the early days of bitnet (the Internet "predecessor").[15] Other research began to call for the creation of dedicated computer crime units.[16]

A new industry emerged with many publications and products directed at various aspects of computer security. Firewalls, encryption systems, operations security, virtual private networks (VPN), physical security, access controls, and biometric security developments are all illustrations of the issues explored. Nearly all of the publications employ the same methodology: Describe the security issue, offer options for a solution, and the technological procedural alternatives for each potential solution. Behavioral approaches and descriptions of problems and trends are virtually nonexistent. One exception is Icove, et al.,[17] who comprehensively focus on security and investigation but also offer some interesting insights about motivations and behaviors. Moreover, the behavioral implications provide some guidance; however, they are limited to observations from a small number of investigations rather than a scientific study of trends or patterns.

Other publications about cybercrime are found in the popular press. Case studies such as *The Cuckoo's Egg*[18] and *Takedown*[19] look at specific instances of network incursion. Stoll[20] documents the case of a computer hacker from Germany who penetrated a wide range of U.S. academic and military computers seeking information to steal and sell on the global national security market. Shimomura[21] describes the investigation, arrest and prosecution of Kevin Mitnik, perhaps the most well known of all hackers, who was released in early 2000 from federal prison for computer crime violations. Both publications provide interesting and unique insights about the capacity to commit cybercrimes as well as the difficulty of investigating these offenses. However, as case studies they offer information about specific offenders, not generalizations about trends in cybercriminality or patterns of offending.

A great deal of effort continues to be dedicated to all forms of computer security, ranging from firewalls to encryption to access control to virus prevention, because of growing problems in hacking/cracking and the use of malicious software. Interestingly, the computer security industry has grown rapidly without fully understanding the nature of cybercrimes and criminals. The effect of this rapid change was that cybercrime, per se, was largely ignored—both by policy makers and the research community.

Increases in Cybervictimization

As computers become increasingly integrated in day-to-day lives and as more people use the Internet, cybervictimization will continue to increase. Furthermore, the ease of finding technical documentation on creating viruses and hacking techniques will lead to larger numbers of technically competent criminals. In short, anyone with a computer and a cause can become a cybercriminal. Therefore, most research in this area focuses on the mechanisms and techniques used rather than on the etiology of the offenders and the offenses they commit. According to Parker, the lack of attention paid to computer crime historically is no accident. "In 1970, a number of researchers concluded that the problem was merely a small part of the effect of technology on society and not worthy of specific explicit research."[22] However, Parker went on to note that "the increase in substantial losses associated with intentional acts involving computers proved the fallacy of this view."[23] The irony is that Parker's observations were made a decade ago, yet there is little substantial progress in understanding and addressing the problem from criminological and investigative perspectives. Furthermore, when Parker's early observations were made, most computing was the province of big business, government and academe. Today, personal computing has changed the entire face of the computer industry.

While there is some debate about who poses the greatest risk as a cybercriminal, the fact remains that anyone who has computing skills may pose a criminal threat.[24] This fact is exacerbated by easy Web access to hacking tools and Web sites devoted to writing viruses and cracking into systems. In the mid-1980s, Van Duyn observed that "insiders pose a far greater threat to the organization's computer security than outside 'electronic invaders' possibly could."[25] His reasoning was that "insiders are familiar with their employers' data processing operations and the type of data each system and application is storing and processing" and therefore know exactly where to look for information. Certainly this logic still has merit. However, the emergence of networking, expansive growth of easily adapted databases integrated with Web pages, and user-friendly protocols are changing this balance.

Many experts conclude that vulnerability from within an organization is the most dangerous and poses the most serious threat. In fact, "one study estimated that 90% of economic computer crimes were committed by employees of the victimized companies." A more recent study conducted in North America and Europe found that 73% of the risk to computer security was from internal sources while only 23% was attributable to external sources.[26] Unlike "outsiders" attempting to break into a system, "insiders" are oftentimes able to more easily circumvent safeguards, reducing their chances of being detected. Moreover, if the employee has authorized access to the information, but chooses to steal or destroy it, then detection is even more difficult. While insider theft remains an important issue, the pervasive advent of networking, personal computing and e-commerce has changed this significantly, bringing more threats from "outsiders." "Insiders" also have a distinct advantage, for not only do they often know immediately where to look for the data, but, if in doubt, "they can reference the systems documentation which usually includes programming specifications, file and record layouts, a data element dictionary, and so on."[27]

The Changing Character of Cybervictimization

From a descriptive perspective, Barrett[28] offers insights about the wide range of cybercriminality which can occur. He provides a foundation about the capacity of computers to be used as criminal instruments as well as instruments of warfare. Interestingly, the dynamics and processes are virtually the same; hence the integrated discussion of criminality and national security is becoming an increasingly prevalent theme in the literature. In many ways, inferences from the National Infrastructure Protection Center[29] can be made that digital crime and digital terrorism are on parallel tracks. This is reinforced by the January 1999 experience of simultaneous attacks on United States Defense Department computer systems originating in Russia. Similar tactics were used by Russian organized crime groups against banks.[30]

One project conducted by the American Bar Association in 1987 found that of the 300 corporations and government agencies surveyed, 72 (24 percent) claimed to have been the victim of a computer-related crime in the 12 months prior to the survey.[31] The estimated losses from these crimes ranged from $145 million to $730 million over the one-year period. The broad range of estimates shows that not only is it difficult to identify and document these crimes, it is even more difficult to place a monetary value on the loss of intellectual property wherein the actual value may not be known for months or years.

The Florida Department of Law Enforcement (FDLE) surveyed 898 public and private sector organizations which conducted business by computer. Of the 403 (44.9 percent) respondents, 25 percent reported they had been victimized by computer criminals.[32] The Florida study found embezzlement of funds by employees to be a major source of the crimes; however, no attempt to estimate losses was made because, according to one of the researchers interviewed, "losses would have been nothing more than a guess." Many experts believe that the true level of computer crime is severely underreported because companies handle these matters internally. This is due primarily to a desire to limit the public's perceptions of the vulnerability of companies to these types of crimes and intrusions.

In perhaps one of the most comprehensive studies on computer security threats and crimes, a survey conducted in 1991 of 3,000 Virtual Address Extension (VAX) sites in Canada, Europe, and the United States found that 72 percent of the respondents reported a security incident had occurred within the previous 12 months and 43 percent reported the incident was criminal in nature.[33] By far the greatest security threats came from employees or people who had access to the computers, however; a number of external security breaches from hackers telephoning into the systems or accessing via networks was reported. The ABA and FDLE studies scarcely mentioned this "external threat" and gave little attention to it as a growing problem. This is not surprising, since networking in the late 1980s was comparatively limited and networking technology was both more expensive and more cumbersome. However, the 1991 United Nations study suggested that external threats via remote access was a problem which would grow in the years to come.

Carter and Katz[34] show a trend of victimization which increased significantly over previous studies, with 98.5 percent of the respondents reporting they had been victimized—43.3 percent reported being victimized more than 25 times. While these numbers seem dramatic, security professionals with whom these results were discussed stated they were surprised at the frequency of admitted victimization, not actual victimization. One respondent stated, "Do we know the national or even local scope of the computer crime threat? Probably not; but it has to be higher than anyone wants to admit."

The 1998 joint survey by the FBI and Computer Security Institute found that for the third year in a row, corporate security directors reported an increase of computer system penetration by outsiders. This represented a 20 percent increase of successful system incursions since 1996.[35] Collectively, these data provide empirical support for the anecdotal evidence: Not only is unauthorized access to and theft from computer systems increasing, but the number of system incursions committed by "outsiders" is increasing.

Hacking and thefts are the best documented offenses, but other forms of cyber-criminality are emerging. Fraud through investment Web sites, theft of identity, and telecommunications are all examples of expanding areas of criminality.[36] Nor is cy-bercrime limited to crimes against property. A recent initiative by the U.S. Department of Justice explored the problem of cyberstalking, noting the rapidly increasing nature of the problem, which is aggravated by the increasing amount of personal information available on the Internet.[37] While largely anecdotal information has been collected on these crimes, little is known about offense patterns and offender characteristics.

TYPES OF COMPUTER CRIME

Defining computer crime sufficiently is a daunting and difficult task. Nevertheless there are, generally, four categories of computer crime, including (1) the computer as a tar-get, (2) the computer as an instrument of the crime, (3) the computer as incidental to crime, and (4) crimes associated with the prevalence of computers. Definitions can become rapidly outdated as new technology has consistently bred new offenses and victimizations.

The Computer as a Target

Crimes where the computer itself is the target include the denial of expected service or the alteration of data. In other words, the attack seeks to deny the legitimate user or owner of the system access to their data or computer. Network intruders target the server and may cause harm to the network owner or the operation of their business.

Data alteration and denial directly targets the computer by attacking the useful information stored or processed by the computer. Altered data may affect business de-cisions made by the company or may directly impact individuals by altering their records. Further, this activity results in the expenditure of great resources to recover the data to its prior state in some circumstances. Although malicious network intruders may alter critical data, the most common source of such damage is an employee of the affected company. The primary difference between data alteration and network intrusion is the intent of the intruder. By reading or "browsing" through confidential files, the intruder actually creates a copy of the file. Thus, mere browsing may be theft, but it does not deprive the owner of the data or the user of the data. This makes the distinction be-tween data alteration and intrusion more meaningful.

The story of Kevin Mitnick (perhaps the poster boy of hackers) perfectly exem-plifies this distinction as he wreaked havoc on countless systems during his hacking career. The prosecution of Mitnick relied on estimates of the value of software he down-loaded but did not alter. Several major corporations placed a total value of hundreds of millions of dollars on the software Mitnick obtained. This amount was determined by a method suggested by the FBI: They directed the companies to estimate the total development costs of the software. This amount was questioned at various stages in Mitnick's trial. Since Mitnick did not deprive the companies of the product of their research and development, it seems that the actual economic harm caused would be less than the total cost. This contention was supported by the failure of a single corporation on the list of Mitnick's victims to report such a loss to the Securities and Exchange Commission, as required for losses suffered by a company that sells stock.

When intrusion is discovered, it often requires the owner or administrator of the affected system to question the integrity, accuracy and authenticity of data on the network. Although the legitimate user of the system and data is not denied access to either, there is no reasonable certainty of the data's security in the system. Security measures often require the removal of Web-based resources and restoration of data from, hopefully, unaffected backup copies.

More direct than the subtleties of a network intruder, the denial of service leaves little room for argument of a negative effect. Although any resource may be denied to the rightful user, the most prominent example of this crime targeting the computer is the network denial of service attack. For example, on February 7, 2000 the Web site of Yahoo! was subjected to an unprecedented attack that effectively removed the site from the Internet for three hours. The initial reaction of law enforcement, security, and even hackers was shock that a site as large as Yahoo could be overwhelmed.[38] Subsequent investigation showed that the attacks had been aimed at choke points that funneled the majority of the site's traffic through a few routers. While not as bad as first suspected, the attack showed that even the largest sites on the Internet were not safe.

Computer vandalism also falls under the category of crimes where the computer is a target. When an intruder removes valuable information from a computer system, the intruder denies the legitimate user or owner access to that information. This could represent a substantial loss of expected revenue. If the data is for direct sale, like a computer program or music, it may be possible to estimate the value of the lost data. However, it is more likely that data disrupted will be provided to the public for good will, to generate advertising income, or for no commercial purpose.

Even though a dollar value cannot be attached to the data, the owner still has a right to present the intended message and be free from disruption. Many organizations, like the University of Cambridge, maintain a Web presence for no apparent commercial purpose. In this case, the University of Cambridge has the distinction of owning the last defaced Web page to be archived at Attrition.org. On May 13, 2001, the Web camera at the University of Cambridge was replaced with the calling card of a computer vandal. The vandal wished to express nothing more important than "Ne0tz owned u!"[39] In another example of computer vandalism, a group named "Hacking for Girlies" defaced the New York Times Web site. The defacement caused the New York Times embarrassment and the loss of advertising revenue for their free Web-based service. The consequences of computer vandalism are similar to data alteration or denial of service; many instances of computer vandalism also include network intrusion. All of these offenses target the computer.

The Computer as an Instrument of a Crime

Unlike crimes targeting the computer, using the computer as the instrument of the crime means that the computer is used to gain some other criminal objective. In other words, a burglar uses crowbars and lock picks as the instruments of crime in a fashion similar to the cybercriminal using computers and networks for crimes such as theft, theft of service, fraud, and exploitation, and threats or harassment.

Theft is defined as the taking of property with the intent of permanently depriving the owner of their property or service. In an environment where data is more easily copied than deleted, depriving the owner of the property permanently is relatively rare. However, theft can also mean taking property with the intent to deprive the owner of the value of the property or stealing securities. Parker, creator of the first computer crime typology, notes that market-sensitive proprietary information, financial information, trade secrets, process technology information, human resources information, customer information, information products, transitory information, and security information can all have value to the owner.[40] To some degree, each of these forms of information requires that the owner either maintains confidence in the integrity of the information or controls the distribution of the information to maintain its value.

Other, more blatant, examples of computerized theft do actually deprive the legitimate owner of a tangible asset. The salami slice technique is a money crime; it is an automated means of stealing assets from a large number of transactions. In the round-down salami technique, the computer is used to round calculated dollar amounts down to the nearest cent. By always rounding down and diverting that amount to a special account, the criminal deprives both merchant and consumer of assets; however, the amounts are often trivial, similar to a slice taken from a salami, too thin to produce a noticeable effect, unless millions of transactions are involved.

Some thefts specifically involve theft of service. Although many services available on the Internet are free, some data and services are considered proprietary. This means the users must pay to use the data or service. The use of these proprietary services without payment is theft. For example, many service providers invest in the ability to meet demand for their service. In the mid-1990s, Internet service provider America Online (AOL) failed to anticipate demand for Internet access. As a result, many customers were not able to connect to AOL servers. To remedy this situation, AOL invested significant amounts of money in increasing their capacity. The amount of the increase was carefully planned to avoid spending too much. The damage from theft of service occurs when the criminal use of service forces the owner to invest in greater capacity to meet the projected needs of legitimate users.

Computers can also be used as instruments to commit fraud. Fraud—fraud using a computer—exploits the trust, guaranteed by law, in a business transaction. The buyer, seller, or peer in a transaction can perpetrate fraud. Shopping cart fraud is an example of consumer fraud against a business. Once purchases are selected, the computer criminal saves a copy of the purchase page and alters the prices. Once the altered prices are in place, the criminal submits the page as normal. Some merchants do not discover the fraud until they match inventory to purchases—possibly a month or more after the merchandise is shipped. Although basic security procedures or well designed shopping cart programs would prevent this, many online merchants do not use either.

Other varieties of fraud found on line are simply high-tech variants of older methods. Old scams have found entirely new audiences of victims on the Internet. Pyramid schemes have found a new source of legitimacy with professional-appearing Web sites and official-sounding Web addresses. In fact, virtually every tired bunko scheme has found new life through the Internet: Perhaps the most common recently is the Nigerian bank scheme, where unsuspecting victims send their bank account numbers overseas with the dreams of getting millions in return.

Computers are now often used as instruments to make threats or harass individuals. The U.S. Department of Justice (DOJ) maintains a Web site that details a range of threatening behaviors conducted on the Internet. In an early case of cyberstalking, a Maryland man, Warren Gray, pled guilty to sending five e-mail messages which graphically threatened the life of his victim and the victim's family. At the same time, Gray slashed the victim's car tires and left a hatchet in the victim's office. In this case, cyberstalking coincided with real-world stalking, but the conviction under Federal law came from the use of "interstate wires" to transmit the threat.

The Computer as Incidental to a Crime

Carter characterizes the computer as incidental to other crimes when "a pattern or incident of criminality uses a computer simply for ease in maintaining the efficacy of criminal transactions."[41] In this category, the computer is not the primary instrument of the crime; it simply facilitates it. These crimes include money laundering, criminal enterprise, child pornography, and luring victims into compromising situations.

Money laundering is needed to provide criminals with the ability to spend their money. Funds can be divided into groups that are too small to be noticed and "smurfed"[42] out of the country to be assembled later in an off-shore bank. Coordinating such a complex scheme is greatly facilitated by using computers.[43] Banks or casinos are closely regulated and heavily penalized for money laundering; however, the enormous volume of financial transactions in the United States makes it difficult for regulators to identify even relatively large questionable transactions. The number of such transactions is likely to increase as more businesses and consumers begin to use electronic fund transfer services.[44]

Criminal enterprises also use computers as incident to the crimes that they commit. Computers appeal to criminal enterprises or businesses for many of the same reasons they appeal to others: They are quick, reliable, very accurate, and perform many business-related tasks far faster than if done manually. Thus, they are used to support many different types of criminal enterprises, including loan-sharking and drug rings. A number of prostitution rings have been found using computers to keep track of customers and payroll.

The production and distribution of child pornography has also benefited from the computer revolution. The Internet has been the key communication medium for the sale and exchange of child pornography on both an international and domestic basis. In September 1998, the largest single child pornography sting operation in history occurred, resulting in the arrest of over 200 people in 21 countries.[45] Code-named "Operation Cathedral," British police coordinated raids in Europe, Australia, and the United States, confiscating more than 100,000 indecent images of children. Most of the images were being traded between child pornographers over the Internet. While most of those arrested were men, some were women who also belonged to exclusive child pornography clubs throughout the world. One U.S.-based club, called "Wonderland," had images for sale depicting children as young as two years of age. The sheer size of the pornography network shocked the police as well as the general public. The United Nations called for a worldwide offensive to curb the exchange of pedophilia on the Internet, a very difficult task considering the vast number of jurisdictions and judicial systems present in the international community.[46]

Some crimes of violence are facilitated through the use of a computer. For example, the Internet has been used to lure victims to pedophiles. Adult users of chat rooms may use the supposed anonymity of the Internet to pose as teenagers to establish a rapport with their intended victim. Numerous "sting" operations have placed law enforcement officers in these same chat rooms posing as children. The Organized Crime Digest reports that a local and federal partnership in Maine has steadily increased the number of charges against distributors of child pornography over the last two and one-half years.[47]

Crimes Associated with the Prevalence of Computers

Targets of these types of crimes are mainly the industry itself, but also include its customers and even people who have avoided information technology. These crimes include intellectual property violations, component theft, counterfeiting, identity theft, and a variety of corporate offenses. Intellectual property violations are often described as piracy. The music trading service Napster has recently caused music piracy to replace software piracy in the public mind as the leading example of this crime. Large-scale software piracy began in Asia. The BSA reports that just one person selling unauthorized copies of some 40 different popular programs in Singapore may have made several million dollars, even though he charged as little as $15 for copies of programs that retailed for as much as $600.[48] Violation of American copyright laws in China—particularly piracy of software, videotaped entertainment, and music—led the United States in early 1995 to announce that it would place a 100 percent tariff on all products entering this country from China unless the Chinese government took action to eliminate such violations.

Extensive software piracy now exists worldwide and is facilitated by the Internet. Dutch bulletin boards[49] provided the nexus of "cracked" games and software during the 1980s. Today, "WaRez D00dz"[50] continue the tradition by racing to provide the first cracked edition of new software—often before it is released officially. Microsoft operating systems are the favorite target of the WaRez D00dz.

The theft of desktop and laptop computers, monitors, printers, scanners, modems, and other computer components has begun to decline in recent years. In 1999, laptop theft accounted for 10 percent of the computer crime reported. This amount dropped in 2000 to 3.9 percent and again in 2001 to 2.3 percent of the total. Although system and component theft has been dropping in significance, the actual dollar value has recently grown. The rapid growth of other areas and the rapidly dropping prices of computer systems are the most likely causes for this decline. While the value of laptops being stolen has dropped, there is significant evidence that laptop computers are now being stolen for the information contained on their hard drives, such as documents and passwords, and not for the hardware itself. Theft of proprietary information is the largest single category of this type of computer crime and accounts for approximately 40 percent of total losses reported.[51]

The full extent of computer theft is unknown because many thefts go unreported and because many police departments consider theft of computer hardware as just another stolen-property crime. Some computer owners do not even know what they own and therefore cannot provide the police with an accurate description, let alone the serial numbers. This is a problem compounded by the inability of some police officers to accurately differentiate among computer equipment and peripherals.

Identity theft has become a major concern for both the public and members of the law enforcement community. Although identity theft can occur without the aid of a computer, the anonymity of the Internet and access to vast numbers of personal information have fundamentally changed the nature of this crime. In a fairly common case, almost 40 people employed by a San Diego pharmaceutical company had their identities stolen by a laboratory aide who had discovered unprotected personnel records at the firm. Before being caught, the thieves obtained 75 credit cards, $100,000 in merchandise, 20 cellular phones, and rented three apartments.

The expanded use of the Social Security number is the primary reason for the ease of identity theft. Three major credit reporting bureaus control the information on all persons applying for credit in the United States: Equifax, Trans Union, and Experian. These companies allow anyone with a name and Social Security number to access credit histories. Credit card companies make the process of credit application little more complicated than supplying this information.

Various corporate crimes also appear to be on the rise as computer use has expanded. The rapid growth of the computer industry has caused many questionable business practices to be developed. Examples of these questionable practices include rebate fraud, grossly one-sided End-User License Agreements (EULAs), misleading advertising, component swapping, reselling refurbished components in "new" systems, simple fraud, and many others. The Federal Trade Commission (FTC) has become involved in actions against several companies that promised mail-in rebates, but could not deliver. Although rebates are a common practice in the industry, the first case to draw widespread attention was the Iomega Zip Drive.™ With the unprecedented demand for the Zip Drive, the rebate fulfillment center contracted to handle the processing of rebates was overwhelmed. A large number of rebates were simply lost, and delays of a year or more were common. Interestingly, with the advancement of re-writable computer disks and CD/DVD burners, and their subsequent affordability to the general public, the demand for "zip drives" has decreased significantly over the past two years.

EULAs are contracts that specify the rights of the consumer when purchasing a license[52] to use software. Originally intended to prevent people from reselling copies of their software, EULAs have become so one-sided as to violate common tenets of contract law and consumer protection legislation. Common elements of the EULAs include a stipulation that the software licensed need not function for any particular purpose, even if that function is advertised. Although it is legal to require an EULA, the terms of that contract do not automatically supercede false advertising legislation. There is also an assumption that an item sold is fit for use.

SUMMARY

Attempts to categorize and label specific types of computer crime have followed traditional methodologies, looking at the computer as a target or instrumentality of the crime as applied to other types of existing legislation. Unfortunately, these types of categorizations and labeling exercises often fall short in grasping the overall milieu in which computer crime is observed. Additionally, they often fail to take into account the behavioral and criminological aspects of digital crime. This may be particularly true when the crime touches some aspect of the Internet, or involves a new type of white-collar scam or sophisticated corporate fraud. Categorizations do help us sort out and define more commonly observed criminal incidents where computers are used. We would like to fit all sorts of different and varied criminal methodologies that involve computers into discrete boxes. Certainly, society has accomplished this task for traditional crime by defining the elements necessary to commit a specific crime. There is a new challenge posed by computer crime: Specific incidents may well fit into a criminal violation and hence meet the basic elements of a crime, while other, more sophisticated criminalities may not. The difficulty in specifically and accurately defining each type and incident of computer crime will continue to plague successful prosecution of those misusing computers.

However, and much more important, the nature of digital crime is so expansive as to include ominous and catastrophic events that cripple our critical infrastructure and threaten our national security. In the post 9/11 era, terrorism has become a real threat to our society and to our way of life. We have attempted to secure ourselves through the use of physical searches for weapons, the employment of new technological sensing devices in critical areas, more visible signs of police and security presence, and a stepped-up military offensive against those in foreign countries who may pose threats. Trying to engage the police in the "war on terrorism" may be futile, as the criminal justice system (and particularly the police) is designed to address crime. The people that pose significant terrorist dangers are often motivated by ideologies that are really not criminal in the traditional sense of the word. They seek destruction and devastation as part of war. The police and the criminal justice system are ill equipped to handle such threats. Sometimes, these terrorists pose significant threats to computer and information systems by targeting our critical infrastructure. Designing a system that will be secure, yet provide easy accessibility to needed data and information, will be a trick. Indeed, securing our information infrastructure may well be one of the most challenging tasks of the future.

REVIEW QUESTIONS

1. What factors led to the explosive growth of digital crime over the past few decades?
2. Describe some of the most common forms of digital crime.
3. What gaps exist in our understanding of digital crime? What can be done to address these gaps?
4. Why is the number of cybervictims growing?
5. Why is computer crime severely underreported?
6. What are the four categories of computer crime? Can you name examples of the types of crimes that fall under each category?

ENDNOTES

1. LEINER, B.M., CERF, V.G., CLARK, D.D., KAHN, R.E., KLEINROCK, L., LYNCH, D.C., POSTEL, J., ROBERTS, L.G., and WOLFF, S. (August, 2000). "A Brief History of the Internet" (ver 3.31). Retrieved February 01, 2001 from the World Wide Web: *http://www.isoc.org/internet-history/brief.html*
2. "Internet Domain Survey, January 2001," Internet Software Consortium (Redwood City, CA, 2001).
3. The material in this first section was adapted from an original paper developed by Carter and Katz-Bannister (2003). The remainder of the material is presented in Chapter 14.
4. PARKER, D. (1999). *Fighting Computer Crime: A New Framework for the Protection of Information.* New York: John Wiley & Sons, Inc.
5. WILLIAMS, W. (1999). "The National Cyberterrorism Training Partnership." *The Informant* 25:3 (pp. 7–11).
6. See *www.earthlink.net/bLink*
7. PARKER, D. (1979). *Crime by Computer.* New York: Charles Scribner and Sons.
8. Bureau of Justice Statistics (1979). *Computer Crime: Criminal Justice Resource Manual.* Washington, DC: U.S. Department of Justice.
9. Bureau of Justice Statistics (1980). *Computer Security Techniques.* Washington, DC: U.S. Department of Justice.
10. Bureau of Justice Statistics (1982). *Electronic Fund Transfer Systems and Crime.* Washington, DC: U.S. Department of Justice.
11. BEQUAI, A. (1983). *How to Prevent Computer Crime.* New York: John Wiley and Sons; COOPER, J.A. (1984). *Computer Security Technology.* Lexington, MA: D.C. Heath and Company; ROACHE, J.Y. (1986). "Computer Crime Deterrence." *American Journal of Criminal Law* 13:2(391); CARROLL, J.M. (1987). *Computer Security.* Boston, MA: Butterworth Publishing; GALLERY, S. (ed.) (1987). *Computer Security.* Boston, MA:

Butterworth Publishing Company; ARKIN, S. (ed.) (1988). *Prevention and Prosecution of Computer and High Technology Crime.* Oakland, CA: Matthew Bender.

12. THACKERY, G. (1985). "Problems of Computer Evidence." In *The Practical Prosecutor.* Vol. 2. Houston, TX: National College of District Attorneys; ROSTOKER, M. and R. RINES (1986). *Computer Jurisprudence.* New York: Oceana Publications; ARKIN, S. (ed.) (1988). *Prevention and Prosecution of Computer and High Technology Crime.* Oakland, CA: Matthew Bender; CONSER, J.A. et al. (1988). "Investigating Computer-Related Crimes Involving Small Computer Systems." In M. PALMIOTTO (ed.). *Critical Issues in Computer Investigations.* 2d ed. Cincinnati, OH: Anderson Publishing Company; HOLLINGER, R.C., et al. (1988). "The Process of Criminalization: The Case of Computer Crime Laws." *Criminology* 26(1):101; CONLY, C.H. (1989). *Organizing for Computer Crime Investigation and Prosecution.* Cambridge, MA: Abt Associates.

13. BEQUAI, A. (1987). *Technocrimes.* Lexington, MA: D.C. Heath and Company.

14. KUSSEROW, R.P. (1983). *Computer-Related Fraud and Abuse in U.S. Government Agencies.* Washington, DC: U.S. Department of Health and Human Services.

15. LANDRETH, B. (1985). *Out of the Inner Circle: A Hacker's Guide to Computer Security.* Bellevue, WA: Microsoft Press.

16. MCEWEN, T. (1989). *Dedicated Computer Crime Units.* Washington, DC: National Institute of Justice.

17. ICOVE, D. et al. (1995). *Computer Crime: A Crimefighter's Handbook.* Sebastopol, CA: O'Reilly & Associates, Inc.

18. STOLL, C. (1988). *The Cuckoo's Egg.* New York: Bantam Books.

19. SHIMOMURA, T. (1996). *Takedown.* New York: Hyperion Books.

20. STOLL, *op. cit.*

21. SHIMOMURA, *op. cit.*

22. PARKER, D. (1989). *Fighting Computer Crime.* New York: Charles Scribner and Sons.

23. *Ibid.*

24. CARTER, D.L. and KATZ, A.J. (1999). "Computer Applications by International Organized Crime Groups." In L. MORIARITY and D.L. CARTER, *Criminal Justice Technology in the 21st Century.* Springfield, IL: Charles C Thomas, Publisher.

25. VAN DUYN, J. (1985). *The Human Factor in Computer Crime.* Princeton, NJ: Petrocelli Books, Inc.

26. U.N. Commission on Crime and Criminal Justice (1995). *United Nations Manual on the Prevention and Control of Computer-Related Crime.* New York: United Nations.

27. VAN DUYN, *op. cit.*

28. BARRETT, N. (1997). *Digital Crime.* London: Kogan Page.

29. *www.fbi.gov/nipc/nipc.htm*

30. SINURAYA, T. (1999). "The Cyber Crime Problem Increases." *Crime and Justice International.* June, pp. 1–10, 32.

31. American Bar Association (1987). *Report on Computer Crime.* Chicago, IL: American Bar Association.

32. Florida Department of Law Enforcement (1989). *Computer Crime in Florida.* An unpublished report prepared by the Florida Department of Law Enforcement, Tallahassee, FL.

33. U.N. Commission on Crime and Criminal Justice (1995). *United Nations Manual on the Prevention and Control of Computer-Related Crime.* New York: United Nations.

34. CARTER, D.L. and KATZ, A.J. (1998). "Computer Crime Victimization: An Assessment of Criminality in Cyberspace." *Police Research Quarterly* Vol. 1, No.1.

35. Computer Security Institute (1999). *Issues and Trends: 1999 CSI/FBI Computer Crime and Security Survey.* San Francisco, CA: Computer Security Institute.

36. Public Interest Research Group (1999). *Identity Theft II: Return to the Consumer X-Files.* PIRG Report online at *www.igc.org/pirg/consumer/xfiles/index.htm.*

37. U.S. Department of Justice (1999). *Cyberstalking: A New Challenge for Law Enforcement and Industry.* A report to the Vice-President. *www.usdoj.gov/ag/cyberstalkingreport.htm*

38. Eunjung Cha, A. and Schwartz, J. (2000, February 8). *Hackers Disrupt Yahoo Web Site.* Retrieved February 14, 2000 from the World Wide Web: *http://www.washingtonpost.com/wp-dyn/business/A23174-2000Feb7.html*

39. Attrition.org (2001, May 13). *Video cam: University of Cambridge* [defaced Web page]. Retrieved August 30, 2001 from the World Wide Web: *http://www.attrition.org/mirror/attrition/2001/05/13/video.cbcu.cam.ac.uk/*

40. Parker, D. (1998). *Fighting Computer Crime: A New Framework for Protecting Information.* New York: John Wiley & Sons, Inc.

41. Carter, D.L. and Bannister, A.J. (2000). *Computer Crime: A Forecast of Emerging Trends.* Presented at the Academy of Criminal Justice Sciences annual meeting in New Orleans, LA.

42. Smurfing in money laundering should not be confused with smurfing in denial of service attacks.

43. Zagaris, B. and McDonald, S.D. (1992). "Money Laundering, Financial Fraud and Technology: The Perils of an Instant Economy." *George Washington Journal of International Law and Economics,* 26(1), 61–90.

44. Walther, S. (1994). "Forfeiture and Money Laundering Laws in the United States: Basic Features and Some Critical Comments from the European Perspective." *Crime, Law, and Social Change,* 21(1), 1–13.

45. Serjeant, J. (1998, September 2). "Police Raid Global Internet Child Porn Club." Reuters.

46. *Ibid.*

47. Anonymous (2001). "Web Stings Hit Child Porn Distributors." *Organized Crime Digest,* 22(12), 3.

48. Anonymous (1992, February-March). "Stalking Asian Software Pirates." *Technology Review,* 95(2), 15.

49. The telephone-based electronic bulletin board systems (BBS) was the primary method for most computer users to communicate and exchange software before Internet access became widely available.

50. Warez d00dz, pronounced "wheres dudes" (like softWARE), are software pirates.

51. Powers, R. (ed.) (2001, Spring). "2001 CSI/FBI Computer Crime and Security Survey." *Computer Security Issues and Trends,* 7, 1–20.

52. Software licenses grant the purchaser limited rights to use the compiled version, but not to reverse engineer or sell copies. Thus, the purchaser does not buy the software; he or she buys the right to use it.

Chapter 2

Digital Terrorism

Chapter Objectives

After completing this chapter, you should be able to:

- Define the concepts of "information warfare" and "cyberterrorism."
- List the four categories of attacks that encompass cyberterrorism and/or information warfare.
- Identify various elements of our critical infrastructure that are potentially vulnerable to cyberterrorism and/or information warfare.
- Define and describe an information attack.
- Describe some of the tactics used in cyberspace to share information and promote terrorist ideologies between and within terrorist groups.
- Define the words "stenography" and "cryptography" and relate their use in information warfare and cyberterrorism.
- Explain the active role of China and al Qaeda in recent cyber attacks against the United States.

INTRODUCTION

Since the beginning of history, warfare has evolved parallel to the development of tools, weapons and technology. In the last century, warfare developed from hand-to-hand and small weapons combat to sophisticated air combat, and now to the development of electronic "smart" bombs that are programmed to destroy their targets. Traditional means of warfare have been further distorted through the means of technology, and also by the escalating events of international terrorist activity. Before September 11, 2001, few would have considered that America's civil aircraft would have been used as weaponry against itself. However, al Qaeda operatives did just that, killing over 2,840 people in a few short hours. It should not be a surprise, then, that military and guerrilla offensives could be waged on many fronts, from the skyscrapers of Manhattan to the digital networks that coordinate our critical infrastructure (e.g., the Internet, computer networks, telephone systems, electricity and water supplies).

Few among the American population have considered a situation involving an attack on our infrastructure. However, this type of attack became a frightening possibility when the lights went out across the northeastern United States on Friday, August 15th, 2003. During the initial hours of the blackout, which affected New York City, parts of Connecticut, Vermont, Ohio, and Canada, confusion reigned and many newscasters covering the outage speculated that it could be a terrorist act. By evening, that scenario had been ruled out and the outage was eventually traced to a power grid failure in Ohio. Regardless, the American public had now seen a glimpse of the very real consequences of such an attack—the cities affected had ground to a virtual halt, oil prices began to rise almost instantly, and panic among the population was evident, especially in the first hours after the outage.

DEFINING THE CONCEPTS

Even though the protection of our national infrastructure is a large part of the national strategy for homeland security,[1] most individuals take for granted that such entities are secure. Perhaps the notion of information warfare or cyberterrorism is not at the forefront of our national public consciousness because it is somewhat nebulous. Information warfare and cyberterrorism are actually very broad concepts that, depending on who is defining them, can encompass a range of activity by a variety of different people. They are also two different conceptual events: Cyberterrorism is a component of information warfare, but information warfare is not necessarily cyberterrorism. For this reason, it is necessary to define these topics as separate entities.

Buzzwords: Information Warfare and Cyberterrorism

Information warfare is an overarching concept that actually encompasses cyberterrorism. Essentially, information warfare is the gathering or use of information to gain an advantage over another party. More specifically, John Alger, the dean of the School of Information Warfare and Strategy at the National Defense University defines information warfare as "those actions intended to protect, exploit, corrupt, deny or destroy information or information resources in order to achieve a significant advantage, objective or victory over an adversary."[2] Still another definition states that information warfare is the "coherent and synchronized blending of physical and virtual actions to have countries, organizations, and individuals perform, or not perform, actions so that your goals and objectives are attained and maintained while simultaneously preventing competitors from doing the same to you."[3]

Information warfare consists of six components: psychological operations, electronic warfare, military deception, physical destruction, security measures and information attacks.[4] Psychological operations (or psy-ops, in popular military lingo) use information to affect the state of mind of the adversary. This could include propaganda, or the spreading of information intended to convince people to subscribe to a certain cause or doctrine. The Internet is a perfect tool for this objective.[5]

Electronic warfare is the denial of information or accurate information to an adversary. This is a tool widely used by terrorist organizations, political hackers, and rival countries via the Internet. Military deception is an age-old attack that generally misleads an adversary about military capabilities or intentions. This type of information warfare does not require that the Internet even exists—it can be carried out by more traditional media.[6]

Physical information warfare involves a physical attack on an information system. Security measures are the methods of protecting an information system so that an adversary cannot breach it. Finally, an information attack is the direct corruption of information without actually changing the physical structure in which it is located.[7]

This should make it clear, then, that information warfare is not limited to those things that can be done with computers. In fact, information warfare is the exploitation or strategic protection of a number of things: telephones, radio signals, radar, electronic devices—anything that can be manipulated in order to control or influence the actions of a decision maker. A more practical definition is that information warfare is any sort of strike or protective measure against an information system, whatever the means. Implanting a virus into a military computer is an information warfare tactic. On the other end of the spectrum, blowing up a cellular phone tower could also be considered information warfare.

In contrast, terrorism is defined as the actual or threatened use of violence by an individual or group motivated by ideological or political objectives. The goal of terrorism is to intimidate or coerce a government or its people.[8] Cyberterrorism, however, cannot be as concretely defined and has spurred significant debate over exactly what it means. The fact is that the word cyberterrorism has been misrepresented in both academic circles and by the media at large. A panel of experts on cyberterrorism was convened in March of 2003, with one stating that "Dropping ATM networks and shutting down e-mail is not terrorism. If I can't get to my e-mail for a few days, I am not terrorized."[9] This illustrates the common misperception that a network disruption is an act of cyberterrorism. This would be considered more of an act of information warfare.

Cyberterrorism is also not defined by the group perpetrating it. Terrorist groups, such as al Qaeda, may use the Internet to further their propaganda, hide their secrets, or recruit new members. However, none of this is considered to be inherently terroristic, and again may be considered more of an act of information warfare.[10] According to one definition, "terrorism is defined by the nature of the act, not by the identity of the perpetrators or the nature of their cause."[11]

BOX 2.1   A Short History of Warfare

In a popular futuristic and thought-provoking book, *The Third Wave,* Alvin Toffler discusses a specific approach to the history of warfare. He describes and explains the development of warfare in three different and separate epochs or waves.

The first, or agrarian, wave produced the first known effective change (or revolution) in the history of mankind. Man began to settle in specific areas and grow food rather than forage and roam large expanses of the land. During the agrarian wave, societies developed and the production of goods and commerce began. Tools were relatively rudimentary and weapons were designed more for personal protection against wild animals and hunting, rather than specifically for killing people. The value of the goods and/or the rapidly increasing value of property (soil) created new conflicts among people . . . the first cause of war.

The second, or industrial wave, marked a significant departure from the manufacturing of simple weapons. Industrial and technological improvement allowed the first weapons for the destruction of multiple persons and buildings (infrastructure). Indeed, this era witnessed the defeat of agrarian-based societies to more advanced industrialized people. Landowners had become industrialized nations. Most importantly, war and defense had become a means for justifying the production of more advanced weaponry, including weapons of mass destruction (e.g., nuclear, chemical, biological). Arbitrary and loosely defined armies had become well structured and highly mechanized forces. Nations were now capable of delivering lethal attacks against entire societies of people, leaving behind large expanses of scorched and uninhabitable land.

The third wave, the information wave, reveals societies based on the rapid exchange of vital and critical information. Accurate and timely communication characterizes successful, thriving, and global societies. War also emulates information importance and is focused on the destruction of critical infrastructure within societies, hence *information warfare.* High-tech weapons "invade" computer systems and networks, aimed at destroying the ability of a nation to operate. Interestingly, the large sophisticated armies of the industrial period are relatively useless as communication and transportation systems, logistical support, targeting, defense networks and the like succumb to electronic attack.

Most importantly, the third wave points to the vulnerability of large information-based nations and suggests how a relatively small, unorganized yet knowledgeable group of individuals could wreak havoc on such a society. Quite prophetic, considering that the book was written over twenty years ago, in 1984!

Source: The Third Wave, Alvin Toffler (New York: Bantam Books, 1984).

Cyberterrorism is specifically a premeditated, politically or ideologically motivated attack or threat of attack against information, computer systems, computer programs, and data that can result in violence against civilian targets.[12] According to Barry Collin of the Institute for Security and Intelligence, cyberterrorism is "hacking with a body count."[13] A 2001 assessment by RAND's National Research Defense Institute concluded that cyberterrorism may also include attacks motivated by political or ideological objectives that can cause serious harm, such as a prolonged loss of infrastructure, like electricity or water.[14] Yet another definition includes severe economic loss as a qualifier for cyberterrorism: If economic loss is harsh enough, a destabilization may occur that can result in serious harm to a society.[15]

Because of the obvious semantic problems presented by the misuse of the terms "information warfare" and "cyberterrorism," it is important to keep these definitions in mind when reviewing the threats that terrorist groups or hostile nations pose to the cybersecurity of the United States. Four categories of attacks that encompass acts of cyberterrorism and/or information warfare will be discussed. These categories include: *infrastructure attacks,* or those attacks designed to destroy a system that includes critical data; *information attacks,* or attacks focused on demolishing or altering the content of electronic files or computer systems; *technological facilitation,* or the use of cyber communication to distribute and coordinate plans for a terrorist attack, incite an attack or otherwise assist in the facilitation of terrorism; and *promotion,* which includes fundraising, solicitation and recruitment.[16]

RISK AND CRITICAL INFRASTRUCTURE ATTACKS

The United States is at a particular risk for cyber attack, whether related to information warfare or cyberterrorism, because of several factors. The first is that the United States continues to occupy a precarious position regarding the Middle East. Several fundamentalist and radical Islamic groups (e.g., al Qaeda, Hezbollah, the Muslim Brotherhood) perceive the United States to be evil. Indeed, much of their radical philosophy attacks modernity itself, characterizing complex communication systems, energy use, and computer networks as threats to fundamental Islam. To make matters worse, recent activities within the Israeli-Palestinian conflict, the 2003 conflict in Iraq and the bombing of Afghanistan after the events of September 11, 2001, have all contributed to anti-American sentiment within the radical Muslim world. Many of these groups have significant experience in launching cyber attacks.[17]

Muslim fundamental and radical groups aren't the only threat to the United States' cybersecurity. Anti-capitalist movements, such as those observed in China and North Korea, have also shown their prowess at engaging American targets in cyber attack. Either type of group could levy a great amount of damage on commercial or government interests using techniques that they have already employed in different cyber realms.[18] Indeed, our country has already suffered very sophisticated attacks from such entities. The question, of course, is whether these attacks were state-supported. In the often confusing and murky world of cyberterrorism and information warfare, the answers to these types of questions are often blurred, as might be expected when secret agencies and spy services are employed.

The second factor that causes significant concern to the United States is the country's unique reliance upon a national information infrastructure. Information infrastructure is composed of five essential components: communications networks, such as those used for phones, satellites and cable networks; equipment used for the provision of information, including televisions, radios, computers and phones; information resources, which might consist of educational or medical programs or databases; applications, like those used for electronic commerce or digital libraries; and people.[19]

The United States, which has identified itself as the most infrastructure-reliant of any nation on earth, is also possibly the most at risk for an infrastructure attack.[20] Critical infrastructure is a particularly attractive target to terrorists, due to the large-scale economic and operational damage that would occur with any major shutdown.[21] The Clinton Administration identified eight areas of infrastructure that constitute a virtual national life support system: telecommunications, banking and finance, electrical power, oil and gas distribution and storage, water supply, transportation, emergency services and government services.[22] President Bush's *National Strategy for Homeland Security* further identifies and characterizes the need for critical infrastructure protection.[23] Many of these areas are interdependent on each other, magnifying the potential effects of a breach of one system.[24]

Banking and financial institutions are also vulnerable to infrastructure attack, as they depend heavily on networks. If one system is breached by an attacker, then all connecting systems can be severely impacted. However, most banking or financial networks tend to be private, with little external access. This helps to mitigate somewhat vulnerability in this sector.

Electrical power and water supply systems rely heavily on electronic sensors that maintain safe levels and aid engineers in shutting off supplies if something were to go wrong. Manipulation of these remote sensors by network intrusion is a threat, especially by those who have legitimately gained access in the past. In fact, "malicious insiders," or those who have been given access to a system for a valid reason, such as employment or research, are the greatest threat to infrastructure. Such an insider would have specialized knowledge of a system, as well as access.[25]

Transportation infrastructure, particularly related to civil air traffic control, is also a concern, particularly after the events of September 11th, 2001. The systems used specifically for civil aviation have in the past been largely custom-designed, which isolates civil aviation systems from most direct attacks. Today, as more and more tasks, including aircraft maintenance, parts manufacturing and flight management systems, are slowly being replaced by commercial-off-the-shelf software, civil aviation systems are very well protected.[26] Security for both new and old systems is generally elaborate, with layers of administrative controls that could thwart even the most technologically sophisticated intruder. Furthermore, most civil aviation technology is designed to withstand system failure or breakdown through the use of redundant systems or separate sub-systems, designed to pick up where the main system left off.[27] The Achilles heel of civil aviation security is its heavy reliance on other types of infrastructure. Air traffic control centers depend on electricity, communications systems, and government services, such as the Federal Aviation Administration. For example, radar operates through simple, dedicated telephone lines. If those telephone lines were to be compromised, the impact could be catastrophic.[28]

There have already been attacks against the United States' critical infrastructure involving many of these systems. For the most part, these have been perpetrated by juvenile hackers, seeking a new thrill or acting as pranksters. None have been directly linked to or proven to be the act of any terrorist organization or foreign country. For example, in March 1997, a teenager hacked into a telephone company computer that serviced the Worcester Airport, located in Massachusetts. Telephone service to the control tower, the airport fire department, airport security, and various other departments was out for more than six hours. The attack caused a ripple effect of delayed and cancelled flights across the country, leading to serious financial losses by the airport and several airlines.[29]

In another infrastructure attack, a disgruntled former Chevron employee disabled the firm's alert system by hacking into the company computers. The attack wasn't discovered until the system failed to notify engineers of a release of noxious chemicals into the air at a plant in Richmond, California. This event put millions of people in the western United States and Canada at risk.[30]

These two attacks were potentially deadly and costly, but were perpetrated by people without political or terrorist agenda. One was motivated by ego, the other by pure revenge. It is particularly disconcerting to think of what someone with a deep-rooted ideological hatred for the United States could do if a cocky teenager can shut down an airport for no specific reason. Possibilities put forth in academic literature include the most heinous visions of disaster:[31]

- Penetration of an air traffic control system in order to send misleading signals to aircraft, causing mid-air collisions.
- Taking advantage of the United States' increasing reliance on telemedicine by intruding into hospital computers and changing prescription dosages, resulting in patient death.
- Entering into computerized commuter and freight train routing systems, causing passenger trains to collide or hazardous materials to be released.
- Destroying government computer systems that process tax returns.

What is the risk of an attack on the U.S. critical infrastructure by a terrorist group or rival nation? Unfortunately, no one really knows how vulnerable our critical infrastructure is. Consider this April 23, 2003, testimony before the United States House of Representatives from Michael Vatis, Director of the Institute for Security Technology Studies at Dartmouth College:[32]

". . . to say that cyber networks are vulnerable does not mean that the critical infrastructures that rely on those networks—such as electrical power, grids, pipelines, telecommunications switching nodes, hospitals, etcetera—are necessarily vulnerable, or that a cyber attack would have a sufficiently long-lasting destructive impact to achieve a terrorist or nation-state's military or political objectives. We still do not actually know the full extent of our critical infrastructure's vulnerabilities to various types of cyber attacks and the extent of their potential impact."

In her testimony before the same group in October of 2001, Terry Benzel, the vice-president of advanced security research for Network Associates, Inc., stated that she was unaware of any analysis of infrastructure that identified its weaknesses, or even the extent to which systems are co-dependent. Benzel referenced a 1997 exercise designed to identify vulnerabilities against infrastructure.[33] Using only hacking tools available on the Internet, National Security Agency hackers successfully gained access to a number of military and infrastructure systems. However, specific vulnerabilities were never disclosed—only the assertion that the United States is at risk on some level for such an attack.[34] Benzel recommended an in-depth study and analysis of infrastructure to the House, to culminate in suggestions and solutions to shore up vulnerabilities.[35] Even after the devastation of 9–11 and the identification of significant national threats, her advice has still not been fully implemented.

INFORMATION ATTACKS

Both information warfare and cyberterrorism create a host of scenarios for cyber attacks. Attacks on infrastructure have already been discussed. There are less destructive forms of cyber attack that terrorist groups or adversarial nations could employ to achieve information warfare objectives. These information attacks are focused on destroying or altering content within a system, and while information may be corrupted and temporarily lost, physical and virtual systems are still preserved. This means that the attack is much less destructive, and more disruptive in nature. However, such an attack can (and most likely would) cause major economic damage and loss.[36] The following represent examples of these types of attack.

Web-site Defacement

India and Pakistan have been feuding over a relatively small strip of land known as Kashmir for over half a century. Cyber attacks are a more recent development in the history of this conflict, and the most visible of these attacks have been perpetrated by pro-Pakistan hacker groups. Since 1995, over 500 Web defacements on Indian sites have taken place, and all have been either political or highly visible to the public. For instance, sites representing the Indian Parliament, television networks, newspapers and academic institutions have all been defaced at some point. These Web sites have been defaced with anti-India images and slogans, with some automatically redirecting Web traffic to pro-Pakistani sites, or in some cases, to Web sites containing pornographic or generally offensive material.[37] This technique has also been used by both Israeli and Palestinian groups, often coinciding with specific political events in the region.[38] Domestically, the White House and the FBI Web sites have both been attacked by single-issue terrorist groups such as the Earth Liberation Front and right-wing hate groups such as the Aryan Nation.

Cyberplagues: Viruses and Worms

These terms are used often used synonymously to describe malevolent computer programs that are capable of running and duplicating themselves. However, there is a subtle difference between the two. A virus is actually a piece of code that attaches itself to other instructions within a computer, like software application codes or booting systems. When the user takes an action to make these host instructions run, the virus starts to run as well. The virus then performs a function and lets the host resume control.[39] Meanwhile, the virus has implanted itself into the memory of the computer, where it searches for new hosts. Each time it finds a new host, it inserts itself and then executes its payload, or function, which may be anything from displaying a smiley face on screen to completely wiping the files from a hard drive.[40] The ILOVEYOU virus, which affected Web development and multimedia files and was spread through Microsoft Outlook address books, hit tens of millions of computer users who opened a seemingly innocuous attachment in their email entitled "Love Letter." The total cost of that virus was over a billion dollars.[41] For more detailed information on viruses and malicious code, please refer to Chapter 6.

The ILOVEYOU virus was eventually traced to a college student, but there have been indications that foreign governments have explored viruses as a means of offensive information warfare. A report from the U.S. Defense Intelligence Agency in 1995 warned that the Cuban military was developing a program to propagate viruses against civilian computers in the United States. China has also developed programs to spread computer viruses.[42]

A worm is a program that reproduces itself over a computer network by breaking into computers much like a virtual hacker. The worm does not need the assistance of an unwitting computer user to be unleashed—rather, they find computers that they are able to penetrate, carry out their attack and then transfer a replica of their code to the next target.[43] Worms run off of weaknesses in popular software in order to reproduce quickly and can have the results of a virus. However, they generally spread much faster, affecting tens of thousands of computers in as little as two to three hours. Estimated costs of worm attacks parallel those of many viruses, with an estimate from a recent attack (Blaster) topping a billion dollars in damage.[44] The Code Red worm in 2001 specifically targeted the White House computer systems that were running on commercial off-the-shelf software.[45] Although this particular attack was not tied to any type of terrorism or specific information warfare agenda, others as noted were.

Distributed Denial of Service Attacks

The denial of service (DoS) attack is an attempt by a cyber attacker to prevent legitimate usage of service. DoS attacks generally take the following forms: destruction or alteration of configuration information for a system; expenditure of resources needed for legitimate operation; and the actual physical modification of network elements. The result of any of these three types of DoS attacks is that a system becomes unavailable for a period of time until the system can be brought back under control.[46]

One of the more common types of DoS attack is the flood attack. In this type of action, the attacker starts the process of establishing a connection to another machine. The connection is never completed, but data structures within the victim computer have been reserved to meet the requirements of that connection. As a result, no legitimate connection may be made while the victim machine is waiting to complete the original phony connection. The DoS instigator can take over other computers and use them to establish a simultaneous attack of bogus connections of one victim computer.[47] DoS attacks have been used against government and defense computers, as well as in the largest attack on e-commerce ever recorded. This attack, in February of 2000, shut down the giants of e-commerce, including eBay, Amazon and Yahoo, for nearly a full day. The economic impact of this attack was astounding.[48] Once again, the attack was not related to any terror or political objectives.

Unauthorized Intrusions

Intrusions are "any set of actions that attempt to compromise the integrity, confidentiality or availability of a computer resource."[49] Theft of classified government information is of particular interest to terror groups or adversarial nations. The consequences of such an attack could have wide-ranging implications. However, this type of attack is very difficult to identify once it has occurred. Unless data has been altered, or administrators are specifically looking for an intrusion, such an attack may go undetected forever.[50] In April of 1998, a group of hackers composed of people from around the globe announced that they had stolen programs off of U.S. Department of Defense computers that essentially ran U.S. military networks and satellites. The software was taken off of a Windows NT server in the Defense Information Systems Agency with the Department of Defense. The hackers claimed that the software could be used to virtually shut down U.S. military operations. The group also claimed to have penetrated National Aeronautics and Space Administration (NASA) computers, as well as Pentagon computer systems.[51] The group claimed that their attack was merely an act of public service—a kind of wake-up call for the United States to realize that if a group of simple hackers could gain access to sensitive information, so too could terrorist groups willing to use that information to their advantage. Detailed information relating to the event is difficult to acquire which heightens anxiety and leads to paranoid visions of extreme national vulnerability.

CYBER AND TECHNOLOGICAL FACILITATION

These final categories of cyber attack are less a physical attack and more of a tactic in information warfare. Facilitation of attack can encompass such things as communication via the Internet by terrorist groups, while promotion of terror might be as simple as recruitment and propaganda.

Facilitation of Attack

Information technology has played a great role in the emergence of networked terrorist groups, such as al Qaeda and Jemmah Islamiyiah. Technology has allowed for reduced transmission time in communication, so that members of an organization all over the globe may coordinate their tasks.[52] Information technology has also reduced the cost of communication. In the past, terrorist networks have had to centralize their major activities to reduce detection often associated by direct travel and telephone communication. This made them more vulnerable to discovery and their operations could effectively be wiped out with just one major raid. However, information technology has allowed these organizations to disperse throughout the world, decentralizing their operations and thereby safeguarding them.[53]

Developments in information technology have also allowed for more complex information sharing among terrorist groups. Organizations now have access to computer conferencing, chatting and Web sites that allow for quick and direct communication.[54] Domestic right-wing groups have historically used Web sites for recruitment and advancement of their philosophies. There are also other tactics for information sharing among terrorist groups.

Data Hiding

Also known as stenography, data hiding includes an assortment of methods for secret communication that can conceal the fact that a message even exists at all. Most practically, data hiding refers to the act of taking a piece of information and hiding it within another piece of data, such as an image, sound recording, or word-processing file.[55] Data hiding is based upon two main principles: The first is that files that contain digital images or recordings may be altered without losing their functionality, and secondly, files may be altered without the effects ever being perceived by the human eye or ear.[56] After the events of September 11, 2001, reports surfaced that revealed that al Qaeda had been transmitting hidden data over the Internet. Hidden maps of terrorist targets and instructions were posted in sports chat rooms and pornographic sites that could be accessed by anyone with an Internet connection.[57] Data hiding is fairly easy to do, given the availability of free programs on the Internet and commercially available software, and is complex enough that it would take an impossible amount of time and energy to find hidden data in every Internet file. It is for these reasons that data hiding is such a valuable tool for terrorists or adversarial nations.

Cryptography

For the most part, cryptography is discussed as a methodology to secure and protect information from unwanted eyes and unauthorized use. The same technology can be used to secure communication between terrorist groups. Cryptography is generally used in conjunction with data hiding. An encryption program scrambles information in a controlled manner through the use of a cryptographic key. Only those with access to the key can read the encoded material. Couriers for the terrorist group al Qaeda have been intercepted while carrying encrypted diskettes. Ramzi Yousef, convicted of the 1993 World Trade Center bombing, had encrypted plans to destroy 11 American airliners. This was only discovered after FBI agents spent over a year decoding files found in Yousef's Manila apartment in 1995.[58]

PROPOGANDA AND PROMOTION

Terrorist organizations and adversarial nations have also used the Internet for purposes of propaganda and recruitment. The Internet is the best tool available for these purposes, mainly because it remains largely unregulated and has the potential to reach so many. Organizations can influence public opinion and generate funding through the use of Web sites, which can offer even greater control over a message than TV or print, due to the interactive nature of the Internet and the direct link between a group and its Web master.

Recruitment and mobilization is an important part of terrorist Web presence. Individuals not directly affiliated with a terrorist group, but who support that group's agenda, may be tapped through the Internet to provide hacking tools, funds, or merely "spread the word." During the al-Aqsa Intifada, Israeli and Palestinian groups each employed this technique to encourage sympathizers to download hacking tools and use them against whichever side they opposed.[59]

Recruiting is made easier by tracking which propaganda is accessed most on a Web site and tailoring messages to fit that particular audience. Terrorist groups can also capture information about those who peruse their Web sites and later contact them. Chat rooms and cyber cafes can also serve as forums to recruit interested members of the public, especially the young. It is no surprise, then, that nearly all terrorist groups have an official presence on the Internet. Even the Palestinian Resistance Movement (Hamas, responsible for literally hundreds of suicide bombings in Israel) can be accessed at *www.palestine-info.net/hamas/*. Hizbollah, a Lebanese Shiite group known best for its involvement in the 1983 bombing of the U.S. Marine Barracks in Beirut, has a site at *www.hizbollah.org*.[60] Again on the domestic side, literally hundreds of sites exist for right-wing hate groups and single-issue terrorist groups. At one point during the late 1990s, there were over 250 sites dedicated just to the emergence and development of state militia groups.

CYBERTERRORISM AS AN ADJUNCT ATTACK

As illustrated previously, not many can agree on exactly what threats cyberterror or information warfare pose to the United States. However, one common theme throughout the literature on this topic is that the threat of cyberterror is at its greatest when considered in conjunction with other terrorist actions. According to testimony of Virginia Governor Jim Gilmore, before the House Science Committee in October 2001, "if a cyber attack occurs simultaneously with either a conventional attack or a weapon of mass destruction attack . . . it can compound and enhance the impact of the original attack."[61]

Cyber attacks are potential force multipliers, which in military terms means that these types of attacks can increase the impact of a terrorist action when combined with more traditional attacks. This is done without escalating the need for manpower or capital on the terrorists' side. For example, if a terrorist organization bombed a building through conventional means, but coupled it with hacking into and disabling 911 systems, the impact of the attack would be exponentially multiplied, as rescue personnel could not respond effectively.[62]

Al-Qaeda and Information Technology

Much of the current interest in cyberterrorism and information warfare has sprung from the events of September 11, 2001 and the subsequent discovery of information technology tools used to plan and coordinate those attacks. Al Qaeda, under the direction of Usama bin Laden (and now his son, Saad bin Laden), appears to have a sophisticated system of communication, surveillance and coordination via computer networks and other information tools. It is widely agreed that members of al Qaeda pose a major threat to the Internet.

In a 2002 interview with *Computerworld,* Sheikh Omar Bakri Muhammed, an Islamic cleric with proven ties to bin Laden, said that al Qaeda was actively planning a "cyber jihad," or holy war, against the United States and its allies. Bakri identified the stock market as a major target, and described how the fundamentalist Islamic groups are assembling cadres of computer science students sympathetic to al Qaeda's cause in places like Pakistan and Malaysia.[63]

In late 2001, the FBI noted a series of network intrusions into emergency telephone and electrical generation systems, water storage facilities, nuclear power plants and gas facilities. Each of the probes had been routed through telecommunications centers in Saudi Arabia, Pakistan and Indonesia—all known operational centers for al Qaeda. In 2002, al Qaeda computers seized in Afghanistan contained information yielded from these probes.[64]

U.S. officials found evidence on these computers that al Qaeda operatives spent considerable time on Web sites that offer software and programming instructions for the digital switches that run critical infrastructure such as transportation and power grids. Because the switches are not meant for public access, they have few security safeguards built into them. An attack using these switches could yield devastating results. When questioned, some captured al Qaeda operatives admitted that they had large-scale intentions to use that information in attacks on the U.S.[65] This information is further confirmed by reports from the FBI (in 2003) that directly points to al Qaeda targeting of commuter rail systems within the United States.

Simple hacking tools, such as LOphtCrack, were also found on al Qaeda computers. LOphtCrack allows a hacker to run combinations of characters at lightning speed in order to try and replicate a password. Other more sophisticated information technology tools, such as data hiding and encryption, were also a common theme in al Qaeda caches.[66]

Al Qaeda uses this technology so effectively, partly because of the structure of the organization. Bin Laden is part of an inner circle that has reverted to using nonelectronic means of communication recently due to the sophistication of U.S. and allied interception. However, outside of this core group exists a loose network of operators who coordinate using the sophisticated information technology already described. These operators are able to participate in the exchange of ideas, information and plans related to the planning and targeting of attacks against the United States and/or its allies. It is this community of terrorists, residing all over the globe and with varying technological knowledge, that poses such a great threat to the United States.[67]

China and Information Warfare

The People's Republic of China is probably not the first threat that comes to mind when discussing information warfare or cyberterrorism. However, tensions between the United States and China remain high, and China is one of the few countries in the world eager to adopt the concept of information warfare. In fact, cyber warfare has been almost totally incorporated into the military lexicon, training, and organization in China.[68] Consider this excerpt from the official Chinese military science handbook:

> "In the near future, information warfare will control the form and future of war. We recognize this developmental trend of information warfare and see it as a driving force in the modernization of China's military and combat readiness. This trend will be highly critical to achieving victory in future wars."[69]

The Chinese government has assembled special hacker forces to engage the United States in online or cyber warfare, and has apparently already used them. In the spring of 2001, a hack into the California power grid was traced back to the Guangdong province in China, where several malicious worms and Trojan horse attacks had also originated. Department of Defense officials didn't think that was a coincidence. Although no proof was ever found that directly implicated the Chinese government or military, conventional wisdom suggests that these attacks had been "ordered."[70]

Further, on April 1, 2001, an American spy plane and a Chinese fighter aircraft collided in midair, leading to the capture of the American plane by the Chinese. The political conflict that followed was accompanied by a wave of attacks on U.S. Web sites by Chinese hacker groups. Approximately 1,200 sites, including the White House, the Air Force and the Department of Energy, were targeted via defacement or denial of service attacks. Again, this was never directly proven to be the work of the Chinese government. However, the attacks were highly visible and China took no action to sanction those who perpetrated them. The attacks were at least tolerated by the Chinese government, although given their hard-line stance on crime in China, it seems more likely that the government directly supported such action.[71]

SUMMARY

China, al Qaeda, domestic right-wing hate groups and numerous other terrorist or nation-state entities all have access to the Internet, and apparently have the tools to perpetrate a variety of cyber attacks against the United States and/or its allies. By the very nature of these technological attacks, our critical infrastructure is most vulnerable. As a result, a great deal of attention has been focused on the topic. Scholars, government officials and reporters alike have speculated on the vulnerabilities of the U.S. to cyber attacks, as well as to the "types" of attacks that may be implemented. As illustrated throughout this discussion, there is a great deal of confusion as to what the threats against U.S. information systems really are. The last major exercise dedicated to testing infrastructure security was "Eligible Receiver" in 1997. Most of the details of the exercise remain classified. What has become public is that a team of "hackers" from the National Security Administration, using only publicly available computer equipment and software, was able to infiltrate Department of Defense systems. The team breached security at the Pacific command center as well as the power grids and emergency communication systems in nine U.S. cities. To make matters worse, the government did not know it was under attack for three days!

Large corporations are also increasingly becoming targets of cyber attacks, ranging from significant intrusions to simple probes. According to the Computer Emergency Response Team Coordination Center at Carnegie Mellon University in Pittsburgh, there were a recorded 76,404 such incidents in the first half of 2003. This number represents a significant jump from the total of 82,094 incidents reported in all of 2002.[72]

Conventional wisdom as well as a host of computer security experts suggest that al Qaeda, unfriendly nations, and other radical groups may well be studying means to attack U.S. economic infrastructure. Such attacks could cause untold damage. While there are no specific threats, it is widely agreed that the use of a cyber attack, whether in the promotion of information warfare or cyberterror, is only a matter of time.

REVIEW QUESTIONS

1. Define the concepts of information warfare and cyberterrorism.
2. What are the six components of information warfare?
3. What are the four major categories of cyberterrorism and/or information warfare?
4. Define critical infrastructure and give some specific examples of these types of systems vulnerable to cyberterrorism and information warfare within the United States.
5. Name and describe various types of information attacks.
6. What are stenography and cryptography?
7. What has the role of China been in recent cyber attacks against the United States?

ENDNOTES

1. See *National Strategy for Homeland Security.* Office of the President: U.S. Government Printing Office, 2002.
2. SCHWARTEAU, WINN. (1996). *Information Warfare.* New York: Thundersmouth Press, p. 12.
3. JONES et al. (2002). *Global Information Warfare: How Businesses, Governments and Others Achieve Objectives and Attain Competitive Advantages.* New York: Auerbach Publication, p. 5. For further information on definitions, refer to DOROTHY E. DENNING. (1999). *Information Warfare and Security.* New York: ACM Press.

4. United States Air Force. "Cornerstones of Information Warfare"; see *http://www.af.mil/lib/corner.html*

5. *See* Jones et al., p. 394.

6. *See* United States Air Force.

7. *Ibid.*

8. Denning, Dorothy. (1999). *Information Warfare and Security.* Reading, MA: Addison-Wesley, p. 68.

9. "Cyberterror Threat Overblown, Say Experts," *Computerworld,* March 14, 2003.

10. Embar-Seddon, Ayn. (February 2002). "Cyberterrorism: Are We Under Siege?" *American Behavioral Scientist,* Vol. 45, No. 6, p. 1036.

11. Thackrah, R. (1987). "Terrorism: A Definitional Problem," *Contemporary Research on Terrorism.* Aberdeen, Scotland: Aberdeen University Press, p. 1043.

12. Pollitt, Mark. (October 25, 1997). "Cyberterrorism—Fact or Fancy?" *Proceedings of the 20th National Information Systems Security Conference*, pp. 285–289

13. Grossman, M. (February 15, 1999). "Cyberterrorism." See *http://www.mgrossmanlaw.com/articles/1999.cyberterrorism.htm*

14. Denning, Dorothy. "Activism, Hacktivism and Cyberterrorism." In J. Arquilla, et al., eds., *Networks and Netwars.* Pittsburgh: RAND 2001, p. 281.

15. Denning, "Cyberterrorism." See *http://www.cs.georgetown.edu/~denning/infosec/cyberterror-GD.doc*

16. Ballard, et al. "Technological Facilitation of Terrorism." *American Behavioral Scientist,* Vol. 45, No. 6, February 2002, p. 1009.

17. Institute for Security Technology Studies at Dartmouth College. "Cyber Attacks During the War on Terrorism: A Predictive Analysis" (September 22, 2001), pp. 1–9.

18. *Ibid.*

19. *See* Jones, et al., pp. 56–57.

20. *See* Jones, et al., p. 67.

21. Testimony of Jim Gilmore, Virginia Governor, before the House Science Committee on October 17, 2001.

22. *See* Denning, "Cyberterrorism."

23. *See National Strategy for Homeland Security.*

24. *See* Jones, et al., p. 71

25. *See* Institute for Security Technology Studies, p. 17.

26. Goodman, Seymour. "The Civil Aviation Analogy: International Cooperation to Protect Civil Aviation Against Cyber Crime and Terrorism." In Sofaer, et al., eds. *Transnational Dimensions of Cyber Crime and Terrorism.* Stanford, CA: Hoover Institution Press, 2001, pp. 77–80.

27. *See* Goodman, p. 78.

28. *See* Goodman, p. 79.

29. *See* Denning, "Cyberterror."

30. *Ibid.*

31. *See* Jones, et al., p. 112.

32. Testimony of Michael A. Vartis, Director of Institute for Security Technology Studies at Dartmouth College, before the House Science Committee on April 8, 2003.

33. Testimony of Terry Benzel, vice-president of advanced security research for Network Associates, Inc., before the House Science Committee on October 10, 2001.

34. *See* Denning, *Information Warfare and Security,* pp. 75–76.

35. *See* Testimony of Terry Benzel.

36. ZANINI, et al. "The Networking of Terror in the Information Age." In J. ARQUILLA, et al., eds., *Networks and Netwars.* Pittsburgh: RAND 2001, p. 44.

37. *See* Institute for Security Technology Studies, p. 5.

38. *See* Institute for Security Technology Studies, p. 6.

39. *See* DENNING, *Information Warfare and Security,* p. 270.

40. *Ibid.*

41. *See* DENNING, "Cyberterror."

42. *See* DENNING, *Information Warfare and Security,* p. 275.

43. *See* DENNING, *Information Warfare and Security,* p. 280.

44. *Ibid.*

45. *See* Institute for Security Technology Studies, p. 10.

46. *See* JONES, et al., p. 398.

47. *See* Jones, et al., pp. 398–399.

48. *See* Institute for Security Technology Studies, p. 11.

49. *Ibid.*

50. *Ibid.*

51. *See* DENNING, *Information Warfare and Security,* p. 226.

52. *See* ZANINI, et al., p. 35.

53. *See* ZANINI, et al., p. 36.

54. *Ibid.*

55. *See* JONES, et al., p. 389.

56. *See* BALLARD, et al., p. 996.

57. *See* JONES, et al., p. 388.

58. *See* JONES, et al., pp. 388–389.

59. *See* ZANINI, et al., p. 42.

60. *See* ZANINI, et al., p. 43.

61. *See* Testimony of JIM GILMORE.

62. *See* EMBAR-SEDDON, pp. 1038–1039.

63. "Al Qaeda Poses Threat to the Net." *Computerworld,* November 25, 2002.

64. "Cyber-Attacks by Al Qaeda Feared." *Washington Post,* June 27, 2002.

65. *Ibid.*

66. Summarized from Public Broadcasting Station interviews, April 24, 2003. See *www.pbs .org/wgbh/pages/frontline/shows/cyberwar/interviews/*

67. *Ibid.*

68. HILDRETH, S. "Cyberwarfare." In BLANE, J., ed., *Cyberwarfare: Terror at a Click.* Huntington, NY: Novinka Books, 2001, p. 14.

69. *See* JONES, et al., p. 221.

70. "Is China Ground Zero for Hackers?" ZDNET, August 28, 2001. See *http://zdnet.com.com/ 2100-1107-504010.html*

71. *See* Institute for Security Technology Studies, p. 8.

72. MCLEMORE, DAVID. "On the Cyberterror Front Lines." *Dallas Morning News,* September 21, 2003, p. 31A.

Chapter 3

The Criminology
of Computer Crime

Chapter Objectives

After completing this chapter, you should be able to:

- Discuss the tenets of choice theory, including routine activities theory.
- Describe the assumptions of deterrence theory.
- Describe the relationship between moral development and digital crime.
- Discuss the impact of personality disorders on digital crime.
- Discuss the major social structure theories that apply to digital crime.
- Discuss the learning and social control theories that apply to digital crime.
- Describe the relationship between terrorism and political theory.

INTRODUCTION

This chapter will focus on the causes of digital crime. There are several theories that have been postulated over the past 100 years to explain crime, but few have been applied directly to digital crime. A theory is an attempt to answer the question "Why?" In this chapter, theories will be presented that attempt to answer the question "Why do individuals commit digital crime?" There have been very few attempts to develop and apply criminological theories to the concept of digital crime. The few attempts that have been made have focused on subculture and learning theories. This chapter will review criminological theories that can explain digital crime. Since few theories have been applied directly to digital crime, this chapter will focus on the classic criminological theories that can be applied to digital crime. In other words, the theories discussed in this chapter were developed to explain crime in general, not digital crime specifically. Through the use of digital crime examples, the reader will be able to see how a particular theory can explain digital crime. In particular, this chapter will focus on choice, deterrence, psychological, social structure, and social process theories.

CHOICE THEORY

According to choice theory, an individual commits a crime because that person makes a rational choice to do so by weighing the risks and benefits of committing the act. If the risks (e.g., apprehension and punishment) outweigh the benefits then the person will not commit the act. The opposite is also true. Choice theory became popular among criminologists in the late 1970s for three reasons. First, the positive school began to be questioned. The positive school was based on the belief that crime-producing traits and factors could be isolated and treatment could be administered to eliminate or control the trait/factor. However, it was being argued at the time that these factors and traits had failed to be identified and isolated after almost 100 years of effort. Individuals became dissatisfied with the positive school and began to offer alternative reasons for why people commit crime. Second, the reported crime rate in the 1960s and 1970s increased significantly. This was evidence to some that what was currently being done to control crime was not working. Therefore, some began to look for other means to control the crime rate besides treatment and rehabilitation. Third, the practice of rehabilitation came under attack.[1] In 1974, Robert Martinson wrote an article reviewing 231 studies of prison programs aimed at rehabilitating inmates. Martinson concluded that "with few and isolated exceptions, the rehabilitative efforts that have been reported so far have had no appreciable effect on recidivism."[2] This finding, which was picked up by the mass media, was used by critics of prison programs to argue against rehabilitation as a primary justification for incarceration. The results of the article are commonly referred to as "nothing works." Since it appeared that the current efforts had failed, many started to call for a change in judicial policy. Many started to emphasize the need for punishment, not rehabilitation, as the primary reason for incarceration.

Based on these reasons, choice theory and its policy implications became popular. Judicial policy started to change focus, on the offense and not the offender. Choice theory argues that since the offender has made a rational choice to commit the offense, the focus should be on the offense committed, not the offender. Policies such as mandatory sentencing and "three strikes and you're out laws" have become popular in recent years and are based on choice theory. The idea is that the way to control crime, including digital crime, is to have offenders fear the punishment and be deterred from committing the act. Since humans are hedonistic, efforts should be placed on making the risks of committing digital crime higher than any benefit derived from committing the offenses. Those who support the use of punishment to control crime assume that the offender is making a choice to commit the act and can be deterred if the risks outweigh the benefits.

Routine Activities

Routine activities theory is based on rational choice. Routine activities theory was developed by Lawrence Cohen and Marcus Felson. Cohen and Felson argue that the motivation to commit crime and the supply of offenders are constant.[3] Many would argue that changes in the crime rates are due to changes in the number of motivated offenders. However, Cohen and Felson argue that there is always a steady supply of offenders who are motivated to commit crime: Changes in crime rates are due to changes in the availability of targets and the absence of capable guardians.[4] This theory is applicable to digital crime because the rapid expansion of the use of computers and the Internet has increased the number of available targets. For example, a person in Egypt can hack into a computer in the United States without ever leaving home. In addition, without adequate software protection, there is frequently a lack of capable guardians to protect people from digital crime.

According to Cohen and Felson, crime occurs when there is a convergence in time and space of three factors:

1. A motivated offender (e.g., a hacker)
2. A suitable target (e.g., a vulnerable computer system)
3. The absence of a capable guardian (e.g., inadequate software protection)[5]

All three factors must be present in order for a crime to occur. In sum, when motivated offenders are present, they make rational choices by selecting suitable targets that lack capable guardianship. This reduces their chances of apprehension.

DETERRENCE THEORY

Deterrence theory flows directly from choice theory. The idea is that offenders, including digital criminals, commit crime because they make a choice to do so. This choice is based on the perceived risks and benefits of committing the criminal act. If the risks (e.g., apprehension and punishment) outweigh the benefits, then the person will not commit the act. The offender will be deterred from committing the criminal act because of the threat of punishment. There are two types of deterrence: general and specific. **General deterrence** seeks to discourage would-be offenders from committing criminal acts because of the threat of punishment. Therefore, general deterrence occurs when would-be offenders choose not to commit a certain act because they fear the sanction that may be imposed. Sometimes offenders are made an example of in order to keep others from committing the same act. For example, an 18th century judge reportedly told a defendant, "You are to be hanged not because you have stolen a sheep but in order that others may not steal sheep."[6] This is an example of general deterrence. **Specific deterrence** is designed to impose a sanction on a convicted offender in order to prevent them from continuing to commit criminal acts in the future. In other words, the sanction should be distasteful to the offender so they do not want to commit any more acts.

There are several assumptions of deterrence theory. First and perhaps the most important assumption is that individuals are rational actors.[7] In other words, offenders weigh the potential risks and benefits of committing a criminal act and then make a conscious decision about whether to commit the offense. As it applies to digital crime, it can be argued that many digital criminals are rational actors, making rational choices to commit a computer crime. Second, offenders must be aware of the penalty for particular crimes.[8] As it applies to computer crime, it is argued that many computer criminals do not know the potential penalties they face for particular crimes. Third, they must view the risks as unpleasant.[9] If a computer criminal does not think apprehension and incarceration is unpleasant then the criminal will not be deterred. Fourth, in order for deterrence to be effective it is assumed that the sanction is swift, certain, and severe. The sanction must be imposed quickly to have the greatest deterrent effect and there must be a high probability that a sanction will be imposed. It is important to keep in mind that it is not the actual certainty, severity, and swiftness of the sanction that serves as a deterrent but the criminal's perception of the certainty, severity, and swiftness of the sanction. If potential computer criminals believe that the certainty of arrest is high for computer crime, then they will be deterred from committing the offense even if there is little chance of arrest in reality. Likewise, if potential computer criminals perceive prison as a terrible place that they do not want to go, then they may be deterred from committing offenses. On the other hand, if a computer criminal does not believe that being incarcerated is anything to fear, then the individual is less likely to be deterred. Therefore, if offenders do not believe that the sanctions in court are severe, then they are unlikely to be deterred from committing criminal acts. Likewise, if they do not believe they will be caught, then they perceive a lack of certainty of punishment and thus are likely to commit the crime. The lack of certainty of arrest and punishment is particularly pronounced when it comes to computer crime. There is generally a low risk of apprehension and punishment.

There is minimal evidence to support the argument that the threat of arrest and punishment deters criminals.[10] In fact, evidence supports the contention that informal sanctions from parents and friends serve as more of a deterrent than legal sanctions.[11] In other words, fearing disapproval from your parents and peers for your actions is more likely to keep individuals from committing those acts than the fear of arrest and punishment.

PSYCHOLOGICAL THEORIES

There are several psychological theories that have been applied to criminal activity. This section will explore the impact of moral development and personality disorders on crime. Moral development theories support the contention that there are differences between the moral beliefs of criminals and noncriminals, while personality disorders argue that there are certain personality characteristics that are predictive of crime.

BOX 3.1   Hijacking the Al Jazeera Web Site

A Web site designer from Norco, California, pleaded guilty to felony charges after admitting to federal authorities that he was responsible for the hijacking of Arabic-language news station Al Jazeera's Web site during the war in Iraq. John William Racine II was charged with wire fraud and unlawful interception of an electronic communication. Al Jazeera Space Channel, based in Doha, Qatar, is an Arabic-language media organization that had registered the domain name *www.Aljazeera.net* through Network Solutions, Inc. in Dulles, Virginia. In addition to its satellite television news service, Al Jazeera provides English and Arabic-language news through its *www.Aljazeera.net* web site. Racine diverted the web site and e-mail traffic for *www.Aljazeera.net* after learning in March 2003 that the Web site contained images of captured American prisoners of war and soldiers killed in action during Operation Iraqi Freedom.

Racine gained control of the *www.Aljazeera.net* domain name by defrauding Network Solutions where Al Jazeera maintained an account for its domain name and e-mail services. Racine then diverted the Web site traffic to another Web site he had designed featuring an American flag in the shape of the continental United States and the words "Let Freedom Ring." Racine also intercepted approximately 300 e-mail messages destined for the *www.Aljazeera.net* domain and diverted the messages to an e-mail account under his control.

Racine admitted to FBI agents that he had contacted Network Solutions by telephone and e-mail in an attempt to gain control of the *www.Aljazeera.net* domain name. He ultimately created a false photo identification card to impersonate an Al Jazeera systems administrator and forged the systems administrator's signature on a Network Solutions "Statement of Authorization" form. Racine then sent the fraudulent documents to Network Solutions by facsimile and induced Network solutions to give him control of the Al Jazeera account.

Racine subsequently changed the *www.Aljazeera.net* account settings and redirected all Web traffic through a dynamic domain name service and ultimately to his Web site containing the American flag. In addition, he rerouted all e-mail traffic to an account he had created on MSN Hotmail using the name of the Al Jazeera systems administrator. While Racine maintained control of Al Jazeera's domain name, Internet users were unable to access the Al Jazeera news Web sites and Al Jazeera was unable to receive e-mail sent to the domain. On March 26, Racine contacted agents of the FBI and admitted that he was responsible for hijacking the Web site and intercepting the e-mail sent to *www.Aljazeera.net*.

The plea agreement includes a sentence of three years' probation, to include 1,000 hours of community service. Additionally, Racine agreed to pay a fine of $1,500 and full restitution to the victims of the offenses.

Which theory do you think applies best to this case?

Source: http://www.cybercrime.gov/racinePlea.htm

Moral Development and Crime

The relationship between moral development and crime focuses on cognitive development. Cognitive development theory assumes that individuals develop in a sequential manner. The individual passes through one step in development, then another step, then another, etc. Kohlberg argues that there are sequential stages in moral reasoning that individuals pass through as they develop. At each stage, the decision of what is right and what is wrong is made for different reasons. Crime, including computer crime, can be explained by arrested development of moral reasoning at certain stages. People stop at a certain stage and do not progress any further.

Kohlberg stated that there are six stages of moral development. They include:

Stage 1: Punishment and obedience orientation stage—what is right is obedience to power and rules and avoiding punishment

Stage 2: Hedonistic orientation stage—right corresponds to seeing one's own needs met, taking responsibility for oneself, and allowing others to do the same

Stage 3: Interpersonal concordance stage—right is having good intentions and motives, and being concerned for others

Stage 4: Law and order orientation stage—right is doing one's duty to society and others, and maintaining the rules of society

Stage 5: Social contract, legalistic orientation stage—right is based on upholding the rules and values agreed upon by society; a social contract

Stage 6: Orientation to universal ethical principles stage—right is an assumed obligation to principles such as justice and equality which apply to all individuals; the individual recognizes the moral rightness of behavior.[12]

The first two stages are usually completed by age 7. Stages 3 and 4 are passed through and completed from preadolescence through adolescence, while the last two stages begin in early adulthood. Where do criminals stop in moral development in comparison to noncriminals? Research has found that criminals frequently fall into stage 1 or 2 of moral development while noncriminals frequently fall into stage 3 or 4.[13] In stage 1, children comply with authority out of fear. Something is viewed as morally right if punishment is avoided. An individual who did not progress through this stage will think that their criminal behavior is permissible as long as they are not punished for it. Obviously, this stage of moral development does not take into account other people or an obligation to society. In stage 2, children define what is right as that which satisfies their needs. That is why it is referred to as the hedonistic orientation stage. At this stage, children define something as right if they are not punished for it (i.e., stage 1) and it satisfies their needs. It is easy to see why it is argued that many criminals have stopped their moral development at stage 1 or 2. Their only concern with whether something is right or wrong is whether they get punished and satisfy their needs. It is not until stage 3 that children begin to take into account the feelings of others. Development to stage 3 insulates people from crime because they have become concerned about others, not just their own needs. Therefore, it is clear to see that individuals who proceed to stage 3 and perhaps beyond are far less likely to commit criminal acts.

Personality Disorders

Psychologists argue that certain personality characteristics of an individual may influence crime. Personality refers to the emotional and behavioral attributes of an individual. Attempts have been made to provide support for the belief that individuals with certain personality types are much more likely to commit criminal acts. These attempts have focused on identifying differences in the personalities of criminals and noncriminals. One attempt at identifying these personality characteristics was completed by Sheldon and Eleanor Glueck after they compared 500 delinquent and nondelinquent boys. Personality characteristics that were conducive to crime included extroversion, impulsivity, lack of self-control, hostility, resentment, suspicion of others, destructiveness, less fearful of failure, ambivalence toward authority, assertiveness, and feeling unappreciated.[14]

Frequently the term "psychopath" or "sociopath" is used in describing some offenders. These terms technically refer to a condition known as antisocial personality disorder. According to the *Diagnostic and Statistical Manual of the American Psychiatric Association,* "the essential feature of antisocial personality disorder is a pervasive pattern of disregard for, and violation of, the rights of others that begins in childhood or early adolescence and continues into adulthood."[15] Some of the characteristics of antisocial personality disorder are (1) repeatedly performing acts that are grounds for arrest, (2) deceitfulness, (3) impulsivity, (4) irritability and aggressiveness, (5) reckless disregard for safety of self or others, (6) consistent irresponsibility, and (7) lack of remorse.[16] Although no research to date has been conducted that analyzes the personality characteristics of computer criminals, it can be argued that certain computer criminals may satisfy the criteria of antisocial personality disorder. However, it is argued that the prevalence of antisocial personality disorder is lower among computer criminals than among other criminals.

Pedophiles and Psychological Theory

Many people wonder why pedophiles commit the crimes that they do; what combination of factors leads a person to want to commit sexual offenses against a child? Unfortunately, there are no easy answers. As discussed in Chapter 7, pedophiles commit their crimes for a variety of reasons and go on committing their crimes, with little hope of rehabilitation. Most experts agree that pedophiles develop a sexual interest over a long period of time. Further, there is a variety of reasons and factors that relate to developing pedophilia, none of which fully cause or explain the crime. Most commonly, pedophiles are exposed to some type of sexual abuse or trauma during their childhood. Another common factor is that they have some type of abuse or other related problem during their sexual development and as a result, develop an interest in children as sexual objects. Interestingly, the advent of the Internet has led to numerous problems in dealing with and detecting pedophiles.

The Internet serves many purposes for the pedophile of today, the least of which is the dissemination of child pornography. This poses a conundrum for theorists: Which comes first—an interest in computers due to existing pedophiliac interests or an interest in pedophilia as a result of viewing these types of images on the Internet? Some of the pedophiles arrested state that they developed an interest in children as sexual objects as the result of seeing such images on the Internet. Others clearly were pedophiles prior to the advent of the Internet and simply learned another technique for obtaining child pornography. In short, the specific reasons why a person becomes a pedophile aren't immediately or clearly understood. Nonetheless, psychological theories posit that a person's sexual interests and sexual paraphilias develop in much the same way as

---

BOX 3.2   Hacking the Telecommunications Industry

On September 6, 2000, Patrick W. Gregory, also known as "MostHateD," was sentenced to 26 months' imprisonment, three years' supervised release, and was ordered to pay $154,529.86 in restitution. Gregory had pled guilty to conspiracy to commit telecommunications fraud and computer hacking. From 1997 though May 1999, Gregory was a member of an online computer hacker organization known as "total-kaOs," and later was a member of another online computer hacker organization called "globalHell." Gregory and Chad Davis, also known as "Mindphasr," co-founded "globalHell" in February 1998. By using stolen unauthorized access devices, such as telephone numbers, personal identification number (PIN) combinations and credit card numbers, Gregory illegally accessed numerous teleconferences provided by victims AT&T, MCI, Sprint, Latitude Communications and various other telecommunications providers.

During the conspiracy, Gregory and other co-conspirators used the unauthorized access devices they stole to set up teleconferences for various members of "total-kaOs" and "globalHell" so that they could communicate with each other and discuss matters relating to telecommunications theft and computer hacking. Gregory admitted he knew that, almost on a daily basis, "total-kaOs" and "globalHell" routinely accessed teleconference services with unauthorized access devices to steal free telephone service in order to share and coordinate their attacks upon protected computers throughout the world. Each of these teleconferences routinely lasted more than six hours.

Gregory also used these unauthorized access devices to listen in on and/or disrupt teleconferences of legitimate third parties using the telecommunications services of these victim companies. For example, in October 1998, Gregory, using stolen teleconference access information from Latitude Communications, gained access to the Dallas Community College District's teleconference system and caused teleconference classes at the college to be disrupted, and caused a telephone charge in excess of $18,500.00 to be made to the college.

Which theory do you think applies best to this case?

Source: http://www.cybercrime.gov/gregorysen.htm

other interests and our personalities—through a process of learning, cognitive reinforcement, and psychological development. Thus, the specific reasons why a person
becomes a pedophile are different from case-to-case, but the process is relatively common. The best explanation for this interest is psychological and cognitive in nature.

SOCIAL STRUCTURE THEORIES

The first set of social theories that will be discussed in this chapter can be classified
as social structure theories. When originally developed, social structure theories focused
on why lower class individuals are more likely to commit crime than middle and upper
class individuals. However, modifications and expansions of the original theories have
moved away from this distinction and have attempted to explain criminal behavior by
all social classes (e.g., general strain theory). This is important in the study of digital
crime because many offenders come from the middle and upper classes. Traditionally,
these theories focus on socioeconomic conditions and cultural values as two prominent factors that impact crime. In this section, two major subtypes of social structure
theory will be discussed: strain theory and subculture theory.

Strain Theory

One major type of social structure theory is strain theory. Originally, strain theorists
saw crime as a result of a lack of opportunity, in particular economic opportunity. Today,
modern day strain theories are much broader than the original theories. At the time of
the development of strain theory, it was argued that U.S. society instills in citizens a
desire for financial success but does not provide all individuals equal opportunity to
achieve that success. Those who do not have an equal opportunity are strained and thus
more likely to be criminal. The most prominent strain theory is the one presented by
Robert Merton.

Merton: Strain Theory
There is a unique combination of cultural goals and the means to obtain them in every
society. According to Merton, the cultural goal of American society is economic success.[17] It is argued that the primary goal of citizens in the United States is material wealth.
This goal is promulgated through a variety of mechanisms including the media, cultural transmission, and other mechanisms. Along with the goal, there are institutionalized means to obtain the goal such as education, occupation, and deferral of gratification.
However, not everyone has equal access to the institutionalized means to obtain financial
success. Members of the lower class have less access to education and good jobs than
members of the middle and upper class. Strain theory is sometimes referred to as blocked
opportunity theory. In other words, people are blocked in their ability to access education and a good job. Therefore, there is a discrepancy between a person's desire to
obtain economic success and their ability to do so. These individuals suffer from strain.

If an individual is strained, how do they adapt to the strain? Merton developed
five modes of adaptation.[18] The modes of adaptation vary in their acceptance or rejec-

tion of the cultural goal of economic success and the institutionalized means to obtain the goal. They also vary in the propensity for criminal behavior. The first mode of adaptation is **conformity.** A conformist both accepts the cultural goal of economic success and accepts the institutionalized means to obtain it. A conformist is highly unlikely to commit criminal acts. It is also the most common mode of adaptation.

The second mode of adaptation is **ritualism.** A ritualist rejects the cultural goal of economic success but accepts the institutionalized means to obtain the cultural goal. One response to strain is to lower your aspirations. This is what a ritualist does. They have lowered their aspiration for financial success but still abide by the means to obtain it, such as employment and education. It is unlikely that a ritualist will commit criminal acts as well.

The third mode of adaptation is **innovation.** An innovator accepts the goal of economic success but rejects the institutionalized means to obtain it. In this instance, the individual innovates new means to obtain economic success besides education and employment. One such means is likely to be criminal activity. The innovator may commit such offenses as computer crime, fraud, drug dealing, robbery, burglary, auto theft, bribery, prostitution, among others in an effort to obtain financial success. This is the mode of adaptation that is most likely to lead to criminal activity and most likely to include computer criminals. Basically, the person wants to be financially successful and will commit criminal acts that help to obtain this goal.

The fourth mode of adaptation is **retreatism.** A retreatist rejects both the cultural goal of economic success and institutionalized means to obtain it. These individuals do not aspire to financial success, nor are they concerned with getting an education and employment. These individuals frequently escape into drug addiction and may commit crimes to support their drug use but they do not aspire to financial success. Therefore, their strain is reduced by abandoning both the goal and the means to obtain it.

The fifth mode of adaptation is **rebellion.** A rebel rejects both the cultural goal and means but substitutes new goals and means to obtain them. This adaptation is likely to lead to crime and can be represented by some gangs, militias, cults, and counter-cultures. Criminality is likely to occur with this mode of adaptation, but it will not be as prevalent as criminal activity among innovators.

White-Collar Crime and Strain Theory

White-collar crimes such as money laundering, corporate espionage, and the numerous varieties of Internet fraud schemes described in Chapter 5 fit neatly into the strain theory school of criminology, which suggests that crime and deviance is largely the result of blocked legitimate opportunities. In this sense, individuals who engage in such schemes can be viewed as "innovators" who pursue illegitimate means in order to achieve the conventional goal of material success.

While Merton's original formulation of the theory focused on the blockage of legitimate opportunities experienced predominantly by those in the lower economic classes, contemporary strain theorists have sought to extend strain theory in order to explain the instrumental crimes of middle- and high-class individuals by defining what they have termed the "relative deprivation" experienced by persons of higher economic status. That is, individuals who already enjoy a certain degree of monetary success may engage in instrumental crimes such as money laundering, espionage, or fraud simply because they *perceive* goal blockage in their attempt to secure ever-increasing wealth. From this perspective, "relative deprivation" offers an explanation as to why crimes such as money laundering and/or corporate espionage are primarily committed by individuals who may already be materially successful.

Agnew: General Strain Theory

A more modern version of strain theory is general strain theory. General strain theory was developed by Robert Agnew and tries to explain why individuals who feel stress and strain in their lives are more likely to commit crimes. Agnew's theory does not focus on economic success as the prominent goal in U.S. society, but instead offers a broader explanation of crime than focusing exclusively on the lower class. Agnew argues the crime is due to negative affective states. Negative affective states can include anger, frustration, disappointment, depression, and fear, which are obviously experienced by all classes.[19]

According to Agnew, these negative affective states are caused by several different sources of strain. First, strain can be caused by the failure to achieve positively valued goals. This is similar to the strain discussed by Merton in that it is the result of a disjunction between aspirations (i.e., what one aspires to) and expectations (i.e., what one can expect to achieve). Second, strain can be caused by the disjunction between expectations and achievements. This is different than the first source of strain because it does not focus on aspirations, but on expectations. This disjunction between expectations and achievements frequently occurs when people compare themselves to peers who seem to be doing better than they (e.g., financially or socially). Based on this disjunction, individuals may feel a sense of inequity. Third, strain can be caused by the removal of positively valued stimuli from the individual. The loss of a positively valued stimuli can include the loss of a boyfriend or girlfriend, the death of a relative, the loss of a job, or the divorce of parents, to name a few. Fourth, strain may due to the presentation of negative stimuli. Examples of negative stimuli include family conflict, school failure, child abuse, and stressful life events. These sources of strain may have a cumulative effect on people in reality. The greater the intensity and frequency strain experiences become for an individual, the more likely the person is to turn to crime.[20]

Subculture Theory

A **subculture** is a set of values, norms, and beliefs that differ from the dominant culture. The main tenet of subculture theory is that criminals, including computer criminals, hold values, norms, and beliefs that are in opposition to those held in the dominant culture. These individuals behave in a manner that is consistent with their values, norms, and beliefs, which many times will bring them in conflict with the law. When originally developed, subculture theories attempted to explain gang formation and crime. However, certain types and examples of computer crime can be due to the existence

---

BOX 3.3   Identity Theft and Software Piracy at Kinko's

On July 11, 2003, Juju Jiang pled guilty to computer fraud and software piracy charges. In pleading guilty to computer damage, Jiang admitted that, between February 14, 2001 and December 20, 2002, without the permission of Kinko's Inc., he installed special key logging software on computer terminals located at Kinko's stores throughout Manhattan to surreptitiously record key stroking activity on those computers, and collect computer usernames and passwords of Kinko's customers.

Jiang also admitted that he then used the confidential information he obtained to access, or attempt to access, bank accounts belonging to other persons, and fraudulently open online bank accounts. In addition to the computer damage charges, Jiang also pled guilty to computer access–device fraud. Jiang admitted that he fraudulently possessed more than 15 computer usernames and passwords belonging to other persons, to access their bank and financial services accounts, open online bank accounts in their names, and transfer the funds to unauthorized accounts.

Jiang also pled guilty to two counts of software piracy for his online sale of copies of Microsoft Office 2000 Professional Edition, in violation of Microsoft's copyrights of its software.

Which theory do you think applies best to this case?

Source: http://www.cybercrime.gov/jiangPlea.htm

---

of subcultures. In this section, the original subculture theories will be discussed, including Cohen's delinquency and frustration theory and Cloward and Ohlin's differential opportunity theory. Although these theories were developed to explain gang crime, the concept of subculture formation certainly plays a role in explaining computer crime.

Cohen: Delinquency and Frustration Theory

Cohen believed that individuals from the lower class had different values, norms, and beliefs than members of the middle class.[21] Despite this, Cohen argued that the goal of lower class youth is middle class membership. However, lower class youth face developmental handicaps which place them at a disadvantage in being able to obtain their goal of middle class membership. These developmental handicaps include lack of educational preparation and inability to delay gratification.[22] Since the lower class has different norms and values than the middle class, lower class families are incapable of teaching their children the proper socialization techniques necessary for middle class membership. Instead, they socialize their children to be members of the lower class, which puts them at an obvious disadvantage in trying to obtain middle class membership.

So how do these youth plan on achieving middle class membership? The primary means to obtain middle class membership is education. However, since these youth have been socialized to be part of the lower class, they frequently have difficulty in school. Schoolteachers and administrators are members of the middle class and hold the values, norms, and beliefs of the middle class. The standards used in school to evaluate youth were called middle class measuring rods by Cohen.[23] These standards and values included ambition, responsibility, deferred gratification, courtesy, ability to control aggression, constructive use of time, and respect for property.[24] Basically, lower class youth are being evaluated by measures grounded in middle class values and norms to which they are not accustomed. These middle class measuring rods made it difficult for children to succeed at school.

If lower class youth fail at school they will not be able to obtain their goal of middle class status and membership. Inability to obtain the goal of middle class status is known as status frustration. Since the juvenile is not performing well in school, he seeks individuals like himself to associate with. In other words, the juvenile starts to associate with others who are failing in school and facing status frustration. These youth form delinquent subcultures and gangs. In these gangs, the youth develop new norms, values, and beliefs to abide by. They also establish new means to obtain status. Cohen argued that the norms, values, and beliefs of the middle class are inverted by these youth:[25] They will do the opposite of what the middle class values, valuing what is abhorred by the middle class. This leads to behavior that is nonutilitarian, malicious, and negativistic.[26] The delinquent behavior of these youth did not serve a purpose. They committed unprovoked assaults and stole items they did not need or want. Since they will not be able to obtain their goal of middle class status, the youth gang develops new means to obtain status, including using violence and committing criminal acts. Cohen argued that this criminal behavior is actually a protest against the norms, values, and beliefs of the middle class culture.[27]

Cloward and Ohlin: Differential Opportunity Theory

Cloward and Ohlin focused on serious delinquency committed by urban, male gang members.[28] Cloward and Ohlin argued that there were two goals that lower class youth pursue: economic success and/or middle class membership.[29] They argued that youth who had little ability to achieve these goals through legitimate means would form delinquent subcultures/gangs in an effort to obtain the goals. Cloward and Ohlin argued that the work of Merton and Cohen—previously discussed—was too simplistic. Merton and Cohen made it seem that if an individual could not achieve a goal, then they would commit a crime.

Cloward and Ohlin believed that illegal opportunities are stratified unequally, just like conventional opportunities.[30] In other words, there is an illegitimate opportunity structure just like there is a legitimate opportunity structure for success. The legitimate opportunity structure involves education, hard work, and a good occupation; not everyone has access to this structure to obtain economic success. Cloward and Ohlin argued that not everyone has access to the illegitimate opportunity structure, either. The illegitimate opportunity structure includes stable criminal enterprises in neighborhoods in which criminal mentors exist to assist youth in becoming successful criminals. These types of opportunities do not exist in every neighborhood, and thus not everyone has access to the means to be a successful criminal. Where youth do not have access to the ability to obtain their goals through legitimate means, then delinquent subcultures/gangs are likely to be established with a different set of values, norms, and beliefs.

Hackers and Social Structure Theories

A previously noted, a subculture is a group response to some conflict with the dominant culture. Conflicts can arise from blocked ambitions, general lack of guidance, or the need to choose new goals in the face of despair. Classic works of criminology from Merton[31] explained crime in terms of the "strain" caused by an individual being unable to meet their goals. Two of Merton's methods of adapting to strain, innovation and rebellion, offer substantial guidance to understanding the hacker subculture. When goals are blocked, an individual can find new and creative ways to pursue goals. The adaptation of innovation is often associated with crime. For example, lower class members are confronted with a society that promotes material goals and the trappings of success. Crime becomes an alternative to achieving the "needs" dictated by society. Upper class members tend to adapt by engaging in white-collar crime. This individual response can be noncriminal as well. The "nerd boom" of the information technology age has created an alternative means to social approval. As one hacker T-shirt proudly proclaims: "Stop laughing computers are cool now" [sic].[32] Rebellion is the other adaptation. Although rebellion can also be associated with crime, it is not necessarily revolution. Rebellion simply describes frustrated people deciding to ignore society's goals as well as the means that they cannot access to achieve society's goals.

Building on Merton's work, subsequent criminologists, notably Cloward and Ohlin,[33] developed an extensive understanding of youth culture and the collective rebellions of juvenile gangs. The key to Cloward and Ohlin's work is recognition that gangs (collective rebellion) offer alternative opportunity structures. When opportunity structures are blocked for one group (e.g., school, employment, business power, political power), a subset of that group may create an alternate economy with alternate opportunity structures (e.g., gang, drug economy, violent power). Howard Becker further develops the idea of subculture by contrasting the values of a subculture of marijuana-smoking jazz musicians to the dominant culture that labels them as criminals. It is particularly interesting that the jazz subculture does not deny that marijuana is illegal; rather, they rely on a common justification that marijuana relaxes them and improves their music (pursuit of a higher goal). Thus, the two elements of resolving conflict with the dominant culture can be alleviated through participation in a subculture. Opportunities for social acceptance and self-efficacy are provided through social interaction while learning the skills of hackers. The goals of the dominant culture (e.g., education, financial success) are replaced with the goals of the subculture (e.g., hacking skill, participation in a higher cause).

By rejecting the goals and opportunities of the dominant culture, the hacker subculture provides the context in which hackers situate their actions. It forms their ethics distinct from those of the dominant culture and the laws of the dominant culture. Mills'[34] concept of vocabularies of motive can help explain the mutual agreements and stated principles of hackers. A key concept of Mills' work is that motives are not inner needs but the products of one's environment, or social context, defined through interactions. Accordingly, hacking would not be considered an instinctive activity. The act of hacking requires elaborate preparation, resources, and extensive knowledge, often obtained through socialization within the hacker subculture. The hacker subculture, therefore, provides a way to understand a very abstract action as personally rewarding. Hackers seem to experience a feeling of power and control not found in real life, relatively hard to understand as a rewarding experience to most nonhackers. In the following excerpt, a reporter asks a hacker about Web site defacements:

> "Defacing a site to me is showing the admins, government [and others] that go to the site that we own them," wrote "soupnazi," one of the founding members of the Keebler Elves, in a chat with ZDNN. "They wouldn't even know we were in [their systems], if we didn't deface [them]."[35]

Although hackers are rewarded and encouraged in their activities by the hacker subculture, these same activities may be indefensible when confronted with the values of the dominant culture.

When captured, many hackers attempt to convince authorities of the rightness of their actions. Confessions are common, but usually take the form of justification. The influence of the hacker subculture has convinced them that their actions are just. Reconciling the hacker subculture's values with the values enforced by society is often a traumatic process. Numerous authors[36] depict hackers as behaving very differently after being taken into custody. Hafner and Markoff present Kevin Mitnick as cold and vindictive while hacking, but prone to weeping and nausea when captured.

The sudden removal from the support and justifications of the hacker subculture and the redefinition of their actions is a difficult transition, especially for young hackers. In the following excerpt, hacker Kenneth Sooyna, begins a diatribe against Agent Steal, an informant hacker accused of trying to entrap Mitnick, with a grudging acceptance of Steal's initial plea bargain:

```
>to agent steal, justin peterson or what ever you call yourself,
>i forgive you for snitching on mitnick.
>i'm sure many of us would snitch if put under
>extreme pressure or under other circumstances.[37]
```

The agreed-upon values of the hacker community provides the social context for the hacking activities that violate the standards of the normative culture. The disjunction between the morals of the hacker subculture and the morals of normative society helps to define the activities of "criminal hackers."

SOCIAL PROCESS THEORIES

Social process theories focus on the relationship between socialization and crime. In particular, social process theories analyze the impact of certain factors such as peer group relationships, family relationships, and failure in school on crime. All of these factors

---

BOX 3.4   Russian Organized Hacking

On July 25, 2003, Alexei V. Ivanov was sentenced to a term of imprisonment of 48 months to be followed by three (3) years of supervised release. Ivanov had pled guilty to numerous charges of conspiracy, computer intrusion (i.e., "hacking"), computer fraud, credit card fraud, wire fraud, and extortion. The charges stemmed from the activities of Ivanov and others who operated from Russia and hacked into dozens of computers throughout the United States, stealing usernames, passwords, credit card information, and other financial data, and then extorting those victims with the threat of deleting their data and destroying their computer systems. In sentencing Ivanov, the district judge described his participation as a "manager or supervisor" in an "unprecedented, wide-ranging, organized criminal enterprise" that "engaged in numerous acts of fraud, extortion, and intentional damage to the property of others, involving the sophisticated manipulation of computer data, financial information, and credit card numbers." The district judge found that Ivanov was responsible for an aggregate loss of approximately $25 million.

Which theory do you think applies best to this case?

Source: http://www.cybercrime.gov/ivanovSent.htm

---

are related to crime. Individuals who associate with criminal peers are at significant risk of committing crime themselves. Likewise, individuals who were brought up in an unnurturing, dysfunctional family are at greater risk of committing crime. Finally, individuals who drop out of school are also at risk for committing crime. Two branches of social process theory will be discussed in this section: learning theory and social control theory.

Learning Theory

According to learning theory, individuals commit crime, including computer crime, because they learn the attitudes, skills, and rationalizations necessary to commit these acts. Many times this learning takes place in interaction with parents and peers. Criminals are different from noncriminals in the extent to which they have been exposed to definitions and situations that portray criminal acts as appropriate. There are three learning theories that will be discussed: Sutherland's differential association theory, Akers' differential reinforcement theory, and Sykes and Matza's techniques of neutralization/drift theory.

Sutherland: Differential Association Theory

The first learning theory to be presented is Sutherland's differential association theory. At the time of Sutherland's work, social structure theories such as strain were popular. However, he argued that criminal behavior is a function of learning, not the inability to obtain economic success. He presented nine formal propositions which demonstrate that social interaction and learning leads to criminal activity.[38]

1)   *Criminal behavior is learned.*[39] Sutherland argued that criminality is not a function of a biological or psychological malady or a function of the social structure, but learning.

2)   *Criminal behavior is learned in interaction with other persons in a process of communication.*[40] This communication is verbal and involves interaction with others.

3)   *The principal part of the learning of criminal behavior occurs with intimate personal groups.*[41] Learning involves interaction with significant others such as parents, siblings, and peers. Therefore, families and peers have the greatest influence on learning criminal behavior and attitudes. Sutherland did not see much of a role for movies and newspapers to serve as a medium to learn criminal behavior. However, Sutherland developed his theory prior to development of television and video games.

4)   *When criminal behavior is learned, the learning includes (1) techniques of committing the crime, which are sometimes very complicated, sometimes very simple; and (2) the specific directions of motives, drives, rationalizations, and attitudes.*[42] In the process of learning criminal behavior, an individual will learn how to commit the offense. The individual also learns the attitudes necessary to commit crimes as well as appropriate rationalizations which may justify their behavior.

5)   *The specific direction of motives and drives is learned from definitions of the legal codes as favorable or unfavorable.*[43] Sutherland argued that an individual may be surrounded by persons who define the legal codes as rules to be observed. In this case, crime is unlikely because the individual believes the law is something to be followed. However, some individuals associate with people whose definitions of the legal code are favorable to the violation of the legal codes. Obviously, crime is much more likely in the latter situation.

6)   *A person becomes criminal because of an excess of definitions favorable to violation of the law over definitions unfavorable to violation of the law.*[44] This is the principle of differential association. Sutherland argued that people learn definitions favorable and unfavorable to the violation of the law. When an individual, through association with others, has obtained more definitions that are favorable to the violation of the law than unfavorable then crime is likely to occur. In other words, the individual has learned to commit certain crimes. This principle is important because it can help to explain why criminals may think that some crimes are appropriate while others are not. For example, an individual may think that committing fraud via the Internet is appropriate but robbery is wrong. How can this be justified? According to Sutherland, the individual has received enough definitions in interaction with others to believe that committing fraud via the Internet is appropriate. On the other hand, the same individual has not received enough definitions to believe that robbery is appropriate to commit as well. Think of definitions favorable to violation of the law on one side of a scale while definitions unfavorable to violation of the law are on the other side. If an indi-

vidual receives enough definitions favorable to the violation of the law then the balance will be tipped in favor of committing the crime. The balance can vary from offense to offense and action to action, however.

7)   *Differential associations may vary in frequency, duration, priority, and intensity.*[45] Differential association varies on the quality and quantity of social interactions. Therefore, associations with criminal and noncriminal behavior vary in those respects. Frequency and duration means that more attention will be paid by an individual to definitions obtained in interaction with those with whom they have frequent contact, and have had contact with for a long period of time. Priority involves the importance of the relationship to the individual and the importance of criminal or noncriminal behavior to the individual. Intensity involves the prestige of the source of a criminal or noncriminal pattern and the emotional reactions related to the associations.[46]

8)   *The process of learning criminal behavior by association with criminal and anticriminal patterns involves all of the mechanisms that are involved in any other learning.*[47] In other words, learning criminal behavior is not different from learning any other behavior.

9)   *While criminal behavior is an expression of general needs and values, it is not explained by those, since noncriminal behavior is an expression of the same needs and values.*[48] Sutherland argued that thieves steal in order to obtain money, but workers work to obtain money as well. Therefore, one cannot say that an individual committed a criminal act in order to get money, because that is the same reason why another individual works at a restaurant. In other words, the need for money explains lawful behavior as well as it explains unlawful behavior.

Therefore, Sutherland argued that the accumulation of an excess of definitions obtained in interaction with intimate social groups which say it is OK to commit certain criminal acts leads to criminality.

Akers: Differential Reinforcement Theory

The second learning theory to be presented is Akers' differential reinforcement theory. Sutherland did not apply a learning theory to his theory of differential association. Instead, he stated that criminal behavior is learned like any other behavior. He did not explain how other behavior or criminal behavior is learned.

Akers integrated differential association and operant conditioning.[49] Basically, Akers applied a learning theory to the work already presented by Sutherland. Operant conditioning argues that behavior is controlled by the consequences of that behavior. Individuals receive positive and negative reinforcements for their behavior. A positive reinforcement is a reward and is designed to increase the behavior being rewarded in the future. For example, if a child is given money for cleaning up her room, then the presentment of this positive reinforcement is likely to lead to the child cleaning up her room in the future. On the other hand, a negative reinforcement is a punishment and is designed to decrease the behavior in the future. For example, if a child is caught skipping school and is punished by a parent, then it is unlikely that the juvenile will skip school in the future. Therefore, a person's behavior is controlled by the rewards and punishments they receive for their behavior.[50] Learning theorists argue that rewards are more powerful in shaping behavior than punishments.

Sykes and Matza: Techniques of Neutralization/Drift Theory

The third learning theory to be presented is Sykes and Matza's techniques of neutralization/drift theory. Sykes and Matza also argued that the process of becoming a criminal is a learning experience. They posited that most criminals hold conventional values, norms, and beliefs, but must learn to neutralize the values before committing crimes.[51] Most criminals are not committed to a criminal lifestyle and only commit criminal acts on rare occasions. However, these same criminals hold values and beliefs which state that criminal behavior is wrong. How can they commit criminal acts and still hold conventional values? The individuals use techniques of neutralization, which shield them from any sense of guilt. These techniques of neutralization allow individuals to drift into criminality and then back into conventional behavior. That is why this theory is sometimes referred to as drift theory. Sykes and Matza argue that the techniques of neutralization are learned and come before the criminal act. There are five techniques of neutralization.[52]

1. *Denial of responsibility:* This occurs when an individual states that their behavior was an accident or resulted from forces beyond their control, such as unloving parents, bad companions, or living in a criminogenic neighborhood.[53] Saying "I did not mean to do it" reflects denial of responsibility.

2. *Denial of injury:* This technique of neutralization occurs when an individual denies the wrongfulness of their action or believes the offense does not really cause any harm.[54] Saying "I did not really hurt anybody" reflects this technique of neutralization. This technique of neutralization can be applied to many instances of computer crime where the computer criminals do not feel that anybody is truly hurt by their criminal activity. An example can include the propagation of a worm that does not actually damage anything and is more of a nuisance than anything else. The computer criminal may argue that no one really got hurt.

3. *Denial of victim:* This occurs when an individual believes that the victim had it coming or the victim caused the offense to occur.[55] Saying "They had it coming to them" reflects denial of victim. This is certainly reflected in some computer crimes, especially recent malicious attacks on several companies' computers by ex-employees.

4. *Condemnation of the condemners:* This occurs when the individual shifts the blame to others by focusing attention on the motive and behavior of those who disapprove of his or her actions.[56] Basically, the individual is challenging those who are condemning the actions by arguing that the police are corrupt and parents take out their frustrations on their children. Asking "Why is everybody picking on me?" reflects this technique of neutralization.

BOX 3.5 Cyber-Harrassment

On May 16, 2002, Raymond Blum, the former Chief Technology Officer for Askit.com, a Manhattan-based computer consulting company, was arrested on charges of transmitting threats via the Internet to his former employer at Askit. As Chief Technology Officer, Blum had access to all computer system passwords and information necessary to operate Askit's computer networks. In February 2002, shortly after Blum's departure from the company, Askit began to experience computer and telephone voicemail problems. There was unusual network traffic on its computer system which caused its computer network to fail; Askit's e-mail servers were flooded with thousands of messages containing pornographic images; and Askit's voicemail system was altered so that certain customers calling the company were directed to a pornographic telephone service.

Following the intrusions directed against their computer and voicemail systems, Askit's chief executive officer and its president began receiving threatening communications in various forms. For example, the president received an e-greeting card containing an image of a box which, shortly after being displayed on the president's computer screen and accompanied by a creaking sound, opened to display a voodoo doll with skeleton-like features. The doll had pins stuck through various parts of the doll's body and was wearing a name tag which identified the doll as being the president.

Which theory do you think applies best to this case?

Source: http://www.cybercrime.gov/blumArrest.htm

---

5. *Appeal to higher loyalties:* This occurs when the individual's peer group takes precedence over the rules of society.[57] Saying "I did not do it for myself, but for my friends" reflects appeal to higher loyalties.

Cressey's classic work, *Other People's Money,* describing the cognitive processes experienced by his sample of convicted embezzlers, compares favorably to Sykes and Matza's attempt to explain youthful deviance in their techniques of neutralization/drift theory. Similar to the "techniques" employed by juveniles in order to escape or "drift" from the norms associated with conventional behavior, Cressey found that many of his sampled embezzlers had successfully "neutralized" their embezzlement prior to committing the actual crime by convincing themselves that they were only temporarily "borrowing" the money, or that he/she was justifiably "owed" the money in exchange for years of underpaid, faithful service to the employer.

Social Control Theory

Social control theory seeks to answer the question, "Why *don't* individuals commit crime?" Social control theory assumes that people will violate the law. So why don't they? The answer to this question, according to social control theorists, lies in the strength of an individual's ties to conventional individuals and society. Those who have close ties with their families and noncriminal friends as well as those who possess high self-esteem are unlikely to commit criminal acts. These individuals are bonded to the larger society. Individuals who are not bonded to the larger social order are free from constraints to violate the law.

Reckless: Containment Theory

Walter Reckless believed that individuals have both internal and external forces which operate when they make decisions to avoid or commit crime.[58] Some internal forces inhibit someone from committing criminal acts, while others encourage criminal behavior. The same goes for external forces; some inhibit, while others encourage criminal acts. Reckless identified four motivating and restraining forces for crime. First, inner pushes and pulls lead an individual toward committing crime. These include an individual's desires, needs, and wants, including money. They also include feelings of restlessness, hostility, and the need for immediate gratification.[59] Second, inner containments inhibit criminal behavior. These are internal personal controls that lead someone to not commit criminal acts. Inner containments include self-esteem, a strong sense of responsibility, internalized moral codes, tolerance of frustration, and positive goal orientations. It is argued that inner containments are the most powerful inhibitors to crime. If an individual is internally restrained from committing criminal acts because of their belief system, it is highly unlikely that this individual will commit criminal acts.[60]

Third, Reckless identified outer pressures and pulls which lead to criminal behavior. These are factors in the environment that may lead to crime. External pressures include the influence of one's peer group, unemployment, and living conditions. Therefore, associating with criminal peers, not having a job, and living in substandard conditions serve as external pressures on individuals to commit criminal acts. External pulls include the rewards for committing criminal acts such as status and financial gain.[61] Fourth, outer containments inhibit criminal behavior and include forces that provide discipline and supervision including parents, police, schools, and the criminal justice system.[62]

As stated previously, inner containments are more effective at inhibiting criminal activity than outer containments. This makes sense, since outer containments are not always present prior to the commission of criminal acts, while inner containments such as internalized moral codes are. In conjunction with these containments and pressures and pulls, an individual's self-image and self-esteem is a major predictor of which of these forces will dominate someone's behavior. Therefore, if an individual has a strong self-image, then inner containments will dominate the person's behavior. However, if an individual does not have a strong self-image, it is more likely that pressures and pulls will dominate their behavior. In other words, a strong self-image insulates individuals from crime.

Hirschi: Social Control/Social Bonding Theory

According to Hirschi, people usually do not commit criminal acts because they fear that criminal behavior will damage their relationships with their parents, friends, families, teachers, and employers.[63] Therefore, individuals do not commit criminal acts because they are bonded to the larger society. When these bonds are broken or diminished, criminal behavior is likely. Hirschi stated that there were four elements of the social bond: attachment, commitment, involvement, and belief. Attachment involves the emotional and psychological ties a person has with others. It includes sensitivity to and interest in others as well as a sense of belongingness. A person who is attached to the larger society is insulated from crime. Hirschi argued that attachment is the most important element of the social bond.[64]

Commitment involves the time, energy, and effort expended in conventional lines of action. For example, an individual who has worked hard to get a good education is not likely to jeopardize his efforts by committing crime. The same goes for individuals who have good jobs. These individuals are committed to conventional lines of action and are not likely to jeopardize their positions in order to commit crime. Therefore, the more conventional assets a person has—such as an education, job, home, etc.—the less likely they will be to commit crime.[65] Involvement includes heavy involvement in conventional activities, which leaves little time for illegal behavior. The phrase "Idle hands are the Devil's workshop" applies here. Individuals who are busy with working, going to school, raising children and other conventional actions are far less likely to commit crime than those who are less involved. Individuals who are involved do not have the spare time necessary to indulge any temptation to commit crimes.[66] Belief involves believing in the moral legitimacy of the law and authority, understanding that the law is something that should be followed. Belief is the level of an individual's acceptance of conforming values and actions.[67]

Hirschi argued that individuals do not commit crime because they are bonded to society. Therefore, those with a weakened bond because of a lack of attachment, commitment, involvement, and belief are likely to commit crime. If individuals do possess these elements of the social bond, then they are insulated from crime.

Gottfredson and Hirschi: Self-Control Theory

In a later control theory, Gottfredson and Hirschi argue that a person's tendency to commit crime can be found in their level of self-control.[68] Self-control involves a person's ability to control their own behavior. Basically, they proposed that individuals who commit crime have limited self-control. These people have a tendency to be impulsive, insensitive, and focused on immediate gratification.

What causes people to have limited self-control? Gottfredson and Hirschi argue that lack of self-control is caused by inadequate child rearing.[69] Self-control, according to Gottfredson and Hirschi, is instilled in people by age eight and is relatively constant thereafter. They suggested that parents must be willing to monitor their child's behavior, to recognize inappropriate behavior when it occurs, and to punish the inappropriate behavior.[70] If this occurs consistently, the child will develop a high level of self-control. Over time, the child will internalize the monitoring by the parents. If the parents are unwilling or unable to do this, then it is likely they will produce children who lack self-control. When this occurs, criminal activity is likely—however, not guaranteed.

Gottfredson and Hirschi also integrated elements of rational choice theory into the development of their theory. Individuals with low self-control must be presented with the opportunities to commit criminal acts in order for crime to occur. If an individual has low self-control but there is no criminal opportunity, then crime will not take place. On the other hand, if criminal opportunity presents itself to an individual with low self-control, then crime is likely to occur.

Virus Writers and Social Process Theories

Social process theories are probably best when used to explain the crimes committed by virus writers and those who propagate and spread viruses. The first empirical observation to take into account when examining the phenomenon of why people engage in virus writing is that there is no common profile of a "typical" virus writer. As discussed in Chapter 6, a common misperception is that virus writers are 13-year old brainiacs that unleash their wrath on society for no apparent reason. In reality, a virus writer could be that kid or a 35-year-old computer programmer looking to increase their salary. This tends to limit the explanatory power of social structure theories because virus writers can come from many walks of life and are typically wealthy enough to afford the computer machinery necessary to practice their trade. Further, not all virus writers are in it for the money or for the fame. The reasons why virus writers write and propagate viruses can be for money, fame, attention, competition, and simply for a perverse sense of fun.

What is undeniable in the development of a virus writer is that a certain level of technical competency is required. While it is true that virus creation tools exist that make it easier to write viruses, one does not become a virus writer overnight. As such, all virus writers must learn how to write and propagate viruses. The learning process that they go through is similar to any other learning process. The learning includes learning how to write the code necessary to create a virus, but as important is learning how to become a good virus writer. In the world of virus writers, competition and bravado play an important role in conditioning the person, as does learning the tools and tactics of the trade. Some writers do so to prove their computer programming capability. Anecdotal, yet unproven, stories of virus writers who have programmed a "quality" virus and found fame and fortune as the result of their prowess abound. Other virus writers achieve fame because their virus infects a large number of computers and makes it into the media spotlight. However, prior to the fame and supposed fortune of the virus writer, the person goes through a learning and social conditioning process.

When the writer first enters the world of the virus writers, they are treated with disdain and as the newcomer that they are. If they enter chat rooms and exchange information and curiosity about virus writing, they are often ridiculed and subjected to a social conditioning process where they learn the practice through trial and error and also learn how to be a better virus writer or face ridicule from their peers. Once they have established their reputation, they often engage in banter with other self-proclaimed virus writers. They learn to show their accomplishments and show others how successful their virus is "in the wild." Others receive financial rewards and eventually develop into for-profit virus writers. Still others enjoy the thrill of infecting other people's machines, hacking into secure systems via their Trojan horses, and enjoy reading about their exploits online and in the media.

Nonetheless, they all share a common learning experience in order to ply their trade. This learning experience is unique compared to other forms of criminal learning in that the significant peers that teach them will likely never see them face to face. Most of the learning takes place in chat rooms, on bulletin boards, and via distance learning. As social learning theory posits, the learning is reinforced both positively and negatively over its course, which serves to reinforce the technical competency of the virus writers. Positive reinforcement includes the thrill experienced by propagating the virus and infecting systems; it can include notoriety and kudos received from their peer group—like graffiti writers they also love to see their moniker appearing with their work; and finally there can be financial rewards. Negative reinforcements include receiving hostility from other virus writers (eventually ending up with an online competition to hack the other's system), receiving ridicule and disdain for their viruses and exploits online, and being sought out by law enforcement. If caught, they may discontinue their activity, but the other forms of negative reinforcement they receive may serve to make them want to become more proficient.

Once confronted or apprehended because of their virus-writing activity, virus writers use the same justifications and excuses consistent with techniques of neutralization theory. A common statement by virus writers is that it is the computer user's or system's fault that they were infected, not the virus writer's (blaming the victim). They state that if the victim had their security up to par, they would not have become a victim in the first place. They also note that such neophytes have no business being online or using their computer if they don't know how to protect themselves. In fact, virus writers tend to show disdain for the average "Internet surfer." Another common theme in the comments of virus writers is that they aren't really doing any harm and, in fact, are performing a public service by pointing out the security holes in the software and computer systems (denial of injury/denial of the victim). Some claim that there aren't really any victims of viruses, they are simply ill prepared to conduct commerce or surf online. Another typical justification is that they are really doing good by showing the greed and incompetence of software vendors (especially Microsoft) and other corporations (condemn the condemners). Finally, many virus writers claim that they really didn't intend to cause any harm by writing their virus. These techniques of neutralization can be seen in several of the anecdotal items contained in Chapter 6, especially the interview with the Dark Avenger.

TERRORISM AND POLITICAL THEORY

The term terrorism has been defined in a number of ways by a variety of scholars. For the most part, each definition has yielded a limited understanding of the actual phenomenon. This is particularly true when analyzing the current wave of international and technological situations in contemporary global affairs, such as those occurring in the Middle East and those involving digital crime and digital terrorism. In the popular mind, terrorism is viewed as the illegitimate and violent actions of specific groups that violate the authority of rightfully established political entities.[71] Terrorism, in general, always has a political agenda. This agenda may be motivated by various political

---

BOX 3.6   Cisco Stock Fraud

On November 26, 2001, former Cisco Systems, Inc., accountants Geoffrey Osowski and Wilson Tang were each sentenced to 34 months in prison for exceeding their authorized access to the computer systems of Cisco Systems in order to illegally issue almost $8 million in Cisco stock to themselves. The two pled guilty to one count of computer fraud, agreed to the forfeiture of assets that the government had seized from the defendants (including stock already liquidated for $5,049,057, jewelry and an automobile), and agreed to pay restitution in the amount of the difference between $7,868,637 and the amount that the government will recover from the sale of the seized items.

Osowski and Tang admitted that between October 2000 and March 27, 2001, they participated in a scheme to defraud Cisco Systems in order to obtain Cisco stock that they were not authorized to obtain. As part of the scheme, they exceeded their authorized access to computer systems at Cisco in order to access a computer system used by the company to manage stock option disbursals, used that access to identify control numbers to track authorized stock option disbursals, created forged forms purporting to authorize disbursals of stock, faxed the forged requests to the company responsible for controlling and issuing shares of Cisco Systems stock, and directed that stock be placed in their personal brokerage accounts.

Which theory do you think applies best to this case?

Source: http://www.cybercrime.gov/Osowski_TangSent.htm

---

ideologies, separatist ethnic movements, or radical religious philosophies, but always the purpose of achievement is a specific set of political objectives. Although vague, as to explaining who terrorists are, this definition does provide a conceptual framework concerning what terrorism is.[72] It can be reduced, simply to a choice among violent means—not a choice between violence and nonviolence, but a manifestation of violence against people to achieve a goal. By extension, terrorists often apply extreme, random acts of violence against the innocent (e.g., attacks on symbolic institutions such as schools, churches, and synagogues; bombings of common gathering places such as cafes, shopping malls, and office buildings; and the killing of individuals that represent legitimate governments such as soldiers, police officers, and political leaders), in an attempt to instill fear in the general population. Thus, terrorism is used as a methodology for political action. As Hoffman argues, terrorism is fundamentally and inherently "political." Terrorism is "ineluctably about power: the pursuit of power, the acquisition of power, and the use of power to achieve political change. Terrorism is thus violence—or, equally important, the threat of violence—used and directed in pursuit of, or in service of, a *political aim*."[73]

The psychological, economic, strategic and political consequences of violence associated with terrorism is often much more prominent than the attack itself. Short-term effects of terrorism involve an immediate psychological effect on society, but are relatively benign compared to the long-term impact, which includes a widespread realization of vulnerability. In fact, the consequences of terrorism tend to have a higher value as time goes on.[74] For instance, the economic impact of the September 11th attack on the World Trade Center Building (2001) was first estimated at a real cost of just over $10 billion. However, looking at the much more involved secondary costs—such as loss of service, impact on the stock market, declining investor sentiment, economic failure of the airline industry, rebuilding of structures, and loss in tourism dollars to the world and specifically New York—the estimated cost exceeds $2 trillion.[75] Essentially, the real impact of terrorist events can be measured in the creation of an atmosphere of chaos, fear and panic in the target population.

No one understood this phenomenon better than Karl Marx. His early work (in 1887) argued that political change could not be achieved without conflict.[76] Indeed, he believed that epochs of history changed as groups of people bound by loss of status and class revolted against ruling elites. In Marxist thought, successful revolutionary strategy began with a core group of leading individuals dedicated to the cause. This group, the vanguard, represented the front lines of violent activity. It was the express purpose of the vanguard to violently confront private property owners and wealthy elites with the opposites elements that maintained their ruling status—replace trust, order and security with chaos, fear, and panic. To the dedicated Marxist, the vanguard represented contemporary terrorist groups. Interestingly, a century and a half later, Franz Fanon argued that no government would willingly give up power and wealth; therefore, this power and wealth had to be taken violently. Fanon suggested that the international act of colonization was in itself an act of violence and thus had to be confronted with violence.[77] Accordingly, governments under attack must respond with stricter measures against the general public (the masses). Since there is no clearly identifiable enemy, governments must resort to more harsh and brutal treatment of the indigenous population in order to ferret out the hardcore vanguard members. Constitutional rights become suspended, unwarranted searches become commonplace, torture replaces interrogation, and innocence gives way to presumption of guilt. At the point that rule of law erodes and the masses react against the ruling government, revolution begins, spurring yet another epoch in human history. To Marx, contemporary terrorists represent the vanguard.[78]

The acts of terrorism aimed at critical information infrastructure (what we call cyberterrorism or digital terrorism) are simply new tactics to accomplish the same end. The modern and complex societies of today are built on information exchange, global processing, and reliance on computerization and telecommunication. What were suppose to be the hallmarks of advanced societies to increase democratic and free thought have now become huge vulnerabilities. Government and business depend on these critically vital systems, making them prize targets for individuals aimed at destroying normalcy. To compound the problem, these systems have been built by information elites that control them. Government and society have been more than happy to place the burden of development and maintenance of computer systems with a few individuals having narrow educational fields and a keen understanding of complex information systems. Indeed, there has been safety in the fact that few of the masses actually understood much of the critical infrastructure on which our society depended upon for vital existence. All of that changed, however, as the interconnectivity of systems became commonplace through the marvels of the World Wide Web and the Internet. Heretofore closed and secured systems became vulnerable to outside attack, relatively unsophisticated juvenile hackers could close down business enterprise with seeming ease, and the "experts" were mystified in ways to prevent such attacks. Digital terrorism has become a reality as sophisticated terrorists understand new tactics that can render airplanes helpless to navigate, force railroads and commuter trains to stop, make electric and water plants idle, and stop local and global communication. In the past, having a tactic that could do so much damage was relatively closed to terrorist groups. Today, they provide some of the most frightful and devastating scenarios relating not only to specific violent actions, but also the to the extreme vulnerability of our country and our world. Terrorism that attacks our critical information infrastructure may not only attack our country, but also the world, in one massive strike. Retrospectively, Karl Marx may well have been correct. It will be through force that revolution is sparked and accomplished; it is specific acts of violence (and terrorism) that will erode safety, security and peace and substitute chaos, fear and panic.[79]

S U M M A R Y

In this chapter, the major criminological theories that can be used to explain digital crime have been presented. Several different areas of criminological thought can be used to explain digital crime. First, it can be argued that some computer criminals commit their offenses due to rational choice and a lack of fear of apprehension. Second, it can be argued that restricted moral development and the presentation of a personality disorder may lead a person to commit digital crime. Third, strain and subculture theories can be applied to digital crime. Fourth, learning and social control theories can explain some types of digital crime as well. Fifth, political theory can be used to explain acts of terrorism. Although little theoretical development has occurred in the area of digital crime, several current criminological theories have applicability to this phenomenon.

R E V I E W   Q U E S T I O N S

1. According to choice theory, why do individuals commit digital crime?
2. What are the major assumptions of deterrence theory?
3. Which psychological theories can be applied to digital crime?
4. What are the five modes of adaptation? Which is most likely to lead to the commission of digital crime?
5. What are the nine propositions presented by Sutherland?
6. What are the four elements of the social bond?
7. How does self-control affect digital crime?

E N D N O T E S

1. SIEGEL, LARRY J. *Criminology: Theories, Patterns, and Typologies,* 4th ed. St. Paul, MN: West, 1992.
2. MARTINSON, ROBERT. "What Works? Questions and Answers About Prison Reform." *The Public Interest,* Vol. 35, 1974, pp. 22–54.
3. COHEN, LAWRENCE and MARCUS FELSON, "Social Change and Crime Rate Trends: A Routine Activities Approach." *American Sociological Review,* Vol. 44, 1979, pp. 588–608.
4. *Ibid.*
5. *Ibid.*
6. KADISH, SANFORD H. and MONRAD G. PAULSEN, *Criminal Law and Its Processes.* Boston: Little, Brown, 1969, p. 85.
7. WALKER, SAMUEL. *Sense and Nonsense About Crime and Drugs: A Policy Guide,* 4th ed. Belmont, CA: West/Wadsworth, 1998.
8. *Ibid.*
9. *Ibid.*
10. PATERNOSTER, RAYMOND. "The Deterrent Effect of Perceived and Severity of Punishment: A Review of the Evidence and Issues." *Justice Quarterly,* Vol. 42, 1987, pp. 173–217.
11. GREEN, DONALD. "Measures of Illegal Behavior in Individual-Level Deterrence Research." *Journal of Research in Crime and Delinquency,* Vol. 26, 1989, pp. 253–275.
12. KOHLBERG, LAWRENCE. *Stages in the Development of Moral Thought and Action.* New York: Holt, Rinehart and Winston, 1969.
13. HENGGELER, SCOTT. *Delinquency in Adolescence.* Newbury Park, CA: Sage, 1989.
14. GLUECK, SHELDON and ELEANOR GLUECK. *Unraveling Juvenile Delinquency.* New York: Commonwealth Fund, 1950.
15. *Diagnostic and Statistical Manual of Mental Disorders,* 4th ed., p. 645.
16. *Ibid.*
17. MERTON, ROBERT K. *Social Theory and Social Structure.* Glencoe, IL: The Free Press, 1968.
18. *Ibid.*
19. AGNEW, ROBERT. "Foundation for a General Strain Theory of Crime and Delinquency." *Criminology,* Vol. 30, 1992, pp. 47–87.
20. *Ibid.*
21. COHEN, ALBERT K. *Delinquent Boys: The Culture of the Gang.* New York: The Free Press, 1955.
22. *Ibid.*
23. *Ibid.*
24. *Ibid.*
25. *Ibid.*
26. *Ibid.*
27. *Ibid.*
28. CLOWARD, RICHARD and LLOYD OHLIN. *Delinquency and Opportunity.* New York: Free Press, 1960.
29. *Ibid.*
30. *Ibid.*
31. MERTON, ROBERT K. "Social Structure and Anomie." *American Sociological Review,* Vol. 3, 1938, pp. 672–682.
32. Jinx Hackwear (2003). *StopLaughing T-Shirt.* Retrieved August 24, 2003 from the World Wide Web. *http://www.jinxhackwear.com/scripts/details.asp?affid=-1&productID=2*

33. CLOWARD, RICHARD and LLOYD OHLIN. *Delinquency and Opportunity.*
34. MILLS, C.W. "Situated Actions and Vocabularies of Motive." *American Sociological Review,* Vol. 5, 1940, pp. 904–913.
35. LEMOS, R. (1999). *Does the Media Provoke Hacking?* Retrieved from the World Wide Web: *http://www.zdnet.com/zdnn/stories/news/0,4586,2288043,00.html*; S. LEVY. (1984). *Hackers: Heroes of the Computer Revolution.* New York: Dell Publishing.
36. HAFNER, K. and J. MARKOFF. *Cyberpunk: Outlaws and Hackers on the Computer Frontier.* New York: Touchstone, 1991; J. LITTMAN, *The Watchman: The Twisted Life and Crimes of Serial Hacker Kevin Poulsen.* Boston, MA: Little, Brown and Company, 1997. SLATALLA, M. and QUITTNER, J. (1995). *Masters of deception: The gang that ruled cyberspace.* New York: Harper Collins Publishers.
37. SOOYNA, KENNETH. (personal communication, Nov. 21, 1998).
38. SUTHERLAND, EDWIN H. and DONALD R. CRESSEY. *Criminology,* 10th edition. Philadelphia: J.B. Lippincott Co., 1978, pp. 77–83.
39. *Ibid.*
40. *Ibid.*
41. *Ibid.*
42. *Ibid.*
43. *Ibid.*
44. *Ibid.*
45. *Ibid.*
46. *Ibid.*
47. *Ibid.*
48. *Ibid.*
49. BURGESS, ROBERT and RONALD AKERS. "Differential Association—Reinforcement Theory of Criminal Behavior." *Social Problems,* Vol. 14, 1968, pp. 128–147.
50. *Ibid.*
51. SYKES, GRESHAM M. and DAVID MATZA. "Techniques of Neutralization: A Theory of Delinquency." *American Sociological Review,* Vol. 22, 1957, pp. 664–670.
52. *Ibid.*
53. *Ibid.*
54. *Ibid.*
55. *Ibid.*
56. *Ibid.*
57. *Ibid.*
58. RECKLESS, WALTER C. "A Non-Causal Explanation: Containment Theory." *Excerpta Criminologica,* Vol. 1, 1962, pp. 131–134.
59. *Ibid.*
60. *Ibid.*
61. *Ibid.*
62. *Ibid.*
63. HIRSCHI, TRAVIS. *Causes of Delinquency.* Berkeley, CA: University of California Press, 1969.
64. *Ibid.*
65. *Ibid.*
66. *Ibid.*
67. *Ibid.*
68. GOTTFREDSON, MICHAEL and TRAVIS HIRSCHI. *A General Theory of Crime.* Stanford, CA: Stanford University Press, 1990.

69. *Ibid.*

70. *Ibid.*

71. TAYLOR, ROBERT W. and HARRY E. VANDEN. "Defining Terrorism in El Salvador: La Matanza." *The Annals of the American Academy of Political and Social Sciences,* 463, September 1982, p. 1.

72. *See* RICHARD SCHULZ. "Conceptualizing Political Terrorism: A Typology." *Journal of International Affairs,* 4:8 (Spring/Summer 1978); and BRUCE HOFFMAN. *Inside Terrorism.* New York: Columbia University Press, 1998.

73. HOFFMAN, BRUCE. *Inside Terrorism.* New York: Columbia University Press, 1998, p. 2.

74. *See* MARTHA CRENSHAW. "The Logic of Terrorism: Terrorist Behavior as a Product of Strategic Choice." In WALTER REICH, ed., *Origins of Terrorism: Psychologies, Theologies, and States of Mind.* Princeton, NJ: The Woodrow Wilson International Center for Scholars, 1998.

75. Institute for the Analysis of Global Security-IAGS, 2004.

76. MARX, KARL. *Das Capital.* Moscow: Progress Publishers, 1887.

77. *See* FRANZ FANON. *The Wretched of the Earth.* New York: Grove Press, 1963 and *A Dying Colonialism.* New York: Grove Press, 1965.

78. COHEN-AMAGOR, RAPHEL. "Foundations of Violence, Terror and War in the Writings of Marx, Engels, and Lenin." *Terrorism and Political Violence,* Volume 1, Issue 2, Summer 1991, pp. 1–24.

79. MARX, KARL. From his speech at Amsterdam in 1872.

Chapter 4

Digital Criminals and Hackers

Chapter Objectives

After completing this chapter, you should be able to:

- Distinguish between computer crime, criminal hacking, and noncriminal hacking.
- Explain why hackers think that the term "hacker" does not refer to criminals.
- Identify hype and exaggeration of hacking incidents found in the media.
- Recognize the role media hype plays in influencing young hackers.
- Classify hackers into broad categories based on activities and expression of ideas in online communication or statements made in person.
- Describe the role of technology that drives the hacker subculture.
- Explain how subcultural status depends on an understanding of technology achieved by the hacker and his or her knowledge of the ethics and values held by hackers.
- Predict hacker actions based on their type.
- Explain the terminology used to describe hackers in the media.

INTRODUCTION: WHAT IS A HACKER?

At this point in most texts, a reader might expect to see a quick definition of a hacker. In some sense, this entire chapter is the definition of "hacker." Originally, the word hacker referred to an unorthodox problem solver and master programmer; in fact, these original hackers made the machines and the programs that are vital to modern society.[1] Recognizing this fact, some media sources have championed terms like "computer cracker" and "black hat" to describe criminal hackers. Some sources even directly equate computer criminals and hackers. The consensus of computer crime experts is that most computer criminals are insiders to the victim organization, not hackers seeking to gain entry.[2] The one thing that is clear is that there is no universal agreement as to the meaning of the word "hacker" or "computer criminal." However, there is a *popular* consensus that hackers are bad people who do bad things.[3]

This chapter presents a view of hackers that is intended to assist investigators and law enforcement officer in understanding the way hackers think. Many descriptions of motive and interpretation of hacker actions come directly from hackers themselves. At no time should this chapter be read to condone breaking the law. Although sympathetic to a hacker's sensibilities, it is not sympathetic to harm caused intentionally, or through negligence. Hackers have established their own set of values; these values often conflict with the laws and values of the greater society. Rather than simply reaffirm our distaste for the illegal actions of some hackers, this chapter presents the hacker's understanding of these actions in an attempt to help investigators predict, effectively investigate, and appropriately respond to the intention of the criminal, not media-induced hysteria or uninformed prejudice.

The Original Meaning of "Hacker"

The origin of the term hacker is contentious. The Massachusetts Institute of Technology (MIT) claims a tradition of the use of the word before computer hackers existed. The word "hack" had long been used to describe the elaborate college pranks that MIT students would regularly devise. These "hacks" ranged from benign (hiding the incoming university president's office door with a bulletin board) to elaborate (building a full-sized replica police car on top of a domed building complete with working light bar and a ticket for parking illegally).

Among early MIT hackers, a hack was "a project undertaken or a product built not solely to fulfill some constructive goal, but with some wild pleasure taken in mere involvement."[4] When one of the early MIT computer hackers used the term 'hacker,' "there was serious respect implied. [T]o qualify as a hack, the feat must be imbued with innovation, style, and technical virtuosity."[5] The limitations of the hardware available made this creative problem solving necessary for the earliest computer hackers. "To top [a] program, someone else might try to do the same thing with fewer instructions—a worthy endeavor, since there was so little room in the small 'memory' of the computers in those days . . . This could most emphatically be done by approaching the problem from a whole new angle that no one had ever thought of before, but that in retrospect made total sense."[6] Thus hacking was most closely associated with creative, unorthodox problem solving to overcome the limitations of early computers. At that time, computers only existed in major universities, business research parks, and government installations. People with access to computers had a tremendous investment in not harming the few computers available. Thus, a hacker, in the classical sense, is someone who has mastered the art of programming to the point that he or she can simply sit down and "hack" in a program that works.

What Did Hackers Become?

Prior to the mid-1980s, the word hacker was obscure, known only to a few eccentric researchers in universities and corporate research parks. The 1983 film *War Games* spawned a boom in home hacking. "Unfortunately for many true hackers, however, the popularization of the term was a disaster . . . The trouble began with some well-publicized arrests of teenagers who electronically ventured into forbidden digital grounds, like government computer systems."[7] These well publicized arrests included the 414 Gang (from Milwaukee—area code 414). "'414 Private' was the home board for the first *group* to attract conspicuous trouble, the teenage '414 Gang,' whose intrusions into Sloan-Kettering Cancer Center and Los Alamos military computers were to be a nine-day-wonder in 1982."[8] The other notorious hacker crackdown culminated in the Operation Sundevil arrests in 1990.

Old school hackers never worried about breaking computer laws; there were none. The new generation that usurped the word hacker was defined—almost from the beginning—by crime. Contemporary hackers, with Internet access, have enormously more power available through easy network access, user-friendly hacking tools, and powerful home computers.

Retaking the Word: Hacker

It wasn't until much later, during the early 1990s, that the original hackers of the previous generation received recognition and began the dispute over the word hacker. Most of the original hackers had started their own high-tech companies or assumed leadership in research programs. The high-tech boom of the 1990s made many of them popular culture heroes. People working in the high-tech sector started to care about the early triumphs in information technology. It started to become more important to hackers to redeem the word hacker. Several factors contributed to this renewed interest:

- Increased computer use in the general population
- Popularization of the Internet
- Popular culture recognition and even reverence of nerds
- Popular fiction like the Cyberpunk books and computer movies
- The zealous promotion of computer Media sources like *Wired* Magazine

The computer media wanted to prove their connection to the "wired world" by picking up speech patterns and opinions of the computer world's stars. Many of these stars were hackers. Aaron D. Ball, a hacker and supporter of then-imprisoned Kevin Mitnick, stated:

```
>An entire community of people has been calling
>themselves hackers since before there was
```

```
>security to break.  These people call those who
>make a practice of breaking security 'crackers',
>and tend to think of them as nuisances more
>than anything else.  This isn't to say that a True
>Hacker doesn't break security;  he may well do so
>---it's just that being a peeping tom isn't his goal
>in life.⁹
```

Wired magazine, recognizing the disputed use of the term hacker, pioneered the popular use of the term cracker through editorial policy. *Wired* tried to establish credibility among the important figures of the early computer culture by refusing to stigmatize the word hacker.

What Do Hackers Do?

Hackers have been accused of breaking into NORAD, the North American Aerospace Defense Command.[10] Hackers have been accused of electronically stealing millions of dollars from major banks.[11]

Not all hacker activities are illegal. Basic First Amendment activities like communication and association are probably the most frequent online activities of hackers.[12] Similarly, not all illegal online activities are hacking. Pedophilia and child pornography draw as much disgust from most hackers as they do from law enforcement. Hackers and the law enforcement community come into conflict over activities like system intrusions and subsequent illegal acts.

Law Enforcement's Point of View: Illegal Actions and Damage

Although the fine points of labeling hacker activities will be covered in more depth later in the chapter, for now, general descriptions will suffice. Hackers explore computers. When the computer belongs to the hacker or when the hacker has legitimate access to the computer, there is no crime. When the hacker does not have permission to use the computer or network, the action is called system intrusion. Federal statute makes it a crime to knowingly use false credentials or access devices (which include passwords). Virtually any system intrusion requires that use of such a device.[13] Further, federal statute also makes it a crime to illegally access or damage a "protected" computer.[14] In this case, illegally accessing a computer connected to the Internet is a federal crime. During the process of an intrusion, data may be intentionally or unintentionally altered. Numerous other crimes may be committed, depending on the effects of such data alteration.[15] Worst-case scenarios include damage to financial networks (carrying billions of dollars each day); alteration, deletion, or exposure of health records; and compromise of safety-related systems. The potential for serious economic harm or catastrophic loss of life is very real in computer intrusion when data is altered.

The primary difference between simple network intrusion and data alteration is the intent of the intruder. By reading or "browsing" through confidential files, the intruder actually creates a copy of the file. Thus, mere browsing may be theft, but it does not deprive the owner of the data or the use of the data. To hackers, this makes the distinction between data alteration and intrusion more meaningful. It may be impossible for an investigator to determine if data has been altered. While criminally altered data may be used for fraud, like manipulating stock prices, or simply to deny the expression of the owner's idea, as with Web page defacements, the simple intruder may not cause actual harm. The problem for law enforcement is that it is often hard to determine the intent of an intruder. Substantial effort must be invested in assuring that data has not been altered or that no malicious intent is present. Law enforcement officers and investigators know that malicious intent is not always necessary for a crime to occur. Sometimes simple negligence or innocent mistakes can cause actual harm. Fundamentally, the law does not recognize a hacker's right to explore the systems, confidential data, and computer resources of others. This basic difference in perceptions makes understanding and predicting hacker actions difficult for law enforcement.

The Hacker's Point of View: Prosocial Hacking

The concept of a hacker subculture was introduced in Chapter 3. Essentially a subculture is a group of individuals within a larger culture. These individuals develop different attitudes and sometimes appearances from the dominant culture. Sometimes members of "deviant" communities define their activities as beneficial or "prosocial."[16] The hacker subculture is a group of like-minded individuals who share a set of values, defined in the hacker ethic. It exists through real-world communication, but also through common pursuits and common styles in virtual interactions.[17] The subculture's definitions of prosocial hacking define it and differentiate its activities from computer crime. For example, hackers report learning experiences, including creative problem solving, and educating others about security vulnerabilities.[18] In the following example, hacker Social Mysfyt, responds to a request for a shortcut to hacker prowess. In so doing, Mysfyt appeals to one of the most fundamental tenets of the hacker subculture: learning.

```
>"hacker" means many things to many people, however i
>believe that one of the only *common* threads is the DRIVE
>to learn more and do more.  by asking for help in getting
>started this person already defeated themself in a *game*
>he knew nothing about.  if you don't have the initiative
>and heart to push yourself to find all the answers
>possible first, you'll never amount to anything
>
>From: "social mysfyt" <snip!>
>Subject: Re: [mitnick] help me out! II
>Date: Thu, 2 Dec 1999 22:44:47 -0500
```

This and numerous similar comments from hackers support the idea that hackers can act in ways that support a higher cause.[19] Hackers understand the crime as a positive action under the "higher" goals supported by the subculture.

Kevin Mitnick's Story

The story of Kevin Mitnick perfectly exemplifies this distinction. Kevin Mitnick clearly broke the law by accessing computer systems without permission. The ensuing debate over Mitnick's case resulted from delays in this (at the time) novel area and the final punishment.[20] Hackers felt that the sentence was too harsh and the prosecution felt that the final punishment was too light because of the obscure nature of what they believed was a serious underlying offense.

The prosecution of Mitnick relied on estimates of the value of software he downloaded but did not alter. Several major corporations placed a total value of hundreds of millions of dollars on the software Mitnick obtained. This amount was determined with a method suggested by the FBI; they directed the companies to estimate the total development costs of the software. This amount was questioned at various stages in Mitnick's trial. Since Mitnick did not deprive the companies of the product of their research and development, it seems that the actual economic harm caused would be less than the total cost. Interestingly, none of the corporations victimized by Mitnick reported such a loss to the Securities and Exchange Commission, which is required by law.

On the other hand, the corporations had no way of knowing if the data had been altered. They may have devoted significant effort to re-establishing their confidence in the data. It is also possible that Mitnick could have sold the information to rival companies; there is no evidence or even suggestion that he did so. However, the initial estimate of value may have reflected this fear. Delays caused by the intrusion may have reduced the market advantage of some of the corporations affected. So the calculation of actual damages is very difficult. In the three years Mitnick spent awaiting trial, the value of a Sun Microsystems operating system (Solaris™) dropped from an estimated prerelease value of several million dollars to essentially free. Delay spent to verify the integrity of data after an intrusion may have had a direct financial impact on its owners.

When intrusion is discovered, it often requires the owner or administrator of the affected system to question the integrity, accuracy and authenticity of data on the network. Although the legitimate user of the system and data is not denied access to either, there is no reasonable certainty of data's security in the system. Security measures often require the removal of Web-based resources and restoration of data from (hopefully) unaffected backup copies.

A HACKER BY ANY OTHER NAME . . .[21]

Although it borders on political correctness for crooks, there is some actual value to understanding the distinctions of a name drawn in the hacker community.[22] Perhaps most important, hackers themselves sometimes use these terms to draw distinctions based on fine points of motivation and action that can be valuable to an investigation. Such information may allow an investigator to include or exclude a suspect from an investigation. There are certain actions that a hacker simply would not perform. For example, a malicious attack that serves only to back up an extortion threat would be very un-hacker-like. Other hackers would probably be more cooperative in the investigation of such an incident. On the other hand, an attack that demonstrated technical skill in a novel way and embarrassed law enforcement or corporate interests would create solidarity among hackers and great status for the perpetrator.

Computer Criminals vs. Hackers

Although a violation of the law is still a crime, juries may be more sympathetic to the motive of exploration versus personal profit. It is also hard to prosecute a "pure" hacker under Federal statutes because the sentencing guidelines are driven by financial damages. These facts alone justify recognizing a distinction; this does not mean excusing an illegal action. It simply means recognizing a fundamentally different reality for investigation and prosecution.

There is little said in mainstream analyses that distinguishes hackers from computer criminals.[23] In fact, some well respected computer crime fighters flatly deny that there is a distinction.[24] Others acknowledge the illegality of the actions, but point to a radically different set of motivations.[25] However, in the underground hacker media, the distinction is a subject of primary importance.[26] Emanuel Goldstein, editor of *2600: The Hacker Quarterly,* has addressed the distinction between hackers and computer criminals in three ways. First, he minimized the criminal damage caused by hacking, implying that very little actual harm is caused. Second, he defended the criminal actions of hackers based on their motives and adherence to hacker subcultural values, which were not viewed as criminal by Goldstein. Third, he disavowed hackers who commit crimes that violate hacker values, such as crimes of financial gain.[27] Thus, it appears that at least some elements of the hacker subculture do not condone what they define as computer crime.

The majority of hacker online actions are perfectly legal; it is hard to imagine committing a crime with every key stroke. Basic activities like communication and information sharing as well as illegal activities all fall within the range of hacker behavior. All of these behaviors can be called hacking. The distinction between hackers who commit crimes and other computer criminals rests upon the attitudes with which a hacker approaches the activity. For various reasons, the hacker subculture accepts actions that violate law. These actions may be called criminal hacking. However, some actions are not accepted by the subculture. These and criminal hacking behaviors may be called computer crime. The point of confusion lies in the fact that criminal hacking is considered to be computer crime by law enforcement, but is considered perfectly acceptable hacking by the hacker subculture. Figure 4.1 shows the overlap of these concepts.

Hacking Criminal Hacking Computer Crime

FIGURE 4.1   The relationship between hacking, criminal hacking, and computer crime.

Definitions of computer crime that equate all hacking with criminal behavior are both offensive to hackers and inaccurate. Similarly, definitions that deny that any meaningful criminal action is committed by hackers are absurd to law enforcement and also inaccurate. This Venn diagram depicts a subset of hacker behavior that is illegal, but condoned by the hacker subculture (labeled criminal hacking). The reality of computer crime and obscurity of perpetrator motives makes this abstract system of defining hackers and computer criminals unworkable in the field. As a consequence, less clear-cut labels are often applied.[28]

Crackers

A cracker is a malicious hacker. There is no final authority on who determines when or how a hacker becomes a cracker. There is no clear way to cross the line back to hacker, either.

In response to a computer incident, John Gilmore, co-founder of the Electronic Frontier Foundation, said:

> As usual, the computer underground is doing a service to the country by making it clear just how shallow the government's understanding of computer security is. They are quite curiously refraining from damaging anything in their intrusions but the egos of the bureaucracies involved. As usual, the first response of the Feds is to threaten dire punishment for the messengers. But they are being prodded into actually attempting to keep serious attackers out, a novel idea somewhat overdue for consideration.[29]

Gilmore's recognition of the possible benefit of even vandalous intrusion echoes the hacker community's divergent values. There is no room for this view in the generally accepted concept of property rights, but the hacker community has a different understanding of their actions. Most hackers claim to benefit the systems they intrude upon because they do not destroy data and alert system administrators to security flaws.

White Hat vs. Black Hat

The current fashion for describing hackers is to use a new set of terminology recognized the "gray" areas of determining malicious hacking. Thus, "white hat hacker" describes an "ethical" hacker. A gray hat hacker is someone who typically behaves in an ethical manner, but sometimes violates accepted ethics. Finally, a black hat hacker is a "malicious" hacker (i.e., a cracker or computer criminal using hacker-like methods). These labels do not conflict with the typology presented earlier in this chapter; they simply describe the motives of contemporary—i.e., Internet—hackers.

White Hat Hackers
White hat is a term used to describe an ethical hacker. The term white hat was needed because so many former or "reformed" hackers entered the computer security field. Eventually, computer science graduates employing hacker-like methods also spurred

the need for the term. The reality existed before the label. There was a long and lively debate about hiring "former" hackers. Other examples of white hat hacking include:

- Software testing by manufacturers
- Independent verification of software function and security
- Reverse engineering
- Training

Tiger teams, a term borrowed from the military, described a hacker or team of hackers hired to "test" the defenses of an organization. These white hat hackers follow a strict code of loyalty to their employers. The use of tiger teams is based on the theory that "only a hacker can beat a hacker." There is a great deal of common sense to the notion of testing defenses with the types of attacks used by an enemy. Several computer security/risk management companies have security services units that actually have white hat hackers on their rolls. A short list includes the "A" list of the field: KPMG, Kroll, Computer Associates, Gartner Group's, ICSA Labs (anti-virus division of Tru Secure), and Cambridge Technology Partners.

Gray Hat Hackers

A gray hat hacker is someone who typically behaves in an ethical manner, but sometimes violates accepted ethics. The term "Gray Hat" came into usage to describe a usually ethical hacker who sometimes indulged in illicit activity. A typical gray hat is a penetration tester who would not attack a client, but hacks and intrudes recreationally. A gray hat may also occasionally violate the hacker ethic against hacking for profit

---

BOX 4.1   Penetration Testing

Penetration testing is looked upon with suspicion by hackers because it is a little too close to law enforcement. Penetration testing is an acceptable use of skills by older hackers as long as they don't develop too comfortable a relationship with law enforcement. It seems to violate the hacker ethic against hacking for profit. Some hacker purists won't do it. However, free penetration testing is unquestionably a prosocial activity to hackers.

The business ethic of a tiger team is based on survival. Loyalty to the company hiring the team is essential to ever being hired again.

- Information discovered during the testing must not be disclosed to anyone but the employer.
- Only intrude where invited, otherwise you become a "bad guy."
- Where the methods are exactly the same, only the intention separates good guys from bad guys.
- White hats often even associate with black hats to keep current.

(other than being paid to do penetration testing for a willing client). A typical contemporary interpretation of the hacker ethic usually includes the following elements:

- Do not profit from intrusion.
- Do not intentionally harm a computer system.
- Attempt to inform a system administrator of security flaws.
- Hackers are not bad guys; computer criminals are bad guys.

Black Hat Hackers

A black hat hacker is essentially a cracker or malicious hacker. The term black hat does not apply to all computer criminals. Only network intrusion and other "hacker-like" activities committed in conflict with hacker ethics qualify as black hat activities. At first the term was not used by hackers (malicious or otherwise), but it has since been used by some hackers to describe themselves.

HACKERS AND THE MEDIA

Since the first public awareness of hackers, a deluge of lurid news stories has blurred the line between hacker and computer criminal. Early second-generation hackers (i.e., bedroom hackers), took control of computer systems and left taunting messages to legitimate users. Hackers became the focus of fear for a society struggling to come to grips with the nascent information age. Old school hackers largely ignored the upstarts but resented the media's use of the word hacker applied to electronic trespassers and vandals. "It was understandable that the journalists covering these stories would refer to the young perps as hackers—after all, that's what the kids called *themselves.*"[30]

There is also a tendency in the media toward publishing the lurid or frightening aspects of crimes, including hacker crimes.[31] An example is a list of credit card numbers found on Kevin Mitnick's computer when he was arrested. The press often reported that there were approximately 20,000 credit card numbers contained in the file. The press consistently failed to report that the same file was publicly available in online newsgroups; the file was years out of date; and there was no indication that Mitnick used or tried to use any of the credit card numbers. According to Mitnick, the card numbers were a source of information for later use in guessing the system for credit card number generation.[32] Although his possession of credit card numbers, names, and expiration dates constitute access device fraud, there is no reason to believe that any harm could be caused by this outdated information that was, at that point, publicly available.

When citing worst-case scenarios for hacking or network intrusion, the alteration of medical records always comes up. In a review of "shockers," author Jonathan Littman reported that a Berkeley researcher discovered a medical facility in the San Francisco Bay Area with open telephone lines to medical records. An examination of medical records will show a great deal of personal information, but beyond the threat to privacy, alteration of those records by a single character can be fatal (in the case of blood-type). It is easy to understand why the alteration of medical data has received such attention.

The problem is that there has never been a recorded instance of a hacker corrupting medical records and killing a person. The lurid nature of the story and the implied threat to readers changes the threat of hackers from a remote curiosity to an immediate threat, and therefore sells. Unfortunately, aspiring hackers often become acquainted with media portrayals of hacking before they begin to interact with actual hackers.[33]

FEAR, UNCERTAINTY, AND DOUBT—FUD

According to the New Hacker Dictionary, FUD was defined by Gene Amdahl after he left IBM to found his own company. "FUD is the fear, uncertainty, and doubt that IBM sales people instill in the minds of potential customers who might be considering [Amdahl] products." The idea, of course, was to persuade them to go with safe IBM gear rather than with competitors' equipment. Thus, FUD is a long standing tradition in the computer world. It is made possible by the necessary ignorance of the vast majority of users; after all, not everyone can be a guru-level hacker. Hacker-related FUD is spread by the computer security industry. Brian Martin of the former Hacker News Network once stated "[b]y instilling FUD in the minds of consumers, the vendor obliquely promises dire consequences if the intended target does not buy their goods."[34]

Hacker-related FUD is a condition created by the need to convey interesting "news." In discussing the maligned image of hackers, a common theme is expressed by Brian Martin: "[T]he use of FUD in a marketing campaign is often subtle and hard to spot. Worse, this underhanded tactic is often problematic in trying to counter. Rather than fighting against incorrect facts or misguided opinions, you find yourself battling vague assertions, self-serving maxims, and half-truths."[35] As with other media exposure, FUD campaigns and lurid stories feed into the hacker subculture, and influence "newbie" hackers as to what hackers do.

THE EVOLVING HACKER SUBCULTURE

The Hacker Ethic

The hacker ethic is an evolving but integral part of the hacker subculture. Its oldest and purest form was derived from the unwritten rules of behavior and beliefs of the earliest hackers. In his book, *Hackers,* Steven Levy compiled these ideas and recorded them.

1. Access to computers—and anything which might teach you something about the way the world works—should be unlimited and total. [p.40]
2. All information should be free. [p.40]
3. Mistrust authority—promote decentralization. [p.41]
4. Hackers should be judged by their hacking, not bogus criteria such as degress, age, race, or position. [p. 43]
5. You can create art and beauty on a computer. [p.43]
6. Computers can change your life for the better. [p.45][36]

When hackers left the university setting, they were forced to adapt aspects of their behavior to their new environments. Therefore, we see an evolution of the hacker ethic to fit the expanded domain of later hackers.

This evolution is demonstrated in the Hacker Manifesto. The manifesto introduces a new type of hacker. It evokes the angst of young hackers exploring network from home computers. They were sometimes isolated and almost never enjoyed the supportive environment and encouragement of the previous generation of hackers. They first began to feel oppressed by the dominant culture. This excerpt is taken from the end of the manifesto:

> Yes, I am a criminal. My crime is that of curiosity. My crime is that of judging people by what they say and think, not what they look like. My crime is that of outsmarting you, something that you will never forgive me for.
>
> I am a hacker, and this is my manifesto. You may stop this individual, but you can't stop us all . . .[37]

The Mentor, author of the Hacker Manifesto, was a member of the Legion of Doom (LOD), the most prominent hacker group of the 1980s.[38]

The New Hacker Dictionary offers a more contemporary definition of hacker ethic. It stresses the importance of information sharing and the requirement of no harm:

1. The belief that information-sharing is a powerful positive good, and that it is an ethical duty of hackers to share their expertise by writing open-source and facilitating access to information and to computing resources wherever possible.
2. The belief that system-cracking for fun and exploration is ethically OK as long as the cracker commits no theft, vandalism, or breach of confidentiality.[39]

The requirement to do no harm may be an evolutionary step in hacker subculture. Previously, hackers existed in the ivory tower of universities; then the crime of curiosity was described in the Hacker Manifesto; and now above, an ethic of minimizing damage has been added. The prohibition against damage was also prominently a part of the story of Phiber Optik, a prominent hacker in the late 1980s and a media star and hacker martyr in the 1990s.[40] According to the report, Phiber Optik damaged an electronic bulletin board system as part of a prank; however, the incident affected him deeply and thereafter he tried to follow the hacker ethic in a way that was more consistent with Raymond's, above.

There is considerable evidence that not all hackers adhere to the hacker ethic in all of their activities. Hafner and Markoff allege that Kevin Mitnick attacked and damaged the computer of a shipping company that refused him access.[41] Also, a cursory search of hacker stories reveals numerous articles detailing the criminal actions of Web vandals, thieves, and stalkers.[42] Hackers who act outside of the hacker ethic are simply criminals.

Although both groups indulge in illegal activities, adherence to the hacker ethic and pursuit of subcultural goals define the difference between computer criminals and criminal hackers. Noncriminal hackers' activities (i.e., those encouraged by the subculture) may be deviant by the standards of the dominant culture, but they are not criminal. The great difficulty in differentiating these three groups is that human behavior is dynamic and contextual. There is therefore no simple dichotomy between hackers and computer criminals. However, historical background can provide contexts for a better understanding of the different hacker "types."

HACKER TYPOLOGY

This typology reflects some of the terminology in common use in the hacker subculture. Very few hackers would use these terms in a precise manner to differentiate themselves from other hackers, but as is common with academic typologies, it reflects observed reality, rather than strict linguistic use. Although there are pronounced differences among the types of hackers presented in this typology, all share certain characteristics. These characteristics can be distinguished by the historical era of the hacker type, although history is not the sole characteristic. Depending on how new hackers are brought into the hacker subculture and their experiences as hackers, they may have a strong affinity to any of the types presented. The common characteristics that form the basis of comparison for hacker types are:

- "Access to resources," or the ability of a type of hacker to access computer hardware or information
- "Enculturation," or the degree to which a type of hacker is expected to adhere to the values of the hacker subculture
- "Skill," or the ability to understand and manipulate a computer

The typology presents qualitative descriptions of the level of each characteristic found in each type rather than a numeric, or quantitative, value. In Table 4.1, an arrow up or down indicates relatively more or less of a concept, respectively. A dot indicates the inapplicability of a concept to a given type; each of these is explained after the table. There are three major types of hacker: old school, bedroom, and Internet. The latter two have subtypes. For bedroom hackers, the subtypes are larval hackers (also called

TABLE 4.1   Typology of Hackers

	Resources	Enculturation	Skill
Old school	•	↑	↑
Bedroom hacker	↓	↑	↑
Larval Hacker	↓	•	↓
warez D00dz	↓	↓	•
Internet hacker	↑	↑	↑
Script kiddies	↑	↓	↓
Hacktivists	↑	•	•

newbies) and warez D00dz. For Internet hackers, the subtypes are script kiddies and hacktivists.

All of the hacker types are not covered in the same level of detail here. This presentation focuses on the contemporary hacker type: the Internet hacker. Even though Internet hackers are by far the most common type today, other types still exist and their historical influences can clearly be seen in the hacker subculture.

Old School Hackers

The Massachusetts Institute of Technology (MIT) is famous for the birth of hacking in the late 1950s, although U.C. Berkeley, Carnegie Mellon and Stanford simultaneously spawned hackers. Hackers first developed in the earliest days of computers, when researchers had to experiment with computers to see what they could do. Invariably, this was accomplished at universities or corporate research campuses. There was no concept of home computers in those days.

Skill (↑)

These same researchers recognized that they had written the book on computers and were under no obligation to follow the book. They solved problems on the fly and often just "hacked" out programs to do so. Hacker ethos was different from corporate or engineering ethos. The latter required understanding and a plan before a solution. Hackers just worked with the problem and depended on their own intimate knowledge of the machine and software to discover the most direct solution. Levy based his hacker ethic on the "old school" hackers of MIT.[43]

Resources (•)

Old school hackers traditionally had almost unlimited access to computer hardware, but could not readily access knowledge bases because this knowledge had not yet been discovered. Further, although access to hardware resources was unlimited, the capabilities of the hardware were very limited.

Enculturation (↑)

The ultimate goal of these early hackers was to reduce the number of programming instructions needed to solve problems or to produce results. The quest for efficiency became so embedded in the early hacker culture that it persists, even after the machines have reached the point where it is no longer strictly necessary. This trait may be at the root of the hacker's legendary cleverness and tendency to brag about good hacks. Quick and clever solutions gave hackers their name.

Like their programming skills, the ethic evolved in the absence of another option. What began as an obvious and convenient conduct became an ideology. Most of the imperatives of the hacker ethic revolved around access to or distribution of computer knowledge. When norms blocked access to the computer, hackers determined that information must be free. Since the old school hackers created the first hacker ethic in a cooperative environment, each saw that following the ethic would produce the best results, and simply followed it. This represents a level of enculturation not seen in newer hackers.

Contemporary Old School Hackers

Although the old school hacker type concentrates on the first generation of hackers, there are contemporary equivalents. It is hard to imagine a low level of computer resources in the Internet age, but given the extreme skill possessed by modern old school hackers, they may find their resources constricting. Like the first generation, they must often invent the knowledge they need to pursue their goals. Further, modern old school hackers tend to form collectives with supportive environments like the first generation. For example, L0pht Heavy Industries has presented many unique discoveries and software tools. These contemporary old school hackers hold more closely to the original hacker ethic than later types. This type is most clearly continued in the collaborative "open-source" community that supports projects like Linux.

BOX 4.2   The Open Source Movement

The open source movement keeps the ideals of the early hackers alive. The human-readable version of a computer program, called source code, is shared with anyone who cares to modify or improve it. Free, or "open," source code also allows other programmers to make their own creations compatible with other, existing programs since they know how those programs work. Most software purchased today tightly controls access to the source code. The source code to Windows™ is a closely guarded trade secret of the Microsoft® corporation. When you purchase a copy of Windows™, you receive the computer-readable version of the program, called object code.

> The basic idea behind open source is very simple: When programmers can read, redistribute, and modify the source code for a piece of software, the software evolves. People improve it, people adapt it, people fix bugs. And this can happen at a speed that, if one is used to the slow pace of conventional software development, seems astonishing.
>
> We in the open source community have learned that this rapid evolutionary process produces better software than the traditional closed model, in which only a very few programmers can see the source.

Guarding the source code allows corporations to prevent some unauthorized (and uncompensated) use of their intellectual property. It also gives them more control over the function and compatibility of their software. One of the general benefits of this technique is that security flaws are not as obvious to would-be attackers. The open source movement claims that there is no true advantage to this technique, called security through obscurity. Rather, the open source movement claims that by quickly discovering and quickly fixing security holes, open source software actually provides greater overall security and fewer bugs.

Quote Courtesy of the Open Source Initiative, *http://www.opensource.org/*

Bedroom Hackers

In the early 1980s, when home computers became widely available, hacking expanded from the universities and research parks. Many children and young adults in the 1980s received home computers and were left, largely unsupervised to explore them. These machines were often placed in the bedroom of their owner. Some people began to explore the capacities of their computers and learn. Many quickly exhausted the possibilities of their isolated machines and sought more. These "bedroom hackers" used their new-found computer skills to gain access to other people's systems. Electronic bulletin boards flourished and disseminated techniques and passwords to allow hackers to explore the network. Phone phreaks, a counterculture movement of the 1960s and 1970s, had been exploring the phone system for years by the time hacking moved out of the universities. Phone phreaks found ways to learn about the phone system much like hackers had learned about computers, but had none of the utopian influences of the universities. Out of common interest and necessity, phone phreaks entered the hacking scene and spread their own techniques, revolutionary politics, street culture, and outright criminality to the bedroom hackers. By the mid-80s, hackers and phreaks were virtually indistinguishable.

BOX 4.3   Phone Phreaks Bring Technology and Attitude to Hacking

- *Telephone technologies (boxes).* Phone phreaks created devices that produced effects on the phone system. The blue box was used to produce a 2600 Hz tone, gaining access to the toll network for the placement of calls without charge. The red box simulates the noise of a quarter, nickel, or dime being dropped into a pay phone, allowing free pay phone calls. Other boxes exist or may simply be part of phreak lore. *Note:* These devices no longer work on the North American phone system, but they did during the days of the bedroom hacker.

- *Counterculture of the 1960s and 70s.* There was an affinity for political subversives and Vietnam war protestors with the phone phreaks. Many freaks were members of the youth culture movements of this period. In fact, one famous phreak, Cheshire Catalyst, edited the TAP (Technical Assistance Program) newsletter founded by Abbie Hoffman.[44]

- *Phone company lore.* Phone phreaks did not restrict themselves to the technology of the Phone Company (there was only one back then[45]). This interest was the beginning of social engineering (see below).

- *Paranoia.* Years of hiding from Bell System security and listening in on phone conversations taught phreaks that privacy was an illusion on the phone system. "Ma" Bell heard everything.

- *"ph"onetic spelling.* Phone phreaks regularly replace the letter "f" with "ph." Phonetic spelling may be the basis of "'leet speak."

Skill (↑)

Although few of the bedroom hackers reached the level of virtuosity of the old school hackers, there were a number of extremely skilled and knowledgeable "elite" bedroom hackers. With the addition of the phone phreaks' knowledge, they have surpassed the old school hackers in many regards. Certainly, their skills were more suited to intrusion than the old school hackers. Bedroom hackers excelled at phone-related feats and found effective, nontechnical means to explore the electronic landscape. These techniques testify to the influence of both old school hackers and phone phreaks.

Techniques

War dialing is a technique to discover computers with modems. War dialers take their name from the 1983 movie *War Games*. The lead character, played by Matthew Broderick, used a program to dial numbers until he found a computer to "play" with. To find other computers, war dialers dial a sequence of numbers.

The practice of social engineering was introduced by phone phreaks; the technique is based on the use of the telephone. The idea is to acquire sensitive information from the human running the machine rather than using advanced computer skills to beat the electronic security. Employees reveal passwords, internal information, and even execute the commands for the hacker. Social engineering is essentially a confidence scam.

Dumpster diving, or trashing, is a fairly direct way to obtain information. A person enters a dumpster and looks for useful information. This technique was introduced

---

BOX 4.4   Social Engineering Tactics

Different tactics are used by social engineers. If one technique fails, it is often possible simply to call back and get a fresh start with a new representative from the company and use any information gained from the failed attempt.

Camaraderie: "Hey, this is Joe out here on a pole. I forgot my order sheet. Can you look up the service on this pair? If I have to drive back to the shop, I'll be behind all day."

Bluster: "This is Supervisor Wilson. I need to reset service flags on this account now . . . Of course I can't do it myself! I'm up a pole trying to fix what your technicians did to this setup."

Technical detail: "Hello, who am I speaking to? . . . Okay Roger, this is Bill at the Tulsa switch. You have a problem with trunk 6. It's okay, we haven't lost calls yet. Go to frame 009 and count up 16 and over 10. That's the bugger as near as we can tell . . . Oh—it has a little pen-shaped device on it? That means that it is being monitored. Let's route around it by switching the pair attached. Here's what you do . . ."

by phone phreaks. The telephone company was a favorite target of dumpster divers. Telephone company trash yielded technical manuals, notes, technical bulletins, and a plethora of information useful to a phone phreak. Aside from the direct access to phone technology from castoff manuals, even small scraps of office minutia were highly prized (names, schedules, internal information). Such information could be used to further social engineering.

Marathon hacking sessions are such a fixture in the popular imagination that hacker stories that start with "Bleary-eyed, staring at monitor" are as much of a cliché as mysteries that start "It was a dark and stormy night." "During the hours . . . [of hacking], a hacker attained a state of pure concentration."[46] It takes time to "warm up" when hacking. Hackers have described this time as "loading" their "memory" with all the necessary variables. "When you had all that information . . . it was almost as if your own mind had merged into the environment of the computer . . . Sometimes it took hours to build up to the point where your thoughts could contain the total picture, and when you did get to that point, it was . . . a shame to waste it." The cyberpunk novels so popular with hackers make this entry into the computer an explicit act.[47] The cyberpunk characters live the reality analogized in the minds of hackers. A key feature of the cyberpunk genre is the projection of human consciousness into the virtual world to explore and manipulate free from physical constraints. Obsessive hacking approaches this state.

Resources (↓)

Bedroom hackers are characterized by limited resources. Although the personal computer brought computing access to an entirely new, and orders of magnitude larger, portion of the population, access to the large, powerful computers was still restricted. Further, the possibilities of the early home computers[48] were quickly exhausted. Unlike old school hackers, bedroom hackers did not turn inward and obsessively attempt to optimize their programs; they turned outward. Old school hackers knew that they had the best equipment available and conceded to the inevitable. Bedroom hackers were painfully aware of new and richer fields at the other end of a telephone line. This fed the craving for more access and fresh fields to explore, with the addition of an illicit thrill. The two keys were illicit access and free phone calls.

Enculturation (↑)

Levy describes the hacker ethic implicitly adopted by the old school hackers. Hackers will not harm the computers they explore, nor will they destroy the data they find (1984). Some bedroom hackers, like Phiber Optik, respect this ethic. The corollary to the hacker ethic is disrespect for those who hoard knowledge or seek to unfairly restrict computer access. The Mentor described this corollary in the Hacker Manifesto:

> This is our world now . . . the world of the electron and the switch, the beauty of the baud. We make use of a service already existing without paying for what could be dirt-cheap if it wasn't run by profiteering gluttons, and you call us criminals. We explore . . . and you call us criminals. We seek after knowledge . . . and you call us criminals.[49]

Bedroom hackers were willing to steal services that facilitate exploration, yet tend to hold a self-conscious ethic about profiting from such activities. Bulletin board systems (BBSs)[50] gave bedroom hackers the first chance to forge a society in a primitive online environment. A BBS uses phone lines to allow users to log in and read or leave files (philez) for other users. BBSs need phone access. The primary communication of bedroom hackers is a file composed and thought out in advance, not rapid e-mail or chat. Bedroom hackers reached their zenith before e-mail moved out of the universities. These Philez (see 'leet speek below) became the standard of communication through telephone bulletin board systems (BBSs). The reliance on long distance telephone lines may be the primary reason for the alliance between hackers and phone phreaks.

Larval Hackers (Newbies)

Larval hackers are a subtype of bedroom hacker. There are contemporary equivalents in the Internet era, but fundamental differences in technology and resources make larval hackers part of the bedroom hacker culture. Larval hackers tend to be excited about exploration, but based on the source of their introduction to hacking (e.g., the media) they are easily misguided or diverted to cracking, vandalism, baseless bragging, or other vices (as determined by more experienced hackers). Larval hackers seem to not know where to start, but to want to start immediately.

Novices have existed since the "old school" days, but there they were socialized to respect the machines and the rights of others under the direct supervision of more experienced hackers. At the zenith of the bedroom hacker era, novices had no such guidance and were often rejected until they proved their worth by finding useful information or committing a notable hack (see "Enculturation"). A group called the Legion of Doom maintained a "secret" BBS where only elite hackers could peruse the

---

BOX 4.5   " 'leet speek" and "k-rad"

Bedroom hackers created a hacker society apart from corporate research parks and universities. They created their own dialect called eleet ('leet) speek or k-rad. In k-rad, numbers were substituted for visually similar letters. Capital letters were freely and randomly used. For instance, "elite hackers" became 31337 HaKorZ. There is no definite pattern for the replacements; they are just inserted upon the whim of the writer. There are different reasons for 'leet speek. Foremost, much of the interaction between 'leeto hackers happened on line. It required typing. Shortcuts and abbreviations became the norm. It is also true that many bedroom hackers were teenagers, and still in school. Their spelling and typing skills were deficient. Finally, repetitious speech becomes boring and tends to get embellished. Whatever the reasons for the growth of elite speak, it served to further differentiate the hacker subculture from the dominant culture. Many of the "philez" on BBSs in the 1980s were written, at least partially, in elite speak.

accumulation of hacker/phreaker knowledge (as well as the usual brags and boasts) amassed by the group. Newbies had to find a way into the secret hack site to be considered adequate.

Skill and Resources (↓)

Larval hackers are characterized by limited knowledge. They are unsocialized in the hacker subculture and may unknowingly violate the hacker ethic. They tend to be eager to prove their skill and acquire status. The lack of general access to resources allowed more experienced hackers slowly to dole out knowledge if they decided the larval hacker had the right attitude and thus, socialize them to the values of the hacker subculture.

Enculturation (•)

Hackers established a social hierarchy based on eliteness. Although there was no single way to become elite, it usually involved either slowly learning how to hack from a more elite hacker or demonstrating virtuosity with an amazing hack. According to Slatalla and Quittner, Phiber Optik was almost instantly recognized for his broad knowledge of the phone system and catapulted to the highest levels of hacker society, membership in the Legion of Doom.[51] Other hackers patiently learned at the gentle hands of "mentors," or in the harsh give-and-take world of hacker BBSs.

Even though many hackers were happy to share knowledge, even the most generous could become overwhelmed with larval hackers who only sought the most direct route to power. One of the ways to attract the attention of an elite hacker was to offer something of interest. In this passage, two larval hackers approach Phiber Optik to explain what they have found, and trade access for knowledge.

> You have to be a little brave to even suggest calling a guy like that. You have to be pretty sure of yourself, not afraid at all that the guy is going to hang up on you, or worse, listen to what you say and then ridicule you . . . They want him to teach them not only about the phone system, but also about all the sophisticated computers he's cracked, about the rare commands he can type, about the way his mind works . . .
>
> [F]or the first time since he hacked into the computer, [he] tells another living human the computer's phone numbers . . . They tell him they have access to a computer . . . and they want to know what it is, what it's capable of doing.[52]

In a process that repeated this transaction thousands of times, with innumerable hackers, larval hackers became the foot soldiers of bedroom hackers. When a bedroom hacker had either exhausted the local exchanges for war dialing or had drawn the attention of the telephone company security, he relied on larval hackers to discover new computers. Repetitive or dull jobs could also be traded for information, new systems to explore, or access to more elite circles. Larval hackers could devote time on their computers and their parents' phone lines to dialing new exchanges. In return, larval hackers received attention, access, knowledge, and social status. "[P]eer recognition from other hackers or friends is a reward and goal for many hackers, signifying acceptance into the community and offering places in a hierarchy of more advanced hackers."[53]

In the mid-80s, underground boards sprang up like digital fungi. ShadowSpawn Elite. Sherwood Forest I, II, and III. Digital Logic Data Service in Florida, [administred] by no less a man than "Digital Logic" himself; Lex Luthor of the Legion of Doom was prominent on this board, since it was in his area code. Lex's own board, "Legion of Doom," started in 1984. The Neon Knights ran a network of Apple-hacker boards: Neon Knights North, South, East and West. Free World II was run by "Major Havoc." Lunatic Labs is still in operation as of this writing. Dr. Ripco in Chicago, an anything-goes anarchist board with an extensive and raucous history, was seized by Secret Service agents in 1990 on Sundevil day, but up again almost immediately, with new machines and scarcely diminished vigor.[54]

This basic exchange of information also served to slowly socialize larval hackers as they gained knowledge. If a larval hacker abused information or became reckless, he would be frozen out of further information. Because information was scarce, the culture of hacking became an important mediator of its spread.

Warez D00dz

Warez D00dz (pronounced: wârz dōōdz) trade pirated software. Other forms of hackers value exploration and discovery. In contrast, warez D00dz value the acquisition of massive amounts of software with broken copy protection. They collect and archive this software, called cracks. They prize recognition of their activities and collections. Many warez sites contain software with such a limited purpose that it could not possibly be of direct interest to most warez D00dz.[55] Although they do not share hacker ethics, warez D00dz share a common origin and many subcultural elements.

Skill (•)

Unlike other hackers, skill level is difficult to quantify because it does not have the primary importance for status. Among warez D00dz, esteem may be granted for demonstrating skill by rapidly cracking copy protection (0 day release). It may also be granted for operating a fast site with an extensive collection of cracked software. Skill can range from extensive to non-existent, even for "elite" warez D00dz.

The skills required for cracking software protection are fairly narrow. This bypasses the slow, but rewarding, building of skills and sense of mastery that accompanies learning how to hack. One basic technique is to compare the Windows registry before and after installation and defeat registry entries that block full use. This makes "trial" versions and limited-function versions into full versions. More sophisticated warez D00dz used software tools called debuggers to watch the code of the software operate and spot the commands that defeat copying. This is more of an art than a science, so disseminating skills and techniques is difficult. Paul, a hacker, suggested that most elite warez D00dz are actually trained programmers who crack software for their own personal reasons.[56] Advanced cracking requires a fairly detailed understanding of the way a computer operates. Source code (readable by humans) must almost directly correspond to object code (not readable by humans). The programming language, assembly,[57] is

---

BOX 4.6   Cracking Protection in the Major Leagues

Cryptanalysis is beyond Warez D00dz, but they can adapt the work of old school hackers like Dr. Edward Felten. Dr. Felten led a Princeton University team that defeated the Secure Digital Music Initiative (SDMI) "water-marking" scheme for rights management. Under legal threats, the team did not release the report at an academic conference.

The Sovereign Copy Protection: Cryptography

In 2000, SDMI organized a challenge to the cryptologic community, offering a prize up to $10,000 to anyone who "can remove the watermark or defeat the other technology on our proposed copyright protection system." Felten, Wallach, et al. sued in federal court and eventually appealed the decision to the second circuit.

The Secure Digital Music Initiative (SDMI) sponsored in part by the Recording Industry Association of America (RIAA) attempts to cryptographically "lock" rights management software to music. Attempting to defeat SDMI is a criminal violation of the Digital Millennium Copyright Act (DMCA). DMCA prohibits the creation of devices or services that circumvent copyright protection (§ 1210).

---

unique to each chip or chip family. Making the jump from patching the Windows™ registry to editing assembly code is difficult for warez D00dz because they do not have the intermediate steps that hackers have to see results as they progress.

Enculturation and Resources (↓)

The earliest warez activities simply involved swapping games or other software. In keeping with the hacker ethic, expensive software that could be cheaply and easily copied, was. Digitized information can be copied. Without steps to prevent it, it can be copied easily. Copy protection was invented. Warez D00dz were born in the ensuing debate about the morality of copying software. At the beginning their actions and culture mirrored that of bedroom hackers. Old school hackers and like-minded individuals despised anything that separated the user from the operating machine. Others found innumerable justifications to try to break the copy protection. "Software is too expensive." "We only copy software we wouldn't buy anyway." "We only do it to try out new programs." It is a "backup copy in case the disk becomes damaged." As the warez scene developed, it grew away from the bedroom hackers.

Warez D00dz do not follow the cardinal virtue of the hacker subculture: share information. Their activities are specific and conscious violations of law. In the early days, a warez BBS was always in danger of discovery and closure (with arrest for the system operator). Warez sites could also be overwhelmed quickly. Leeches download only, and do not contribute. Leech time was wasted access to a scarce resource (i.e., the warez board). Thus, elite warez boards remained cloaked in secrecy. Unlike elite hacker boards, information was not distributed through the economy.

The Contemporary Scene

The warez scene has evolved since the 1980s, when it was closer to hacker culture. The contemporary warez scene has expanded to include:

- Music and movies
- MP3s (volume counts)
- Digitally compressed movies (0 day release)
- Cable and satellite descrambling
- DVD decoding
- Peer-to-peer networking
- Console games

However, most of the warez scene does not pursue the technology like other forms of hackers. There is still frequent common cause among the two groups, though. The warez scene supports the efforts of hackers who create peer-to-peer networking technology (e.g., Gnutella), cryptographic attack programs (e.g., DeCSS), and the work of hacktivists and civil libertarians (e.g., Secure Digital Music Initiative).

Internet Hackers

Contemporary hackers have Internet access. Through this connection they have virtually unlimited access to knowledge and virtually unlimited access to resources prized by the bedroom hackers. Where the bedroom hackers relied on the subculture to maximize scarce resources, Internet hackers rely on the subculture for the sense of community and organization to give meaning to their activities.

While there are remnants of the previous types of hackers, they appear to be products of their times. Old-school ethics and style still exist in groups like L0pht Heavy Industries, a Boston-based hacker group. L0pht has devoted considerable effort to warning Microsoft and Microsoft users about potential security flaws. Microsoft replied that these problems were only theoretical. L0pht responded by creating scripts to exploit these flaws and distributing them via the Internet. The L0pht motto is "Making the theoretical practical." Originally, L0pht members did not profit from their work; they worked for the satisfaction of forcing the software industry to fix its flawed products and admit its faults. Like the hackers of old, they simply could not stand intentionally imperfect systems. Also, like many of the original old school hackers, L0pht eventually turned to lawful applications of their skills. L0pht has recently merged with @stake security to provide security solutions for profit; beyond even white hat hacking, they have created a business.

Resources (↑)

The technology of choice for the contemporary hacker is the Internet. Bedroom hackers are in their twilight, but the research revealed that files have been archived on Web servers to maintain the historical connection with the hackers and phreaks of old. The relatively low cost of Internet access and the proliferation of powerful home computers may greatly affect the traditional alliance between hackers and phone phreaks. The existence of powerful home computers means there is no longer a need to connect to a host mainframe via long distance phone lines. The Internet allows rapid communication and information on archival services without toll connections to electronic bulletin boards (BBSs).

Enculturation (↑)

Given the vast information and communication resources available to Internet hackers, it makes sense that enculturation cannot be controlled through the restriction of information. Thus, the enculturation of Internet hackers often begins with media exposure. To some extent, all new computer users explore the capabilities of their new environment. The more driven users often attempt to push beyond normal systems functions through trial and error. Those with a flair for such activity or a more subtle understanding of their machine-environment seek a context in which to understand their activities and skills. Many bypass the hacker culture and seek socially approved avenues to advance their knowledge. Other novice computer users feel the thrill of illicit discovery or the power of manipulating others. This latter group may become Internet hackers or their more spiteful variant, script kiddies.

The availability of information has produced a different dynamic among hackers. Enculturation is now more a process of directing the boundless possibilities for exploration than an avenue to acquire specific knowledge. Many areas of society now suffer from information overload. Information is so common and so easy to acquire that the primary task of most individuals is deciding how much attention to pay and seek the information that may be useful in a slurry of trivial or irrelevant information. Television viewers are familiar with this phenomenon. With hundreds of channels available, an individual program looses its ability to hold the viewer's attention. Older viewers may remember generally finding enough choices with only a few broadcasters in their market. Now, the expression "there's nothing on TV" has never been more wrong, but everyone identifies with the sentiment. The online community also knows this phenomenon. Early Web surfers simply explored the Internet and accepted what they found; now, there is a pervasive sense that virtually any information sought is on the Web somewhere. No act is too deviant to suppose that it would not be depicted. No information is too illicit or dangerous to find.

Now a potential hacker who wants to learn has only to bring up a Web page or use an online bookstore. The monumental efforts of bedroom hackers to acquire and compile information have been replaced by a one-click purchase at amazon.com. The hacking subculture is still relevant, but fundamentally altered by both the progressing technology of the digital environment and the motivating force that drives novice hackers.[58] Internet hackers form a subculture to socialize and seek an understanding of the knowledge they so easily acquire. In essence, the Internet hacker culture does not teach so much as it directs members toward interesting areas.

Although there are notable cases of mentoring in the hacker subculture, a review of Internet hacker communication does not provide any evidence of such close

relationships.[59] However, the communication does reveal evidence of a form of enculturation. Hacking is about exploration and discovery; experienced hackers show little
desire to deprive larval hackers of the opportunity to discover for themselves.

```
>>HI....it is on udp      when i do a port scan i have run
>>in to port 23 with udp and i cant log in to it with my
>>telnet program  can you tell me how i can log in to a udp
>>telnet?????????
>>thanx   and im sorry  to ask here but know one elss would
>>know........
>
>No.  This is not the place to ask.
>alt.2600 is significantly closer to the place to ask, but
>*please* just RTFRFC instead.
>Or search the web.
>Or learn Perl.⁶⁰ [ellipses original]
```

Aaron Ball uses the term "RTFRFC." It is an adaptation of "Read the F---ing
Manual" (RTFM), referring to a document called a Request for Comment (RFC). RTFM
is a standard response to questions that could be answered by reading the manual.
Aaron's response is typical of experienced hackers. The Internet presents numerous ways
to find information. Posting questions without attempting to find the information is dis-
paraged in Internet hacker culture. In another example of self-help mentoring, Lewis
DePayne, one of Kevin Mitnick's co-defendants, administers a "gentle reminder" to a
young hacker interested in a movie adaptation of Mitnick's story.

```
>TelePhreak . wrote:
>>i know this probably has been posted many times before
>>but can you please post the lists of actors.
>>(e.g: Actor   -   Person in real life)
>
>Lazy asshole.  Open up your web browser and cruise the
>iMDB database.  Then post the results to this list
>yourself.⁶¹
```

The Internet Movie Database is a relatively well known resource. Even without
specific knowledge of IMDB, a search for "cast" and "Takedown" on any major search
engine would have answered his question.

Skill (↑)
It is likely that today's hackers are the most skilled in history. With access to the compiled works of old school and bedroom hackers, as well as the technical knowledge–base
of the Internet, hackers' knowledge is limited only by their ability to find, organize,
and comprehend it. As one hacker put it:

"I went to the interview and they said 'do you know SQL Server?' and I said 'yeah.' After the interview, I went outside and called Andy to ask him what the hell SQL server was. He said 'some Microsoft thing like [a Web database query system], don't worry you can do it.' On the way home I stopped at a book store and bought 'Learn SQL server in 7 days.' I read it that night and was setting up their stuff the next day. By the end of the week I had it done and even undid the stupid stuff I did the first day."[62]

Script Kiddies

The script kiddie is someone looking for the easy kill. They are not out for specific information or targeting a specific company. . . . It is this random selection of targets that make the script kiddie such a dangerous threat. Sooner or later your systems and networks will be probed, you cannot hide from them. I know of admins [system administrators] who were amazed to have their systems scanned when they had been up for only two days, and no one knew about them. . . . Most likely, their systems were scanned by a script kiddie who happened to be sweeping that network block [sequential group of Internet addresses].[63]

Script kiddies are often described as a scourge or pestilence on the Internet. A well administered system with good security policies has little to fear from most script kiddies, but even such a system is vulnerable to a distributed denial of service attack launched from a point-and-click program. Distributed denial of service attacks use unsuspecting, zombie computers to attack a victim. Persons with inoffensive and frankly uninteresting information on their Web sites may become unwitting accomplices in the script kiddies' attack. Unsecured, home computer systems with cable modems provide easy targets for script kiddies. When equipped with a software program called a client or zombie, the system becomes a weapon to be used against more secure sites.

Script kiddies seem to be primarily concerned with bragging and attacking each other or anyone else who draws their wrath. The attacks are often simple exploits of well known vulnerabilities, but can disrupt Internet Relay Chat (IRC) channels. Chat rooms are often raided by script kiddies who provoke verbal attacks (a process known as trolling) and retaliate by "punting" the user out of the chat room. Web page hacking is also a favorite activity of script kiddies and script kiddie groups. The altered Web pages often contain little more than rants, nonsense, or shoutz to friends and insults to enemies and law enforcement.

Enculturation (↓)

Script kiddies are the Internet era equivalent of larval hackers. However, the fundamental difference between script kiddies and larval hackers is instant gratification. Unlike larval hackers, script kiddies do not have to rely upon older, and more restrained, mentors. Script kiddies download other people's programs to perform their attack. They often care little for the underlying technology or intricacies of the glitches they exploit. Script kiddies resemble larval hackers, but they do not share the curiosity of the latter.

Like all Internet hackers, they have access to resources including powerful tools and readily available knowledge.

Where larval hackers may cause harm, script kiddies revel in it. If larval hackers are incompletely socialized hackers, script kiddies do not desire entry into the hacker subculture. The distinction between larval hackers and script kiddies is largely a matter of definition at the initial stages. Some script kiddies do evolve into Internet hackers, as larval hackers grow into hackers. However, this does not appear to be the reason that script kiddies start, unlike larval hackers.

Skill (↓)

The term script kiddie comes from their use of premade tools or scripts. Script kiddies do not have enough skill to write their own programs or explore new exploits for themselves. They download an attack program and attempt to get it to run. Many such programs exploit long-known vulnerabilities, but some system administrators do not update their software. Internet hackers dismiss the actions of script kiddies as unskilled.

Resources (↑)

Like all Internet hackers, script kiddies have virtually unlimited access to cheap or free computing power, and nearly boundless information. Many script kiddies do not have the motivation or discipline to acquire it. Of all the hacker types, script kiddies are the most defined by the resources they use rather than their own abilities. Most script kiddie tools are limited to a single purpose with few options to avoid overloading the script kiddie or requiring them to read directions. A typical script kiddie scenario may involve three tools. First come the tools used to build a database of vulnerable target systems. These systems are then scanned by another tool to determine if they have known vulnerabilities. Once the vulnerable systems have been identified, the kiddie strikes with yet another tool. Without the high level of resources available from the Internet, script kiddies would not exist.

Hacktivists

Recently, there has been an increase in the political activity of self-identified hackers. Hackers have combined to challenge the treatment of their peers by the government.[64] Early cases like those of Phiber Optik, charged in 1992 and eventually serving one year in federal prison, drew the attention of hacktivists who also rallied around Kevin Mitnick. Other examples include Kevin Poulsen, a convicted hacker, who now writes a column for a Web-based magazine. Poulsen has used his column to speak out about Mitnick's case numerous times. Phiber Optik has spoken out on a radio show he cohosts. Emmanuel Goldstein, editor of *2600: The Hacker Quarterly,* used the resources of his magazine to start an e-mail list for the intention of assisting Kevin Mitnick.

The common characteristic of hacktivists is the use of hacker skills and attitudes to convey a political message. The term "hacktivism" came from an article entitled "Grassroots Hacktivism," written by convicted hacker Kevin Poulsen in 1998. The article was a response to an intrusion on the New York Times' Web page by a group calling itself "HFG." At first glance, the HFG message was moronic.

```
"F1RST OFF, WE HAVE TO SAY.. WE OWN YER DUMB ASS.
4ND R3MEMB3R, DUMB ASS 1S OFT3N CUTE 4SS. AND WE L1KE
CUTE ASS."
```

A deeper examination showed actual political content with clear influence from the hacker subculture. The computer language used to format and write Web pages (Hypertext Markup Language: HTML) allows hidden comments to assist Web page writers. HFG used these comment lines to explain their real purpose, but excluded anyone who didn't know how to read them. A hint on the page directs attention to the comments:

```
PS: OUR COMMENTS ARE MORE 'LEET THAN OUR TEXT. DOWNLOAD
THE SOURCE TO TH1S PAGE AND PONDER OUR W1ZDOM.
```

```
<!—Just because we type in all caps and use 'elite' speak doesn't mean—>
<!—we are kids, or we don't own your dumb ass.  For everyone who calls—>
<!—us immature kids, it shows one more person has underestimated us.—>
<!—And worse, what does that say about their security? That "immature—>
<!—kids" were able to bypass their 25,000 dollar firewalls, bypass—>
<!—the security put there by admins with XX years of experience or a—>
<!—XXX degree from some college.  Nyah Nyah.—>
```

HFG claimed to attack the New York Times because of the overly personal and biased treatment of the Mitnick story by one of the Times' reporters, John Markoff. A Markoff story recited old facts, later discredited, but received the front page. Markoff also co-authored a book with the "hero" of his articles, Shimomura.

```
<!— The injustice Markoff has committed is criminal. He belongs in a—>
<!— jail rotting instead of Kevin Mitnick. Kevin is no dark side—>
<!— hacker. He is not malicious. He is not a demon. He did not abuse—>
<!— credit cards, distribute the software he found, or deny service—>
<!— to a single machine.  Is that so hard to comprehend?—>
```

Mitnick's supporters, who range from fellow cyberpunks to respected civil libertarians, believe the hacker has been unfairly singled out to bear the full brunt of the federal government's prosecutorial power. Together, they've formed a burgeoning grassroots movement built on such staples as bumper stickers, picketing, and fundraising.

Skill (•)

Hacktivists skill ranges from very low to very high. At the high end of the skill continuum, the Cult of the Dead Cow has provided technical assistance to the Hong Kong Blondes in their protests against China's human rights policies. Some countries limit their citizens' access to the Internet—and thus to information—by using a firewall to block sites that provide prohibited information. Even repressive countries recognize the economic, research, and technological value of Internet connectivity and do not block all access.[65] The latest software from the Cult of the Dead Cow, called Peekabooty, adapts security technology to overcome restrictions on citizen access to the Internet. A user in a country that censors the Internet connects to the ad hoc network of computers running Peekabooty. A small number of randomly selected computers in the network retrieves the Web pages and relays them back to the user. As far as the censoring firewall is concerned, the user is simply accessing some computer not on its "banned" list. The retrieved Web pages are encrypted using the de facto standard for secure transactions in order to prevent the firewall from examining the Web page contents. Since the encryption used is a secure transaction standard, it will look like an ordinary e-business transaction to the firewall.

Peekabooty is a complex piece of software. It is designed to fit on one 1.44 MB floppy disk. Using only that space, it implements peer-to-peer networking using the most up-to-date encryption. Further, it is designed to be user friendly and language adaptable. In short, it is a remarkable demonstration of skill.

At the other end of the skill continuum, some hacktivists have only minimal skill. They can barely manage mailing list software or post Web pages to the Internet. Recent Web page hacks serve as evidence of a growing political agenda. Using the same, low-skill methods as script kiddies, many hacktivist Web page hacks target servers with weak security. Unlike script kiddies, politically active, skilled hackers seek high-volume sites, which are usually more secure, to spread their message. For instance, Portuguese hackers cracked the Indonesian government's Web page to protest the government's actions in East Timor. In other cases, messages about Kevin Mitnick have appeared on cracked sites, ranging from the New York Times to UNICEF.

Enculturation (•)

Hacktivists often subordinate the values of the hacker subculture to their political goals. For instance, the prohibition against hacking for personal gain does not prevent hacktivists from using hacking to spread their ideology regardless of the quality of the hack. Although it is entirely possible to conduct hacktivism while maintaining the values of the hacker subculture, as with the Cult of the Dead Cow, it further diffuses constraining effects of the subculture by replacing the underlying motivation with political goals.

Resources (↑)

Like all of the Internet hackers, hacktivists have virtually unlimited access to cheap or free computing power and nearly boundless information. These resources are turned toward political ends rather than standard goals of the hacker subculture. In many cases, the normal facilities of the Internet serve hacktivists better than hacker files and tools. For example, e-mail list communication kept supporters of Kevin Mitnick in touch until he was released. Web sites serve as platforms for publicizing political causes. They do not have to be hacked, when access is so cheap and easy. Because so many of the activities of hacktivists are entirely legal, they are among the most accessible of hacker types.

SUMMARY

There are important reasons to understand the hacking subculture when considering computer crime. The fundamental differences in motivation from computer criminals require a categorically different approach to controlling hacking-related crime. Understanding the way hackers define themselves and the history that inspires them can be an important tool to predicting their actions and gauging appropriate responses to criminal hacking. Hackers understand their history in distinct eras and often hold older hackers in high regard. The typology presented in this chapter is not necessarily the "official" view of hacker society; however, all of the elements are consistent with the general understanding held by hackers (if such a consensus can ever be said to exist). The organization of information presented in the typology may assist nonhackers in understanding the historical development of hacking. Further, the influence of each historic element can still be seen in hacker society today.

Showing a sophisticated understanding of these issues can increase hackers' respect for law enforcement. This increased respect can cultivate connections and information that may be valuable in solving crimes. Prevention efforts can also benefit from properly gauging the audience. Script kiddies and larval hackers will require a different approach from experienced (i.e., enculturated) hackers. Perhaps most usefully, understanding the mental processes of justification in the hacker's language and beliefs gives law enforcement an upper hand when dealing with hackers. It may be one of the few advantages available to law enforcement.

REVIEW QUESTIONS

1. Explain why hackers do not consider themselves to be criminals. How can someone break the law, but not feel deviant?
2. Explain the hacker ethic. Can individual hackers deviate from the hacker ethic? Do all hackers hold the same understanding of that ethic?
3. Explain the difficulty of prosecuting true hackers. How does a suspect's strict adherence to the hacker ethic make prosecution difficult? How does it remove the threat of actual harm?
4. Explain the influence of the media on the development of the hacking subculture. Do all hackers agree with the way the media handles hacking? Why or why not?
5. Do all hackers share the same background? How do resources, enculturation and skill help to differentiate hackers?

ENDNOTES

1. LEVY, S. (1984). *Hackers: Heroes of the computer revolution.* New York: Dell Publishing; DUFF, L. and GARDINER, S. (1996). Computer crime in the global village: Strategies for control and regulation—in defence of the hacker. *International Journal of the Sociology of Law,* 24(2), 211–228; HAFNER, K. and LYON, M. (1996). *Where wizards stay up late: The origins of the Internet.* New York: Touchstone.

2. ICOVE, D., SEGER, K., and VONSTORCH, W. (1995). *Computer crime: A crimefighter's handbook.* Sebastopol, CA: O'Reilly & Associates; GOLLMAN, D. (1999). *Computer security.* New York: John Wiley & Sons, Inc.; PARKER, D. B. (1998). *Fighting computer crime.* New York: John Wiley & Sons, Inc.

3. CHANDLER, A. (1996). The changing definition and image of hackers in popular discourse. *International Journal of the Sociology of Law,* 24(2), 229–251.

4. LEVY, *ibid.*

5. LEVY, *ibid.*

6. LEVY, *ibid.*

7. LEVY, *ibid.*

8. STERLING, B. (1992). *The hacker crack-down: Law and disorder on the electronic frontier.* New York: Bantam Books.

9. BALL, AARON D. (personal communication, Dec. 7, 1998).

10. HAFNER, K. and MARKOFF, J. (1991). *Cyberpunk: Outlaws and hackers on the computer frontier.* New York: Touchstone.

11. FLOHR, U. (November, 1995). *Bank robbers go electronic.* Retrieved May 5, 2004 from the World Wide Web: *http://www.byte.com/art/9511/sec3/art11.htm*

12. LOPER, D.K. (2000). The criminology of computer hackers: A qualitative and quantitative analysis. *Dissertation Abstracts International,* 61 (08), AAT 9985422.

13. 18 U.S.C. § 1029 et seq.

14. 18 U.S.C. § 1030 et seq.

15. WALL, D.S. (2001). Cybercrimes and the Internet. *In* D.S. WALL (ed.). *Crime and the Internet* (pp. 1–17). New York: Routledge.

16. BECKER, H.S. (1963). *Outsiders: Studies in the sociology of deviance.* New York: Free Press.

17. LOPER, *ibid.*

18. LOPER, *ibid.*

19. For further discussion of the "benefits" of illegal activity, *see* GRABOSKY, P. and SMITH, R. (2001). Telecommunication fraud in the digital age: The convergence of technologies. *In* D.S. WALL (ed.), *Crime and the Internet* (pp. 29–43). New York: Routledge.

20. LEVI, M. (2001). "Between the risk and the reality falls the shadow": Evidence and urban legends in computer fraud. *In* D.S. WALL (ed.), *Crime and the Internet* (pp. 44–58). New York: Routledge.

21. Portions of this material have been submitted for publication elsewhere.

22. WILLIAMS, M. (2001). The language of cyberspace. *In* D.S. WALL (ed.), *Crime and the Internet* (pp. 152–166). New York: Routledge.

23. MANN, D. and SUTTON, M. (1998). Netcrime: More change in the organization of thieving. *British Journal of Criminology,* 38(2), 201–229.

24. PARKER, D.B. (1998). *Fighting computer crime.* New York: John Wiley & Sons, Inc.

25. BARRETT, N. (1997). *Digital crime: Policing the cybernation.* London: Kogan Page.

26. GOLDSTEIN, E. (1993, June 13). Hacker testimony to House subcommittee largely unheard. *In* THOMAS, J. and MEYER, G. (eds.) *Computer Underground Digest, 5.43.* DeKalb, IL: Editor. Retrieved February 26, 2000 from the World Wide Web: *http://venus.soci.niu.edu/~cudigest/CUDS5/cud543.txt*

27. GOLDSTEIN, E. (1996). Knowledge is strength. *2600: The hacker quarterly,* 13(4), 4–5.

28. CHANDLER, A. (1996). The changing definition and image of hackers in popular discourse. *International Journal of the Sociology of Law,* 24(2), 229–251.

29. GILMORE, J. (1999, June 4). Crackers do for gov't what critical infrastructure report couldn't. *RISKS Digest, 20* (43). Retrieved August 22, 2003 from the World Wide Web: *http://catless.ncl.ac.uk/Risks/20.43.html#subj5*

30. STERLING, *ibid.*

31. FURNELL, S. (2002). *Cybercrime: Vandalizing the information society.* Boston: Pearson Education.

32. MITNICK, K.D. (2000). *Off the Hook for February 8, 2000* (Emmanuel Goldstein, producer). New York: WBAI Radio. [Radio/Web simulcast]. Retrieved March 9, 2000 from the World Wide Web: *http://www.2600.com/offthehook/rafiles00/020800.ram*

33. LITTMAN, J. (1997, September 18). *Hacker shocker: Project reveals breaches galore.* Retrieved from the World Wide Web: *http://www5.zdnet.com/zdnn/content/zdnn/0918/zdnn0010.html*

34. MARTIN, B. (1999, August). *The newbie's guide to fear, uncertainty, and doubt.* Hacker News Network. Retrieved August 1999 from World Wide Web: *http://www.hackernews.com/orig/fud.html*

35. MARTIN, *ibid.*

36. LEVY, *ibid.*

37. BLANKENSHIP, L. (1986). *The hacker manifesto.* Retrieved March 21, 2000 from the World Wide Web: *http://viaduct.custom.net/glitch/manif.htm*

38. STERLING, *ibid.*

39. RAYMOND, E.S. (August 13, 2003). *The jargon file, version 4.4.4.* Retrieved August 30 from the World Wide Web *http://www.catb.org/~esr/jargon/*

40. SLATALLA and QUITTNER, *ibid.*

41. HAFNER and MARKOFF, *ibid.*

42. ELLISON, L. (2001). Cyberstalking: Tackling harassment on the Internet. *In* D.S. WALL (ed.), *Crime and the Internet* (pp. 141–151). New York, NY: Routledge.

43. LEVY, *ibid.*

44. Abbie Hoffman was a political activist and founder of the Youth International Party ("Yippies"). He was one of the Chicago Seven, who went on trial after violence erupted at the 1968 Democratic National Convention in Chicago.

45. The Bell System was dominant, but there were much smaller local—and a few regional—companies.

46. LEVY, *ibid.* at p. 37.

47. CHANDLER, *ibid.*

48. E.g., Commodore 64, TRS 80, or Apple 2e.

49. BLANKENSHIP, *ibid.*

50. The first personal computer BBS was started by Ward Christensen and Randy Seuss in February 1978 in Chicago.

51. SLATALLA and QUITTNER, *ibid.*

52. SLATALLA and QUITTNER, *ibid.* at pp. 28–29.

53. JORDAN, T. and TAYLOR, P. (1998). A sociology of hackers. *The Sociological Review, 46*(4), 757–780 at p. 768.

54. STERLING, *ibid.* pp. 87–88.

55. VERTON, D. (2002). *The hacker diaries: Confessions of teenage hackers.* Berkeley, CA: McGraw-Hill.

56. Paul –name withheld– (personal communication, 1999).

57. Assembly languages differ depending on the architecture of the processor used; that is, each family of processors uses a different assembly language. That is one of the reasons why Macintosh software cannot be used on PCs.
58. MATT "BARCODE" LEWIS (personal communication, October 30, 2001).
59. LOPER, *ibid.*
60. RICHARDB3 (personal communication, October 27, 1998) and AARON D. BALL (personal communication, October 27, 1998).
61. DePAYNE, LEWIS. (personal communication, October 5, 1998).
62. ERIC B. (personal communication, 1999).
63. Honeynet Project (21 July, 2000). *Know your enemy: The tools and methodologies of the script kiddie.* Retrieved September 13, 2003 from the World Wide Web: *http://project .honeynet.org/papers/enemy/*
64. TAYLOR, P. (2001). Hacktivism: In search of lost ethics? *In* D.S. WALL (ed.), *Crime and the Internet* (pp. 59–73). New York: Routledge.
65. HEINS, M. (2001). Criminalizing online speech to "protect" the young: What are the benefits and costs? *In* D.S. WALL (ed.), *Crime and the Internet* (pp. 100–112). New York: Routledge; and AKDENIZ, Y. (2001). Controlling illegal and harmful content on the Internet. *In* D.S. WALL (ed.), *Crime and the Internet* (pp. 113–140). New York: Routledge.

Chapter 5

White Collar Crimes

Chapter Objectives

After completing this chapter, you should be able to:

- Describe how computer technologies have altered the ways in which embezzlement is committed.
- Describe how computer technologies have increased the opportunities to commit money laundering.
- Describe how computer technologies have affected the crime of corporate espionage.
- Describe how computer technologies and the increasing use of the Internet have affected identity and fraud crimes.

INTRODUCTION

Historically, the field of criminology has emphasized the need to explain the occurrence of what has commonly been referred to as traditional "street crime." Crimes such as homicide, rape, armed robbery, and aggravated assault have garnered a vast amount of public and media attention, and criminal justice policies have been designed mainly to counteract these personal violent crimes. Whether or not this emphasis has been due to the very real fear that these types of crimes engender in citizens or the media's constant fixation with the "gory details" such crimes produce has been a matter of some debate; what is clear is that the public's common perception of what constitutes "crimes" as well as who is the common "criminal" have been formed largely in relation to traditional street crimes.[1] As a result, crimes that do not fall under traditional definitions or those that are committed by persons who do not fit the public's common perception of the typical "criminal" have received much less attention.

Noted criminologist Edwin Sutherland was the first to highlight these disparities in the late 1940s, and he attempted to describe and define a class of behaviors very different from those of traditional street crimes, including acts committed by corporate executives, corrupt politicians, and unscrupulous professionals. He defined these acts as "white-collar crimes," and he suggested that they are largely ignored because the perpetrators of these offenses comprised society's elite—people with the economic wherewithal and status to shape the criminal law in their favor and avoid detection and punishment.[2]

This chapter will describe the ways in which the computer revolution has altered the techniques used to commit some of the most common white-collar offenses, specifically embezzlement, corporate espionage, money laundering, identity crimes, and fraud. The large-scale dissemination of computer and information technologies seems to have created greater opportunities for the white-collar offender, and law enforcement officials are now faced with the unenviable task of looking for loopholes in the ever-expanding technologies used to commit white-collar offenses.

EMBEZZLEMENT

Embezzlement has been defined as the unlawful misappropriation for personal use of money, property, or some other thing of value that has been entrusted to an offender's care, custody, or control. Embezzlement is essentially a theft in violation of a trust. As such, embezzlement has been recognized as a crime since English common-law traditions dating back to the 15th century.[3] The embezzler usually is engaged in some type of fiduciary relationship with the victim, either as an employee, guardian, or trustee. Traditionally, embezzlement has involved the physical theft of money or property by employees or others engaged in managing the assets of persons or organizations.

Embezzlement has been the subject of considerable research and debate in regards to both its definition as a traditional white-collar offense and the motivations behind embezzlement schemes. Although Sutherland specifically used embezzlement as an example in his early portrayal of white-collar offending, historically the embezzler has not been a person of high social status. Rather, he or she has typically been a person engaged in managing the financial affairs of societal elites. Historically, the typical embezzler is a low-level financial institution employee, usually a female bank teller engaged in stealing financial deposits directly from bank customers. In this regard, some have argued that the embezzler has more in common with the traditional street robber than the corporate executives or professionals originally highlighted by Sutherland in his depiction of white-collar offenders. So too, unlike most other white-collar offenses, embezzlement schemes are often carried out by individual offenders rather than by corporations and other organized entities. These disparities aside, most researchers have historically categorized embezzlement as a white-collar offense, probably because the offense involves a violation of professional trust in which deception rather than physical force is used to carry out the act.

Donald Cressey, in his classic embezzlement study *Other People's Money,* identified a four-step process that described the motivations common to his sample of convicted embezzlers. Prior to the commission of the crime, the embezzler often finds themselves experiencing financial problems that cannot be solved through legitimate financial means. The offender then identifies embezzlement as an avenue through which to alleviate his or her financial problems. The embezzler must also possess the technical knowledge necessary to carry out the embezzlement scheme. Finally, the embezzler will use "neutralization techniques" in order to overcome any lingering shame or guilt associated with stealing money that has been entrusted to their care. These techniques may involve the intention of paying the money back before anyone notices its absence, or justifying the theft based on the belief that the "rich" individuals or organizations that have entrusted the money to the embezzler's care will not miss the funds. Freed from these considerations, the embezzler commits the theft in order to solve his or her financial problems.[4]

The advent of the computer age and the ubiquitous use of computers in the management, allocation, and tracking of both personal and business finances have transformed the methods used by embezzlers to misappropriate cash and/or property. Today, the computer provides the most available means to commit embezzlement, and knowledge relating to the manipulation of large-scale computerized financial databases has become the primary tool of the embezzler.

With regard to other computer crimes, embezzlement can be classified as a "computer-assisted" crime rather than a "computer-focused crime." Computer-assisted crimes are those where the computer is used in a supporting capacity. The specific crime, such as embezzlement, predates the introduction of computers. In contrast, computer-focused crimes have emerged more recently as a direct result of computer technology (e.g., hacking).[5] Anderson has classified the modern-day embezzler as an "internal perpetrator," or an authorized user of computer systems who uses legitimate access to computer files to commit theft. Because embezzlers have been authorized to use computer systems and resources, they are among the most difficult computer criminals to detect and apprehend.[6]

While the crime of embezzlement appeared centuries before the computer revolution, the use of computer technology does appear to have altered both the commission of the act and the profile of those who embezzle. First, the traditional embezzler was often limited by the physical nature of the theft act. That is, there was a limit to how much cash and or property the embezzler could actually steal because the act involved taking and transferring cash or other material goods. Modern embezzlement schemes using computerized records often may not involve the physical theft of anything. The embezzler's take is predicated only on his or her abilities as they relate to the misappropriation of data files, and millions of dollars can be stolen with simple keystrokes.

Second, the advent of technologically driven financial management techniques may have narrowed the pool of potential embezzlers to those individuals who possess the specialized skills required to use computer information systems. In this regard, modern-day "technical elites" who steal from their employers and organizations may more closely resemble the societal elites originally identified by Sutherland as typical white-collar offenders. Indeed, more recent studies of convicted embezzlers seem to suggest that rather than experiencing financial problems, many technically elite embezzlers are simply motivated by a desire for a more affluent lifestyle.[7] Nonetheless, the examples listed below of recent embezzlement cases involving the misuse of computer technologies can be used to illustrate the widely varied nature of both the perpetrators of modern day embezzlement and their victims, including private businesses, government agencies, and individuals:

- Thirty-six-year-old Daniel Gruidl of Minnesota pled guilty to computer fraud charges related to the embezzlement of funds from his employer, Vital Signs of Minnesota Inc. Grudl felt that he was underpaid, so he simply used false passwords in order to log onto the company's computerized payroll system. He proceeded to give himself raises and bonuses that totaled over $108,000. The scam went undetected for two years.[8]

- Don McCorry worked as a Senior Financial Manager in charge of government employee retirement accounts in Fairfax, VA. McCorry altered computer records of employee withdrawals from their retirement accounts by reassigning monies to his personal retirement account, labeling them "emergency" withdrawals in his own name. McCorry embezzled over $1.1 million over a four-year period. When he was arrested, investigators confiscated a Mercedes-Benz, a $50,000 art collection, a $100,000 wine collection, and fifty suits valued at $10,000 from his residence.[9]

- A computerized payroll glitch at a North Carolina hospital resulted in a hospital cook being paid $787 an hour over a three-month period. The cook failed to report the overpayment, stating that she believed the glitch to be a "gift from God."[10]

- Cleveland stockbroker Frank Gruttadauria defrauded 50 prominent business executives and investment clients over a 15-year period. He exaggerated the values of client investment portfolios by altering computerized financial statements. Clients believed they had $277 million in assets, but their accounts totaled barely $1 million in actual value. One individual investor appropriated about $120 million to Gruttadauria. $60 million was actually invested, and the actual cash value of his holdings upon detection of the scam was $8,000.[11]

CORPORATE ESPIONAGE

Corporate espionage involves any theft of proprietary business information through spying or deception, particularly the theft of "trade secrets." Trade secrets encompass any proprietary information that produces value to a commercial enterprise because it provides competitive advantages over business rivals.[12] The informational targets to be stolen through corporate espionage schemes are wide and varied, including detailed customer lists, product specifications, research and development data, computerized source codes, memoranda detailing corporate strategies, pricing lists, and technology and computer systems data.[13]

Corporate concerns regarding espionage and the theft of business secrets have grown over the course of the last two decades. Several related factors have combined to increase the occurrence of corporate espionage and heighten awareness of the problem. First, the corporate community's increasing use of information and computer technologies to conduct business has provided corporate spies easier access to valuable proprietary information. In particular, the ubiquitous use of e-mail as a means of intra-office communication has made employee exchanges readily accessible to potential corporate spies who possess the technical expertise to crack such networks. In addition, global commerce has increasingly been conducted electronically over the Internet (i.e., "e-commerce"), which has created a wealth of accessible corporate data available to cyberspace hackers.[14] These factors have worked to make the theft of corporate information much easier. It is no longer necessary for corporate thieves to steal information physically, since most valuable corporate secrets usually exist solely in computerized form.

As a result of these factors, the incidence of and costs associated with corporate espionage have risen sharply. A recent survey by the American Society for Industrial Security (ASIS) estimates that Fortune 1,000 companies lost close to $45 billion dollars to corporate spies in 1999 alone.[15] Indeed, some analysts estimate that losses from business espionage have doubled since the early '90s. The average company detects 2.45 cases of corporate espionage per year, with each incident costing approximately $500,000. Technology companies appear to be particularly vulnerable. Fortune 1,000 tech firms report an average of 67 espionage attacks per year, costing these firms an average of $115 million annually.[16]

While the dawn of the information age has increased the use of spy tactics among domestic corporate rivals, global political and military trends have also played a role in elevating the costs related to corporate espionage. With the end of Cold War rivalries between the U.S. and Soviet militaries, nations have increasingly concentrated espionage efforts toward the theft of trade, rather than military, secrets. So too, the end of U.S.-Soviet hostilities helped to created a vast network of former military spies—individuals highly skilled in espionage tactics—available for corporate hire.[17] The result has been an increase in the use of corporate espionage by nations looking for competitive advantages for their domestic industries. The National Counter-Intelligence Agency estimates that U.S. businesses lost $44 billion to the theft of trade secrets by international spies between 1996 and 1997.[18]

Corporate spies can be divided into two distinct groups.[19] Most corporate espionage schemes are conducted by business "insiders," persons who have legitimate access to a company's computer networks, such as employees, information technology personnel, or corporate executives. Limited research suggests that up to 85 percent of all such schemes are carried out by these insiders, whose motivations extend from blackmail and monetary concerns to a simple lack of loyalty or job dissatisfaction.[20] The remaining acts of corporate espionage are performed by corporate "outsiders," or persons who crack into a corporation's computer data networks without any form of legitimate access rights. Outsiders may penetrate computer systems via the Internet, or by gaining access to internal computer networks. Outsiders include domestic spies hired by corporate competitors, as well as foreign nationals hired by adversarial governments intent on gaining a competitive advantage over American firms. At the extreme, these types of spies may access proprietary information simply by entering the workplace facility and visually stealing computer passwords or gaining physical access to computer server rooms.[21]

Outside the realms of insiders and outsiders, the growing employment of independent contractors by large-scale corporations has created unique problems in regard to corporate espionage schemes. Independent contractors are individuals hired by a corporation to perform specific, limited jobs, such as database management, product introductions, or programming changes. These individuals (often referred to as "kites") more closely resemble temporary workers rather than full-time employees, and their resulting lack of loyalty and long-term commitment to the hiring corporation may make them vulnerable targets for information for competing firms. "Kites" may also be hired by competing firms because they have specific knowledge concerning competitor operations.[22]

Companies that have been victimized by corporate espionage schemes can pursue a civil action against the offending firm; however, civil suits often turn into lengthy affairs and the invariable costs incurred through civil courts are prohibitive. The case involving Silicon Valley software firms Cadence Design Systems and Avant! Corporation provides a prime example of the painstakingly slow and costly process involved in resolving domestic espionage suits (see Box 5.1 below for a timeline of events surrounding the case and its eventual outcome).[23] The case originated with an internal investigation conducted by Cadence Design Systems in 1995.[24] Over the course of the preceding four years, several top Cadence executives had left the company to form a rival firm, Avant! Corp. Both companies write software code that helps computer engineers design silicon chips used in advanced computer systems. Cadence executives claimed that Avant! executives had stolen Cadence source code in order to develop software that was producing over $100 million in sales by 1996. The civil and criminal trials took eight years to resolve.[25]

In response to these concerns, as well as the belief that the problem of corporate espionage had grown with the increasing use of computers in the workplace, Congress enacted the Economic Espionage Act of 1996. Under the act, corporations who suspect that they are victims of espionage schemes may request an FBI investigation. If such an investigation reveals criminal wrongdoing, the U.S. Attorney's office of the Department of Justice can prosecute the offending firm for theft of trade secrets.[26]

The Economic Espionage Act outlines two separate offenses related to corporate spying. First, the act attempts to enforce espionage crimes originating from foreign governments and businesses by creating criminal penalties for those who steal, destroy, or knowingly receive stolen trade secrets that would benefit foreign governments. Individual offenders may be fined up to $500,000 and/or face a prison sentence of up to fifteen

BOX 5.1   Cadence Design Systems vs. Avant! Corporation

June 1994	Avant! sales reach $39 million after former Cadence Vice President Gerald Hsu joins three other former Cadence executives to head up Cadence rival Avant!
August 1995	During a routine site visit to an Avant! customer, Cadence engineers notice similarities between Avant! code and Cadence code that they had developed years earlier. Four thousand lines of identical code are identified, including grammatical and program errors.
December 1995	Santa Clara Co. District Attorneys conduct a search and seizure at Avant! headquarters. Cadance files a formal civil complaint in U.S. District Court. The complaint contends that four Avant! executives conspired to steal trade secrets and copyrighted information over a three-year period.
April 1996	Avant! and six employees, including the Chairman and Chief Executive Officer, are indicted on criminal charges in Santa Clara County, CA.
March 1997	Cadence fails in its attempt to obtain a preliminary injunction against Avant! intended to stop the sale of software allegedly pirated from Cadence source code.
July 1997	Judge stays the civil suit against Avant! in consideration of the pending criminal charges.
September 1997	Preliminary injunction granted against Avant! barring the company from selling software developed from allegedly stolen source code.
February 1998	Avant!'s Chief Financial Officer resigns.
November 1998	Grand jury convenes to consider criminal indictment against Avant! employees.
December 1998	Federal judge extends preliminary injunction against Avant! barring it from selling newer version of software.
May 2001	Eleven Avant! employees and executives plead no contest to criminal charges related to trade secret theft. Individual fines range from $27,000 to $2.7 million.
July 2001	Avant! ordered to pay over $200 million in restitution and court costs to Cadence.
November 2002	Cadence agrees to settle all civil claims against Avant! and its employees in exchange for $265 million in damages. The companies agree to a reciprocal licensing agreement covering the software in question.

years. Under this portion of the act, corporations may be fined up to $10 million. Second, the act enforces domestic espionage between competing U.S. firms by making the theft of trade secrets related to or included in a product involved in interstate commerce a federal crime. Individual offenders may be fined up to $250,000 and/or face a prison sentence of up to ten years. Under this portion of the act, corporations may be fined up to $5 million.[27]

MONEY LAUNDERING

Money laundering is the act of concealing the source of assets that have been illegally obtained. The primary object in laundering is to hide the source and ownership of such funds through the creation of a seemingly legitimate history or paper trail. Like embezzlement, money laundering is an "old" crime whose opportunities have expanded greatly with the increasing use of technology in the marketplace. It is impossible to know the extent to which money laundering occurs; however, experts estimate that about $300 billion in cash is laundered each year. The amount of illegal money laundering associated with the drug trade alone is thought to be anywhere from $5 to 15 billion annually.[28]

Traditionally, money laundering was accomplished through three primary means: (1) Cash that was illegally obtained could be physically transported from its place of origin to a jurisdiction that had less stringent banking and reporting requirements. Although the money would eventually be "lost" in the eyes of law enforcement in this new jurisdiction, the act of physically moving cash from one place to another is time-consuming, dangerous, and cumbersome for the launderer. (2) The launderer could quickly transform hard currency into legitimate real property, such as real estate, commercial interests, or personal luxuries.[29]

The problems with transforming illegally gained assets in this manner are two-fold. First, the large-scale purchasing of property is ostentatious, and authorities may notice changes tending toward a suddenly lavish lifestyle. Second, many criminals may have difficulty spending all of their ill-gotten cash, given the exorbitant profits in some illegal enterprises (e.g., large-scale drug trading). (3) Launderers often turned to a method commonly referred to as "smurfing." Smurfing involves the division of large amounts of cash into smaller denominations so as to conceal its common origin. The launderer would enlist several persons to deposit relatively small amounts of cash into several different accounts scattered over a geographic area. In this way, the launderer could successfully avoid federal reporting requirements regarding large-scale cash deposits.[30]

The increasing use of technology, especially telecommunications and the Internet, has provided a wealth of new opportunities for the money launderer. Obscuring the origin and owner of large amounts of cash is now a keystroke away. In order to understand the impact that technology has had on money-laundering crimes, it may be useful to view the advancement of technology in this area in two distinct phases. During the 1960s and '70s, governments, banks, and other financial institutions increasingly used telecommunications networks to move large amounts of cash.[31] These electronic cash transactions, or "electronic funds transfers" (EFTs), served to digitize the financial marketplace. Telephone lines and computer networks substituted for the physical transport of cash and other financial instruments.

Money is swiftly and easily moved both legitimately and illegitimately across these computerized networks. Currently, there are two primary cash transfer institutions. FedWire is the electronic payment network created by the Federal Reserve System. Over 250,000 transactions are performed on the system per day. CHIPS is a clearinghouse payment system created by private banking companies. This consortium moves over $866 billion per day.[32]

The electronic revolution that has occurred in the banking industry, especially the large-scale movement of cash in electronic forms, has made laundering easier. Because money transfers now involve electronic messages rather than physical cash, it is easier for the launderer to move money in a series of transactions over a short period of time. Smurfing can be accomplished by one individual at a keyboard rather than a large group of smurfs over a wide geographic area. So too, money that can be moved electronically is also easier to integrate into the mainstream banking system.

While the introduction of telecommunications and computer technologies in the 1960s and '70s served to increase the ease with which money could be laundered, the current explosion in e-commerce and the influence of the Internet may provide launderers even greater opportunities in years to come. The biggest concern for law enforcement officials is the recent introduction of anonymous electronic cash exchange systems, or "e-cash."[33] E-cash is digital money that may be exchanged over the Internet. It is an electronic replacement for cash. E-cash comprises an electronic series of numbers that have intrinsic value in some form of currency.[34] E-cash may be likened to the serial numbers located on hard currency, except in the case of e-cash there is no hard currency, only the related electronic numbers. Interest in the use of e-cash has grown in conjunction with the Internet, largely because it can be exchanged with increased speed and efficiency. On line businesses can also increase e-commerce profits through its use.

Authorities fear that the increasing use of such "cashless" systems may promote unique "cyberlaundering" schemes that are more difficult to detect and defend against. Researcher Mark Bortner describes a hypothetical scenario whereby the anonymous nature of e-cash and the ease with which it can be accessed through the Internet provides "cyberlaunderers" easy opportunities:[35]

> Doug drug dealer is the CEO of an ongoing narcotics operation. Doug has rooms filled with hard currency that is the profits from his illegal enterprise. This currency needs to enter into the legitimate mainstream economy so that Doug can either purchase needed supplies and employees, purchase real or personal property or even draw interest on his ill-gotten gains . . . Doug employs Linda launderer to wash the dirty money. Linda hires couriers ("smurfs") to deposit funds under different names in amounts between $7,500 and $8,500 at branches of every bank in certain cities . . . In the meantime, Linda launderer has been transferring these same funds from each branch and depositing the money with Internet banks that accept E-cash . . . Once the hard currency has been converted into digital E-cash, the illegally earned money has become virtually untraceable—anonymous. Doug drug dealer now has access to legitimate electronic cash.

Law enforcement authorities have several tools at their disposal to enforce money laundering crimes. The oldest among these is the Bank Secrecy Act of 1970 (BSA). The BSA requires banks and other financial institutions to file records concerning suspicious financial transactions over $10,000 (e.g., large cash deposits, foreign bank exchanges, cross-border currency transports). In addition, the 1986 Money Laundering Control Act works to close certain loopholes in the BSA that were exploited by launderers in the past. Specifically, the Money Laundering Control Act requires banks and other financial institutions to report any suspicious banking transactions (including possible "smurfing" schemes) regardless of the monetary amount of any single transaction.[36]

Finally, the U.S. Treasury Department's Financial Crimes Enforcement Network (FinCEN) serves as a "central clearinghouse" for intelligence and information sharing on money laundering.[37] FinCEN's main objective is to provide law enforcement agencies the analytical tools necessary to identify and prosecute money laundering cases. FinCEN uses two primary avenues to accomplish this goal. First, FinCEN provides direct case support to over 150 local law enforcement agencies, and coordinates efforts with the International Association of Chiefs of Police (IACP), the National White Collar Crime Center (NWCCC), and the National Association of Attorneys General (NAAG). This support specifically involves developing linkages from the various aspects of money laundering cases so that prosecutions can occur. Second, FinCEN provides secondary support to local law enforcement agencies in the form of training, office space, and database research access. FinCEN officials have termed this support a "platform approach" to solving money-laundering cases, whereby federal resources are used to aid local law enforcement efforts directly.

Over the course of the last 13 years, FinCEN has provided law enforcement and regulatory agencies over 50,000 analytical case reports involving over 200,000 money laundering suspects. In recognition of the increasingly "borderless" nature of "cyber-laundering," FinCEN also spearheads efforts to promote international cooperation in the fight against laundering. FinCEN develops these international partnerships through Financial Intelligence Units (FIU), or centralized money-laundering analysis agencies located across the globe.[38] These FIUs appear to be of increasing importance, given the inherently global nature of international terrorists attacks and these organization's vital interest in maintaining adequate monetary resources in order to foster new terrorist networks and fund future terror attacks.

IDENTITY THEFT

The recent emergence of identity crimes as a primary public and law enforcement concern can be viewed as indicative of the more general patterns of growth we have witnessed in computer crimes during the course of the last several decades. The exponential growth in the incidence of identity theft can largely be attributed to the creation of opportunities that are directly linked to technological and commercial advances. These advances have produced an alarming rise in the fraudulent use of individual information such as Social Security numbers, dates of birth, and credit card numbers by thieves who are intent on using this information for personal gain, and they have forced law enforcement agencies to redirect scarce resources in order to mitigate the threat.

Statistical trends reveal the feverish pace of growth in identity theft crimes. Experts estimate that personal losses related to identity theft reached $745 million in 1997 alone, a figure that represents a 68 percent increase in losses tied to identity theft over only a two-year span.[39] Credit thieves victimize approximately 1,000 individuals per day, and national estimates indicate that 350,000 to 500,000 persons annually experience monetary losses connected to identity crimes.[40] Trans-Union Corp., one of the three primary credit-reporting bureaus, indicates that about two-thirds of all consumer inquiries to the company's fraud division in 1997 involved possible identity theft crimes, or over 43,000 complaints per month.[41] In 1999, the Social Security Administration received over 62,000 allegations involving the misuse of Social Security numbers alone.[42] These explosive growth patterns are clearly beginning to strain law enforcement resources at the federal level—identity theft has been the primary charge in over 90 percent of all arrests made by the Secret Service's Financial Crimes Division since the mid-1990s. Losses related to closed identity theft cases by the Division topped $248 million in 2000, with potential losses tied to other reported cases nearing $1.5 billion.[43]

These trends can partly be attributed to the increasing use of Social Security numbers as personal identifiers. Social Security numbers, rarely referred to by those under retirement age decades ago, are now used as a means to conduct a wide range of business transactions, most notably the opening of new lines of personal credit. The use of Social Security numbers as personal identifiers, however, has not been limited to credit transactions. We are now asked to include the number on an ever-increasing array of forms, including medical records, motor vehicle driver's licenses, educational and employment records—some car dealers will even ask for it prior to allowing a customer to test drive a vehicle. Obviously, theft opportunities increase in relation to the number of times that consumers are required to use Social Security numbers as personal identifiers by commercial and governmental enterprises.

Moreover, growth trends in identity theft have strongly paralleled the advent of "e-commerce," or the use of on line technologies to conduct both consumer-based and business-to-business transactions. Today's consumer—ardently pounding out key strokes and "surfing" commercial Web sites—is far more likely to be asked to provide his or her Social Security number at their virtual "checkout" than was the more traditional pedestrian shopper of previous decades.

Identity thieves use a variety of methods to steal personal information. Heading up the list of low-tech means is "dumpster diving," or rummaging through private or commercial trash receptacles in search of discarded bills or pre-approved credit applications.[44] Other low-tech methods include the direct theft of mail, which may include a veritable treasure trove of personal information, contained on bank statements and unwanted telephone calling cards. Some thieves even complete change of address forms in the name of unwitting victims in order to divert and more easily access personal mail. "Shoulder surfing," or eavesdropping on conversations and cash transactions that involve the disclosure of personal identifiers, provides an avenue for low-tech thieves who are unwilling to steal documents outright.[45] While these theft techniques provide

---

BOX 5.2   Recent Identity Crime Prosecutions

- Federal agents arrested a former employee at a Long Island software company who allegedly originated a crime ring that eventually cost consumers $2.7 million. The suspect sold the credit reports of over 30,000 people, including names, Social Security numbers, and other credit information, to black market identity thieves who used the information to fraudulently obtain a wide variety of consumer goods. Each victim's credit history was sold for only $30.

- A defendant was recently convicted in federal court for fraudulently obtaining the names and Social Security numbers of high ranking military officers from internal government Web sites and using the information to apply on line for credit cards and other lines of credit. He was sentenced to 41 months in prison and ordered to pay over $186,000 in restitution.

- A former temporary employee of an insurance firm was convicted for using policyholders' bank account information to deposit over $764,000 in counterfeit bank checks.

- Seven defendants were recently convicted in an identity theft–drug smuggling scheme. The suspects used stolen Social Security numbers to garner employment and identification documents that were used to facilitate the smuggling of heroine and methamphetamine from Mexico. A number of the defendants also used their stolen identities to claim earned income tax credits on IRS tax forms.

---

opportunities for everyday thieves, more organized and technologically based methods have been used by sophisticated thieves intent on stealing mass quantities of personal information. These schemes may involve hacking information from corporate databases used for on line transactions or the bribing of employees who have internal access to customer identifiers.

Once personal identifying information is obtained, thieves can ransack a victim's financial status and destroy their credit history with frightening ease. For example, they may be able to open a new credit account using stolen Social Security numbers, names, and date of birth. The victim, of course, is left with the unpaid bills and delinquent accounts. Depending on the amount of personal information stolen, thieves may even be able to create entirely new bank accounts in your name, writing "hot" checks that are eventually traced back to the victim's credit history. Others have been victimized by thieves who have established wireless phone service, bought cars and other expensive consumer goods, and filed for bankruptcy under assumed identities in order to avoid paying past due accounts (see Box 5.2).[46]

Federal law enforcement agencies and the criminal justice system have begun to respond to the increasing threat posed by identity thieves through new legislation and consumer awareness programs. In 1998 Congress passed the Identity Theft and Assumption Deterrence Act. The law makes it a federal crime when someone:

Knowingly transfers or uses, without lawful authority, a means of identification of another person with the intent to commit, or to aid or abet, any unlawful activity that constitutes a violation of federal law, or that constitutes a felony under any applicable state
or local law.[47]

Violations of the law may be punishable by up to 15 years in prison. While the act clearly
signifies a growing recognition of the costs associated with identity crimes, the impact
of these and other laws aimed at curtailing identity theft may be largely symbolic for
many of those victimized. The reality is that identity crimes remain extremely difficult
to prosecute once detected. A large number of cases are detected too late for officials
to investigate adequately. These cases are extremely labor intensive, and often require
collaborative effort on the part of federal, state, and local law enforcement agencies
for successful prosecution. So too, the actual monetary losses involved in many individual cases of identity theft may be considered too small for dedication of a large
amount of prosecutorial resources.[48]

Given the difficulties inherent in detecting and prosecuting identity crimes, many
experts believe that the establishment of consumer awareness and monitoring programs
may be the most viable avenue toward thwarting the growth of identity theft. To this
end, the Federal Trade Commission (FTC) has established the Identity Theft
Clearinghouse. The clearinghouse collects identity theft complaints and provides victims referral information and other resources aimed at helping them restore their credit
history and financial status. The clearinghouse has also established a hotline for consumers who believe they have been victimized in an identity crime.[49]

INTERNET FRAUD SCHEMES

The Internet has increasingly been used as a vehicle for interpersonal communications,
research, consumer spending and business-to-business transactions over the course of
the last decade. This growth has provided the public with previously unparalleled opportunities for personal and economic advancement, and has created entire new industries in the process. These advances, however, have also produced fresh opportunities
for fraud and abuse on line. Interestingly, many fraud schemes committed over the
Internet are simply new takes on old themes—chain letter hoaxes, confidence schemes,
and bait-and-switch con games that are now performed over an electronic medium rather
than in person or over the telephone. Whether in old or new form, it is clear that the
increasing use of the Internet has given rise to an alarming growth in fraudulent schemes.
According to the official reporting rates of the National White Collar Crime Center,
consumer complaints concerning on line fraud have risen from 16,838 in 2000 to over
75,000 complaints in 2002, over a 400 percent increase in just two years.[50] These Internet
fraud schemes encompass a wide range of offenses, including financial institution fraud,
investment fraud, communications fraud, and confidence schemes. This section will
briefly define and describe the first three above-mentioned types of Internet fraud, as
well as discuss various types of confidence schemes in more detail.

Financial institution fraud involves attempts to conceal the truth from deposit and lending institutions so as to gain monetarily.[51] Examples of financial lending institution fraud include credit/debit card fraud and identity theft. Credit card fraud is one of the most widely reported Internet frauds, and identity theft has become a primary concern for law enforcement personnel and the public alike (see Chapter 10 for a discussion concerning enforcement efforts against identity theft). Investment frauds are "deceptive practices involving the use of capital to create more money," including traditional stock market investment schemes and pyramid business schemes designed to defraud individual consumers, all of which can be conducted on line.[52] Communication frauds involving new and different forms of technology have skyrocketed through thefts of wireless phone codes and other satellite communication devises.[53]

While all types of Internet fraud have experienced recent growth, frauds that involve a breach of personal trust, or what have been traditionally referred to as confidence schemes, may be among the most widely practiced and familiar to the general public. These schemes now typically use email communications or on line sites as a primary medium rather than the mail or telephone. The most widely perpetrated Internet confidence schemes include on line auction fraud, the Nigerian "419" fraud, chain letter hoaxes, and what are known as "urban legends" passed along through electronic mailings.

On line auction fraud is the most widely reported type of Internet fraud by a large margin. Sixty-four percent of all reported Internet fraud is auction fraud, and the Internet Fraud Complaint Center (IFCC) received over 30,000 auction fraud complaints in 2001. Losses related to on-line auction fraud surpass $4,000,000 annually; the average loss per complaint is $776.[54] Individuals and/or businesses participating in on line auctions can be defrauded in several ways. The most prevalent form of on line auction fraud is nondelivery of goods. In most cases, the victim of nondelivery has very little recourse if payment for the item has already been received by the would-be seller. Most on line auction buyers do not have a physical address or description of the perpetrator. Sellers may also purposely misrepresent the item to be auctioned in terms of its quality or characteristics. This can be accomplished through simple item descriptions or the altering of item pictures. "Shill bidding" is the use of intentional fake bidding on the part of the seller in order to artificially inflate an item's auctioned price. Finally, "fee stacking" occurs when the seller adds hidden charges to the cost of the item prior to delivery, most often through inflating the shipping cost. The costly nature of these schemes is detailed in Box 5.3, which provides excerpts from case summaries provided by the IFCC of two of the most extensive schemes recently investigated by federal law enforcement authorities.[55]

Another highly publicized on line fraud scheme has been dubbed the Nigerian 419 scheme by authorities. Since its origination in 1989, the on line e-mail letter scheme has cost individuals and businesses an estimated one billion dollars globally. The scheme is named "419" after the relevant Nigerian criminal codes that are involved. The scheme encompasses numerous different e-mails forwarded by Nigerian nationals in which the correspondence outlines nonexistent opportunities for recipients to receive Nigerian government funds in exchange for advance fees.[56] The following is an excerpted summary of the content of these fraudulent emails detailing the scheme from Interpol:[57]

BOX 5.3   Prominent On Line Auction Fraud Cases

CASE #1   The CATCH Task Force successfully prosecuted Raj Trivedi for victimizing more than 700 individuals throughout the world with his Internet fraud scheme of advertising high-tech products, accepting payment, and then failing to deliver the merchandise advertised. Losses from these frauds were over $992,000. Trivedi victimized consumers who went to his Web site to purchase electronic equipment (e.g., computers and camcorders) that Trivedi advertised on the auction Web sites eBay, uBid, and Yahoo. In March 2002, Trivedi was sentenced to three years in prison and ordered to pay restitution to his victims, who averaged $1,200 in individual losses.

CASE #2   The case against Teresa Smith of Massachusetts represents one of the largest on line auction fraud schemes on record. Smith was the subject of over 300 individual complaints stemming from frauds occurring from April 2001 through October 2002. Her scheme was simple: She would defraud her victims by selling a computer, requiring them to pay up front, and then not sending any of the auctioned merchandise. Smith then refused any type of refund request. During the investigation it was discovered that Smith had spent the victims' money on living expenses, a new vehicle, and advertising costs associated with the scheme. Smith would change her on line identity any time complaints were reported against her. The scheme was finally detected after investigators uncovered over $800,000 in fraudulent proceeds. Smith is currently awaiting sentencing.

The letters explain that the money is from delayed approved contract payments by the Nigerian administration to certain companies or individuals who have abandoned their claims. The letter alleges that the present military government is now paying these claims. The signatories claim to be acting as middle men and request that the victim supply signed and stamped blank company letterheads and invoices together with detailed account information so that monies can be transferred in advance of payment in order to pay taxes and bribe relevant officials in charge of the supposed proceeds. Obviously, no money is ever received, resulting in a total loss of bank deposits from the victim.

The IFCC received over 16,000 complaints about the scheme in 2002 alone. Largely as a result of this scheme, Nigeria ranks second behind only the United States in losses associated with Internet fraud schemes.[58]

Chain letter hoaxes and "urban legends" comprise another highly publicized and common form of Internet fraud. Chain letter hoaxes over the Internet are simply on line versions of age-old schemes designed to perpetuate the forwarding of e-mails. Often, these letters ask the recipient to forward the e-mail message to as many people that they can in exchange for a specified sum for each forwarded e-mail.[59] Chain letter hoaxes are typically less costly than other forms of on line fraud because the recipient is simply duped into believing that they will receive compensation that is not forthcoming. These hoaxes have included claims that prominent businesses will compensate recipients for forwarded emails, including Microsoft, Outback Steak House, Victoria's Secret, Newell Company, Nokia, Old Navy, and McDonalds, among others.[60] These claims are

BOX 5.4   Common On Line "Urban Legends"

Needles on Gas Pumps

Some persons have been affixing hypodermic needles to the underside of gas pump handles in the Jacksonville, FL area. These needles appear to be infected with the HIV virus. In the Jacksonville area alone there have been 17 cases of people being stuck by these needles over the past five months. We have verified reports of at least 12 other cases around the country . . . Evidently, the consumers go to fill their car with gas, and when picking up the pump handle get stuck by infected needles . . . IT IS IMPERATIVE TO CAREFULLY CHECK THE HANDLE OF GAS PUMPS EVERY TIME YOU USE ONE!

Cyanide-Laced Deposit Envelopes

I hesitate to be an alarmist, but if anything like this happened to one of my family or friends I would not be able to forgive myself for not passing this along . . . A woman died recently from licking the deposit envelope at a Bank of America ATM. It was laced with cyanide. Investigators stated that they went back to the ATM in question and found six other envelopes in the slot . . . Please, I implore you to use extreme caution when using those envelopes. The radio station advised that you should first spit on the envelope, and then close it . . . I know this sounds gross, but better gross than DEAD.

Poison Perfume Samples

I was sent an email at work about someone walking up to you at a mall parking lot and asking you to sniff perfume they are selling at cut-rate prices. This isn't really perfume but ether, and you will pass out and they will take your wallet and all of your valuables. This is not a prank e-mail. This is true! I could have very well been a victim. PASS THIS ALONG.

Rat Feces

A stock clerk was sent to clean up a storeroom at his work place. When he got back there, he was complaining that the storeroom was really filthy, and that he had noticed dried mouse or rat droppings in some areas . . . A couple of days later, he started feeling like he came down with a stomach flu, achy joints, and headache. He went to bed and never woke up. Within two days he was ill and weak. His blood sugar count was down to 66. He was rushed to emergency where he suffered from complete organ failure. He died shortly before midnight . . . There is a virus that lives in dried rat droppings (much like Hanta virus). Once dried, these droppings are like dust and can be easily digested. ALWAYS carefully rinse off the tops of any canned foods or soda . . . A family friend recently died from drinking a can of soda!

never true, because currently there is no software in existence that is capable of tracking the number of times that an e-mail is forwarded and then subsequently compiling a report back to a central tabulator.[61] So-called urban legends are myths designed to create a generalized panic among e-mail recipients. These messages typically entail grandiose claims of impending danger arising from commonplace activities. Box 5.4 details some of the more common urban legends currently circulating on line. Rest assured, none of the claims are true.[62]

The Computer Fraud and Abuse Act (CFA) has become the primary vehicle for the prosecution of Internet fraud crimes. The CFA was initially enacted by Congress in 1984, primarily as a means to protect classified information contained on government computers. The scope of the CFA was expanded in 1986, and again in 1996. The 1996 amendments to the Act worked to incorporate *all* computers that are involved in interstate and/or foreign commerce under the Act.[63] Essentially, the CFA covers most fraudulent business practices that are conducted over the Internet.

SUMMARY

This chapter has defined and described how the growth in computer technologies has affected five major criminal offenses, including embezzlement, money laundering, corporate espionage, identity crimes, and fraud. The traditional crimes of embezzlement and money laundering have clearly become more prevalent, and modern technologies have increased opportunities to commit both crimes. In terms of embezzlement, the computer has allowed individuals increased access to funds manipulation and has eliminated problems related to the material bulk of moving large quantities of cash. Money laundering is now easier because of two primary reasons: (1) electronic funds are easier to conceal while maintaining anonymity, and (2) the advent of "cashless" banking systems such as e-cash has made detection of such crimes much more difficult.

In addition, computer technologies have created a wide array of new avenues to the pilfering of corporate secrets, including trade technologies, research and development strategies, and customer lists. Computerized corporate data is easier to access, and the prevalent utilization of electronic mail in business environments has given corporate thieves expanded opportunities. So too, the end of the Cold War has created a cadre of former spies who can provide foreign firms the skills and expertise necessary for stealing domestic trade secrets.

Finally, the traditional crime of fraud has taken on new forms as a result of the information revolution. In particular, the Internet has increasingly been utilized as a platform to perpetrate fraud, especially in on line auction schemes, financial institution frauds, and the transmission of "urban legends."

REVIEW QUESTIONS

1. Identify and describe the similarities and differences between corporate espionage offenders who are "insiders" and those who are "outsiders."
2. What is the Bank Secrecy Act of 1970? How has the advent of computer technologies created ways around this act?

3. What are "urban legends"? How have these "legends" changed over the course of the last two decades?

ENDNOTES

1. REIMAN, J. (1995). *The Rich Get Richer and the Poor Get Prison.* Boston: Allyn & Bacon.
2. SUTHERLAND, E. (1940). "White-Collar Criminality." In *White Collar Crime: Classic and Contemporary Views.* G. GEIS, R.F. MEIRER, and L.M. SALINGER (eds.). New York: Free Press (pp. 29–38).
3. GREEN, G.S. (1997). *Occupational Crime,* 2nd ed. Chicago: Nelson Hall.
4. CRESSEY, D.R. (1953). *Other People's Money: A Study in the Social Psychology of Embezzlement.* Glencoe, IL: Free Press.
5. FURNELL, S. (2002). *Cybercrime: Vandalizing the Information Society.* Boston: Addison-Wesley.
6. ANDERSON, J.P. (1980). "Computer Security Threat Monitoring and Surveillance." James P. Anderson Co.: Fort Washington, PA.
7. *Ibid.,* 3.
8. FIEDLER, T. (1999). "Man Admits Helping Himself to Raises; Embezzlement Trial is the First Computer Fraud Case to be Heard in Minnesota." *Star Tribune* (Minneapolis, MN), June 24.
9. GLOD, M. (2002). "Ex-Fairfax Official Gets 14 Years in Theft." *Washington Post,* November 23.
10. KANE, D. (2002). "Millions Vanish Through Theft, Embezzlement at North Carolina Agencies." *Knight Ridder/Tribune Business News,* November 24.
11. MURRAY, T.D. and CANIGLIA, J. (2003). "Broker's Victims Start Over; Gruttaduria's Investors Still Hurting, Rules Not Changed." *Cleveland Plain Dealer,* February 16.
12. HUDSON, J.E. III. (2002). "Trade Secret Theft Threatens Everyone with Corporate Espionage Escapades." *Houston Business Journal,* October 4.
13. ROBINSON, S.W. *Corporate Espionage 101.* SANS Institute, 2003.
14. KONRAD, R. (2000). "Leaks and Geeks: International Espionage Goes High-Tech." *C/Net News.Com,* September 21.
15. *Ibid.,* 14.
16. *Ibid.,* 14.
17. *Ibid.,* 14.
18. *Ibid.,* 12.
19. *Ibid.,* 13.
20. *Ibid.,* 13.
21. *Ibid.,* 13.
22. *Ibid.,* 13.
23. BOWMAN, L.M. (2001). "Avant Ordered to Pay $182 Million." *C/Net News.Com.,* July 19.
24. SWARTZ, J. (1997). "Felony Charges Halve Avant's Stock." *The San Francisco Chronicle,* April 16.
25. BURROWS, P. (1997). "A Nest of Software Spies?" *Business Week,* June 15.
26. *Ibid.,* 14.
27. *Ibid.,* 12.
28. LYMAN, M.D. and POTTER, G.W. (2000). *Organized Crime.* Prentice Hall: Upper Saddle River, NJ.
29. *Ibid.,* 28.
30. *Ibid.,* 28.

31. GRABOSKY, P.N. and SMITH, R.G. (1998). *Crime in the Digital Age.* The Federated Press: New Brunswick, NJ.
32. *Ibid.,* 31.
33. BORTNER, R.M. (1996). "Cyberlaundering: Anonymous Digital Cash and Money Laundering." Presented as a final paper at the University of Miami School of Law.
34. *Ibid.,* 33.
35. *Ibid.,* 33.
36. *http://fincen.gov*
37. *Ibid.,* 36.
38. *Ibid.,* 36.
39. LEASE, M.L. and BURKE, T.D. (2000). "Identity Theft: A Fast-Growing Crime." *FBI Law Enforcement Bulletin,* 69 (8).
40. *Ibid.,* 39.
41. HOAR, S.B. (2001). "Identity Theft: The Crime of the New Millennium." *USA Bulletin* (March).
42. *Ibid.,* 41.
43. *Ibid.,* 41.
44. *Ibid.,* 39.
45. *Ibid.,* 41.
46. Excerpted from HOAR, S.B. (2001). "Identity Theft: The Crime of the New Millennium." *USA Bulletin* (March).
47. (2002). Federal Trade Commission Bulletin. "Identity Theft: When Bad Things Happen to Your Good Name." (February).
48. *Ibid.,* 41.
49. *Ibid.,* 47.
50. (2003). IFCC 2002 Internet Fraud Report.
51. *Ibid.,* 50.
52. *Ibid.,* 50.
53. *Ibid.,* 50.
54. (2001). IFCC Internet Auction Fraud Report (May).
55. *Ibid.,* 54.
56. (2003). Professionals Against Confidence Crimes. "Interpol Warning: Nigerian Crime Syndicates Letter Scheme Fraud Takes on New Dimension."
57. *Ibid.,* 56.
58. *Ibid.,* 50.
59. *http://www.scambusters.org*
60. *Ibid.,* 59.
61. *Ibid.,* 59.
62. *Ibid.,* 59.
63. (2001). *GigiLaw.Com.* "The Expanding Importance of the Computer Fraud and Abuse Act."

Chapter 6

Viruses and Malicious Code

Chapter Objectives

After completing this chapter, you should be able to:

- Identify and distinguish the various types of viruses and malicious code.
- Understand the differences between the differing types of viruses, including file viruses, boot viruses, macro viruses, and network viruses.
- Understand the differences between a virus and worm. Additionally, understand how a worm operates in comparison to a virus.
- Understand the definition and operation of a Trojan horse and how it is different from a standard virus.
- Describe adware and spyware, and the controversy concerning whether or not these types of programs are in fact viruses.
- Describe and understand other types of malicious code and attacks, including denial of service attacks and blended threats.
- Describe and understand the true threat posed by viruses, the extent of the virus and malicious code problem, and virus hoaxes and their effect on computers and productivity.
- Understand who the virus writers are and why they write viruses.

INTRODUCTION

There is perhaps no other area of computer crime that creates more fear, misperceptions, and attention than computer viruses. The immediate popularity of personal computing, rapidly developing technology, and a general lack of oversight and regulation have combined to create the concomitant development of software and malicious programs as well. None of the first personal computers, early versions of DOS (disk operating software), or first networks was designed with security in mind.[1] As a result, law enforcement, virus security experts, and network managers continually play catch-up with an ever-growing list of viruses and malicious code. The market for virus protection software, firewalls, and computer security expertise is a multibillion dollar industry that relies on the same fears that drive many to purchase home security systems. The question is, how serious is the virus problem, and what is really necessary to deal with the problems viruses and other types of malicious code present? Indeed, in the years preceding the turn of the century, virus hype definitely outpaced virus damage. However, in recent years, several high-profile worms have caused millions of dollars of damage to numerous businesses and personal computer users.

Initially, viruses were spread primarily through floppy disks, with the infections being spread by infecting multiple computers via the same diskette. Today viruses and other types of malicious code are primarily spread over the Internet through a variety of mechanisms including e-mail, e-mail attachments, downloadable files, Web pages, newsgroups, peer-to-peer file transfers,[2] instant messaging,[3] digital pictures, and several other techniques and tactics.[4] The Internet was designed for the rapid propagation of data, making no distinction between good or bad data.[5] As such, viruses and other types of malicious code take advantage of the very conveniences and features that make the Internet so appealing. The true cost of viruses is unknown; estimates range from very little true damage to wild estimates claiming that viruses cost billions of dollars annually. A recent survey of security experts from the government, private industry, and universities revealed that 85 percent had experienced some type of security breach in the prior year. An additional 35 percent of the respondents claimed over $375,000,000 million dollars in losses to hackers and viruses. Finally, the respondents reported that an average virus outbreak took approximately 20 person-days or less to recover and cost the company between $10,000 (median) and $120,000 (average) in estimated direct costs.[6] Nonetheless, there is no centralized database that collects information on the damage that viruses cause.

At the outset, it is important to note that this chapter is not designed to provide the reader with substantial technical knowledge concerning viruses or virus prevention and computer security. It is simply an overview of the types of viruses, malicious code, and security problems that exist, with some relevant examples and some material on the investigation and prosecution of virus writers. This chapter focuses almost exclusively on common computer systems and windows-based viruses that the casual and neophyte reader will be familiar with. Viruses and malicious code can infect other operating systems and hardware, but that is beyond the focus of this chapter. Finally, this chapter is not written for expert computer users or experts in the virus writing and virus prevention fields. Instead, it offers a layman's approach, designed for people unfamiliar with the complexities of the virus problem.

Although no reliable estimate exists, there is probably no other area in computers where more time, energy, and resources are spent than on antivirus protection. This has led to the creation of the pseudo-virus expert. This is the person who proclaims expertise in office workgroups around the world, claiming that they know about viruses and how to prevent them. Most commonly, this is the person who can download patches and update antivirus software, with little real knowledge of viruses. There are many reasons behind this, most prominently the "false authority syndrome" so aptly described by Rob Rosenberger, a well-known virus expert (see Box 6.1). Hence, the author of this chapter wants to make it perfectly clear that he is no virus expert and wishes to avoid false authority syndrome at all costs. Instead, the author, like most people who express legitimate concern about viruses and malicious code, is a student of the virus industry. This chapter provides a nontechnical look at viruses and malicious code, and is designed to give the reader the knowledge of viruses they need to be discriminating about what they hear, read, and learn about this area. Often there is more bark than bite in most of the viruses that plague our computers.

BOX 6.1   Computer Viruses and "False Authority Syndrome"

The following account is from Rob Rosenberger, a virus expert and myth debunker concerning what he terms "False Authority Syndrome."

True Story

A couple of years ago I dropped by the Software Etc. store in Fairview Heights, Illinois just to browse. Another customer had come in before me and told an employee about a problem with his video monitor. The employee warned the customer that he had contracted a newly discovered computer virus, which he proceeded to describe in great detail.

I interrupted the employee. "Sir, you have it completely wrong. That virus doesn't exist. It's the latest hoax."

"Oh, no," the employee replied. "We've got e-mail reports from our sales headquarters telling us to keep our eyes open for it."

To which I countered, "Some upper-tier sales manager has been duped and is telling you BS. McAfee Associates and others have issued public statements dismissing that virus as a hoax. What you've described simply cannot be done by any virus. Period."

I then turned my attention to the customer. "Stop listening to this guy. You don't have this magical virus he's describing because it simply doesn't exist. You have some other problem with your video monitor." What credentials does this salesman hold in the field of computer viruses? He may have flipped burgers at a McDonald's restaurant two weeks ago, for all we know.

Most people who claim to speak **with authority** about computer viruses **have little or no genuine expertise.** Some virus experts describe it as "False Authority

Syndrome"—the person feels competent to discuss viruses because of his job title, or because of his expertise in another computer field, or simply because he knows how to use a computer.

I want you to question the credentials of anybody who talks about computer viruses. Indeed, I want you to question my credentials in this field!

The U.S. Air Force highlights the concept of False Authority Syndrome in *Tongue & Quill,* their official publication on effective writing:

> "*Nonexpert opinion* or assumed authority—Don't be swayed (or try to sway someone else) based on the opinion of an unqualified authority. The Air Force is chock-full of people who, because of their position or authority in one field, are quoted on subjects in other fields for which they have limited or no experience." (As this Air Force publication notes, False Authority Syndrome can attack people in all fields of expertise.)

Computer salesmen, consultants, repairmen, and college computer teachers often succumb to False Authority Syndrome. In many cases a person's job title sounds impressive, but his or her job description at most may only include references to vague "computer security" duties.

People without impressive job titles suffer from False Authority Syndrome, too. A user who contracts a virus, for example, will often turn around and confidently tell other people how to avoid them. He or she may even rise to the position of "office virus expert."

False Authority Syndrome plays on two important desires. First, people genuinely like to help others; second, they like to feel in control of their computers. Users easily succumb to the effects of False Authority Syndrome when driven by these natural desires.

"Marcello," a typical user who took a hoax for real, posted a message on CompuServe warning users not to read any messages with "Good Times" in the subject line (lest they contract the so-called Good Times virus). Ironically, Marcello *used* the words "Good Times" in the subject line of his own warning message!

At least one virus expert sent Marcello a playful reply telling him to "stop infecting people" with the Good Times virus. Confronted with details about the hoax, Marcello replied, "Thank you for your help, and I'm sorry, because I was duped, but anyway I was worry *[sic]* about my computer and a lot more from *[sic]* my job."

So-called "Office Virus Experts"

A rule of thumb: The first employee attacked by a computer virus will quickly rise to the position of office virus expert. "Trust me, I know what I'm talking about. I've *been* there."

Sadly, managers often overlook more competent people when naming office virus experts. The guy who practices safe computing is a nobody, but all hail the jerk who barely survived an attack.

(continued)

BOX 6.1   continued

Experts Believe *ILoveYou* Cost $2.7 / $4.7 / $6.7 / $8.7 Billion

Legend: experts around the world believe the ILoveYou virus in May 2000 caused $2.7 billion, $4.7 billion, $6.7 billion, or $8.7 billion in damages. *Reality:* Computer Economics, Inc. concocted the first three estimates as a publicity stunt during the peak of *ILoveYou* hysteria. They concocted the fourth estimate after the hysteria died down. *Reason experts are duped:* No statistically accepted metrics exist to gauge virus costs—and no statistically valid data exists to gauge worldwide virus proliferation. Therefore, any cost estimate is as good as any other cost estimate. *Fallout:* The antivirus industry can cite yet another plausible-sounding estimate.

Conclusion

I don't want to dispel any particular computer virus myths someone may have told you—that's not my goal here. Rather, I want you to *question a person's expertise* if he or she claims to speak with authority on computer viruses. This way we can prevent all the "blind leading the blind" techno-babble. And we can reduce the number of people who believe all the myths out there.

In summary:

- Most people have little or no expertise in the field of computer viruses.
- People with little or no expertise often fall prey to False Authority Syndrome.
- False Authority Syndrome contributes significantly to the spread of fear and myths about computer viruses.

Visual Developer editor Jeff Duntemann sums it up best: "If people exercised greater discretion in who and how and to what degree they place their trust, we would know more as a community—and we would know it better. There would be fewer paths for bad or phony knowledge."

Source: http://vmyths.com/fas/fas1.cfm

Most virus writers and attackers are opportunistic, and like other criminals choose to attack systems at their weakest and most vulnerable points.[7] As such, the SANS Institute and the National Infrastructure Protection Center (NIPC) at the FBI created the top 10 vulnerabilities list to help organizations and security experts in identifying the most problematic security holes in Windows operating systems. The list is contained in Table 6.1 and depicts the consensus of opinion of security experts from the government and private industry. SANS and the FBI claim that the overwhelming majority of successful attacks target one or more of these 10 vulnerable services.[8] This chapter reviews the nature of viruses and other types of malicious code through an examina-

---

TABLE 6.1   The SANS/FBI Top 10 Vulnerabilities in Windows Systems

Top Vulnerabilities to Windows Systems

W1 Internet Information Services (IIS)

W2 Microsoft SQL Server (MSSQL)

W3 Windows Authentication

W4 Internet Explorer (IE)

W5 Windows Remote Access Services

W6 Microsoft Data Access Components (MDAC)

W7 Windows Scripting Host (WSH)

W8 Microsoft Outlook and Outlook Express

W9 Windows Peer to Peer File Sharing (P2P)

W10 Simple Network Management Protocol (SNMP)

---

tion of what these programs are, and their effect on infected systems. An examination of the threat posed by viruses, real and imagined, is undertaken with a particular emphasis on the ultimate effect viruses and malicious code have on society. This chapter will explore who the virus writers are and why they write viruses in the first place, and review investigative procedures and prosecution of virus writers—and all of the difficulties faced by law enforcement in this area.

VIRUSES AND MALICIOUS CODE

There is a great deal of confusion surrounding the definition and categorization of viruses and other types of malicious code. In fact, there is an entire vocabulary of virus writing and antivirus detection that must be understood prior to engaging in any discussion of viruses and their impact. As such, several terms and issues associated with this area must be discussed prior to the coverage of the subject matter in this chapter. To begin, viruses and malicious code must be understood from several perspectives and variables, the most important of which is the potential damage that viruses and malicious code can cause. Damage can include triggered events that cause computer operations to be disrupted, clogging or disrupting e-mail or network operations, deleting or modifying files, accessing and sharing confidential information, performance interference and degrading, compromised security, and damage to the computer's software and hardware.[9] As such, many viruses and malicious code are graded based on the potential damage they can cause and their overall impact on computer operations at the individual level and across the world.

In a similar vein, the level of vulnerability or exposure is an additional defining characteristic of viruses and malicious code. Vulnerabilities include the ability of an attacker to execute commands on a victim's computer or network, the ability to access data on a remote system, the ability to take control of a system and assume another's identity, and the ability of the attacker to deny service to legitimate traffic on a given system or systems.[10] These are essentially the universal vulnerabilities that attackers exploit in order to propagate a virus or engage in some type of malicious attack. In essence, computer systems and software can be graded in terms of their exposure to these vulnerabilities (see Table 6.1). In making assessments of how secure or unsecure a system or computer is, exposure assessments describe a state of operations which are not universal vulnerabilities, but describe how exposed a system is to a potential attack. The degree of exposure is determined by how easy it is for an attacker to conduct information gathering on a system, how easy it is to hide attack activities on a system, how easy it is to access a system and compromise its operation, and how many points of entry or security holes are present in a given system. In other words, exposure refers to the potential problems or security holes that are present that would allow an attacker to exploit the vulnerabilities described above.

In addition to the vulnerabilities and exposures described above, there are numerous terms used in describing viruses and their potential impact. The most common term used to describe how a virus is operating and the effect it is having is listing the virus as "in the wild." The "wildness" of a virus measures the extent to which a virus is spreading among computer users and systems. This measurement includes the number of infected independent sites and computers, the geographic distribution of infection, the ability of current technology to combat the threat, and the complexity of the virus. The true number of virus infections and malicious code attacks can never be ascertained with any degree of reliability and validity. However, several firms and independent organizations propagate lists of the most active viruses and the number of reported infections. One such list utilizes a Delphi technique (a survey and analysis of experts) to ascertain the number of viruses that are in the wild and which are most damaging. Viruses in the wild are those that are spreading as a result of normal day-to-day operations on and between the computers of unsuspecting users. Further, to make the list, two or more virus experts must report problems with the virus.[11] The April 2004 Wildlist reported 303 viruses currently in the wild; however, as is the case with most computer statistics, this number changes almost daily.

Viruses and malicious code are simply programs, and like any other program they are designed for a specific function. A virus or malicious code program is written for a variety of noncriminal purposes including advertisements, jokes, and political messages. However, less humorous and more malicious intentions include destroying data and information, information acquisition and identity theft, surreptitious control of a remote machine, or the shutdown of a legitimate business or Web site. The virus program delivers a payload; this is part of the virus program that delivers the malicious intent or other device. The virus is executed by some type of payload trigger which causes the virus or malicious code to deliver its contents or execute its commands. The trigger can be something the user does, such as opening an e-mail attachment or downloading a file; it can be triggered by some event such as a date or condition on a computer; or it can self-execute based on code written into the virus program. Early viruses were simple code, but recently viruses have become increasingly sophisticated and written to avoid detection. Some viruses are encrypted, which is a method of scrambling or encoding data to prevent reading or tampering with the data. The level of encryption and the strength of the encryption has increased substantially in recent years. Only individuals with access to a password or key can decrypt and use the data, and this allows the virus to hide itself from virus scanners—that is, the encrypted virus jumbles its program code to make it more difficult to detect. Some viruses also use "stealth," making them appear not to exist on a machine or hide their tracks from scanning software. Like a cyber Cold War of sorts, virus detection software writers and virus writers engage in a never-ending battle to stay one step ahead.

The development of virus construction tools by virus writers allows a larger number of less sophisticated computer users to write and create viruses. A virus construction set is a utility program intended for creating new computer viruses. Virus construction sets allow generating of source code of the viruses, object modules and/or infected files themselves.[12] Another tool developed by virus writers known as a mutation engine allows viruses to change their code each time they infect a new machine. Known as a polymorphic virus or malicious code, these programs do not have any constant section of code. In most cases, two strains of the same "polymorphic" virus will not have a single coinciding element of code. A polymorphic virus can change its pattern when it replicates, avoiding detection by simple virus scanning techniques. Viruses are also polymorphic if they cannot, or can but with great difficulty, be detected using the so-called virus masks or indicators; in other words the scanner looks for parts of nonchanging virus specific code. The virus changes in two main ways: by encrypting the main code of the virus with a nonconstant key with random sets of decryption commands, or by changing executable virus code.[13]

The type of encryption or operating algorithms used in a virus can vary substantially. The technical complexity of this area continually increases and changes. One area of interest is termed the TSR (terminate and stay resident) capability of the virus. This essentially means that the virus is able to leave itself in system memory, intercept some events, and in the process run infecting routines on files and sectors of the disk. Resident viruses stay in memory and are active until power down or until operating system reboot. Nonresident viruses do not infect computer memory and are active for an limited time only. Some viruses leave small parts in the memory which do not spread the virus; these viruses are considered nonresident.[14] Resident viruses are active regardless of whether or not the infected program is running and remain viable until the next reboot, even if all the infected files are deleted from disk. It is also largely impossible to get rid of such viruses by restoring all the files from distribution disks or backup copies: The virus simply remains active and infects the newly created files. This is also true for some boot viruses as well—even formatting the disk doesn't necessarily remove viruses, as they will continued to infect the disk repeatedly after formatting.[15] Hence the TSR capability of the virus is an important factor in classifying and determining the potential seriousness of a given virus.

Another feature of the operating algorithm of a virus is the use of stealth algorithms. Stealth allows the virus to remain hidden on a system and cover its tracks during and after the infection process. Yet another operating algorithm that can be used to grade or distinguish a virus is the use of self encryption and polymorphism. These are used to make the virus detection and removal procedure as complicated as possible.[16] Polymorphic viruses are exceedingly difficult to detect and they have no permanent signatures, that is, none of their code fragments remain unchanged. Often, a comparison of two samples of the polymorphic virus will yield few, if any, similarities in the code of the virus, making it impossible to program an antivirus solution. This may be achieved by encrypting of the main body of the virus and making modifications to the decryption routine.[17]

The destructiveness of a virus ranges from virtually harmless to extraordinarily dangerous and malicious. Some viruses have no real effect on the operation of the computer or the data and information stored on the computer; their payloads consist of some message being displayed or silly program being run. Other viruses can seriously disrupt the operation of the computer, rewriting commands, altering normal system operation, and changing boot routines and other malicious commands. Additionally, some viruses intentionally target the information and data on a system, resulting in lost data, data destruction, erasure of vital information in system areas, even inflicting damage to hardware.[18]

History and Development

There is a great deal of controversy surrounding the origins of computer viruses, who is responsible for creating the first computer virus, and who can claim responsibility for discovering and eliminating the early viruses. One author contends that the first viruses (although no one called them that at the time) appeared in the late 1960s and early 1970s on early versions of Univac and IBM machines.[19] Occasionally, on the mainframes in operation at that time, programs appeared that cloned themselves, occupied system resources, and lowered the productivity of the system. These programs, known as "rabbits," did not copy themselves from system to system and remained strictly local phenomena, mistakes or pranks by system programmers. The first incident which may be called an epidemic of "a computer virus" happened on a Univax 1108 system. The virus called "Pervading Animal" merged itself to the end of executable. However, the first recognized versions of what could be termed the modern virus appeared on early PC machines in the middle to late 1980s, correlating largely with the enormous growth of the PC industry.

The earliest viruses infected boot sectors and floppy disks, performing such functions as playing Yankee Doodle Dandy on the speakers and deleting letters in documents.[20] Early viruses were extraordinarily easy to detect when compared with the viruses of today; each virus contained recognizable code that became known as the virus' signature. Once the signature was detected and identified, antivirus software could then be programmed to detect, isolate, and eliminate the virus.[21] The first vastly spread virus was a bootable virus called "Brain,"[22] which spread via floppy disks.[23] The virus was created in Pakistan by brothers Basit and Amjad Farooq Alvi. They left a text message inside the virus with their name, address and telephone number. According to the authors of the virus they were software vendors, and wanted to know the extent of piracy in their country. Unfortunately, their experiment left the borders of Pakistan.

The first counterpunch by virus writers was to encrypt the code within the virus, thus hiding their signatures by writing them in indecipherable code.[24] In order to complete the infection, the encrypted virus needed to return to its original state in order to replicate and infect. The decryption routine written into the virus could be identified and used as a virus signature, allowing detection by antivirus software.[25] MtE (MuTation Engine) is the first known polymorphic generator. It was released in 1991 and shocked antivirus researchers with its very complex polymorphic algorithm.[26] Polymorphic routines still encrypted the virus, but the encryption routine was randomized by a mutation engine.[27] The first polymorphic virus appeared in the early 1990s and was known as "Chameleon,"[28] but polymorphic viruses became really serious with the introduction of the "Tequila"[29] virus in April 1991.[30] The polymorphic virus took off two years later. A host of these viruses spread with the help of the burgeoning Internet.

Several things combined to aid the spread of viruses: the rapid growth of the Internet; the rapid growth and availability of personal computers; the availability of the polymorphic engine; and the availability of virus creation tools that first hit in July of 1992. The first viral code construction set for IBM PC compatibles was called VCL (Virus Creation Laboratory).[31] This set allows the user to generate code to produce viruses. The program used a Windows™ interface and a menu system that allowed the virus writer to choose virus type, objects to infect (COM or/and EXE), presence or absence of self-encryption, measures of protection from debugging, inside text strings, and an optional ten additional effects.[32] The created virus can then use a variety of means for infection by adding its body to the end of file, replacing files with its body destroying the original content of a file, or becoming companion viruses.[33] The introduction of the polymorphic engine and the VCL automated and simplified the virus writing process so that any teenager with a computer and a cause could write a virus.

At the end of 1992, the first virus specifically designed for Windows™ was released.[34] With the release of Windows 95™, the first "virus epidemic" was soon to follow (in 1996) with the widespread release and propagation of macro viruses. The Concept[35] virus was an innocuous virus that spread very rapidly and was a wake-up call for Microsoft and the anti-virus industry.[36]

The main problem with trying to give the exact definition of a virus is that virtually all the unique features of a virus—such as incorporating with other objects, stealth behavior, potential danger, and potential for spread—may be found in other nonvirus programs.[37] A second difficulty is that viruses are operating-system and software-system specific.[38] One author maintains that it is only definable through the specification of several necessary conditions. For example, the ability of the virus to produce copies of itself, the capability to incorporate itself into other files and systems (networks, files, executable objects, etc.), and the capability to further contaminate other systems are all potential necessary conditions to be able to define a computer virus.[39] Some authors claim that viruses are a form of artificial life possessing all of the properties of a live organism. They can propagate, adapt themselves to different environments, and self-transmit in an effort to move and relocate.[40] Ironically, legendary computer guru Peter Norton announced that computer viruses did not exist, declaring them to be mythical.[41]

Mobile code is code that can be transmitted across a network and executed on the other end of a transmission. Mobile code may be created using one of numerous mobile code systems, including Java, ActiveX, safe Tcl, Visual Basic, Visual Basic for Applications (VBA), and scripting.[42] Mobile code has become quite routine on most Web pages and is also used in a growing number of Internet-capable programs. The positives of mobile code can be turned against the user and used in an attack that is quite difficult to detect.

Viruses

The classification or categorization of computer viruses and malicious code is ongoing. There is some disagreement concerning the exact terminology used and what is and what is not considered a virus or malicious code. Nonetheless, there is an active attempt by several antivirus vendors and the federal government to have some standard classifications of viruses and other types of malicious code. Viruses can be categorized based on the environment they operate in, the operating system they are targeted at, the type of encryption and operating algorithms used, and their destructive capabilities.[43] Other types of malicious code include worms, Trojan horses, adware or spyware, logic bombs, denial of service attacks, and blended threats. This list is not necessarily complete nor is there universal agreement on the exhaustiveness and mutual exclusivity of the list. Nonetheless, the list does comprise the majority of the types of viruses identified in the current literature.

Viruses operate in four primary environments: file viruses, boot viruses, macro viruses, and network viruses.[44] File viruses infect their targets in several ways: as a parasite, as a companion, or through file system–specific features known as link viruses. File viruses use a particular operating system to propagate, and they can infect virtually any type of executable file. These viruses can overwrite the contents of a target executable with its own code, destroying the original contents of the files. This method is the simplest and results in system failures and other problems because the infected file simply stops working. As such, these are relatively easy to detect and remove. Parasitic viruses also change the contents of the infected files, but they latch onto the file and leave it operational. Kaspersky (2003) contends that these types of viruses include "prepending" viruses (saving themselves at the top of file), "appending" (saving themselves at the end of file), and "inserting" (inserting themselves in the middle of file).[45] The insertion methods vary as well, by moving a fragment of the file toward the end of file or by copying its own code to such parts of the file which are known to be unused ("cavity" viruses). Companion viruses do not change the infected files; instead, they clone the target file so that when run, the companion virus runs instead of the original file. Link viruses, like companion viruses, do not change the physical contents of files, but when an infected file is started, they "force" the OS to execute their code. This is achieved by modifying the necessary fields of the file system.[46] Viruses can also infect other areas of a computer, including compiler libraries, object modules and source code—however, these types of viruses are extraordinarily rare.

Boot viruses attack either the boot sector of the system, the master boot record, or change the system pointer to an active boot sector. Gap boot viruses infect the boot sector of a floppy disk and the boot sector or Master Boot Record (MBR) of a hard disk. Boot viruses operate based on the algorithms of starting an operation system upon power on or reboot—after the necessary hardware tests (of memory, disks etc.) the system loader routine reads the first physical sector of a boot disk (A:, C:, or CD-ROM, depending on the options in BIOS Setup) and passes the control to the virus. In the case of a diskette or CD-Rom infection, the virus attacks a boot sector, analyzes the operations and boot routine of the computer, and substitutes the virus code in the place of the normal operating code. In the case of a hard disk target, the target is a boot sector on the hard disk. The virus passes control from the computer to virus in that particular sector. Upon infecting the disk, the virus in most cases moves the original boot sector to some other sector of the disk. If the virus size exceeds the size of the sector, then the target sector will contain the first part of the virus, the rest of it placed in the other sectors.[47] Diskette infecting is accomplished when the virus rewrites the original boot sector code with its own code. Hard disks can be infected when a virus writes itself over the master boot record (MBR) code or the boot sector code of the boot disk (C: drive, usually), or modifies the address of the active boot sector in the disk partition table.[48]

Macro viruses are most commonly associated with common business software and infect documents, spreadsheets, databases, and presentation files. Macro viruses take advantage of macro languages built into common systems of business software, most notably Microsoft Office™. Macro viruses transfer themselves from one infected file to another within a given system and cross over to other systems, typically via attachments or shared files. Macro functions within a file or processing program can operate without user intervention. Macro viruses generally use an auto-macro present in the file, a standard system macro (associated with some menu item) that has been redefined, or the macro of the virus is pulled automatically after a certain key or key combination has been pressed. If a Word document is infected, when opening it, the program calls the infected automatic macro and then executes the virus code. If the virus contains macros with standard names, they take control after a user executes the corresponding menu item (File/Open, File/Close, File/Save, etc.). If some symbol of the keyboard is redefined, the virus activates itself only after the corresponding key has been pressed.

Most macro viruses contain all of their functions as standard macros of the software program they infect. However, there are viruses that use the techniques of hiding their code and keeping their code as a nonmacro entry. For example, when activated, a Word macro virus will move the macro code into the common macros contained in the program with the help of the macro editor contained in the program. The virus then creates a new macro, inserts its own code inside the macro, and then saves this macro with the code in the document. On exit from Word the global macros (including the macros of the virus) are automatically saved to a DOT file of the global macros (this file is usually called NORMAL.DOT). The next start of the Microsoft Word™ editor activates the virus at the moment when Word loads the global macros, in other words, immediately.[49] The virus then redefines one or several of the standard macros and then intercepts the commands of typical file operations. When routine commands are executed, the virus infects the currently open file. To do this, the virus converts the file to the template format and then saves its macros, including the auto-macro to the file. For example, once the virus infects the macro called File/Save, then every DOC file becomes infected. If the File/Open macro becomes infected, then the virus records itself into the file whem it is being read from the disk.[50]

Network viruses attack the networks themselves or e-mail systems of the networks in order to spread themselves. Network viruses make extensive use of networking protocols and capabilities of local and global access networks to multiply. The main operating principle of the network virus is its capability to transfer its code to a remote server or workstation on its own. Network viruses also are capable of running their code on remote computers or at least "pushing" users to run the infected file.[51] Network viruses essentially spread themselves on a computer network, and as a rule, like companion viruses, don't change files or sectors on disks. They infiltrate computer memory from the network, calculate and record network addresses of other computers, and then send copies of themselves to the network addresses.

Worms

Computer viruses have progressed from urban myth to annoyance to major threat. However, even with all the damage that computer viruses have done, they pale in comparison to what we have seen and have yet to see from the computer worm.[52] A computer worm is also a piece of software that copies itself elsewhere. However, unlike a virus, it does not attach itself to, or modify, other files. The worm is a stand-alone piece of code; although it may need to use another program to spread, it does not change that program in any way. The term worm is taken from the book *Shockwave Rider* and refers to a self-replicating piece of code (called the "tapeworm") created by a character in that book.[53] In contrast to a traditional virus, a worm is a program that makes copies of itself from one disk drive to another, or by copying itself using e-mail or another transport mechanism. The worm may do damage and compromise the security of the computer. It may arrive in the form of a joke program or software of some sort or may be spread through e-mail and networks without much active user intervention. These programs spread in a computer network and, similar to virus companions, don't change files or sectors on disks. They penetrate the computer's memory from a computer network, calculate network addresses of other computers and send their own copies to these addresses. Worms sometimes start files on the system disks, but generally can't apply themselves to computer resources (with the exception of main memory).

The first known Internet worm was the Morris worm. This worm crippled the Internet for several days in 1988 by exploiting buffer overrun flaws common in several pieces of software. A buffer overrun occurs when a program does not check the length of an input string against the amount of memory it has available to store that string. If the entered string is too long, then it overwrites other memory in the computer. In the case of the Morris worm, the string contained garbage data, followed by

BOX 6.2   The Melissa Virus

The Melissa virus first appeared on the Internet in March of 1999. It spread rapidly throughout computer systems in the United States and Europe. It is estimated that the virus caused $80 million in damages to computers worldwide. In the United States alone, the virus made its way through 1.2 million computers in one-fifth of the country's largest businesses. David Smith pled guilty on December 9, 1999 to state and federal charges associated with his creation of the Melissa virus and was sentenced in 2002. Smith admitted spreading the Melissa virus, which infected more than one million personal computers in North America and disrupted computer networks in business and government.

Prosecutors noted that the Melissa virus demonstrated the danger that business, government and personal computer users everywhere face in our technological society. "Far from being a mere nuisance, Melissa infected computers and disabled computer networks throughout North America. There is a segment in society that views the unleashing of computer viruses as a challenge, a game. Far from it; It is a serious crime."

"Computer criminals may think that they operate in a new frontier without boundaries, where they won't be caught. Obviously, that's not true," said investigators. "We've responded by breaking down traditional borders among federal, state, county and local law enforcement. In this case, it helped us to make an arrest in less than a week." Attorney General Janet Reno stated, "This plea is a significant marker in the Justice Department's efforts to stop computer crime. In light of society's increasing dependence on computers, the Department will vigorously investigate and prosecute computer crimes that threaten our computer infrastructure."

Smith admitted in state and federal court that he created the Melissa virus and disseminated it from his home computer. Smith acknowledged in his federal plea agreement that the Melissa virus caused more than $80 million in damage. He was eventually sentenced to 20 months in federal prison followed by three years of supervised release, 100 hours of community service, a fine of $5,000 dollars, and was prohibited from accessing a computer of any kind. He said that he constructed the virus to evade antivirus software and to infect computers using the Windows 95™, Windows 98™ and Windows NT™ operating systems and the Microsoft Word 97™ and Word 2000™ word processing programs.

According to Paul Zoubek, Director of the state Division of Criminal Justice, the Melissa virus appeared on thousands of e-mail systems on March 26, 1999, disguised as an important message from a colleague or friend. The virus was designed to send an infected e-mail to the first 50 e-mail addresses on the users' mailing lists. Such e-mails would only be sent if the computers used Microsoft Outlook™ for e-mail. Because each infected computer could infect 50 additional computers, which in turn could infect another 50 computers, the virus proliferated rapidly and exponentially, resulting in substantial interruption or impairment of public communications or services. According to reports from business and government following the spread of the virus, its rapid distribution disrupted computer networks by overloading e-mail servers, resulting in the shutdown of networks and significant costs to repair or cleanse computer systems.

(continued)

BOX 6.2   continued

Smith described in state and federal court how, using a stolen America Online account and his own account with a local Internet service provider, he posted an infected document on the Internet newsgroup "Alt.Sex." The posting contained a message enticing readers to download and open the document with the hope of finding passcodes to adult-content Web sites. He acknowledged that each new e-mail greeted new users with an enticing message to open and, thus, spread the virus further. The message read: "Here is that document you asked for . . . don't show anyone else ;-)."

Opening and downloading the message caused the Melissa virus to infect victim computers. The virus altered Microsoft word processing programs such that any document created using the programs would then be infected with the Melissa virus. The virus also lowered macro security settings in the word processing programs. The virus then proliferated via the Microsoft Outlook™ program, causing computers to send electronic e-mail to the first 50 addresses in the computer user's address book.

Source: http://www.usdoj.gov/criminal/cybercrime/meliinfo.htm

---

instructions for the computer to send the same message to other available machines. The worm was supposed to spread slowly, and in a controllable fashion, but, due to a bug in the code, it spread much faster than anticipated. This brought about the first large scale denial of service (DoS) condition on the Internet itself. An infected machine could have its resources entirely controlled by the worm in as little as one hour. The courts were not impressed by Morris' actions, and sentenced him to three years probation, 400 hours community service, and $10,050 in fines.[54]

In sum, a worm is self-propagating malicious code program that does not necessarily require user intervention to spread. Unlike a virus, which requires that a user run a program or execute a command, a worm self-propagates and infects systems in a very short period of time. The Code Red worm infected more than 250,000 systems in just nine hours on July 19, 2001.[55] Some worms include built-in DoS attack payloads or Web site defacement payloads, while others have dynamic configuration capabilities. However, as noted by the CERT® Coordination Center, the biggest impact of these worms is that their propagation effectively creates a DoS because of the huge amounts of scan traffic that the worm generates.[56] Additionally, worms cause a great deal of collateral damage such as crashing routers, overloading networks, and creating meaningless and repetitive tasks for the computers they infect.[57]

Trojan Horses

A Trojan horse is commonly an unauthorized program contained within a legitimate program that performs functions unknown (and probably unwanted) by the user.[58] Trojan horses typically masquerade as something desirable, a joke program, a legitimate software program, or some other type of executable file that the user wishes to install and

BOX 6.3   Could Your Computer Be a Criminal?

PCs hijacked to send spam, serve porn, steal credit cards

by Bob Sullivan
MSNBC

July 15—One thousand home computers hijacked and used to serve up pornography. Perhaps tens of thousands co-opted by the "SoBig" virus, many of them turned into spam machines. Hundreds of other home computers loaded with secret software used to process stolen credit cards. If your biggest computer crime fear was lost or stolen files, think again: Someone may be using your PC to commit crimes.

A curious spam mail went out and disappeared without much fanfare on June 25. Playing on a familiar prank, the e-mail urged recipients to visit "Windows-update.com" and download a security fix for their computers. Those who fell for the ploy were tricked into downloading a Trojan horse program. The malicious software steered the victim computer into an Internet Relay Chat room, where a computer criminal playing the part of the Pied Piper awaited to issue instructions to the now enslaved PC.

Joe Stewart, senior intrusion analyst with Lurhq Corp., played along with the Windows-Update spam. For one hour that day, he was in the chat room, too. And during that hour, he watched as about 800 PCs were drawn in. There, the hacker loaded them with more software, a small "bot" program which could be used by other chat room members. But what for?

Hiding Behind Innocent PCs

Internet credit card thieves have a major barrier to cross when they sell stolen card numbers: "Hot" cards become "cold" very quickly, as victims get wise and call to cancel their accounts. No one wants to pay for stolen credit cards that have been canceled. So the thieves have written a number of automated programs, or "bots," that quickly verify the validity of a credit card number. One such bot simply checks to see if a supplied account number follows the mathmatical formulas designed by credit card companies to prevent random account numbers from being used for fraud, called a "checksum." Windows-Update.com victims had this checksum bot placed on their machines, ready for use by an eager credit card thief looking to test out stolen numbers.

Only one machine would be used at a time, Stewart said. The moment one "bot" computer was disconnected, presumably by a victim who discovered the problem, another was ready to take its place. But each PC that was used in the scheme was an unwitting accomplice to credit card fraud.

"Maybe you don't think you have anything on your machine worth stealing," Stewart said. "Well, you do. Your bandwidth and your disk space."

For years, computer intruders have had their fun at the expense of innocent computer users by seizing control of their machines. Such zombies were a central part of the

(continued)

BOX 6.3   continued

the first famous major Internet attacks, which knocked Web sites like Yahoo.com and CNN.com off line in 1998.

But such attacks have for the most part been limited to pranks until just recently, when a new spate of malicious computer programs with obvious criminal intent have been unleashed. More and more, experts say, these are for-profit pranks.

"We're definitely seeing a paradigm shift," said Richard Smith, the well known computer sleuth who last week helped uncover a widespread scheme that turned about 1,000 PCs into an elaborate system that served up porn Web sites. "There's a real problem here. With hijacked computers, there's a lot of bad things you can do with them. I think we're just at the beginning."

Beware of Geeks Bearing Gifts

At the core of the problem is the type of computer virus known as a Trojan horse. It takes its name from the well known Greek myth, and functions much the same. Trojan horses sneak onto a victim's computer by appearing to be something benign, like a software update. Unlike the Melissa and LoveBug worms, Trojans don't spread themselves far and wide, and they don't call attention to themselves. These programs simply lie quietly on victims' computers, but now those computers are at the beck and call of the Trojan author.

Five years ago, hacker groups like the Cult of the Dead Cow released Trojans with names like "Back Orifice" to much fanfare, but they were often used just to perform spooky tricks like opening and closing victims' CD-ROM doors. This new batch of Trojan writers have far more serious crimes in mind, Smith said.

"It seems to me that when the (music industry) starts going after people, they will just start storing songs on other people's computers. And what if there's kiddie porn stored on someone else's computer?" Smith said.

The Trail Gets Cold

Using an army of hijacked computers to commit crimes or send out spam obscures the computer criminal's tracks effectively—and rotating rogue programs among the machines makes shutting down criminal operations tricky for Internet service providers. Smith actually discovered the porn ring when he was investigating a "phishing" e-mail, a note sent out which appeared to be a request from PayPal.com for users to update their password information on a Web site. The site was actually controlled by people intent on stealing the data.

Such "phishing" e-mails are common now, and the corresponding Web sites are normally shut down within hours when investigators like Smith complain to the Web host provider. But this site stayed up for days because its location was constantly changing—from one innocent victim's computer to another.

"I got an IP address for it, but the host didn't know what was going on, and finally I said, 'Oh my God, it moved.' It is much harder to do anything about this. The hacker gained a week on us," Smith said.

Another disturbing fact about the new wave of programs: They are simple and small, and nearly impossible to spot with an untrained eye, said Oliver Friedrichs, senior manager at Symantec's Security Response Team. The hijackings will likely go unnoticed by victims who aren't running up-to-date antivirus software and personal firewalls, he said.

"When this thing is running, you're really not going see it on your system," he said.

Spam, Virus, Hacking Worlds Converge

The trouble really started when the worlds of spam and computer viruses began to converge, said Mark Sumner, chief technology officer at antivirus firm MessageLabs Inc. For years, virus writers were content to just get attention by causing a nuisance. But now, some have discovered that clever virus programming can be profitable—by enabling spammers to hide their trails and send out e-mail from hijacked computers, for example.

"There's never been any money in writing viruses but now there's the potential of commercial gain," Sumner said.

The SoBig virus, first released in January, probably ushered in this new era of Trojan horse programs. From the start, Stewart said, it was designed to enable spammers to sneak their e-mail software onto unwitting home users' computers who have high-bandwidth connections to the Internet. SoBig is now in its fifth iteration, the most recent released on June 24, the same day as the Windows-Update spam. The coincidence has some researchers, including Smith, thinking that all these Trojan horse incidents might be related—that the SoBig virus was used both to hijack PCs for spam and for serving up porn.

But even if one group is behind the recent spate of incidents, consumers should be aware that virus writers will likely seize on this new way of doing business, experts say. Whatever is successful in the computer underground world is immediately imitated.

"The possibilities are growing as to what your machine can be used for," Stewart said. "The likelihood that people will encounter (Trojan horses) is pretty high. Whether they infect you or not depends on the computer user."

Source: http://www.msnbc.com/news/939227.asp

run. Just like the Trojan horse of history, however, there is a hidden purpose and program hidden within the desirable file. The hidden program typically waits for some computer event to occur, a date to be reached, or some other type of trigger, and then delivers its payload.[59] The hidden payload can open a back door for the virus writer, can destroy files or disks, or can simply display a message of some type. In the case of an attachment, as the user executes the file, the infection occurs simultaneously and silently. The Trojan horse is a program that neither replicates nor copies itself, but causes damage or compromises the security of the computer. In many cases, a legitimate program has been altered by the placement of unauthorized code, the Trojan horse, within legitimate code.[60] Typically, an individual e-mails a Trojan horse to you. However a growing number of attacks are accomplished through port scanners looking for installed Trojans by attackers that did not install the Trojan themselves. In other words, it is possible to conduct scans for Trojans in a systematic fashion and then exploit the security holes uncovered through the scans. There is a variety of ways that a Trojan can be installed on a user's computer, including via ICQ chat, IRC chat, through attachments, through actual physical access to a machine, via a Web browser or e-mail program, and through file sharing.[61]

Trojan horses can be viruses or remote control programs that provide complete access to a victim's computer and, as such, are one of the most accessible weapons that hackers use to conduct attacks.[62] If a certain type of Trojan horse is installed and initialized on a system, that computer is now completely open to anyone who knows to connect to it using the Trojan horse as a server.[63] The person responsible for the initial installation is not the only person who can be privy to the knowledge that a Trojan horse resides on the target computer—there are port scanners designed to find remote control Trojans already planted on systems.[64] Therefore, anyone who utilizes the port scanner and finds the installed Trojan horse can have access to the victim's computer or system. A remote-control Trojan is not a traditional virus; it is a self-contained program designed to invisibly execute commands issued from a remote user.[65] Trojans work by utilizing a client part and a server part. When the victim (unknowingly) runs the server on its machine, the attacker will then use the client to connect to the server and start using the Trojan.[66] Most Trojans use auto-starting methods, so even when you shut down your computer they're able to restart and give the attacker access. New auto-starting methods and other tricks are discovered all the time, ranging from "joining" the Trojan into some executable file that is often used like explorer.exe, to modifying the system files or the Windows Registry.[67]

Perhaps the most popular and widely used Trojan horse is the Backdoor Sub Seven Trojan.[68] Upon a successful installation, the Sub Seven Trojan allows a remote attack virtual control over an infected machine. This Trojan comprises distinctly separate programs that work to overtake the victim's computer. The first program is called the Sub Seven server and is run on the targeted computer to allow the attacker to connect to the victim and gain access to the computer. The editserver portion of the Trojan defines the characteristics of the infection and determines whether to notify the attacker when the victim computer is on line. This part of the program also allows the attacker to monitor and change the settings through which the attack occurs. In other words, the attacker can connect to the victim's machine and install a different configuration of the Sub Seven server that uses alternate ports, different techniques for autostarting, and allow the attacker free access to alter and control the victim's system.[69] Once installed and operating, attackers can initiate a variety of attacks, including the ability to restart Windows, reversing mouse buttons, recording sounds from the microphone attached to the compromised machine, record images from an attached video camera, change desktop colors, opening/closing the CD-ROM drive, record screen shots of the victim's computer and turn the victim's monitor on and off.[70] The attacker can also obtain characteristics of the hardware and software installed on the compromised machine and access stored information on the computer, including passwords and other personally identifying information. Finally, the Sub Seven Trojan installs a port redirector and the port scanner that allows an attacker to hack into other systems by configuring ports on an already infected computer to point to new targets.[71]

There are numerous types of Trojans, and similar to viruses there is no universal agreement on the naming and categorization of all of the types. Danchev (1999)[72] lists several types of Trojans, including:

- *Remote Access Trojans*—These are probably the most common as they give attackers the power to do more things on the victim's machine than the victim possibly could, even while sitting in front of the machine. These Trojans can give the attacker complete access to a victim's computer as well as access to files, passwords, data, etc.

- *Password-Sending Trojans*—These Trojans attempt to steal all of the cached passwords and also look for other passwords entered on a computer while the victim is on line and then send them to the attacker's e-mail address, which in most cases is located at some free Web-based e-mail provider.

- *Keyloggers*—These Trojans log the keystrokes of the victim and then let the attacker search for passwords or other sensitive data in the log file. Most of them come with two functions like on line and off line recording and can be configured to send the log file to a specific e-mail address on a daily basis.

- *Destructive*—The only function of these Trojans is to destroy and delete files. They can automatically delete core system files (for example, dll, .ini or .exe files). The Trojan can be activated by the attacker or sometimes works like a logic bomb, and starts on a specific day and at a specific time.

- *Denial of Service Attack Trojans*—The main idea is that if you have 200 users infected and start attacking the a secondary victim simultaneously, this will generate a great deal of traffic (more then the victim's bandwidth, in most cases) and access to the Internet will be shut down. A variation of this Trojan is the mail-bomb Trojan, whose main aim is to infect as many machines as possible and simultaneously attack specific e-mail addresses with random subjects and contents which cannot be filtered.

- *Proxy/Wingate Trojans*—These Trojans turn the victim's computer into a proxy/wingate server (zombie) available to the whole world or to the attacker only. It's used for anonymous Telnet, ICQ, IRC, Internet access, etc., and also to register domains with stolen credit cards and for many other illegal activities. This gives the attacker complete anonymity and the chance to commit crimes from a remote computer. If caught, the trace will lead to a victim's computer and not the attacker.

- *Software Detection Killers*—Some Trojans will kill ZoneAlarm, Norton Anti-Virus and many other popular anti-virus/firewall programs designed to protect users. Once they are disabled, the attacker will have full access to your machine, to perform some illegal activity, use your computer to attack others, and often disappear.

BOX 6.4   Disgruntled UBS PaineWebber Employee Charged with Allegedly Unleashing "Logic Bomb" on Company Computers

A disgruntled computer systems administrator for UBS PaineWebber was charged today with using a "logic bomb" to cause more than $3 million in damage to the company's computer network, and with securities fraud for his failed plan to drive down the company's stock with activation of the logic bomb. Roger Duronio, 60, of Bogota, N.J., was charged today a two-count Indictment returned by a federal grand jury, according to Assistant U.S. Attorney William Devaney.

The Indictment alleges that Duronio, who worked at PaineWebber's offices in Weehawken, N.J., planted the logic bomb in some 1,000 of PaineWebber's approximately 1,500 networked computers in branch offices around the country. Duronio, who repeatedly expressed dissatisfaction with his salary and bonuses at Paine Webber, resigned from the company on Feb. 22, 2002. The logic bomb Duronio allegedly planted was activated on March 4, 2002.

In anticipation that the stock price of UBS PaineWebber's parent company, UBS, A.G., would decline in response to damage caused by the logic bomb, Duronio also purchased more than $21,000 of "put option" contracts for UBS, A.G.'s stock, according to the charging document. A put option is a type of security that increases in value when the stock price drops. Market conditions at the time suggest there was no such impact on the UBS, A.G. stock price.

PaineWebber promptly reported what had happened to government investigators and the U.S. Attorney's Office, and has been helpful and cooperative in the investigation by the U.S. Secret Service's Electronic Crimes Task Force. "Cybercrime against financial institutions is a significant issue," Christie said. "Although the damage was contained in this case, the potential for catastrophic damage in other cases is always there. We will prosecute cyber criminals and put them in prison."

The Indictment alleges that, from about November 2001 to February, Duronio constructed the logic bomb computer program. On March 4, as planned, Duronio's program activated and began deleting files on over 1,000 of UBS PaineWebber's computers. It cost PaineWebber more than $3 million to assess and repair the damage, according to the Indictment.

As one of the company's computer systems administrators, Duronio had responsibility for, and access to, the entire UBS PaineWebber computer network, according to the Indictment. He also had access to the network from his home computer via secure Internet access.

Duronio is charged in Count One of the Indictment with securities fraud, which carries a maximum penalty of 10 years in federal prison and a $1 million fine. He is charged in Count Two with Fraud and Related Activity in Connection with Computers. That charge carries a maximum prison sentence of 10 years and a fine of $250,000 or, alternatively, two times the gain made by the defendant or the loss suffered by the victim.

Source: http://www.usdoj.gov/criminal/cybercrime/duronioIndict.htm

Adware and Spyware

Although not technically viruses or malicious code, adware and spyware have become a frequent topic of debate in regard to privacy concerns on the Internet. Adware and spyware are programs that can be contained in e-mail attachments, downloaded as part of another software program, or downloaded from a Web site. Adware is a type of program that is, essentially, a pain to the user that manifests itself in several ways, including changes to the browser, redirecting startup pages on the Internet browser, replacing the search function within the browser, and generating pop-up ads and frames that can be difficult to delete or shut down. Spyware programs are applications that send information via the Internet to the publishers or programmers for marketing purposes without obvious notification to users.[73] Spyware can send a variety of information about the user's computer hardware, software, browsing habits, and other personal information to the host marketer or programmer. Spyware is typically installed in addition to some other type of functional software, more often than not downloaded software that is distributed as freeware. The software operates independently of the spyware and is the visible and useful component of the downloaded package. Spyware serves as an information gatherer which maintains, monitors, and sends user and/or computer information in the background.[74] Some programs that get installed as companion software, technically not spyware, can cause a great deal of frustration for the user—especially if the user chooses to uninstall the companion software or spyware. Programs have been known to replace the searching engine function in the Internet browser, directing the user to their own preferred Web sites. Spyware can also lead to annoying pop-up ads that users have difficulty disabling.

Spyware typically takes advantage of the fact that many software users do not read the end user license agreement (EULA) or fine print during installation. If they did, they would see legal disclaimers and permissions to share information and install the spyware. As noted by Post (2002), spyware EULAs are worded in such a way that they contain so much information and disclaimers, that the average person can't understand what the software and spyware does and doesn't do.[75] Further, the data that is gathered is not specifically identified and how the data is going to be used is not specifically spelled out. Many people, upon finding out that they installed the spyware and were not really aware of it, feel that the spyware is malicious. The real fun starts when a user attempts to uninstall the spyware and programs that they downloaded. Often, the entire hard drive has to be scrubbed and the operating system reinstalled because the downloaded program made numerous, and complex changes to the computer. As a result, there is now spyware killer software available, as well as Internet security software that allows you to monitor and deter adware and spyware. Another way spyware is installed is through the use of cookies. A cookie is a file that contains information about a program, a Web site, the user, or the user's computer. Cookies enable faster browsing and, when they are from a legitimate Web site, can be beneficial to the Web site and the user. However, in the case of some spyware, the cookie contains uniquely identifiable data, such as the user's name, computer specifications, installation version, and other personally identifying information that the user might not wish to share.

Denial of Service Attacks

A denial of service (DoS) attack uses multiple systems to attack one or more victim systems or Web sites with the intent of denying service to legitimate users wishing to log on or utilize the attacked server. In essence, the attack sends phony requests to the server overloading it and preventing legitimate traffic. The degree to which the attack is automated, or self-sustaining and replicating, dictates how rapidly the attack denies service to the server or Web site. These attacks are remarkably effective due to the interdependency of computers and security on the Net and due to the limited resources of the Internet.[76] The attack tools are increasingly being distributed through "zombie" machines that are compromised on university campuses. In the week of February 7, 2000, several distributed denial of service attacks on several prominent Web sites, including Yahoo!, E*Trade, Amazon.com, and eBay were launched. In these attacks, multiple computers are instructed by a rogue program to bombard the target site with nonsense data. This bombardment soon causes the target site's servers to run out of memory, and thus cause it to be unresponsive to the queries of legitimate customers.[77] As described in the box item, these attacks can be used in a coordinated fashion to attack and destroy businesses and antispam companies.

Blended Threats

Blended threats combine the characteristics of viruses, worms, Trojan Horses, and malicious code with server and Internet vulnerabilities to initiate, transmit, and spread an attack. By using multiple methods and techniques, blended threats can rapidly spread and cause widespread damage. Recent blended threats have launched denial of service attacks, defaced Web servers, and Trojan horses planted on machines for later use in future attacks. The blended threat spreads through multiple methods; the infection routine can vary as well. These threats can scan for vulnerabilities in a system (such as buffer overflows, HTTP input validation vulnerabilities, and known default passwords to gain unauthorized administrative access), exploit the vulnerabilities, and then use the machine to further spread the attack. The attack spreads within human intervention and attacks systems and networks from multiple points, attempting to infect executable files, change the access rules for the machine, make numerous registry changes, and further exploit the machine into harming other machines and extending the attack.

Blended threats exploit one or more vulnerabilities as they infect a system and may perform additional network attacks such as a denial of service against other systems.[78] The essence of a blended attack is the multiple payloads and multiple targets that are part of the virus' programming. Many experts predict that blended attacks will increase in the near future. An example of a blended attack was the Code Red Worm, released to the wild in July of 2001. The worm replicated to thousands of systems in a matter of a few hours; estimates put the infection as high as 300,000 machines within the first 24 hours. This worm did not need to create a file on the remote system in order to infect it, but existed only in memory of the target system.[79] Blended threats are effective because most current security products cannot prevent the attack—they can only

---

BOX 6.5   Spam Block Lists Bombed to Oblivion

"Bad guys have broken out the nuclear weapons," victim says

by Mike Brunker
MSNBC

Sept. 24—Denial of service attacks by "zombie armies" of compromised computers have put two more spam-blocking lists out of business, adding to the body count in what one victim described as an "all-out war" raging in cyberspace.

The Operators of the Monkeys.com and Blackhole.compu.net "block lists"—used by Internet service providers and businesses to filter out incoming spam before it reaches end users—both announced this week that they are abandoning the services in the face of distributed denial of service attacks (DDOS) that have targeted antispam sites offering the lists this summer.

"It just wasn't feasible to run this (list) and make ourselves a large target anymore," said Bill Larson, network administrator for the Tennessee-based Internet Service Provider Compu-net Enterprises.

In withdrawing from the field of battle, they join Osirusoft.com, which announced earlier this month that it would no longer host the Spam Prevention Early Warning System, also known as SPEWS.

Other block list providers, including SpamCop.net, Spamhaus.org and the Spam & Open Relay Blocking System (SORBS) also have reported being subjected to increasingly intense DDOS attacks from thousands of compromised computers known as "zombies."

Mysterious Forces Behind Attacks

The "zombie army" is being marshaled by mysterious opponents of anti-spam forces who use virus-infected e-mail and hacking techniques to take control of machines from unknowing users, most of whom haven't taken the precaution of installing firewalls or anti-virus software to protect them from intruders.

Ron Guilmette, who operated the Monkeys.com block list for more than a year and a half before shutting it down Monday night, said in a news group posting announcing the list's demise that he had "underestimated both the enemy's level of sophistication, and also the enemy's level of brute malevolence."

Guilmette, of Roseville, Calif., told MSNBC.com on Wednesday that his mail, Web and DNS servers were bombarded by data packets directed at Monkeys.com from "more than 10,000 machines" in DDOS attacks that lasted for 10 days beginning on Aug. 19 and then resumed again late last week.

He said that while his "small fry" operation was more susceptible than some of the bigger lists like SPEWS and Spamhaus, none of the antispam services are impervious.

"All of these services are now under criminal attack, which is premeditated and financially driven," he said. "It's all-out warfare and the bad guys have broken out the nuclear weapons."

(continued)

BOX 6.5   continued

In the case of Compu-Net, Larson said he made the decision to cease operating the list not because of a DDOS attack, but because of an escalating case in which someone was forging company e-mail addresses on spam, causing many thousands of messages to "bounce" back and threatening to overwhelm the company's e-mail servers.

Threats to Servers, Selves

In addition to the bounced e-mail, Larson and other members of Compu-Net staff were forced to handle a flood of abuse complaints from people who wrongly believed the company was spamming them and deal with "threats against ourselves, our servers and our Internet connection," he wrote in a posting to the news.admin.net-abuse.e-mail (NANAE) news group.

And he feared that the DDOS attacks that have targeted other block list operators would be next.

"As an ISP, if we got hit by a denial of service attack that lasted a week or 10 days, we would be out of business," Larson said, explaining the decision to cut and run.

Earlier this month, the cyberattacks forced Joe Jared, who had been hosting the Spam Prevention Early Warning System, also known as SPEWS, at his Osirusoft.com Web site, to suddenly pull the plug on the popular but controversial block list.

Jared's action blocked access to the SPEWS.org Web site, though mirror sites with the list continued to operate, enabling network administrators to reconfigure their systems to query the alternate sites.

Other block lists, which are used by Internet service providers and businesses to filter out the majority of incoming spam before it reaches the end users, have come under siege from distributed denial of service (DDOS) attacks this summer. The bombardment of massive amounts of data has intermittently prevented subscribers or users from gaining access to lists at Web sites of SpamCop.net, Spamhaus.org, Monkeys.com and the Spam & Open Relay Blocking System.

Attacks More Systematic, Intense

DDOS attacks have been used against antispam sites before, but this summer's onslaught appears to be more systematic and intense than anything seen before.

"There's not much doubt in my mind that the various attacks are the work of the same person or organization," Julian Haight, president of Seattle-based SpamCop.net, which has been under attack intermittently since mid-July, told MSNBC.com earlier this month.

While it's not clear who is behind the campaign, suspicion has focused on renegade spammers, who have an obvious motive.

"These block lists have become more and more effective as they've become focused, so they've started to hit home," said Jesse Dougherty, director of development with software solution provider ActiveState.

The block lists have alienated some in the Internet community by blocking users who have nothing to do with spam, either accidentally or, in the case of SPEWS, as a deliberate tactic aimed at pressuring Internet service providers to crack down on spammers on their networks. But because the attacks are targeting multiple sites rather than just one or two, most experts say spammers are more likely culprits.

"It has been suggested to me that the person (behind the attacks) could be a site that I've erroneously blamed for spam, but given the amount of resources being put into it I'd certainly vote for the spammer," said Haight.

An Extra $30,000 on Bill

Haight, who said that SpamCop was knocked off line periodically in the early days of the attack in mid-July, said it will cost about $30,000 this year to pay for a content distribution network capable of withstanding such assaults.

Britain's Spamhaus.org also has been able to withstand steady attacks that began more than 2½ months ago, chief executive Steve Linford told the Boston Globe earlier this month.

"We're usually under attack from 5,000 to 10,000 servers at once," Linford was quoted as saying. "They're extremely large attacks that would bring down just about anything."

Some security experts, and many in the anti-spam community, believe that spammers have been behind recent viruses that have placed malicious "Trojan horse" programs on vulnerable computers, creating the network of "zombies" that can be remotely ordered to launch such attacks.

And while there is no hard evidence, some believe that the "sobig" family of viruses may be recruiting for the zombie army.

Guilmette, the former provider of the Monkeys.com block list, said the electronic bombardment of his site began "at 11:27 p.m. Pacific Time on Aug. 19, which coincidentally or not was the same day that sobig.f started to make the rounds."

Big ISPs Seen as Culprits

While the escalating attacks have the antispam community up in arms, there is no indication that law enforcement yet considers them to be serious.

"I went to my local police and I had to twist their arms just to get them to take a report," said Guilmette, adding that he called his local FBI office and left a message but was never called back.

But the longtime spam fighter said he bears more of a grudge against big ISPs like AT&T and UUNet, because they are in a better position to halt the attacks.

"If www.whitehouse.gov had been under attack for 10 days, you can bet your ass that the big providers would have gone to the lower level ISPs and and asked them to shut off the machines that were part of the zombie army that was doing the attacking," he said. "In my case they told me all I could do was try to ride it out and hope for the best."

Source: http://www.msnbc.com/news/959094.asp

detect the threats once they have arrived on the system or simply alert that an attack has taken place.[80] Many anti-virus products do not scan Windows memory, which is exactly where Code Red was targeted. This means blended threats such as Code Red, which reside solely in memory, might remain undetected and if detected would probably only result in an alert rather than block when a signature matches. As such, once the administrator receives an alert, the worm has already infected the machine.[81] Many businesses and universities have resorted to shutting down their systems and networks entirely when new worm threats become apparent. Patches and detection routines are then downloaded and the systems are restored within a few days.

EXTENT OF VIRUSES AND MALICIOUS CODE ATTACKS

The number of known viruses surpassed 70,000 in January 2002. Of those, 26.1 percent are macro viruses, 26.1 percent are Trojan horses, 19.2 percent are executable and 6.8 percent are script viruses. Other virus types (Unix, boot sector, Internet worms, file, Macintosh and multipartite) account for the remaining 21.8 percent. During 2001, 79 percent of infections reported to Sophos were due to executable viruses, 12 percent were due to script viruses and 4 percent were due to macro viruses. The remaining 5 percent of infections were due to Trojan horses, Unix, and boot sector viruses. The number of new viruses discovered every month continues to increase. In the last quarter of 2001, the Sophos virus lab was processing around 1,200 new viruses each month.[82]

Every six months, Symantec produces the *Internet Security Threat Report,*[83] which provides an update about Internet threat activity, including network-based attacks, a review of known vulnerabilities, and highlights of malicious code. The report noted the following trends:

Attack Trends
• The top ten attack sources account for nearly 80 percent of all attack activity.
• Network-based attacks were 19 percent higher.
• The severe event incidence rate declined by 52 percent among managed security service customers.
• Eleven percent of companies suffered from at least one severe event, down from 23 percent in 2002.
• Most attacks occurred between 1 p.m. and 10 p.m. GMT (from 8 a.m. to 5 p.m. EST).
• Remote execution of commands is becoming more common.

Malicious Code Trends
• Blended threats increased 20 percent.
• Sixty percent of malicious code submissions were blended threats.

- Speed of propagation has increased.
- Linux systems may be targeted for future attacks.
- There has been increased theft of confidential data.
- New infection vectors:
  - Instant messaging
  - Peer-to-peer services—19 new attacks identified (up from four in 2002)

Vulnerability Highlights

- Eighty percent of all vulnerabilities discovered are remotely exploitable.
- Web application vulnerabilities are up 12 percent.
- Attacks are being released faster.
- Areas to watch for new vulnerabilities:
  - Integer error
  - Timing analysis
  - Microsoft Internet Explorer
  - Microsoft IIS

Current Issues

- In August 2003, Blaster worm exploited a vulnerability 26 days after it was discovered.
  - The cost of eight days of massive worm attacks in August may be up to $2 billion dollars.

As noted in this section, some viruses can cause widespread damage and affect thousands of networks and machines. Undoubtedly, the greatest cost is loss of work hours and time spent patching systems, not to mention productivity lost from everyone having to chat and e-mail their friends about the latest threat. Even so, a growing number of experts and publications raise the idea that viruses, for the most part, are more hype and hoax than actual malicious threat. For example, perhaps the largest virus hype to date concerned the Michelangelo virus in the early 1990s. In the lead-up to March 6, 1992 (Michelangelo's birthday and the supposed date of the virus payload release), the media coverage and doom saying about the virus was so intensive that millions of people around the world refused to turn on their computers at all for the entire period around March 6th. McAfee claimed at the time that anywhere "from 50,000 to five million" computers were infected, a statement that was far from the truth.[84] The airwaves were flooded with supposed virus experts predicting the shutdown of governments and business worldwide. In the end, relatively few machines were infected and the virus eventually lived on to become urban legend. The hype of potential viruses and the damage that people believe viruses can cause feeds into the larger problem of virus hoaxes.

BOX 6.6   E-mail Hoaxes

SEND THIS TO ALL OF YOUR FRIENDS, DO NOT DELETE THIS MESSAGE, IMPORTANT ALERT. These are but a few of the opening lines of many e-mails commonly received daily via the Internet. Most of these messages are relatively harmless, but some have a more sinister purpose. Some people think that many of the scams and hoaxes are new, when they are classically old schemes being perpetuated in a new format, cyberspace. To most, these are harmless annoyances that quickly find their way into the cyber trash bin. The undeniable cost is lost productivity and time spent on sifting through the increasing volume of these junk e-mails, typically referred to as spam. There is a growing body of information on the Internet concerning spam and e-mail hoaxes. In general, these e-mails can be grouped into five general categories: spam, chain-mail, hoaxes, virus hoaxes, and fraud.

Spam

Spam is the generic term (also called unsolicited commercial e-mail [UCE] and junk e-mail) for any e-mail that is sent to a large group of people, typically as an advertisement or other solicitation. If your e-mail address falls into the hands of a "spammer," you will undoubtedly receive ever-increasing unsolicited advertisements. Most spam is easily deleted and is simply annoying. There are several Web sites with detailed information on spam, federal legislation, and other problems with these e-mails:

> *http://do-not-spam.com/*
>
> *http://spam.abuse.net/*
>
> *http://members.aol.com/e-mailfaq/e-mailfaq.html*
>
> *http://www.cauce.org/*

Chain-mail

This is simply traditional chain letters that have found a new medium. If you believe in good or bad luck, you can forward these to your friends. These are increasing because forwarding them is relatively easy using e-mail.

Hoaxes

There are almost too many hoaxes to document. Some of the more popular ones involve people spending $250 for a cookie recipe, people having their kidneys removed while they sleep, and people receiving cash awards and gift certificates by forwarding e-mail. There is no way for a company to track who you send e-mail to and they are not giving away free computers, vacations, or cash. Check out these hoaxes at the Web sites listed below.

> Information on medical hoaxes: *http://www.quackwatch.com*
>
> Department of Energy's Web site for debunking myths and legends: *http://ciac.llnl.gov/ciac/CIACWelcome.html*

Offers current information about hoaxes being propagated on the Internet:
http://urbanlegends.about.com/culture/urbanlegends/library/blhoax.htm

Entire websites dedicated to urban legends:

http://www.urbanlegends.com/

http://www.nonprofit.net/hoax/hoax.html

http://www.snopes.com

Virus Hoaxes

We are spending much more time de-bunking hoaxes than handling real virus incidents.

—*The U.S. Dept. of Energy Computer Incident Advisory Capability (CIAC)*

We have all gotten well intentioned e-mail warnings about some virus that is possibly the worst ever found. Many people simply delete these messages. Others forward the e-mails on in the chance that this virus could be a real threat. E-mail hoaxes promote fear. They make you pause. They waste your time. They scare some people into not using technology to its fullest extent for fear of contracting a dangerous virus. Virus hoaxes are defined as deliberate or unintentional e-mail messages warning people about a virus or other malicious software program that simply doesn't exist.

Most hoaxes contain one or more of the following characteristics:

- Warnings about alleged new viruses and their damaging consequences
- Demands for the reader to forward the warning to as many people as possible
- Pseudo-technical "information" describing the virus
- Bogus comments from officials: FBI, software companies, news agencies, etc.

One of the better ones forwarded concerned a virus that was "infecting all digital cellular phones" and that I shouldn't answer any phone calls that caller-id couldn't track or I would get the virus. In short, there are numerous hoaxes that are propagated concerning viruses. In fact, there is more worry about viruses than is necessary. Rob Rosenberger maintains an excellent informational Web site on viruses, hoaxes and real, and offers sound advice concerning them at *http://www.vmyths.com/*

Symantec's Web site for virus hoaxes: *http://www.symantec.com/avcenter/hoax.html*

McAfee's Virus Hoax Center: *http://www.mcafeeb2b.com/asp_set/anti_virus/library/hoaxes.asp*

F-secure Corporation Web site: *http://www.datafellows.com/virus-info/hoax/*

(continued)

BOX 6.6   continued

Fraud

These are the most dangerous e-mails you will receive. Do yourself a favor and don't give out your credit card, send money, or involve yourself in any of these schemes. Age-old pyramid schemes involving cash, stocks, or even golf balls never work and are in fact illegal. Reputable charities and organizations do not solicit contributions or sell merchandise via e-mail.

The Federal Trade Commission (*http://www.ftc.gov/bcp/conline/pubs/alerts/doznalrt.htm*) has recently identified the 12 scams that are most likely to arrive in consumers' e-mail boxes. The "dirty dozen" are:

1. Business opportunities
2. Bulk e-mail
3. Chain letters
4. Work-at-home schemes
5. Health and diet scams
6. Effortless income
7. Free goods
8. Investment opportunities
9. Cable descrambler kits
10. Guaranteed loans or credit, on easy terms
11. Credit repair
12. Vacation prize promotions

Information on frauds and scams: *http://www.scambusters.org*

Tips for Survival

There is no surefire, 100 percent accurate way that can determine whether or not an e-mail is a hoax or not. Virtually any chain e-mail you receive (i.e., any message forwarded multiple times) is more likely to be false than true. Be skeptical. You can easily check the Web sites listed above for information on these Internet hoaxes. Any time the message tells you to forward this to everyone you know, it is probably a hoax and should be placed where it belongs, in your e-mail trash.

Virus Hoaxes

As described in Box 6.7, there is a variety of Internet and virus hoaxes. Hoaxes are spread and believed by unsuspecting users for a variety of reasons. Gordon, Ford, and Wells (1997) note that in all the hoaxes they examined, the hoax was far more interesting and popular than the reality behind the virus or hoax. Perhaps the most common reason hoaxes are believed is a blind trust in authority. As noted previously, false authority syndrome can lead some people to proclaim themselves as virus experts. Often, well intentioned users forward these bogus warnings to everyone in their address book. Additionally, virtually every workgroup has a "techie" person that many people go to with computer-related problems and technical questions. If such a person chooses to spread a hoax, or even if the hoax comes from a friend of the user, it is believed without much investigation or question. As some true virus experts note, this problem is magnified in the cyberspace environments, where little thought is given to authentication of sources: If you proclaim yourself to be an expert loudly and often enough, you are often accepted as such.[85] Another reason hoaxes can spread rapidly and become believable is the excitement generated by being the first person to e-mail everyone that a new and threatening virus is out there and feeling that you are performing a public service by notifying everyone. Even bright, well reasoned people can be drawn in by an effective hoax—as Barnum so adequately noted, there's a sucker born every minute. Other reasons include a general lack of skepticism, a desire for attention and recognition, and a lack of knowledge concerning viruses and computer systems.

BOX 6.7   The Teddy Bear Virus Hoax

A virus hoax that continually makes the rounds of e-mail systems is the teddy bear or jdbgmgr.exe hoax. The text of the e-mail warning about the alleged virus is as follows:

Dear All:

I'm sorry about this; but I received this E-mail from a client regarding a virus that was inadvertently passed on to everyone in their address book. I followed the instructions and YES, IT WAS ON MY COMPUTER.

Since you are in my address book, I am sending this on to you as a precaution. NORTON 2002 DID NOT DETECT IT!

Here are the instructions on how to check for this virus and delete it if you have it to. It only took a few minutes, following these instructions. Be sure to notify all in your address book too (which will take longer than deleting the virus from your computer).

Since you are in our address book, there is a good chance you will find it in your computer too unless you have an Apple or MAC. The virus (called jdbgmgr.exe) is not detected by Norton or McAfee anti-virus systems. The virus sits quietly for 14 days before damaging the system. It is sent automatically by messenger and by the address book,

(continued)

BOX 6.7   continued

whether or not you sent E-mails to your contacts. Here's how to check for the virus and how to get rid of it:

YOU MUST DO THIS

1. Go to Start, Go to Find or Search option.
2. In the File Folder option, type the name: jdbgmgr.exe
3. Be sure you search your C: drive and all sub-folders and any other drives you may have.
4. Click "Find Now".
5. The Virus has a Teddy Bear icon with the name jdbgmgr.exe. DO NOT OPEN IT.
6. Go to Edit (on menu bar), choose "Select All" to highlight the file without opening it.
7. Now go to File (on the menu bar) and select Delete. It will then go to the Recycle Bin.
8. Go to the Recycle Bin and Delete it.

IF YOU FIND THE VIRUS, YOU MUST CONTACT ALL THE PEOPLE IN YOUR ADDRESS BOOK, SO THEY CAN ERADICATE IT IN THEIR OWN ADDRESS BOOKS.

To do this:

1. Open a new e-mail message.
2. Click the icon of the address book next to the "TO".
3. Highlight every name and add to "BCC".
4. Copy this message, enter subject, paste to e-mail.

I am very sorry about this nuisance. This age of technology is not that great sometimes. We are victims!

The problem is that the jdbgmgr.exe file is an actual working file in the Windows system: It is the Microsoft Debugger Registrar for Java. The actual Windows Jdbgmgr.exe has a teddy bear icon as described in the hoax, lending further credence to the user.

Deleting the file may have little or no effect. However, enough correspondence has been generated that Microsoft has issued a bulletin and a patch for those who deleted the file. According to the virus myths Web site, *www.vmyths.com*, people fall victim to this hoax for several reasons. First, the basic chain letter identifies an obscure file found on tens of millions of PCs—and it offers simple instructions on how to *find* the file in question. Second, the file uses a teddy bear as its associated icon, giving the impression an immature hacker drew it. Finally, gullible users will assume they found a dangerous virus—simply because they found a file on their PC. They will then fall victim to false authority syndrome when they rewrite the chain letter before sending it to their friends.

Sources: Virus Myths *http://www.vmyths.com/*; Symantec's Web site for virus hoaxes: *http://www .symantec.com/avcenter/hoax.html*; McAfee's Virus Hoax Center: *http://www.mcafeeb2b.com/asp_set/ anti_virus/library/hoaxes.asp*; and F-secure Corporation Web site: *http://www.datafellows.com/virus -info/hoax/*

Authoring a virus hoax takes relatively little technical skill other than good salesmanship. However, the hoax can be as costly or costlier than an actual virus. It is estimated that virus hoaxes could cost an organization as much as a genuine virus incident.[86] One source claims that a virus hoax could cost as much as $41.7 million.[87] The cost of a virus hoax is difficult to determine, but clearly the hoax could result in loss of productivity for those "affected" by it, could result in increased network traffic from people spreading the hoax, and could also result in damage to systems by those who erroneously delete files off their system, resulting in increased tech support time to repair the damaged systems.

Spotting a virus hoax is relatively easy in some ways, as they tend to have several commonalities. Several virus experts conclude that most hoaxes:[88]

- Contain a warning message about a virus or some other malicious code
- Are usually from an individual, occasionally from a company, but never from the cited source
- Warn not to read or download the supposed virus and preaches salvation by deletion
- Describe the virus as having horrific destructive powers and often the ability to send itself by e-mail
- Usually has many words in caps and exclamation marks
- Urge the reader to alert everyone they know and forward the e-mail along
- Seek credibility by citing some authoritative source as issuing the warning
- Claim the source says the virus is "bad" or has them "worried"
- Seek credibility by describing the virus in baseless technical jargon

VIRUS WRITERS AND VIRUS EXPERTS

Numerous authors have attempted to characterize virus writers and elaborate the reasons why people write and spread viruses. One train of thought contends that virus writers go through a progression from students and schoolchildren to young adults and college students to professional virus writers. At each stage, the destructive capability of the virus and the technical expertise of the writer increases.[89] In this theory, the motivations for virus writing also change from recognition from peers and experimentation, progressing to revenge and social notoriety.

The virus writers and those who wish to write viruses have a variety of resources from which to learn their trade and propagate viruses. There are numerous virus-maker journals, newsletters, bulletin boards and Web pages devoted to virus writing and virus creation tools.[90] Sarah Gordon, currently at Symantec, has consistently taken a more conciliatory view. In a survey of virus writers, she claims that:

> . . . The virus writer has been characterized by some as a bad, evil, depraved, maniac; terrorist, technopathic, genius gone mad, sociopath. This image has been heightened not only by the media, but by some of the actions of the virus writers themselves. Public communications from the writers, in the form of echo-mail messages, often seem to indicate they are intent on doing as much damage as humanly possible. Their electronic publications have in the past reinforced this, and the very fact that they release viruses may seem to confirm it: These people are bad. [But it can be argued that] this is a gross oversimplification of the situation, and that the virus writing aspect of these individuals is not sufficient to characterize them into one group simply labelled "unethical people."

Most virus writers obviously have numerous justifications and rationalizations for why they choose to write viruses. Not all experts agree on the seriousness of the virus problem, with many noting that most viruses are relatively harmless and easily removed.[91] Trojan horse programs allow those without a comprehensive understanding of multiple operating systems, networking concepts and programming languages to routinely attack remote systems. The largest group of attackers, comprising over 95 percent of the attacker population, is referred to as "script-kiddies," individuals with limited knowledge of operating systems and networks.[92] This group doesn't write code or create viruses; instead, they use precompiled programs like Trojan horses to do the work for them, which afford the attackers access to other computers to pilfer files, change settings or launch denial of service attacks.[93]

BOX 6.8   Interview with a Virus Writer—Inside the Mind of Dark Avenger

by Sarah Gordon

About three years ago I was introduced to the man known as Dark Avenger. Having just purchased a PC, and finding myself the proud owner of not only the PC but of the Ping-Pong virus as well, I found my way to the Fidonet virus echo. Watching the information fly back and forth, suddenly there appeared a new name—Dark Avenger. I was intrigued by his style and the hype surrounding him. At some early point of participation in the forum, I commented that I would like to have a virus named after me, hoping to draw his attention. Had I understood at that time quite what viruses actually entailed, I would not have made that statement. As I talked with antivirus researchers and product developers, I began to understand the issues. I also talked to virus writers. Having a background in juvenile corrections, I found their attitude typical of youths in crisis. Their response to public mail demonstrated the attitude so prevalent in interaction between rebellious teenagers and authority figures. Their private mail (which I have not and will not disclose) resembled the private conversations I'd had when counseling in a one-on-one situation: frustation, anger and general dissatisfaction followed by small glimpses of conscience—often resulting in a decision to at least consider the consequences of their actions. Some, like their more traditional counterparts, never made it to that final stage, but at least we had some stimulating discussions. I've had, and continue to have, detailed conversations with virus writers, focusing on the reasons behind their misdirected creativity.

Time passed, and still Dark Avenger continued to haunt me. Why had he not responded to me like the majority of virus writers? Despite several failed attempts to contact him, he remained elusive.

Enter the MtE

With the release of the now-infamous Mutation Engine, I found Dark Avenger had indeed noticed me. The demo virus which accompanied the engine contained the text: "We dedicate this little virus to Sara Gordon, who wanted to have a virus named after her." Many people asked me about this, and I became quite accustomed to people assuming I knew Dark Avenger personally. The fact of the matter is, at that time, he was still a mystery. How could I explain to people that I "knew" him, yet had never spoken with him? I'm not a programmer, yet I knew him from looking at his viruses. I have no formal background in computer science, but I could understand what he was doing and how he was feeling, despite some people arguing that there is no such thing as "instinctive hacking." Few people believed me at that point; yet the fact is, at that time, I had never spoken with him directly.

When I learned Christopher Seeley was talking on a semi-regular basis to someone identified by both Alan Solomon and Vesselin Bontchev as Dark Avenger, I sent him a message to pass on to (dav). The message was written slowly and laboriously in Bulgarian, and I briefly stated that I would like to ask him some questions.

His response came quickly. I immediately recognized the author as the creator (not necessarily distributor) of the viruses attributed to him. We exchanged several electronic messages, routed through various gateways. Eventually—with the assistance of various intermediaries—I was able to speak "live" (or at least electronically) with Dark Avenger.

Since that time we have exchanged many messages, this interview being an edited compendium of our messages and conversations taking place over a five-month period. He agreed to allow me to ask him these questions, and I agreed to allow him to remove any questions or responses he was not comfortable answering or making public.

Who is the Dark Avenger? Many people have asked me: "Is Vesselin Bontchev the Dark Avenger?"; in fact, one of the reasons I became so intent on finding the Dark Avenger was to learn the answer to this question. I can state unequivocally that the Dark Avenger is not Vesselin Bontchev. Neither is he a crazed technopath, nor a maniac intent on destroying the world. He has very little in common with the usual crop of virus writers I have talked to. He is, all in all, a unique individual.

(continued)

BOX 6.8 (continued)

August 1992

> **Sara Gordon:** Some time ago, in the Fidonet virus echo, when you were told one of your viruses was responsible for the deaths of thousands, possibly, you responded with an obscenity. Let's assume for the moment this story is true. Tell me, if one of your viruses was used by someone else to cause a tragic incident, how would you really feel?
>
> **Dark Avenger:** I am sorry for it. I never meant to cause tragic incidents. I never imagined that these viruses would affect anything outside computers. I used the nasty words because the people who wrote to me said some very nasty things to me first.
>
> **SG:** Do you mean you were not aware that there could be any serious consequences of the viruses? Don't computers in your country affect the lives and livelihoods of people?
>
> **DA:** They don't, or at least at that time they didn't. PCs were just some very expensive toys nobody could afford and nobody knew how to use. They were only used by some hotshots (or their children) who had nothing else to play with.
>
> I was not aware that there could be any consequences. This virus was so badly written, I never imagined it would leave the town. It all depends on human stupidity, you know. It's not the computer's fault that viruses spread.
>
> **SG:** It is said many people working for the government and companies in Bulgaria had computers at that time. Isn't this correct?
>
> **DA:** I don't know who said that, but it's not true. Actually, at that time, most of the people in Bulgaria did not even know what a computer was.
>
> **SG:** Did you have access to modems at that time? Did you ever make use of virus exchange systems to send your viruses? I've seen your name on some of the mail coming from those systems.
>
> **DA:** At that time, I did not have access to a modem. At that time there were no virus exchange systems, I think. I've been on some of them, but that was much later. I never made any "use" of them, I was just fooling with them. I've been on almost no VX systems using that name. If you saw it somewhere, probably it was just some impostor, not me. When I have called any of them they (the sysops) insist I have written many more viruses. It's very difficult, when you're (dav) [Dark Avenger] and you upload a virus, to make out that you didn't write it.
>
> **SG:** Did you ever call the virus systems using your real name?
>
> **DA:** Not a real name but a name that sounded like a real person.
>
> **SG:** Why didn't you ever contact me?
>
> **DA:** I did. I left you a message once. Well, it was not to you, but I put something in it for you.
>
> **SG:** Yes, I remember that one. Something about: "You should see a doctor. Normal women don't spend their time talking about computer viruses." I answered it, if you recall?

DA: Yes. You said: "I do not want to be a normal woman, at least not in Bulgaria."

SG: Yes, but why didn't you talk to me directly?

DA: I didn't know you wanted to talk to me. Why didn't you send me mail?

SG: I was afraid of you. Anyway, why did you dedicate that virus to me?

DA: You said you wanted it.

SG: People have wondered why you wrote your first virus. Why did you write it and do you have any regrets about it?

DA: I wrote it because I had heard about viruses and wanted to know about them, but nobody around me could tell me anything. So I decided to write my own. I put some code inside it that intentionally destroys data, and I am sorry for it. I started working on it in September 1988.

SG: Couldn't you have asked someone who had a virus to show it to you?

DA: I knew nobody who had a virus. In fact, I think that at that time, nobody in Bulgaria had one.

SG: Where did you hear about viruses? What in particular caught your interest?

DA: There was a magazine called *Computer for You,* the only magazine in Bulgaria at that time. In its May 1988 issue there was a stupid article about viruses, and a funny picture on its cover. This particular article was what made me write that virus. Of course, this was not the first time I heard about viruses. I was interested in them, and thinking of writing one a long time before that. I think the idea of making a program that would travel on its own, and go to places its creator could never go, was the most interesting for me. The American government can stop me from going to the U.S., but they can't stop my virus.

SG: It has been stated by Valery Todorov that he wrote his first virus, WWT, because he was curious as to whether he could write one or not, but that he wrote his second virus because Vesselin Bontchev (often called the Number One Enemy of Dark Avenger) gave him the idea. Did you get any ideas from other people's viruses? Have you ever written a virus with someone else?

DA: No, but for someone else, yes.

SG: For who?

DA: For you.

SG: How do you feel about the destruction of data?

DA: I think it's not right to destroy someone else's data.

SG: If you think that, then why did you put destructive code in your viruses?

DA: As for the first virus, the truth is that I didn't know what else to put in it. Also, to make people try to get rid of the virus, not just let it live. At that time, I didn't think that data in PCs could have any great value.

SG: Do you mean the data in PCs in Bulgaria is of no value?

DA: As I said (or did I?), at that time there were few PCs in Bulgaria, and they were only used by a bunch of hotshots (or their kids). I just hated it when some

(continued)

BOX 6.8   (continued)

asshole had a new powerful 16Mhz 286 and didn't use it for anything, while I had to program on a 4.77Mhz XT with no hard disk (and I was lucky if I could ever get access to it at all).

Actually, I don't know why I'm saying all this. The real answer is: I don't know. And I didn't care. I also don't care very much now, I'm afraid. I just want the other people to leave me alone. The weasel (Vesselin Bontchev) can go to hell.

By the way, if you really think you should not break any laws, you can start by purchasing MS-DOS, or turning off all your computers permanently. First law of computer security: Don't buy a computer. Second law: If you ever buy a computer, don't turn it on.

SG: Don't you feel responsible if someone else uses one of your viruses to cause actual harm to a person's machine?

DA: No. If they wanted to cause harm, they wouldn't need my viruses. They could simply type "format c:" or something else that is much more effective.

SG: How can you say this? By writing and distributing the viruses, making them available, you do provide people with the idea and the means, in the same way you were initially provided. By doing this, your actions affect innocent users.

DA: The innocent users would be much less affected if they bought all the software they used (and from an authorized dealer) and if they used it the way they are allowed to by the license agreement. If somebody instead of working plays pirated computer games all day long, then it's quite likely that at some point they will get a virus.

Besides, there's no such thing as an innocent user, but that's another subject.

SG: What about the fact that you're giving people the idea, by creating such clever viruses?

DA: Ideas are not responsible for people who believe in them. Or use them. Or abuse them. Also, I didn't write them to "provide" anybody with anything. The weasel is the one who "provides." I just wrote them for fun. I couldn't care less for all the suckers who see/use them. They were not supposed to make such a big mess.

SG: Still, you have provided them with an insidious weapon. Don't you feel that by providing them with such clever computer tricks, you are contributing to hurting the innocent users?

DA: I don't provide nobody with nothing. The weasel provides.

SG: How does he provide?

DA: He just "provides." That's one of his favorite words. I don't want to talk or think about it.

SG: What do you think about the new crop of virus writers, like Falcon/Skism and nUkE?

DA: They are kids, most of whom seek fame (and achieve it easily with the help of a-v people). Most of them are not good at programming viruses at all.

SG: Well, at least that is some point you and the a-v community agree upon. You have achieved a certain amount of "fame" yourself. How does it make you feel when you see your name in magazines and mail? How do you feel when you see your viruses "defeated" by antivirus programs?

DA: I wrote the virus so it would be killed, like I said. It was not supposed to do all this. I like seeing my name in magazines and in messages. I used to read all the messages about me, but I like it most when I see it printed somewhere. And I liked it a LOT seeing my things in Western a-v programs. First time I saw McAfee Scan was about version 5.0 or so. I liked it a lot. I was just excited, happy.

SG: Where did you get that name, Dark Avenger?

DA: I didn't really "get" the name. I mean, I didn't call myself that. I put those words in the virus and someone else (we both know who) said it was written by the Dark Avenger. He's the one that made me be the Dark Avenger, that name. I didn't use the name until after he called me that. That phrase itself came from some old song from a long time ago, and not from an Iron Maiden song, like some people have said. In many ways, I suppose you could say he made the Dark Avenger.

SG: How long do you think you will continue writing viruses?

DA: I don't. I never planned it.

SG: You misunderstood the question. Are you going to continue writing viruses?

DA: I don't know. It depends on what will happen to me.

SG: What do you mean?

DA: I mean, I will not normally write/spread any destructive or virus code, unless something extraordinary happens. Well, not if they put me in jail. If they do, and I ever get out, I will not be in a mood for programming. It is not/was not a crime to write the viruses, so I don't think this should happen. I just am not interested in writing them now.

SG: Do you know the difference between right and wrong?

DA: Why do you ask me this? In American movies, at the end, always the good guy gets the money, the girl and the applause, and the bad guy gets in jail or something. But in real life, it's not clear who is good and who is bad, and who gets what. It's not black and white. The only thing that is for sure is that good people always lose.

SG: Have you ever considered making an antivirus product, other than the fake doctor.exe which is actually a virus?

DA: I have considered it many times, but antivirus products are as useless as viruses. As for doctor.exe, it's not fake, it really does the job as it says it does.

SG: Why do you say they are useless? Don't you think they help protect users from common viruses?

(continued)

BOX 6.8   (continued)

DA: The users spend much more money on buying such products and their updates rather than on the losses of data damaged because of viruses. The a-v products only help the users to empty their wallets. Besides, viruses would spread much less if the "innocent users" did not steal software, and if they worked a bit more at their workplace, instead of playing games. For example, it is known that the Dark Avenger virus was transported from Europe to the U.S.A. via some (stolen) games.

SG: But viruses have now spread far beyond games. Most viruses are known to come by other routes.

DA: Sure they spread beyond the games. Still, I've never found a virus on any original disk from a package I bought from Borland International.

SG: But I got my first virus from commercial software! Don't you remember my telling that story?

DA: Not from Borland International. Some places you get a virus, some places you don't.

SG: It is said that your fellow Bulgarian, Vesselin Bontchev, did many things to provoke the virus writers. Did he provoke you?

DA: This is quite true, and I don't think he ever denied it. If he did, it would be a lie. There are a lot of people in Bulgaria who know it and can confirm it, but I don't think this was a big contribution to virus writing—his viruses were pretty worthless. He is not a good programmer.

SG: Do you feel that conditions in your country really help create virus writers as was stated by Bontchev in his "factory" paper? What can you tell me about the conditions in your country that contributed to your writing your first virus?

DA: I don't think the conditions in my country help create virus writers any more than conditions in any other country in Eastern Europe. Not after a certain person we both know left the country. As for my first virus, it had nothing to do with it that.

SG: What contribution could "a certain person" have made to assist you (or anyone) in writing a virus? Don't you think that the conditions affecting the economy and computer technology of your country have indeed contributed to the overabundance of virus writers coming from former Eastern Bloc countries?

DA: His articles were a plain challenge to virus writers, encouraging them to write more. Also they were an excellent guide how to write them, for those who wanted to, but did not know how. It never said that he himself wrote some.

SG: According to some people, the story of viruses being such a big problem from Bulgaria begins with: "Soon hackers obtained a copy of the virus and began to hack it . . . some were optimized by hand. As a result, now there are several versions of this virus that were created in Bulgaria—versions with infective length 627, 623, 622, 435, 367, 353 and even 348 bytes." It is said many young people brought Bontchev viruses in those early days.

DA: Sure they did. Do you know the viruses vhp and vhp2?

SG: I think I may have heard of them.

DA: I think you don't want to know about this. I will send you a copy of a book that will tell you all about it. You don't want to hear it, and most of all you don't want to hear it from me.

Source: http://www.research.ibm.com/antivirus/SciPapers/Gordon/Avenger.html

SUMMARY

Several virus thinkers have projected what the future will hold for virus writing, virus detection, and virus prevention.[94] Many of the predictions made during the early 1990s did indeed come true, particularly those that predicted that future viruses would be more polymorphic, have better encryption, and be better able to spread rapidly.[95] Their observations can be characterized into a few, relatively tight categorizations. The first prediction is that we will continue to have problems with polymorphism, mutations, and as-yet undescribed features of future viruses that will confound virus prevention experts and software.[96]

Viruses can flourish and cause the most damage in an environment "friendly" to their existence. A friendly environment is one with a vulnerable operating system, one with complete documentation on the operating system, and the overall popularity of the operating system in the computer world.[97] In other words, security holes in a system can be manipulated to the extent that a virus writer understands the operating system and can exploit the holes and the code of the system. Once that code is exploited, the degree of damage inflicted and the nature and extent of the outbreak is determined by the popularity of the operating system—the number of potential targets. For example, for a virus to be successful, it must be able to spread. If only a small number of people used the targeted software or operating system, then the population available to infect is small as well, and the virus cannot spread.

Several authors, publications, and antivirus firms have described what they believe the future of virus and malicious code attacks will be like. The CERT® Coordination Center has been monitoring attack trends since the early days of virus attacks and offers several trends that they believe will appear in the coming years.[98] First, the level of automation and the speed at which attacks occur and spread is likely to increase. Since the late 1990s, scanning for potential victims and vulnerable systems has become part of major attacks. Recently, scanning has become part of the attack itself, with the virus or malicious code looking for vulnerabilities as they go. Additionally, the attacks have been self-propagating and coordinated with distributed attack tools that make denial of service attacks more efficient. The potential for virus spread without user intervention is best seen through the various stages that viruses came to infect e-mail. Originally, it was thought that viruses could not be deployed via e-mail since e-mails only contained text. With the advent of HTML, Active X, and Java code and the ability to send attachments, the thought was that only by executing the attachment could a user get an infection. Macro viruses and other sneaky tricks demonstrated that even nonexecutable files could infect a user's machine via e-mail, yet it was still assumed that simply reading e-mail could not infect a system. Recent viruses and worms demonstrated, however, that simply previewing e-mail is enough to trigger an infection.[99]

The second trend is the use of increasingly sophisticated attack tools designed to fool antivirus software, hide any forensic tracks, vary the pattern and behaviors of the attack, and substantially alter the virus or code with each new attack. In essence, the attack becomes non-predictable and chaotic, making it extremely difficult to detect or stop new infections. For example, modern viruses typically have more vectors, and this multipartite evolution is likely to continue. Clarkson (2002) describes the possibility of an "Octopus" worm or virus which would be controlled from a central point through which the virus or worm could connect to get additional instructions or updates.[100] The updates would include new vulnerabilities and new encryption routines designed to prevent the virus from being detected. Additionally, virus code could be written to do a "operating system fingerprint" prior to executing itself on a target computer. Hence, unlike the past, the virus could infect different operating systems, different networks, and different software. The future is also likely to see increasing numbers of variants and multiple versions of viruses.[101] The wide availability of mutator engines and virus tool boxes has led to increasing releases of variants, typically from someone other than the original virus creator. A virus could be released with several different exploits, updating earlier versions and adding new functionality as it went.

The next two trends focus on the vulnerabilities of systems and software. The CERT® Coordination Center notes that the number of new vulnerabilities discovered doubles each year, making it difficult for administrators and software engineers to keep up. Further, automated discovery of these vulnerabilities is being written into the code of the attack, making the time frame available to patch very small. This has led many affected systems, businesses, and universities simply to shut down their network in response to a coordinated, automated attack. The other trend involves the primary defense mechanism now common on many networks and personal computers, the firewall. Several holes are being discovered in firewalls and certain types of code (ActiveX controls, Java, and JavaScript) make it difficult to protect vulnerable systems and to discover malicious software.[102] For example, blended threats combine the worst parts of worms and viruses, spreading via worm technology and delivering a virus payload upon deployment.[103] In addition, future Trojan horse–type attacks could be accomplished through a worm, which would then open a security hole in the system that would allow the attacker access to the system. The Trojan would then block off further attempts to enter the security hole and cover its own tracks on the system.[104]

The last two trends are a little more difficult to understand and describe. The best way to describe the fifth trend identified by the CERT® Coordination Center is that security is always dependent on the weakest link in the chain. Security on the Internet and intranets is highly interdependent, and exposure to a potential attack is contingent upon the security, or lack thereof, of other parts of the network. This can be exploited through what is termed an "asymmetric" attack, which involves numerous distributed systems launching an attack against a single victim. Finally, and perhaps most problematic, is the increasing threat from dedicated infrastructure attacks. The interdependency of systems connected to the Internet used to carry out day-to-day business is ever growing and increasingly being relied upon by a variety of businesses, governments, and other operations. These types of attacks fall into four categories: distributed denial of service; worms; attacks on the Internet Domain Name System (DNS); and attacks against or using routers.[105] Denial of service attacks and worms have been described. The attacks on Internet DNS would focus on disrupting or perverting the data and connectivity of the Internet systems that translate domain names to IP addresses. These attacks can result in a redirection of a user to a site determined by the attacker, compromised data on their servers, denial of service, and co-optation or takeover of the domain itself.[106] Routers are specialized computers that direct traffic on the Internet rapidly. These systems could be used as an attack platform, to deny service, and to exploit the trust connection that may exist between routers to speed up service.[107] In sum, any of the attacks described in the final trend could lead to denial of service, compromise of sensitive or personal information, misinformation, and an extreme economic impact, largely from lost revenue and the time and resources necessary to recover.

REVIEW QUESTIONS

1. What is the difference between a virus and other types of malicious code?
2. What are the most common types of viruses?
3. What variables are used to distinguish and classify viruses?
4. What is a Trojan horse? What are the various types of Trojan horses?
5. What is a worm? How do worms differ from traditional viruses?
6. What is a denial of service attack? How do these attacks work?
7. What are virus hoaxes? Why are the hoaxes sometimes more dangerous than an actual virus?
8. Describe the type of person who would write a virus.
9. What trends and what types of virus attacks are likely to increase in the future?

ENDNOTES

1. STEPHENSON, PETER. (2000). *Investigating Computer-Related Crime: A Handbook for Corporate Investigators.* Boca Raton, FL: CRC Press.
2. CHIEN, ERIC. (2003). Malicious Threats of Peer-to-Peer Networking. Symantec AntiVirus Research Center. Available on line: *http://enterprisesecurity.symantec.com/content/ knowledgelibrary.cfm?EID=0*
3. HINDOCHA, NEAL. (2003). Threats to Instant Messaging. Symantec Security Response. Available on line: *http://enterprisesecurity.symantec.com/content/knowledgelibrary.cfm? EID=0*
4. CHIEN, ERIC. (2003). Malicious Threats to Personal Digital Assistants. Symantec AntiVirus Research Center. Available on line: *http://enterprisesecurity.symantec.com/content/ knowledgelibrary.cfm?EID=0* ; CHIEN, ERIC. (2003). Potential Threats to WAP Enabled Devices. Symantec AntiVirus Research Center. Available on line: *http://enterprisesecurity .symantec.com/content/knowledgelibrary.cfm?EID=0*

5. Symantec Corporation. (2003). Internet Security for the Web: Protecting Enterprise Networks from Malicious and Inappropriate Web-Based Content. Available on line: *http://enterprisesecurity.symantec.com/content/knowledgelibrary.cfm?EID=0*

6. Trend Micro. (2002). The Real Cost of a Virus Outbreak: Why Is Antivirus Needed? White Paper. Available on line: *www.trendmicro.com*

7. SANS Institute. (2003). SANS FBI Top 20 List of Vulnerabilities. Available on line: *http://www.sans.org/top20/#threats*

8. *Ibid.*

9. *http://cve.mitre.org/*

10. *http://cve.mitre.org/*

11. WELLS, JOE. (2003). PC Viruses In-the-Wild—September, 2003. Available on line: *http://www.wildlist.org*

12. KASPERSKY, EUGENE V. (2003). The Classification of Computer Viruses. Metropolitan Network BBS Inc., Bern, Switzerland. Available on line: *http://www.avp.ch/avpve/classes/classes.stm*

13. *Ibid.*

14. *Ibid.*

15. *Ibid.*

16. *Ibid.*

17. *Ibid.*

18. *Ibid.*

19. KASPERSKY, EUGENE (1999). Computer Viruses—What are they and how to fight them? Available on line: *http://www.avp.ch/avpve/entry/entry.htm#1-1*

20. *Ibid.*

21. Symantec Corporation. (2003). Internet Security for the Web: Protecting Enterprise Networks from Malicious and Inappropriate Web-based Content. Available on line: *http://enterprisesecurity.symantec.com/content/knowledgelibrary.cfm?EID=0*

22. This virus infects the boot-sectors of floppy-disks during access to them. Location on a disk is in a free cluster which the virus marks as BAD (pseudo-bad clusters). An infected disk gets a new volume label, "(C) Brain". The virus uses a stealth mechanism—when you look at the boot-sector of the infected disk, it shows the unchanged boot-sector.

23. KASPERSKY, EUGENE (1999). Computer Viruses—What are they and how to fight them? Available on line: *http://www.avp.ch/avpve/entry/entry.htm#1-1*

24. Symantec Corporation. (2003). Internet Security for the Web: Protecting Enterprise Networks from Malicious and Inappropriate Web-based Content. Available on line: *http://enterprisesecurity.symantec.com/content/knowledgelibrary.cfm?EID=0*

25. *Ibid.*

26. MtE (MuTation Engine) is the first known polymorphic generator. It was released in 1991 and shocked antivirus researchers by its very difficult (for 1991) polymorphic algorithm.

27. Symantec Corporation. (2003). Internet Security for the Web: Protecting Enterprise Networks from Malicious and Inappropriate Web-based Content. Available on line: *http://enterprisesecurity.symantec.com/content/knowledgelibrary.cfm?EID=0*

28. These are not memory-resident harmless polymorphic viruses that affect .COM-files by using the "Vienna" algorithm. They are encoded and use two interesting algorithms. The first algorithm realizes the property of a polymorphic virus, due to which two strains of the virus would not coincide with high probability even in one byte. The main body of the virus is encoded depending on the timer (1000000h=16777216 variants), and the decoder is selected from more than 3,000,000,000,000,000,000,000 variants (the decoder length is 39 bytes).

The second algorithm fairly successfully complicates the virus tracing—it performs dynamic en/decoding of the virus codes using INT 1 and INT 3.

29. These are memory-resident harmless stealth polymorphic multipartite viruses. They write themselves at the end of .EXE files are executed or closed. These infectors hit MBR on execution of infected files, save the old MBR in the last sectors of C: drive and reduce its size in the Disk Partition Table. The viruses infect RAM on a reboot from the infected MBR only. They hook INT 13h, 1Ch, 21h. According to their internal counters, the viruses display a colorful picture (Mandelbrot fractal set) and the message:

```
Execute: mov ax, FE03 / INT 21. Key to go on!
```

After executing this instruction, the viruses display:

```
Welcome to T.TEQUILA's latest production.
Contact T.TEQUILA/P.o.Box 543/6312 St'hausen/Switzerland.
Loving thoughts to L.I.N.D.A
BEER and TEQUILA forever !
```

30. KASPERSKY, EUGENE (1999). Computer Viruses—What are they and how to fight them? Available on line: *http://www.avp.ch/avpve/entry/entry.htm#1-1*

31. The virus constructor utility VCL.EXE (Virus Creation Laboratory) seems to be the most well known virus creation tool. This constructor can generate source assembler files of the viruses, the OBJ modules and infected master files. VCL contains the standard pop-up menu interface. By using VCL menus, it is possible to choose the virus type, enable or disable self encryption, anti-debugging code, internal text strings. It also is possible to choose up to 10 effects which are called upon virus execution. VCL-based viruses can use a standard way of infection (they append their code to the files while infecting them), they can overwrite the files, or use companion technology.

    The main properties of VCL-viruses are:
    - They are non–memory resident
    - They scan the subdirectory three or the current directory of the current drive while infecting the files
    - They are appending to COM files, or create new COM files or overwrite COM and EXE files.

    Source: http://www.avp.ch/avpve/constr/vcl.stm

32. KASPERSKY, EUGENE (1999). Computer Viruses—What are they and how to fight them? Available on line: *http://www.avp.ch/avpve/entry/entry.htm#1-1*

33. *Ibid.*

34. *Ibid.*

35. This is the first WinWord virus found "in the wild". The virus contains five macros: AAAZAO, AAAZFS, AutoOpen, PayLoad, FileSaveAs. It infects the files that are SaveAs'ed (FileSaveAs).

    These are the text strings in the infected document:

```
see if we're already installed
iWW6IInstance
AAAZFS
AAAZAO
That's enough to prove my point
```
and other. The WINWORD6.INI on infected system contains the file:
```
WW6I= 1
```

On the first execution of the virus code (i.e., on the first opening of the infected file), the MessageBox appears with digit "1" inside, and "Ok" button. *http://www.avp.ch/ avpve/macro/word/concept.stm*

36. KASPERSKY, EUGENE (1999). Computer Viruses—What are they and how to fight them? Available on line: *http://www.avp.ch/avpve/entry/entry.htm#1-1*
37. *Ibid.*
38. *Ibid.*
39. *Ibid.*
40. *Ibid.*
41. *Ibid.*
42. Symantec Corporation. (2003). Internet Security for the Web: Protecting Enterprise Networks from Malicious and Inappropriate Web-based Content. Available on line: *http:// enterprisesecurity.symantec.com/content/knowledgelibrary.cfm?EID=0*
43. KASPERSKY, EUGENE V. (2003). The Classification of Computer Viruses. Metropolitan Network BBS Inc., Bern, Switzerland. Available on line: *http://www.avp.ch/avpve/ classes/classes.stm*
44. *Ibid.*
45. *Ibid.*
46. *Ibid.*
47. *Ibid.*
48. *Ibid.*
49. *Ibid.*
50. *Ibid.*
51. *Ibid.*
52. Symantec Corporation. 2003. Internet Security for the Web: Protecting Enterprise Networks from Malicious and Inappropriate Web-based Content. Available on line: *http:// enterprisesecurity.symantec.com/content/knowledgelibrary.cfm?EID=0*
53. CLARKSON, MICHAEL (2002). Beating the Superbug: Recent Developments in Worms and Viruses. GIAC GSEC Practical (1.4) SANS Institute: Information Security Reading Room. Available on line: *http://www.sans.org/rr/*
54. *Ibid.*
55. CERT Coordination Center (2003). "Overview of Attack Trends." Available on line: *http://www.cert.org/archive/pdf/attack_trends.pdf*
56. *Ibid.*
57. *Ibid.*
58. DANCHEV, DANCHO (1999). "The Complete Windows Trojans Paper." Frame4 Security Systems. Available on line: *http://www.frame4.com*
59. Symantec Corporation (2003). Internet Security for the Web: Protecting Enterprise Networks from Malicious and Inappropriate Web-based Content. Available on line: *http:// enterprisesecurity.symantec.com/content/knowledgelibrary.cfm?EID=0*
60. DANCHEV, DANCHO (1999). "The Complete Windows Trojans Paper." Frame4 Security Systems. Available on line: *http://www.frame4.com/*
61. *Ibid.*
62. CRAPANZANO, JAMIE (2003). "Deconstructing SubSeven, the Trojan Horse of Choice." SANS Institute Information Security Reading Room. Available on line: *http://www.sans.org/rr/*
63. DANCHEV, DANCHO (1999). "The Complete Windows Trojans Paper." Frame4 Security Systems. Available on line: *http://www.frame4.com/*

64. CRAPANZANO, JAMIE (2003). "Deconstructing SubSeven, the Trojan Horse of Choice." SANS Institute Information Security Reading Room. Available on line: *http://www.sans.org/rr/*

65. *Ibid.*

66. DANCHEV, DANCHO (1999). "The Complete Windows Trojans Paper." Frame4 Security Systems. Available on line: *http://www.frame4.com/*

67. *Ibid.*

68. CRAPANZANO, JAMIE (2003). "Deconstructing SubSeven, the Trojan Horse of Choice." SANS Institute Information Security Reading Room. Available on line: *http://www.sans.org/rr/*

69. *Ibid.*

70. *Ibid.*

71. *Ibid.*

72. DANCHEV, DANCHO (1999). "The Complete Windows Trojans Paper." Frame4 Security Systems. Available on line: *http://www.frame4.com/*

73. POST, ANDRÉ (2002). "The Dangers of Spyware." Symantec Anti-Virus Research Library. Available on line: *http://www.symantec.com/avcenter/whitepapers.html*

74. *Ibid.*

75. *Ibid.*

76. CERT Coordination Center (2003). "Overview of Attack Trends." Available on line: *http://www.cert.org/archive/pdf/attack_trends.pdf*

77. HOLDER, ERIC (2000). "Internet Denial of Service Attacks and the Federal Response." Statement of Eric Holder, Deputy Attorney General of the United States Before the Subcommittee on Crime of the House Committee on the Judiciary and the Subcommittee on Criminal Oversight of the Senate Committee on the Judiciary on February 29, 2000. Available on line: *http://www.usdoj.gov/criminal/cybercrime/ccpolicy.html#mv.*

78. CHIEN, ERIC and PÉTER SZÖR (2002). Blended Attacks Exploits, Vulnerabilities and Buffer-Overflow Techniques in Computer Viruses. Virus Bulletin Conference. Available on line: *http://enterprisesecurity.symantec.com/content/knowledgelibrary.cfm?EID=0*; GORDON, SARAH (2003). Virus and Vulnerability Classification Schemes: Standards and Integration. Symantec Security Response. Available on line: *http://enterprisesecurity.symantec.com/content/knowledgelibrary.cfm?EID=0*

79. *Ibid.*

80. *Ibid.*

81. *Ibid.*

82. HRUSKA, JAN (2002). Computer virus prevention: A primer. Oxford, UK: Sophos Plc. Available Online: *http://www.sophos.com/virusinfo/whitepapers/prevention.html*

83. Symantec Corporation (2003). Symantec Internet Security Threat Report. Available on line: *http://enterprisesecurity.symantec.com/content/knowledgelibrary.cfm?EID=0*

84. GORDON, SARAH, RICHARD FORD, and JOE WELLS (1997). Hoaxes & Hypes. Presented at the 7th Virus Bulletin International Conference in San Francisco, California, October 1–3, 1997. Available, on line: *http://www.research.ibm.com/antivirus/SciPapers/Gordon/HH.html*

85. *Ibid.*

86. GROCOTT, DARREN (2003). Virus hoaxes—are they just a nuisance? SANS Security Essentials GSEC Practical Assignment Version 1.2e. SANS Institute Information Security Reading Room. Available on line: *http://www.sans.org/rr/*

87. *Ibid.*

88. GORDON, SARAH, RICHARD FORD, and JOE WELLS (1997). Hoaxes & Hypes. Presented at the 7th Virus Bulletin International Conference in San Francisco, California, October 1–3, 1997. Available on line: *http://www.research.ibm.com/antivirus/SciPapers/Gordon/HH.html*; GROCOTT, DARREN (2003). Virus hoaxes—are they just a nuisance? SANS Security Essentials GSEC Practical Assignment Version 1.2e. SANS Institute Information Security Reading Room. Available on line: *http://www.sans.org/rr/*

89. KASPERSKY, EUGENE (1999). Computer Viruses—What are they and how to fight them? Available on line: *http://www.avp.ch/avpve/entry/entry.htm#1-1*

90. *Ibid;* PEARSON, DAVID (2003). Psst . . . Hey Buddy, wanna create a virus? SANS Institute Information Security Reading Room. Available on line: *http://www.sans.org/rr/*

91. DUCKLIN, PAUL (2001). Is virus writing really that bad? Presented at the Fourth Anti-Virus Asia Researchers (AVAR) Conference 2001, Hong Kong, November 2001. Available on line: *http://www.sophos.com/virusinfo/whitepapers/virubad.html*; ROSENBERGER, ROB *http://vmyths.com/*

92. CRAPANZANO, JAMIE (2003). Deconstructing SubSeven, the Trojan Horse of Choice. SANS Institute Information Security Reading Room. Available on line: *http://www.sans.org/rr/*

93. *Ibid.*

94. BONTCHEV, VESSELIN (April 1994). "Future of Viruses." Virus Bulletin. Available on line: *http://www.virusbtn.com/old/OtherPapers/Trends/*; KASPERSKY, EUGENE (1999). Computer Viruses—What are they and how to fight them? Available Online: *http://www.avp.ch/avpve/entry/entry.htm#1-1*

95. BONTCHEV, *Ibid.*

96. KASPERSKY, *Ibid.*

97. *Ibid.*

98. CERT Coordination Center (2003). Overview of Attack Trends. Available on line: *http://www.cert.org/archive/pdf/attack_trends.pdf*

99. CLARKSON, MICHAEL (2002). Beating the Superbug: Recent Developments in Worms and Viruses. GIAC GSEC Practical (1.4) SANS Institute: Information Security Reading Room. Available on line: *http://www.sans.org/rr/*

100. *Ibid.*

101. *Ibid.*

102. CERT Coordination Center (2003). Overview of Attack Trends. Available on line: *http://www.cert.org/archive/pdf/attack_trends.pdf*

103. CLARKSON, MICHAEL (2002). Beating the Superbug: Recent Developments in Worms and Viruses. GIAC GSEC Practical (1.4) SANS Institute: Information Security Reading Room. Available on line: *http://www.sans.org/rr/*

104. *Ibid.*

105. CERT Coordination Center (2003). Overview of Attack Trends. Available on line: *http://www.cert.org/archive/pdf/attack_trends.pdf*

106. *Ibid.*

107. *Ibid.*

Chapter 7

Exploitation, Stalking, and Obscenity on the WWW

Chapter Objectives

After completing this chapter, you should be able to:

- Understand the nature of victimization that can occur in cybercrime.
- Describe the groups affected by cyber exploitation, stalking, and obscenity.
- Describe the offenders who typically prey on victims in cyberstalking and exploitation cases via the Internet.
- Understand the law and legislation in the areas of cyberstalking, cyber exploitation, and pornography.
- Describe the Supreme Court cases that have recently been decided concerning federal efforts to target cybercriminals and protect children on line.
- Understand and describe the issues with pornography on line, child pornography, and child exploitation facilitated by the Internet.
- Understand and describe the difficulties faced by law enforcement in detecting, investigating, and prosecuting cases of cyberstalking and cyberexploitation.

INTRODUCTION

The Internet allows for communication across national and international boundaries. Not all of this communication is for benign purposes. The ease of use and perceived anonymity that the Internet affords has created the opportunity for certain criminals to exploit, stalk, and commit sex crimes electronically. Further, the nature of crimes committed electronically takes on a different character and presents unique difficulties for law enforcement. For example, physical contact or close proximity does not need to occur for a person to become a victim or for a crime to be committed. A child can be threatened, coerced, intimidated, and exposed to questionable material from offenders anywhere in the world. The crimes that are committed frequently involve multiple victims and offenders and cross national and international boundaries. In sum, the use of the Internet for exploitation, stalking, and obscenity has grown substantially in the past 20 years.

The driving force behind this growth is the vast profit that can be made selling pornography on the Internet. More disturbing is that sexual predators have found their way onto the Internet and have found it to be the perfect tool for exchanging child pornography, trolling for victims, and arranging meetings and tours for sexually deviant behavior. Sex rings of pedophiles have been uncovered that exchange numerous sexually explicit pictures and videos of children. In some high-profile cases, sex rings have been used to transport children across the world for sexual purposes—many times these networks are maintained via the Internet. In addition, pedophiles are using the Internet to arrange meetings with children and have been known to travel hundreds of miles for these meetings. This chapter surveys the nature of exploitation, stalking, and obscenity on the Internet, paying particular attention to the different character these offenses take on when committed over the Web. For every one of the crimes and problems discussed in this chapter there are numerous victims involved. The primary focus of this chapter is on the offenders that commit these crimes, the nature of the offenses, and insight into the reasons why they occur. The aim of this chapter is to provide greater exposure of these types of offenses and offer enough information that the casual reader, computer scientist, and law enforcement officials can work to curb the victimization described. Effective prevention, enforcement, and investigation of the offenses described here necessitates a more complete understanding of the etiology of the offenses and offenders described.

NATURE OF EXPLOITATION ON THE INTERNET

The exploitation of people for sexual and other purposes is nothing new, but the use of the Internet to facilitate these crimes is a recent phenomenon. The explosion of pornography, exploitation attempts, and crimes facilitated by the Internet have caught politicians and law enforcement completely off guard. Some would argue that warnings went unheeded, others that regulation has come far too late, and still others argue that any regulation over Internet use is a violation of free speech and the free exchange of ideas. However, few would argue that that the use of the Internet for exploitation and other offenses is a productive and ethical pursuit. People can be victimized in a variety of ways on line; the focus of this chapter is primarily on sexual victimization and stalking. The primary targets of such crimes are almost exclusively children and women even though, as will be noted below, women stalking men via the Internet is not all that uncommon. Internet sex predators victimize people by enticing them through on line contact for the purpose of engaging them in sexual acts; by using the Internet for the production, manufacture, and distribution of child or other sexually deviant pornography; by using the Internet to expose youth to child pornography and encouraging them to exchange pornography; and by enticing and exploiting women and children for the purpose of sexual tourism (travel with the intent to engage in sexual behavior) for commercial gain and/or personal gratification.[1]

Estimates of the number of children affected by on line crime, child exploitation and abuse, and other Internet-related crimes vary considerably. One estimate puts the number of children who are prostituted in the United States between 100,000 and 3 million.[2] The numbers of children involved in pornography and sex trafficking also are uncertain and probably severely underestimated. The Justice Department reports that the number of child pornography cases being investigated has jumped from around 90 to 300 cases per year.[3] A recent Time/CNN poll of 409 teenagers between the ages of 13 and 17 showed that 66 percent of the girls and 54 percent of the boys had experienced people saying offensive things to them on line. Computer sex offenders frequently roam chat rooms and post sexually explicit material on the Internet to make contact with young children and teenagers. Initial victimization may be indirect and limited to showing a child pornographic sites or initiating sexual conversations in a chat room, by e-mail or instant messages. More aggressive predators will spend time developing close relationships with vulnerable children. Eventually, they may introduce them to photographs of children engaging in "normal" sex with adults, send them gifts, and contact them by telephone. Typically they will try to gain their trust, alienate them from their family, and eventually try to set up a meeting where the child will be victimized. Some on-line sex offenders have gone so far as to send plane tickets to children to fly across the country to meet them.[4] A recent report by UNICEF[5] concluded that one million children enter the commercial sex trade each year worldwide. Some of the statistics offered in the report are staggering:

- In Lithuania, 20 percent to 50 percent of prostitutes are believed to be minors.
- In a Cambodian survey of 6,110 sex workers, 31 percent of those interviewed were youths between the ages of twelve and seventeen.
- There are at least 244,000 women and children who are part of the commercial sexual exploitation trade in the United States.
- There are between 400,000 and 500,000 child prostitutes in India.
- Debt bondage—paying off loans given to their parents or guardians—is often the way young girls enter prostitution in India, Nepal, Myanmar, Pakistan, and Thailand.[6]

BOX 7.1   Keeping Children Safe—WWW.Protectkids.org

Protectkids.org is a Web site dedicated to on line safety for children and to protecting them from unwanted exposure to the variety of threats presented by the Internet. They have a clearinghouse of material dedicated to prevention and offer the following facts about on line safety for kids:

- By the end of 1998, more than 40 percent of all American homes had computers, and 25 percent had Internet access. This trend is expected to continue. Children and teenagers are one of the fastest growing groups of Internet users. An estimated 10 million kids are on line today. By the year 2002, this figure is expected to increase to 45 million, and by 2005 to 77 million.

- Only one-third of the households with Internet access are proactively protecting their children with filtering or blocking software.

- 75 percent of children are willing to share personal information on line about themselves and their family in exchange for goods and services.

- About 25 percent of the youth who encountered a sexual approach or solicitation told a parent.

- One in five U.S. teenagers who regularly log on to the Internet say they have received an unwanted sexual solicitation via the Web. Solicitations were defined as requests to engage in sexual activities or sexual talk, or to give personal sexual information.

- One in 33 youth received an aggressive sexual solicitation in the past year. This means a predator asked a young person to meet somewhere, called a young person on the phone, and/or sent the young person correspondence, money, or gifts through the U.S. Postal Service.

- 77 percent of the targets for on line predators were age 14 or older. Another 22 percent were users ages 10 to 13.

- 75 percent of the solicited youth were not troubled, 10 percent did not use chat rooms and 9 percent did not talk to strangers.

- Only 25 percent of solicited children were distressed by their encounters and told a parent.

- Only 17 percent of youth and 11 percent of parents could name a specific authority, such as the Federal Bureau of Investigation (FBI), CyberTipline, or an Internet service provider, to which they could report an Internet crime.

Source: http://www.protectkids.org/statistics.htm

The sex trade in many countries involves young boys who are offered to European, American, and Asian tourists, sometimes as part of vacation packages. Estimates are that 20–30,000 of Sri Lanka's child prostitutes are boys who are "rented" to tourist pedophiles. Several other countries are known for tolerating an active sex trade of young boys for visiting tourists include the Dominican Republican, Haiti, Egypt, Morocco, and Tunisia.[7]

Women are also targeted by on line predators and other criminals. Many would argue that pornography itself is a victimization or at least an objectification of women. As discussed in this chapter, women are frequently the targets of physical stalkers and are at greater risk of being the victim of a cyberstalker. Additionally, women report feeling higher levels of violation as the result of being stalked, threatened, or harassed on line. Certain factors make some groups more vulnerable than others to on line victimization. First, and most obviously, regular use and access to a computer with Internet capability is necessary to being victimized. The axiom that it is only a matter of time before you see something on the Internet that is pornographic or offensive holds true, and in many cases first exposure is accidental. Older children tend to be at greater risk because they often use the computer unsupervised and are more likely to engage in on line discussions of a personal nature. People that actively participate in chat rooms, trade e-mail messages, and send pictures on line are also more likely to be victimized.

Many people simply use the computer at work and correspondence is limited to e-mails between colleagues and friends. However, a growing number of people spend countless hours using Internet chat and posting to Internet discussion groups. Again, it is only a matter of time before such people cross paths with a victimizer. Troubled or rebellious teens who are seeking emancipation from parental authority can be particularly susceptible to Internet predators. Many sex offenders are well versed in the dynamics of teenage difficulties and know exactly what to say to a troubled teen to get them into a vulnerable position. All adolescents struggle with sexuality and the Internet provides them with a seemingly anonymous and nonthreatening mechanism to ask questions and explore issues of a sexual nature. The problem is that often the teen has no idea who is on the other end of the wire. Most teens feel that victimization is unlikely and that they are safe talking on line. Finally, single people have flocked to the Internet in growing numbers looking for companionship and relationships. While many professional on line dating services exist, many people encounter someone in a chat room or as the result of some other type of Internet conversation. Seeking the thrills romanticized in *You've Got Mail,* these people set up meetings and make themselves vulnerable. While it is likely that most of this interaction is relatively safe, it is also a growing medium for pedophiles and sex offenders to lure their victims off the computer and into a compromising position.

Incidence and Prevalence of Victimization On Line

The potential for victimization on line is probably much higher than most people think. As noted throughout this text, there are numerous ways in which people can experience some type of loss, including fraud, viruses, and malicious destruction of data.

However, several areas of cybervictimization are becoming increasingly common, yet severely underreported and under-investigated, including unwanted or unintended exposure to obscene or pornographic material, harassment, threats, and cyberstalking. To date, there is no central clearinghouse for the collection of data on the numbers of these types of victimizations. One of the more comprehensive examinations of the problems these areas pose was the Youth Internet Safety Survey[8] conducted by Finkelhor, Mitchell, and Wolak and sponsored by the National Center for Missing and Exploited Children. The survey measured several areas of problems that youths reported being exposed to while surfing on line, including:

- *Sexual solicitations and approaches:* Requests to engage in sexual activities or sexual talk or give personal sexual information that were unwanted or, whether wanted or not, made by an adult.

- *Aggressive sexual solicitation:* Sexual solicitations involving off line contact with the perpetrator through regular mail, by telephone, or in person, or attempts or requests for off line contact.

- *Unwanted exposure to sexual material:* Without seeking or expecting sexual material, being exposed to pictures of naked people or people having sex when doing on line searches, surfing the Web, opening e-mail or e-mail links.

- *Harassment:* Threats or other offensive behavior (not sexual solicitation), sent on line to the youth or posted on line about the youth for others to see. Not all such incidents were distressing to the youth who experienced them.

- *Distressing incidents* were episodes where youth rated themselves as very or extremely upset or afraid as a result of the incident.[9]

The research interviewed a nationally representative sample of 1,501 youth ages 10 to 17 who use the Internet regularly. The results indicated that approximately one in five received a sexual solicitation or approach over the Internet in the last year, with one in 33 receiving an aggressive sexual solicitation (a solicitor who asked to meet them somewhere; called them on the telephone; sent them regular mail, money, or gifts). One in four had an unwanted exposure to pictures of naked people or people having sex in the last year. One in 17 was threatened or harassed, and approximately one quarter of the respondents who reported these incidents were distressed by them. Although the respondents reported high rates of victimization, less than 10 percent of sexual solicitations and only 3 percent of unwanted exposures were reported to authorities such as a law-enforcement agency, an Internet service provider, or a hotline. Further, only one-quarter of the youth who encountered a sexual solicitation told a parent; however, almost 40 percent of those reporting an unwanted exposure to sexual material did tell a parent. Few could name resources where they could report these offenses, and in households with home Internet access, only one-third of parents said they had filtering or blocking software.[10]

The results from this research can be viewed in a number of ways. Although the percentages may seem at first glance to be relatively small, the researchers extrapolated estimates of the number of victims based on the sample drawn in the survey. The

TABLE 7.1   Population Estimates and Confidence Intervals for Online Victimization
of Youth[a]

Online Victimization	% Regular Internet Users	95% Confidence Interval	Estimated Number of Youth[b]	95% Confidence Interval[b]
Sexual Solicitations and Approaches				
Any	19%	17%–21%	4,520,000	4,050,000–4,990,000
Distressing	5%	4%–6%	1,190,000	930,000–1,450,000
Aggressive	3%	2%–4%	710,000	510,000–910,000
Unwanted Exposure to Sexual Material				
Any	25%	23%–27%	5,950,000	5,430,000–6,470,000
Distressing	6%	5%–7%	1,430,000	1,140,000–1,720,000
Harassment				
Any	6%	5%–7%	1,430,000	1,140,000–1,720,000
Distressing	2%	1%–3%	480,000	310,000–650,000

[a]Estimates and confidence intervals are based on an estimated number of 23,810,000 regular Internet users between the ages of 10 and 17.
[b]Estimates and confidence intervals are all rounded to the nearest ten thousand.

Source: Finkelhor, David, Kimberly J. Mitchell, and Janis Wolak (2000). *Online Victimization: A Report on the Nation's Youth.* Washington, DC: National Center for Missing & Exploited Children.

results of this extrapolation are presented in Table 7.1 and reveal that between 4 and 5 million youths between the ages of 10 and 17 received a sexual solicitation or approach on line. Another 5.4 to 6.4 million were exposed to unwanted sexual material. Finally, between 1.1 and 1.7 million were harassed on line. The authors note that the survey suggests that youths encounter a substantial number of offensive episodes, many of which are distressing and most of which are unreported.

The survey also reported demographics regarding the types of youths that were targeted for sexual solicitations and approaches. The research reported the following:

- Girls were targeted at almost twice the rate of boys (66 percent versus 34 percent), but given that girls are often thought to be the exclusive targets of sexual solicitation, the sizable percentage of boys is important.

- More than three-quarters of targeted youth (77 percent) were age 14 or older.

- Only 22 percent were ages 10 to 13, but this younger group was disproportionately distressed. They reported 37 percent of the distressing episodes, suggesting that younger children have a harder time shrugging off such solicitations.

- Almost all (97 percent) were persons the youth originally met on line.

- Adults were responsible for 24 percent of sexual solicitations and 34 percent of the aggressive solicitations.
- Most of the adult solicitors were reported to be ages 18 to 25. About 4 percent of all solicitors were known to be older than 25.
- Juveniles made 48 percent of the overall and 48 percent of the aggressive solicitations.
- Slightly more than two-thirds of the solicitations and approaches came from males.
- One-quarter of the aggressive episodes came from females.

TABLE 7.2   Risky Online Behavior (N = 1,501)

Risky Online Behavior in the Past Year	All Youth % Yes
Youth Went to X-rated Sites on Purpose	8
Talked About Sex On Line With Someone Youth Never Met in Person (N = 839)[a]	7
Youth Knew He or She Was Talking to an Adult	2
Adult Knew He or She Was Talking with a Minor	2
Used Credit Card On Line Without Permission	<1
Posted Picture of Self for Anyone to See	5
Sent Picture of Self to Someone Met On Line (N = 839)[a]	12
Posted Some Personal Information for All to See	11
Posted Last Name	9
Posted Telephone Number	1
Posted Name of School	3
Posted Home Address	2
Posted E-mail Address for Anyone to See (N = 1,143)[b]	27
Made Rude/Nasty Comments to Someone On Line	14
Played Joke or Annoyed Someone On Line	14
Played Joke/Annoyed Someone Youth Knew	13
Played Joke/Annoyed Stranger	2
Harassed/Embarrassed Someone Youth Was Mad at On Line	1
Harassed/Embarrassed Stranger	<1
Harassed/Embarrassed Someone Youth Knew	1
Youth Was in Trouble at Home for Something He or She Did On Line	5
Youth Was in Trouble at School for Something He or She Did On Line (N = 1,100)[c]	3

[a]Only asked of youth who reported talking on line with people they didn't know in person.
[b]Only asked of youth who reported having an e-mail address.
[c]Only asked of youth who reported using the Internet at school.

Source: Finkelhor, David, Kimberly J. Mitchell, and Janis Wolak (2000). *Online Victimization: A Report on the Nation's Youth*. Washington, DC: National Center for Missing & Exploited Children.

- In 13 percent of instances, the youth knew where the solicitor lived. Youth stated the solicitor lived nearby (within a one hour drive or less) in only 4 percent of incidents.

The Youth Internet Survey found that a larger number than might be expected of offensive experiences on the Internet are being perpetrated on youths. Although the majority of solicitations do not result in a more serious offense, the sheer number of such encounters is alarming. Although many youths simply ignore such affronts, a significant percentage are severely distressed by the incidents. Complicating things is the fact that the overwhelming majority of these offenses and innuendos go unreported to authorities or the parents of the child.[11] The problems that youths experience on line could be exacerbated by the youth engaging in other risky behavior. However, the percentage of youth engaging in such behavior was relatively small. Finally, the belief by many that such on line offenses are not serious adds to underreporting and lack of attention being paid to these victims.

STALKING VIA THE WWW

Stalking is most often defined as the willful or intentional commission of a series of acts that would cause a reasonable person to fear death or serious bodily injury and that, in fact, places the victim in fear of death or serious bodily injury.[12] Stalking laws have changed recently in response to greater knowledge about the crime being generated through research. Originally, many statutes had a narrow definition of stalking that included a specific intent requirement.[13] However, many states have reformulated their laws to broaden the definition of stalking to include repeated behavior that is harassing, communicating, or nonconsensual communication. In addition, many states have adopted a "general intent" requirement rather a specific intent requirement which allows prosecutions for implied threats and threats that may or may not be considered "credible."[14] Some definitions also take into account the receiver's reactions to the communications, including any reaction that would cause a reasonable person to fear for their personal safety, fear bodily injury or death to themselves or a related person, to suffer substantial emotional distress, or cause a person to become seriously alarmed, terrorized, or tormented by the behavior.[15]

Many stalking laws are broad enough to encompass stalking via e-mail or other electronic communication, defining the prohibited conduct in terms of "communication," "harassment," or "threats" without specifying the means of such behavior. A more specific definition of cyber stalking would be the use of the Internet, e-mail or other electronic communications device to stalk, threaten or harass a person. Other states have specifically defined stalking via e-mail within their stalking or harassment statute. For example, California recently amended its stalking law to expressly include stalking via the Internet.[16]

The true numbers of cyberstalking incidents are unknown, but recent anecdotal evidence suggests that it is a growing problem.[17] The Los Angeles District Attorney's Office estimates that electronic communications were a factor in approximately

---

BOX 7.2   Internet "Cyber Stalker" Pleads Guilty to Federal Charges

Warren Gray, a 19-year old Upper Marlboro, Maryland man, pleaded guilty to five counts of sending threatening e-mails to a Largo High School administrator at the same time as Gray was stalking him last November. In addition to sending five threatening e-mails, Gray admitted that in a two-week period in November he also twice slashed the victim's car tires at Largo High School and left a hatchet in the victim's school office. The e-mails, which were introduced into the court record in federal court, included extremely graphic threats to kill Jones, to harm his family, and to burn down his home. Gray pleaded guilty to five counts of violating Title 18, U.S.C. Section 875, which criminalizes threats sent through the interstate wires. The charges carry a maximum penalty of five years imprisonment and a fine of $250,000 for each of the five counts.

U.S. Attorney Lynne Battaglia stated, "This guilty plea should serve as a notice to criminals who misuse the Internet—we will be moving you from cyberspace to cell space."

Prince George's County Police Department spokesman Royce Holloway stated, "This is another example of the cooperation between local and federal law enforcement in pursuing criminals who exploit the Internet to commit crimes. The citizens of Prince George's County appreciate the effort of the U.S. Attorney's Office in removing these criminals from our community."

This case was investigated by the Federal Bureau of Investigation and the Prince George's County Police Department, including the Department's relatively new computer forensic unit. Battaglia and Richard Mosquera, Special Agent in Charge of the F.B.I.'s Baltimore office, praised the professional and thorough work of the Prince George's Police Department on the investigation.

Source: http://www.usdoj.gov/criminal/cybercrime/gray.htm

---

20 percent of the roughly 600 cases handled by its Stalking and Threat Assessment Unit. The chief of the Sex Crimes Unit in the Manhattan District Attorney's Office also estimates that about 20 percent of the cases handled by the unit involve cyberstalking. Finally, the Computer Investigations and Technology Unit of the New York City Police Department estimates that almost 40 percent of the caseload in the unit involves electronic threats and harassment—and virtually all of these have occurred in the past three or four years. One major ISP receives approximately 15 complaints per month of cyberstalking, in comparison to virtually no complaints of cyberstalking just one or two years ago.

Dynamics and Nature of Stalking and Cyberstalking

The traditional conception of the crime of stalking involves a stranger following some unsuspecting female and showing up for repeated interactions with the person. This conception has been reinforced in popular film in such movies as *Taxi Driver* and host of serial killer movies. However, the true dynamics of stalking have extended far beyond this traditional conception and new definitions and laws have expanded the meaning dramatically. What makes this area of law difficult to enforce is that it is often difficult to distinguish between dangerous stalking behavior and relatively benign harassment or puppy love. Police officers investigating such crimes are as replete with true stalking stories as they are with false reports and overestimations of the dangerousness of the behavior. Many cases of stalking do not even rise to extreme levels of violence or harassment.[18] Nonetheless, all forms of stalking should be taken seriously, as they represent a fundamental threat to a person's physical and psychological well being.

Stalkers have been known to use binoculars, telescopes, cameras equipped with "long lenses," video cameras, hidden microphones, the Internet, public records, and accomplices (both witting and unwitting) to keep track of the whereabouts and activities of those they target.[19] Cyberstalking is simply the electronic form of stalking, where the harassment or threats are directed via the Internet typically using e-mail, chat rooms, bulletin boards, or even Web pages. Most often, due to the distance between users and the anonymity of the Internet, this behavior will not escalate into physical harm, but this does not mean that the pursuit is any less distressing.[20] A recent survey of stalking victims reported that stalkers employed the following tactics most often:

- Followed, spied on, stood outside home or place of work (82 percent).
- Made unwanted phone calls (61 percent).
- Sent unwanted letters or left unwanted items (30 percent).
- Vandalized property (30 percent).
- Killed or threatened to kill a pet (9 percent).[21]

Stalkers, by their very nature, want a relationship with their victims. They want to be part of their victims' lives. And, if they cannot be a positive part of their victims' lives, they will settle for a negative connection to their victims. It is this mindset that not only makes them stalkers, but makes them dangerous. Thus, virtually all stalking cases involve behavior that seeks to make either direct or indirect contact with the victim.[22]

Given the conclusion that general stalking is probably vastly underreported, the true picture of cyberstalking is even harder to assess. The reasons for underreporting are similar to underreporting for all crime: Victims may not consider the behavior dangerous, they may not know that what is happening to them is a crime, they may believe that little can be done about the stalking, or they may feel embarrassed or want to keep the offense secret for some other reason. One estimate is that approximately 200,000 individuals are stalked each year in the United States; however, recent empirical research surveying adults estimated that 1.4 million Americans (approximately 1,000,000 women and 400,000 men) are currently being stalked in the United States—a number seven times greater than the previous estimate of 200,000.[23] These estimates should be interpreted with caution, as they are based on extrapolations from surveys and the definitions of true stalking are not universally accepted. Nonetheless, this staggering estimate reveals a serious problem, especially when the stalking moves on line.

BOX 7.3   Man Convicted of Threatening Federal Judges by Internet E-mail

Carl E. Johnson, 49, of Bienfait, Saskatchewan, Canada, has been convicted on four felony counts of sending threatening e-mail messages via the Internet to federal judges and others. The convictions were announced following a seven-day trial before United States District Judge Robert J. Bryan, in Tacoma, Washington. Johnson was convicted of one count of Retaliating Against a Judicial Officer, one count of Obstructing Justice by Making a Death Threat Against a Judicial Officer, and two counts of Transmitting Threatening Communications in Foreign Commerce. The first three charges were based on death threats posted to the Internet naming two federal judges based in Tacoma and Seattle. The fourth charge was based on an e-mail threat sent directly to Microsoft Chairman Bill Gates. Johnson was acquitted on one count of Obstructing Justice.

In announcing his verdict on Tuesday, April 20, 1999, Judge Bryan stated that he had "no doubt" Johnson was the author of three threatening messages sent over the Internet. Although Johnson had used anonymous remailers and forged e-mail address information in an attempt to disguise his identity, Judge Bryan found that the government's technical evidence proved Johnson's authorship. In response to the defense contention that the statements constituted "free speech" protected by the First Amendment to the United States Constitution, Judge Bryan ruled that the messages were "serious expressions of intention to do harm," and thus "clearly over the line" of protected speech.

The guilty verdicts are the culmination of a two-year investigation by U.S. Treasury agents into anonymous threats posted on the Internet and a scheme to assassinate government officials known as "Assassination Politics." As the testimony and evidence at trial showed, the assassination scheme was first promoted by James Dalton Bell, of Vancouver, Washington, who had proposed to murder IRS employees, had gathered a list of IRS agents' names and home addresses, had contaminated an IRS office with a noxious chemical, and had experimented with other toxic and dangerous chemicals, including nerve agents. Johnson had corresponded with Bell about Bell's "Assassination Politics" concept via Internet e-mail. After Bell's arrest, Johnson vowed in an Internet e-mail message to take "personal action" in support of Bell. On June 23, 1997, Johnson anonymously posted a message on the Internet suggesting that specific sums of money would be paid, in the form of electronic cash, for the deaths of a Federal Magistrate Judge in Tacoma, Washington, and Treasury agents involved in the Bell investigation. Additional threatening messages linked to Johnson continued to appear on the Internet in the months that followed, and Johnson set up a World Wide Web page with a partial prototype of the "Assassination Politics" scheme.

Johnson also issued a death threat to several Judges of the United States Court of Appeals for the Ninth Circuit, again through an anonymous e-mail message. The government was able to identify Johnson as the author of the threatening messages and the Internet assassination Web page through a variety of technical means. In the case of the Ninth Circuit judge's death threat, Treasury agents were able to link the unique characteristics of an encrypted digital signature on the threatening message to encryption "keys" found on Johnson's computer.

Treasury investigators received assistance in the case from Canadian law enforcement agencies who were investigating Johnson for his Internet activities and an unexploded gasoline bomb found in a courthouse in Estevan, Saskatchewan. The trial featured testimony from officers of the Royal Canadian Mounted Police and Canadian Customs, as well as the Canadian Internet Service Provider Sympatico and Canadian telephone company Sasktel. Computer experts from the Treasury Department and Portland Police Bureau also testified.

Johnson was sentenced to 37 months of imprisonment on four felony counts of sending threatening e-mail messages via the Internet to federal judges and others. The retaliation and threatening communication counts carried a possible maximum penalty of five years in prison. The obstruction of justice count carries a maximum penalty of ten years in prison. Johnson also faces additional charges in Canada in connection with the bomb found in the Canadian courthouse.

Source: http://www.usdoj.gov/criminal/cybercrime/Johnson.htm

Most people using electronic forms of communication are much more brazen than they would be face to face; such is the case with cyberstalkers. The medium encourages people to interact in ways in which they would either be too embarrassed to do in person or in ways in which they feel they might not be caught. This is most likely due to the perceived anonymity of the Internet and also because people talking to one another on line are far away from each other physically.[24] Because individuals can mask their identity and remain relatively anonymous when using the Internet, linking the harassment to one individual is difficult and time consuming. Several programs and other techniques exist that can mask the IP (Internet Protocol) address of a person, making it difficult to trace the source of a given communication. Further, anonymous remailers and Internet providers who guarantee user anonymity also complicate any investigative process.

Cyberstalkers employ a variety of tactics on line, most commonly sending unsolicited, hateful, obscene, or threatening e-mail or harassing the victim in on line chat rooms.[25] With newsgroups, the cyberstalker can create postings about the victim or start rumors which spread through the bulletin board system. Cyberstalkers may also set up a Web page(s) on the victim with personal or fictitious information or solicitations to readers. Another technique is to assume the victim's persona on line, such as in chat rooms, for the purpose of sullying the victim's reputation, posting details about the victim, or soliciting unwanted contacts from others. The Internet can provide, both for free and at a cost, a wealth of information about anyone, including their address, phone numbers, e-mail addresses, their neighbors and friends' information, their housing information, credit reports, and personal identifying numbers and passwords. More complex forms of harassment include mailbombs (mass messages that virtually shut down the victim's e-mail system by clogging it), sending the victim computer viruses, or sending electronic junk mail (spamming).[26] Several interesting cases have been documented involving cyberstalking, including these:

- In the first successful prosecution under California's new cyberstalking law, prosecutors in the Los Angeles District Attorney's Office obtained a guilty plea from a 50-year-old former security guard who used the Internet to solicit the rape of a woman who rejected his romantic advances. The defendant terrorized his 28-year-old victim by impersonating her in various Internet chat rooms and on line bulletin boards, where he posted, along with her telephone number and address, messages that she fantasized about being raped. On at least six occasions, sometimes in the middle of the night, men knocked on the woman's door saying they wanted to rape her. The former security guard pleaded guilty in April 1999 to one count of stalking and three counts of solicitation of sexual assault. He faces up to six years in prison.

- A local prosecutor's office in Massachusetts charged a man who, utilizing anonymous remailers, allegedly engaged in a systematic pattern of harassment of a co-worker, which culminated in an attempt to extort sexual favors from the victim under threat of disclosing past sexual activities to the victim's new husband.

- An honors graduate from the University of San Diego terrorized five female university students over the Internet for more than a year. The victims received hundreds of violent and threatening e-mails, sometimes receiving four or five messages a day. The graduate student, who has entered a guilty plea and faces up to six years in prison, told police he committed the crimes because he thought the women were laughing at him and causing others to ridicule him. In fact, the victims had never met him.[27]

Characteristics of Stalkers and Their Victims

Most stalkers are typically male (87 percent), white (80 percent), between the ages of 18 and 35 (50 percent), and are of average intelligence earning above-average incomes.[28] In contrast, most stalking victims are women (78 percent), white (83 percent), between the ages of 18 and 39 (74 percent), and are married (59 percent).[29] The research in this area indicates that the majority of stalkers and their victims (60 percent) had a personal relationship before the stalking began. The majority of these cases (42 percent) involved spouses or partners and another 14 percent had a dating relationship. Nearly 18 percent of stalkers were acquaintances or coworkers of the victim, while only 22 percent were complete strangers.[30] Specific profiles or categorizations have been developed as the result of the study of this phenomenon.

Several categorization schemes exist for classifying stalkers,[31] and the behavior of each type varies to a certain degree. Comprising the largest group of estimated stalkers (47–60 percent), simple obsessional stalkers typically involve a victim and a perpetrator who have a prior relationship. The motivation behind this may be coercion to re-enter a relationship, or revenge aimed at making the life of the former intimate uncomfortable through the inducement of fear. Many simple obsession cases are actually extensions of a previous pattern of domestic violence and psychological abuse. The only difference is that the abuse occurs in different surroundings and through slightly altered tactics of intimidation. Thus, the dynamics of power and control that underlie most domestic violence cases are often mirrored in simple obsession stalking cases. This category of stalker is thought to be the most dangerous and this is the most likely category of stalking to result in murder. Thirty percent of all female homicides were committed by intimate partners, and domestic violence victims run a 75 percent higher risk of being murdered by their partners.

The second largest category of stalkers (43 percent) is the love obsession type, where no prior relationship exists between perpetrator and victim or they are casual acquaintances. Often, the stalker identifies the victim through the media or the Internet. Usually, stalkers in this category seek to establish a personal relationship with the object of their obsession—contrary to the wishes of their victims. Love obsession stalkers tend to have low self-esteem and often target victims whom they perceive to have exceptional qualities and high social standing. These stalkers seek to raise their own self-esteem by associating with those whom they hold in high regard. These types of stalkers are also often suffering from some type of mental disorder or defect. They frequently target celebrities; several famous cases includes Madonna and Jodie Foster. Often, love obsession stalkers are so desperate to establish a relationship—*any* relationship—that they "settle" for negative relationships, explaining why some stalkers are willing to engage in destructive or violent behavior in an irrational attempt to "win the love" (more likely the attention) of their victims.[32]

A third category is referred to as erotomaniacs, meaning that the stalker believes that the victim is in love with them. By definition, erotomaniacs are delusional and consequently, virtually all suffer from mental disorders—most often schizophrenia. This category was the least frequent (less than 10 percent) and differed from the previous two in that these offenders were more likely to be females stalking males. Erotomania stalking cases often draw public attention because the target is usually a public figure or celebrity. Like love obsession stalkers, erotomaniacs attempt to garner self-esteem and status by associating themselves with well known individuals who hold high social status. While the behavior of many erotomaniacs never escalates to violence, or even to threats of violence, the irrationality that accompanies their mental illness presents particularly unpredictable threats to victims. Perhaps the best-known case of erotomania stalking involved a series of incidents perpetrated against the popular late-night talk show host, David Letterman. This woman, first found hiding in Mr. Letterman's closet, believed she was his wife. On numerous other occasions she was caught trespassing on his property. With her young son in tow, she once scaled the six-foot wall surrounding Letterman's property. On another occasion, she was arrested while driving Letterman's stolen car. When questioned by police, she confidently stated that her husband was out of town and that she was going grocery shopping so she would have dinner ready for him upon his return. Despite the treatment she received during her many involuntary stays at a mental institution, she eventually took her own life.[33]

Another, recently developed category, is the vengeance or terrorist stalker. Vengeance/terrorist stalkers attempt to elicit a particular response or a change of behavior from their victims rather than seeking a personal relationship with them. When vengeance is their prime motive, stalkers seek only to punish their victims for some wrong they perceive the victim has visited upon them. In other words, they use stalking as a means

---

BOX 7.4   Individual Pleaded Guilty to Causing Numerous Anonymous E-mail Messages to Be Sent to a Senior, Supervisory-level Employee at the Department of Defense

Trung Ngo, age 32, of Falls Church, Virginia, pled guilty in federal court to a charge of repeated telecommunications harassment. This case is the result of an investigation conducted by the Defense Information Infrastructure Intrusion Investigation Team, a special unit of the Defense Criminal Investigative Service (DCIS), Department of Defense (DoD). He faces maximum penalties of two (2) years' imprisonment, a fine of $250,000, and one (1) year of supervised release.

According to documents filed in court, Trung Ngo, a former DoD employee who was later employed at the General Services Administration (GSA), caused to be sent numerous anonymous e-mail messages to a current senior, supervisory-level defense department employee at the Defense Information Systems Agency (DISA) which were harassing in nature. Trung Ngo had worked as a telecommunications specialist for the victim at DISA from March 28, 1994 through September 30, 1995.

Around September 1995, Ngo was assigned to another organization at DISA. In February 1998, Ngo left DISA, and joined the GSA.

Beginning in April 1998 and continuing through July 1998 Trung Ngo caused to be sent unwanted e-mail messages, sometimes over fifty (50) per day, for the purpose of harassing the victim. The victim received these messages at his DISA e-mail account. In addition, at the end of 1995 the victim began receiving unsolicited magazines, figurines, and other products at his home via U.S. postal mail. Some items had been purchased and some of the magazine subscriptions had been entered in the victim's name.

Source: http://www.usdoj.gov/criminal/cybercrime/ngo_pr.htm

---

to "get even" with their enemies. Most commonly this type of behavior involves fired employees or political stalking (as in the case of some anti-abortionists).

Traditional stalkers and cyberstalkers have several similarities and differences. The similarities primarily involve the motivations for stalking and the demographic and relational characteristics of the offense.[34] In essence, the stalker is motivated by a desire to get close to the victim, control the victim, or punish the victim in some way. The major difference is that while off line stalking necessitates a closer proximity to the victim, cyberstalking can occur from across the nation or the world. Electronic communications technologies make it much easier for a cyberstalker to encourage third parties to harass and/or threaten a victim (e.g., impersonating the victim and posting inflammatory messages to bulletin boards and in chat rooms, causing viewers of that message to send threatening messages back to the victim "author.") Finally, as noted previously, cyberstalkers are much more likely to be brazen than off line stalkers because of the anonymity of the Internet and the lack of close proximity.[35]

Law Enforcement and Legislation Targeting Stalking

California was the first state to enact stalking legislation (in 1990) and today all 50 states and the federal government have antistalking statutes. However, a recent report notes that less than one-third of the states' antistalking laws that explicitly cover stalking via the Internet, e-mail, pagers, or other electronic communications.[36] Nonetheless, many experts feel that existing stalking laws would cover the crime if committed using the Internet or other electronic means. Yet certain types of cyberstalking would most likely fall through the cracks and escape prosecutions. Currently, several federal laws cover the crime of stalking, but several of the statutes are not specifically targeted at cyberstalking. One such statute makes it a crime to transmit any communication in interstate or foreign commerce that contains a threat of injury.[37] This statute does not cover harassment offenses meant to annoy someone. A portion of a telecommunications law makes it a crime to annoy, abuse, harass, or threaten any person via electronic or telephone communication.[38] The Interstate Stalking Act[39] makes it a crime for any person to travel across state lines with the intent to injure or harass another person and, in the course thereof, place that person or a member of that person's family in reasonable fear of death or serious bodily injury. The problem with this law is that it probably would not directly apply to cyberstalking cases. Again, the existing law would most likely apply to cases of cyberstalking, although it would be prudent to be more specific about the crime in future legislation.

Cyberstalking is expected to increase as computers and the Internet become more popular. An Assistant U.S. Attorney reported that in two recent cases of e-mail harassment, he asked an FBI agent to confront the would-be harasser. Upon advising the cyberstalker that such behavior might constitute a criminal offense, both stalkers ceased their harassment.[40] Perhaps the greatest problem in the area of cyberstalking is the lack of enforcement and lack of attention being placed on this crime. Investigators and law enforcement agencies are relatively ill equipped to deal with cyberstalking for a variety of reasons. First, and most prominent, is the lack of reporting on the part of

---

BOX 7.5   New State Cyberstalking Law

On April 1, 2001, amendments to the Michigan criminal stalking law were signed that make it illegal for a person to post a message through an electronic medium, including the Internet, if the sender intends to make the victim feel terrorized, frightened, intimidated, or harassed, and the action causes the victim to suffer emotional distress or feel terrorized, frightened, intimidated, or harassed. Violations of the law constitute felonies and can carry prison sentences of up to two years or fines of up to $2,000. The new law also provides more stringent penalties, up to five years in prison and $10,000 in fines, if the message is a violation of a restraining order, injunction, or condition of release.

Source: Office of Victims of Crime. (2002). National Victim Assistance Academy. Washington, DC: Office of Justice Programs. Available on line: *http://www.ojp.usdoj.gov/ovc/assist/nvaa2002/chapter22_2sup.html*

victims. Again, many people report that they do not think what has occurred is a crime or that they doubt the ability of law enforcement to do anything about the crime. Second, most law enforcement agencies are not trained to recognize the serious nature of cyberstalking and to investigate such offenses. Unfortunately, some victims have reported that rather than open an investigation, a law enforcement agency has advised them to come back if the cyberstalkers confront or threaten them off line. In several instances, victims have been told by law enforcement simply to turn off their computers.[41] Finally, even if reporting were higher, the overwhelming majority of law enforcement agencies are ill prepared to deal with cyberstalking because of lack of resources, lack of investigative tools, and lack of trained personnel. Most large law enforcement agencies now have computer crime units, with extraordinarily busy police officers staffing them. Additionally, cyber evidence processors in local law enforcement agencies and the federal government are already overbooked and understaffed.

OBSCENITY ON THE WWW

The issue of what is obscene has been debated in the court systems of the United States for a long period of time. The growth of the Internet has forced the Supreme Court to revisit this slippery issue that lives somewhere between community protection and freedom of speech. The players are the same: on one side, governmental officials and politicians looking to regulate a sexually oriented industry that they feel is linked to a whole host of other, more serious problems; and on the other side, free speech activists, the American Civil Liberties Union, and those who seek to profit from pornography. It is an old battle. The new battlefield, however, presents unique problems and questions for the American legal system. In the past, pornography, especially the seriously hard core, the bizarre, and the illegal kind of pornography, was kept relatively out of sight and required that purveyors either visit a sexually oriented business, purchase the materials in person, or order them via the mail or over the phone. In terms of monitoring, the government had a relatively easy job of tracking and preventing illegal types of pornography from being circulated in the United States. The Internet changed all of that and essentially made pornography, even the hard core and illegal stuff, widely available to the general public.

The old questions of what is and what is not obscene became somewhat secondary in this new battle over the ability of the government to restrict what is posted on the Internet versus free speech.[42] Interestingly, the battle has focused on what both sides of the argument would agree is a problem—child pornography and access to pornography by children. The difference between the two sides lies in the proposed remedies. It is fair to say that neither side would allow child pornography to be shared, posted, or disseminated. However, adult access became the issue in several Supreme Court cases that examined a variety of federal law passed regarding the access of children to the Internet and the ability of government to regulate the Internet. The government's position has consistently been that the onus of regulation is on Internet Service Providers (ISPs) and the people and businesses who wish to post, sell, or disseminate pornography. Laws were passed that mandated that ISPs had to monitor and regulate certain types of pornography, especially child pornography. Further, anyone who wised to sell or promote pornography had to assure that children were not accessing the material, or face federal charges.

On the other side, the onus is placed firmly on the individuals and on the parents of the children. In short, it is up to the individual to self-regulate access, and it is up to parents to assure that children do not access the materials. As is typical, the law ended up squarely in the middle. The prosecution of Internet-related child pornography and luring cases is increasing. The Department of Justice has found that prosecution of these cases has increased by 10 percent every year since 1995. Many of these cases are international in scope. Box 7.6 shows several of the cases that this unit of the Justice Department has handled.

BOX 7.6   Recent Cases in Obscenity and Child Exploitation Prosecuted by the U.S. Attorney

- *Interstate Transportation of a Minor with Intent to Engage in Criminal Sexual Activity/Child Pornography:* A former substitute teacher in Virginia was sentenced to the maximum of 30 years in prison for his convictions on two counts of interstate transportation of a minor with intent to engage in criminal sexual activity and two counts of possession of child pornography. The defendant befriended young males in the 13- to 16-year age range and lured them into engaging in sexual activity by offering them clothes, money, and other gifts.

- *Child Pornography:* A defendant was sentenced to 120 months (10 years) in prison and three years of supervised release after pleading guilty to all counts of a federal indictment charging him with publishing an advertisement to receive, exchange, distribute, and reproduce sexually explicit visual depictions of minors; transporting visual depictions of minors engaged in sexually explicit conduct; possession of materials containing images of minors engaged in sexually explicit conduct; and forfeiture. The defendant admitted that on July 7, 2000, he was operating an f-serve, or automatic image trader. The defendant's f-serve provided Internet users access to images saved on his computer hard drive of minors engaged in sexually explicit conduct. The defendant published an advertisement in an America Online chatroom indicating he had "hardcore" preteen images available.

- *Child Exploitation:* A defendant in Indiana was sentenced to 151 months' (12 years') imprisonment after he pleaded guilty to production and possession of child pornography. In 2001, the defendant used an 11-year-old minor to engage in sexually explicit conduct in order to produce Polaroid pictures.

- *Child Pornography:* A Maryland defendant was sentenced to 41 months (three years) in prison for possession of child pornography. A federal jury convicted the

(continued)

BOX 7.6   continued

defendant in November 2001 after a four-day trial. The case stemmed from a 1999 investigation by the Maryland State Police based on complaints that a computer user had placed an on line profile on a Web site known as Matchmaker.com soliciting persons to have sex with a minor female child.

- *Child Pornography:* A defendant was sentenced to ten years in prison following his conviction after a bench trial for possessing and distributing thousands of images of child pornography. Among other things, the defendant was convicted of publishing an advertisement to receive, exchange, and distribute child pornography. He was also found guilty of four counts of shipping or transporting child pornography. A German law enforcement official saw the defendant's advertisement on an Internet Relay Chat "channel" and was able to download images of child pornography from the defendant's file server. In February 2000, federal agents executed a search warrant at the defendant's home, and agents seized computer equipment that yielded approximately 5,000 images and digital movies of child pornography.

- *Child Pornography:* A former university professor was sentenced to 15 years in prison for conviction on charges of receiving and possessing child pornography. The defendant admitted to downloading on his office computer tens of thousands of graphic images of minors engaged in sexually explicit conduct. He also admitted possessing two tapes of a minor child he videotaped.

- *Internet Enticement/Child Pornography:* A defendant in Georgia was sentenced to 135 months (11 years) in prison, followed by three years of supervised release, for attempted enticement of a minor over the Internet; interstate transportation of child pornography in an automobile; sending child pornography by computer; and possession of child pornography. The court also ordered forfeiture of the defendant's laptop computer, his digital camera, and his cellular telephone. The defendant used telephones and the Internet to send both adult and child pornography, as well as depictions of bestiality, to federal agents acting undercover as a 13-year-old girl. Agents arrested the defendant when he arrived for his rendezvous with the girl.

- *Sexual Coercion of a Minor:* A defendant was sentenced to 96 months (eight years) in federal prison for sexual coercion of a minor. The defendant pleaded guilty in September 2001 to using the Internet to persuade a minor to engage in a sexual act. The evidence revealed that he began a long-term Internet relationship with a 13-year old girl, who he eventually persuaded to perform a sexual act in front of a Web cam. The images were transmitted over the Internet.

Source: http://www.usdoj.gov/criminal/ceos/inves_prosec.htm

Laws and Legislation Protecting Children On Line

Over the past decade, several laws have been proposed and adopted to deal with the issues of child exploitation on the Internet; some of these laws are reviewed in this chapter. For example, the Child Protection and Sexual Predator Punishment Act of 1998 specifically addressed the issues of on line victimization of children. The law prohibits the transfer of obscene material to minors, and increases penalties for offenses against children and for repeat offenders. Furthermore, the act amends the Child Abuse Act of 1990 by requiring on line service providers to report evidence of child pornography offenses to law enforcement agencies.[43] In 1994, the U.S. Congress extended the Mann Act by enacting the Child Sexual Abuse Prevention Act.[44] This act empowers the Justice Department to penalize U.S. citizens traveling across state or national borders to engage in sexual activity with children.[45] The production of sexually explicit depictions of a minor for importation into the United States is also prohibited.[46] Additionally, a child sex tourism provision was added to the 1994 Violent Crime Control and Law Enforcement Act that makes it illegal for a U.S. citizen or permanent resident to travel in interstate or foreign commerce with the intent to engage in sexual acts with a minor that are prohibited under federal law in the United States. This provision applies even if these acts are legal in the destination country.

There are numerous state laws that prohibit the possession, manufacturing, distribution, and sale of child pornography. In many instances, simple possession is a felony. U.S. federal law on child pornography[47] outlines the prohibited behavior and law concerning the distribution and possession of child pornography.[48] The majority of child pornography offenses are covered by federal law in a number of statutes[49] and prohibit the production, sale, transmittal, and possession of child pornography. Additional federal law covers child luring[50] and the transportation of children for sexual purposes.[51] The same statute prohibits traveling for sexual purposes in the United States and abroad. The publication or posting of any information relating to a child for sexual purposes is also prohibited.[52] This statute would apply any time a child predator communicates on line with another child predator and provides personal information about a minor under 16 for criminal sexual purposes.

Federal law on the sexual exploitation of children[53] prohibits people from using children in the production of sexually explicit material. The law also targets parents who allow or force their children to participate in the production of child pornography.[54] The law also prohibits the exchange of child pornography between people and prohibits the publication of advertisements seeking or offering child pornography.[55] Violations of this law are punishable by 10 to 20 years in prison for first offenders, 15 to 30 years for second offenders, and not less than 30 years for anyone with two or more prior offenses.[56] Additional federal law prohibits the transportation or transmittal, reception, distribution, and possession of child pornography.[57] Violation of the portion of the law relating to transportation, transmittal, and distribution carry a maximum sentence of up to 15 years, but a prior conviction carries a mandatory minimum of five years up to a maximum of 30 years in prison. The possession of child pornography carries a maximum sentence of five years with a mandatory minimum of two years to a maximum of ten years for prior offenders. This law has an affirmative defense provision that requires that a person possessed less than three matters of child pornography, took reasonable steps to destroy the materials, and promptly reported the matter to law enforcement officials.[58]

The Child Online Protection Act (COPA) prohibits anyone by means of a commercial Web site from knowingly making a communication that is "harmful to minors" available to minors under 17 years of age for commercial purposes. The prohibited material includes pictures, writings or recordings that are obscene, or that the average person would find, with respect to minors, appeals to the prurient interest; depicts sexual activity in a patently offensive way; and lacks serious literary, artistic, political or scientific value. The offense is a misdemeanor authorizing up to six months' imprisonment and a $50,000 fine for each violation. In addition, the Attorney General is authorized to collect a $50,000 civil penalty for each violation.[59]

In 1998, Congress enacted the Protection of Children from Sexual Predators Act of 1998 (PCSPA) which established new criminal offenses, amended existing statutes, and provided for enhanced penalties. Three new offenses or definitions of offenses were created:

1. *Use of interstate facilities to transmit information about a minor:*[60] Prohibits the use of the mail or facility of interstate or foreign commerce to transmit information about a minor under the age of 16 for criminal sexual purposes.[61] This statute is in response to a case from Illinois where an individual posted a nine-year-old girl's name and telephone number on the Internet, indicating that she was available for sex. The individual initiating the transmission can be fined, imprisoned up to five years, or both.

2. *Transfer of obscene materials to minors:* Prohibits the use of the mails or a facility of interstate or foreign commerce knowingly to transmit, or attempt to transmit, obscene materials to minors under the age of 16.[62] The individual transmitting the materials may be fined, imprisoned for 10 years, or both.

3. *Definition of sexual activity:* Defines criminal sexual activity to include the production of child pornography.[63] Previously, several cases presented for federal prosecution could not be charged because the individual either transported a minor or traveled to meet a minor to produce child pornography, but not for sexual activity.

The new laws also enacted attempt provisions to several laws,[64] increased penalties for several child sexual offenses,[65] made prosecution for child sexual assault possible for imported child pornography,[66] and increased and expanded sentencing for child sexual offenses.[67] The legislation also imposes the death penalty if the death of a child results from the offense,[68] allows for civil forfeiture relating to these offenses,[69] and places an affirmative responsibility on Internet Service Providers to report child pornographic offenses.[70]

The United States Supreme Court has had the opportunity to review several cases involving child pornography and legislation designed to protect children on line. In *Reno*

v. *American Civil Liberties Union*,[71] the Court examined two provisions of the Communications Decency Act of 1996. The first part criminalized the knowing transmission of "obscene or indecent" messages to any recipient under 18 years of age.[72] Another section of the act prohibited the "knowing" sending or displaying to a person under 18 of any message "that, in context, depicts or describes, in terms patently offensive as measured by contemporary community standards, sexual or excretory activities or organs."[73] The Court decided that these two provisions of the Communications Decency Act, specifically the "indecent transmission" and "patently offensive display" provisions, potentially violated the free speech portion of the First Amendment. The Court specifically noted that the act lacked precision of definition, a requirement when justifying the restriction of free speech. The Court noted that the government has an interest in protecting children from potentially harmful materials; however, the Communications Decency Act attempted to pursue that interest by suppressing a large amount of speech that adults have a constitutional right to send and receive. Of particular interest was the analysis the Court made regarding what could be done in this area. Specifically, the Court concluded that the burden the act placed on free speech was not justifiable, given that currently available filtering software is a reasonably effective method by which parents can prevent their children from accessing material which the parents believe is inappropriate.

In *Ashcroft* v. *Free Speech Coalition*,[74] the Supreme Court reviewed provisions of law aimed at child pornography, specifically virtual child pornography. The ability of users to "morph" or alter images and the ability to literally generate virtual pornography led the United States government to add a provision to the Child Pornography Prevention Act of 1996 (CPPA). The new additions to existing child pornography laws now included computer-generated imagery depicting or conveying the impression that a minor is engaged in sexually explicit conduct.[75] An additional section of the new law prohibited production or distribution of materials pandered as child pornography, even if it was not involving actual children. The Supreme Court decided that these two sections were unconstitutional and overbroad. The Court noted that the CPPA was inconsistent with existing jurisprudence regarding obscene material. The act placed an affirmative burden on anyone who might be charged to prove that the material under questions was not child pornography, either because it was fake or because the actors in question were indeed adults. Taken together, these two decisions effectively invalidated two major pieces of legislation regarding obscenity on line; Attorney General Ashcroft complained that the Court had dealt a severe blow to the ability of law enforcement to fight child pornography.

The next major case the Court would decide examined provisions of the Child Online Protection Act (COPA). The COPA legislation was a specific attempt by Congress to address the free speech concerns raised in the *Reno* v. *ACLU* case discussed above. In *Ashcroft* v. *American Civil Liberties Union*,[76] the Court noted that unlike the Communications Decency Act, COPA applies only to material displayed on the World Wide Web, covers only communications made for commercial purposes, and restricts only material that is harmful to minors.[77] In addition, Congress placed a three-part obscenity test in COPA that drew on a previous Supreme Court decision.[78] The Court, although refusing to examine the overbreadth issue because of a technicality, concluded that COPA's reliance on "community standards" to identify what material "is harmful to minors" does not by itself render the statute substantially overbroad for First Amendment purposes. Finally, and most recently, the Court concluded in *United States v. American Library Association*[79] that the provision of the Children's Internet Protection Act requiring libraries receiving federal assistance to have filtering software was not unconstitutional.

In response to the Supreme Court decisions, Congress enacted the Prosecuting Remedies and Tools Against the Exploitation of Children Today Act of 2003 (PRO-TECT Act),[80] which included a wide variety of provisions relating to the exploitation of children. The PROTECT Act strengthens existing U.S. law by increasing imprisonment penalties to 30 years for convicted sex tourists, criminalizing persons or organizations that assist or organize sex tours, and better enabling federal prosecutors to convict offenders by modifying burden of proof requirements. In addition, the new law establishes parallel penalty enhancements that apply to the production of child pornography overseas. The PROTECT Act is a wide-ranging bill pertaining to the investigation, prosecution, and punishment of offenses relating to children and pornography. The PRO-TECT Act also provides criminal penalties for users of innocent-sounding domain names if the owner knowingly uses the domain name to link to sexually explicit material. If a Web site's domain name deceptively draws people to sexually explicit material, the operator could be imprisoned for up to two years. The sentence is increased to four years if the domain name is intended to attract minors to the material. In addition, an offender of either provision can be fined up to $250,000.

CHILD PORNOGRAPHY

Child pornography can be defined simply as depictions of children in a sexual act or in a sexual way. Most policy makers and researchers conclude that this applies to anyone under 18 years of age. Child pornography contains the same types of sexual activities as those depicted in adult pornography, except that the media contains images or descriptions involving children, children and adults, or children and animals or objects.[81] A narrower definition of child pornography would limit the concept to mean only images depicting sexual acts between real children and other children, adults, or some other sexual depiction. Broader definitions would include depictions of children that are sexually suggestive, drawings of children engaged in sexual acts, sexually graphic writings involving children, cartoons suggesting sex with children, etc. Although certain forms of art and writing fall into a gray area subject to debate, clear visual depictions of children engaging in sexual conduct are child pornography and unilaterally prohibited. One study by the Justice Department found a history of child pornography in three mainstream pornographic magazines, *Playboy, Penthouse,* and *Hustler.*[82] The study found between 6,000 and 9,000 (depending on definitional criteria) child images in the three magazines, most involving sex or violence.[83] Of these depictions, 29 percent involved nudity or genital display, 20 percent involved genital activity, 16 percent included sexual contact with an adult, 10 percent involved the use of force, and another 10 percent involved killing or maiming.[84] Regardless of the definition, child pornography is a serious issue with long-term implications for the offender and child victims that have come to the forefront recently because of the Internet.

There is currently no accurate statistical source that reports the extent of or numbers of arrests involving child pornography. One recent estimate noted that at any given time, there are, on average, around one million sexually explicit pictures of children on the Internet. In just one week in December of 1995, 5,651 messages about child pornography were posted on just four electronic bulletin boards. Included in these messages were over 800 graphic pictures of adults or teenagers engaged in sexual activity with children between eight and ten years of age.[85] Clearly, there is still a child pornography "industry" working internationally that produces materials for sale and consumption. Various sources estimate that child pornography comprises anywhere from 5 to 10 percent of the pornography trade, resulting in profits in the millions.[86] Other sources conclude that the extent and profit estimates of the child porn industry are grossly exaggerated.[87] A search on the Internet reveals that there are numerous Web sites that insinuate child pornography, a substantial number of newsgroups that concern child pornography, and a wide variety of writings and other material concerning how to access child pornography. The most common forms, if a broad definition is used, are altered pictures and stories relating to sexual contact with children—both of which were extremely easy to find and document. More thorough investigation and monitoring reveals that child pornography is commonly posted to several newsgroups and can be accessed at some personal Web sites internationally.[88]

Child pornography exists for reasons similar to other forms of pornography; there is a demand for such materials. In contrast to other forms of pornography, there is little discussion of child pornography being a victimless crime or a protected form of free speech. It is fair to assume that very few people would advocate the ready availability and use of child pornography. Child pornography is clearly an abhorrent and unconscionable act to the vast majority of people; however, to the pedophile the collection and use of child pornography is a source of pride, fantasy, and sexual gratification. Child pornography is used by the pedophile to feed and create sexual fantasies, lower the inhibitions of a child who they are planning to molest, and to blackmail a child into remaining silent.[89] In addition, the pedophile uses child pornography as a profit device and in barter with other pedophiles to add to their collection or access other children to victimize.[90] The supply side of the child pornography trade largely consists of pedophiles willing to molest children as well as possess child pornography. As Campagna and Poffenberger[91] note, the single most distinctive characteristic of habitual child molesters is a compelling interest in collecting child pornography. Habitual child molesters categorize their collections in a sophisticated and elaborate way and typically possess a variety of child pornography in several media, including computer files, videotapes, magazines, amateur pictures, books and novels, drawings and art, and several others.[92] The pedophile also typically keeps an annotated journal or diary to record molestations and other details of their crimes. Once apprehended, the pornography and diary become invaluable evidence for prosecution. To the child molester, their child pornography collection is equated with valuable family heirlooms and investments, as the collections can be traded between pedophiles and used as payment for child prostitution.[93] This underground system used to be maintained through group associations, the mail and by telephone; today, the Internet serves as the primary mechanism.

There exist, unfortunately, several national and international organizations dedicated to pedophiles and child sexual exploitation. The links between members in these organizations serve as a communication network for the exchange of child pornography. The North American Man/Boy Love Association (NAMBLA) advocates sexual and emotional relationships between adult males and underage boys. NAMBLA has chapters in many large U.S. cities and publishes a variety of print media for its members (estimated anywhere between 500 and 1,000 in 1988).[94] NAMBLA also has a Web site and annual meetings. Undoubtedly the membership, or at least those willing to access the Web site, has grown with the expansion of the Internet. Another such organization is the Lewis Carroll Collector's Guild, which publishes the newsletter *Wonderland* four times a year. *Wonderland* is a collection of articles and advertisements than promote interest in photographs and artwork pertaining to nude children on the premise that no exploitation is involved.[95] Several other organizations can be found on the Internet and have been documented by law enforcement officials. The common theme of these organizations is the promotion of sex and children. They are also undoubtedly useful for pedophiles to establish connections with others interested in their questionable practices.

BOX 7.7   The North American Man/Boy Love Association (NAMBLA)

NAMBLA stands for the North American Man/Boy Love Association. They are an organization devoted to furthering what they depict as consensual relationships between men and boys. Their Web page has had several addresses recently, indicative of the unwillingness of ISPs to host their site; however, the message has remained the same. Their Web site describes their mission and their purpose:

> The North American Man/Boy Love Association (NAMBLA) supports the rights of all people to engage in consensual relations, and we oppose laws which destroy loving relationships merely on the basis of the age of the participants.
>
> NAMBLA does not say that ALL children should engage in such relationships.
>
> However we believe that when this does occur society should be able to distinguish between those relationships that are loving, supportive and mutually desired, and those which are harmful and involve force or coercion.
>
> NAMBLA unequivocally condemns all coercive or non-consensual acts, sexual or otherwise, between people of any age.
>
> NAMBLA supports youth liberation and the empowerment of young people in all areas of their lives (not just sexual). We believe that there should also be improved education and the establishment of viable community resources so that young people are better able to manage their own lives and function as productive citizens of this society.

Source: http://www.qrd.org/qrd/orgs/NAMBLA/

The U.S. Customs Service initiated an investigation of the Wonderland group, eventually executing search warrants in 31 cities in the United States and cooperating with international law enforcement, leading to searches and warrants in 13 different countries. At the time, Customs officials noted that it was the most extensive ring of child pornographers ever uncovered, involving as many as 200 suspects around the world, 34 of them in the United States. All of the suspects were members of a perverse network trading in images depicting everything from sexual abuse to the actual rape of children. One of the requirements for membership was a stockpile of several thousand images of graphic child pornography. Customs agents tracked these suspects through cyberspace, sifting through a maze of Internet providers, servers, files and screen names. The case resulted in numerous arrests and seizures of computers and other digital evidence. Such cases challenge the patience and capabilities of law enforcement due to the extensive distances between the conspirators and the difficulties associated with sifting through and processing digital evidence. In testimony before Congress, Deputy Assistant Attorney General Kevin V. Di Gregory stated:

> The trafficking in child pornography by computer users has, in some ways, challenged the progress of nearly eighty years of aggressive child pornography investigation and prosecution. Whereas by the early 1990s the Government had largely eradicated the cottage trade within the United States for this material and distribution was typically limited to trading or sharing between individual pedophiles who actually knew each other, today computer technology has reinvigorated both the commercial and non-commercial distribution of obscene child pornography. This reinvigoration means that child pornography produced in the 60s, 70s, and early 80s is now being re-released and distributed to an audience the size of which pedophiles could not have envisioned ten or twenty years ago. Additionally, the ability to mass market child pornography with little or no overhead to huge populations has created an environment where pressures for new material exist. This demand, unfortunately, is being met by new material from sources which include the Pacific Rim, Mexico, and South America. Our investigation has also resulted in the discovery that substantial amounts of written obscenity containing graphic descriptions of torture, bondage, and rape of children are being posted and distributed on the Internet and on private on-line systems. As the World Wide Web continues to grow, we expect that obscene visual images consisting of fantasy drawings or computer-generated images featuring similar themes of child sexual and physical abuse will also be created and made available for distribution. Obscene material, both written and visual, which can be used to seduce, lure, or train children to perform certain acts, must be highlighted and punished differently.

The fact that there really is no way to gauge how extensive the exchange of child pornography is on the Internet underlies perhaps the most serious problem—that law enforcement is only finding the tip of the iceberg in terms of the actual extent of this problem. As high-profile prosecutions began to occur in the late 1990s, the message to pedophiles and purveyors of child pornography was that anonymity was not assured on the Internet. As a result, efforts to conceal their presence, secure their connections, and encrypt their files has become more prevalent in recent years. Therefore, the job of law enforcement in this area has become increasingly difficult.

The "New" Child Pornographers

In the past, child pornography took the form of pictures, magazines and videotapes—many homemade and collected over long periods of time by pedophiles. Pedophiles now use the Internet for four primary purposes: trafficking child pornography, locating children to molest, engaging in inappropriate sexual communication with children, and communicating with other pedophiles.[96] In the past, the distribution and sharing of child pornography was through clandestine newsletters or tightly controlled networks,[97] whereas today the networking and distribution is on line.

In the summer of 1996, a U.S. federal grand jury indicted 13 individuals from the United States and three from Australia, Canada, and Finland, charging them with orchestrating and participating in an on line molestation of ten-year-old girls. The defendants took part in real-time photo shoots where they typed messages requesting photos of the girls in certain poses, while one member shot photos with a digital camera and transmitted the photos back to the group. The defendants were members of the Orchid Club, a private, on line child pornography group that shared sexually explicit images and videos of girls as young as five. To be a member of the Orchid Club, members had to know the password to access photos and on line chat sessions. Initiation to the club required a potential member to describe a personal sexual experience with a child. After the molestation, members allegedly asked that the camera be aimed at the girl's pubic area, and then inquired about traveling to Monterey, California to molest her themselves.

As noted by Lanning and Burgess,[98] child pornography collectors takes great pride in their collections, sometimes numbering in the thousands of pictures, magazines, or videos. In a recent arrest by the U.S. Customs Service, a computer was seized that contained well over 100,000 images of child pornography.[99] The images were catalogued and filed by age, gender, hair color, sex act, and several other variables. Customs officials estimated that it took endless hours of work to enter and develop the file structure containing the images. In the past, the distribution of such a collection would take endless hours of photocopying, film developing, or video processing. If done commercially, it was relatively easy to track the source. Today the individual with the 100,000 images could easily upload the files to the Internet through a variety of mechanisms and methods and distribute them to the masses in a matter of hours. These images could then be downloaded and saved by anyone and redistributed at a later date. Posting child pornography via Web pages has been curtailed substantially over the past decade; however, the distribution via e-mail, newsgroups, bulletin boards, file transfer protocols (ftps), and other direct connect mechanisms continues. In addition, advanced encryption programs and software are now readily available and make detection even more difficult. These facts inevitably lead to the conclusion that the computer and the Internet are facilitating child pornography and changing the nature of manufacturing, distributing, and collecting child pornography.

Unlike other forms of obscenity or pornography, child pornography laws are actively prosecuted. As noted in the U.S. Attorney General's *Report on Pornography*,[100] substantially more federal cases are prosecuted involving child pornography than for violating federal obscenity laws. The enforcement of child pornography laws is compli-

cated by a variety of factors, including detection, distribution networks, and the definition of child pornography itself. Detecting child pornography is difficult, as those who
actively possess and/or distribute the material take great pains to conceal their crimes.
Many times the pornography is not discovered until after the person has been arrested
for a far more serious sexual offense involving a child, at which point the child pornography is used as evidence but not likely to be prosecuted separately. The Internet has
made detection and prosecution all the more problematic. In the past, distribution networks were characterized as "cottage industries" where child pornography was exchanged
between pedophiles.[101] Today, the Internet has produced what is currently being called
a "global cottage industry." The formal publication and distribution was produced internationally outside the United States, and law enforcement considered the domestic
production of materials under control.[102] Child pornography in the United States was
described as primarily amateur photographs and videotapes being produced by pedophiles
and being exchanged through informal networks.[103] These conclusions must now be considered outdated given the extent and nature of law enforcement activities currently on
the Internet. A secondary issue involves the definition and nature of the material itself.

Lanning and Burgess[104] identified several types of "sex rings" that were used by
pedophiles to produce child pornography, victimize children, and prostitute children.
Once detected, these rings involved multiple children and on occasion several adults.
Recently, U.S. Customs officials recently started the International Child Pornography
Investigation and Coordination Center to aid in the investigation of child pornography.
One recent case involved a child pornography ring that was operating in 22 states and
14 countries, involving over 100 suspects. The suspects in this case and several others
currently under investigation are using large hard disks, digital satellite links, cable
modems, and the most current encryption technology to communicate and distribute
child pornography over the Internet.[105] Operation Cheshire Cat, a joint investigation
between the Customs Service and the English National Crime Squad, involved over
100 members of a major pedophile ring that operated in 21 countries. There are numerous state statutes involving obscenity; the test for obscenity is determined by local
community standards. Between October 1st, 1997 and July 31st, 1998, Customs officials had arrested 183 individuals on new charges, convicted another 189 individuals,
and returned 181 indictments on cases involving the possession, manufacture and/or
distribution of child pornography. Agents and local law enforcement personnel go into
chat rooms, news groups, and Internet relay channels assuming fictitious screen names
to document and engage individuals trading in or posting child pornography. As of June
1998, the FBI had executed 427 searches, filed 246 indictments, made 177 arrests, and
convicted 201 people.

Moving from Pornography to Molestation

The theoretical link between child pornography and child molestation has been re-
searched and debated by several experts.[106] The evidence is mixed. Any causal statements that child pornography causes child molestation are not supported by the current
research. Nonetheless, there are some revealing statistics. One survey found that of

42,000 sex offenders, 42 percent reported the use of pornography either immediately prior to or during commission of the act.[107] Although much of the research in this area is limited and of questionable methodology, the "best" research finds harmful effects of pornography exposure.[108] One field study found that between 77 percent and 87 percent of convicted child molesters used pornography to stimulate themselves, to lower the inhibitions of the child victim, or to teach the child to model the activity in real-life sexual encounters.[109] Several compilations and meta-analyses reveal that the link between pornography and sex offending is present, operates more like a correlate or risk factor than a causal factor, and needs more research.[110]

The specific link between child pornography and child sex offending is more pronounced than the pornography/sex offender link, yet it is still not a causal relationship. A review of the current research and literature on child pornography and the link to child molestation reveals that child pornography is one of several potential facilitators in the crime of child molestation or sexual abuse.[111] We cannot determine at this point whether viewing child pornography produces the impulse to molest children initially or whether child pornography is obtained to satisfy or heighten an already present desire to sexually abuse children. Odds are that both of these statements are true to some extent. Child pornography has been found to stimulate the impulse, provide fantasies, and stimulate pedophiles.[112] Some people are particularly vulnerable to the influence of exposure to pornography, but this exposure in and of itself does not cause their sexually aberrant desires or acts.[113] Importantly, however, several research studies have found that as a group child molesters are more aroused by sexual stimuli which depict children than any other forms of pornography.[114] They use child pornography prior to and during their actual assault[115] as a stimulus and as a tool to entice children into the act.

Sexually abusing children is most commonly assumed to be a learned behavior, with child pornography serving several roles in the learning process. A noted clinical psychiatrist in testimony before Congress outlined the role that child pornography plays in the development of a pedophile.[116] Pedophiles are sexual in nature, highly addictive, compulsive and repetitive, and very difficult to treat; self-control and self-discipline don't stop them. The overwhelming majority use child pornography to stimulate their sexual appetites, which they masturbate to then later use as a model for their own sexual acting out with children. Over time the use of child pornography desensitizes the viewer to its pathology; no matter how aberrant or disturbing, it becomes acceptable and preferred. Some also use it to seduce children into engaging in sexual acts with them. When they introduce it to children, the suggestion is that this is normal behavior and many other young people, like themselves, also use it and do these things. Pedophiles often trade, lend, or sell the pictures they make of young people nude and having sex through an informal network. The pedophiles use the pornography during masturbation and eventually become at risk of conditioning themselves into sexual deviancy. In time the "high" obtained from masturbating to pornography becomes more important than real-life relationships. It makes no difference if one is an eminent physician, attorney, minister, athlete, corporate executive, college president unskilled laborer, or an average 16-year-old boy. All can be self-conditioned into deviancy. The process of masturbatory conditioning is inexorable and does not spontaneously remiss. The course of this illness may be slow and is nearly always hidden from view. It is usually a secret part of the man's life, and like a cancer, it keeps growing and spreading. It rarely ever reverses itself, and it is very difficult to treat and heal. Denial on the part of the addict and refusal to confront the problem are typical and predictable. The presence of child pornography creates the potential of many types of harms in the community in creating sexual predators or pedophiles and later their victims.[117] Eventually, the sexually addicted male may move into actual molestation which is recorded and used for further fantasizing and reinforcement.

In conclusion, pedophiles use child pornography for several reasons:

- For personal sexual stimulation
  - Child pornography provides a powerful erotic stimulus to achieve sexual arousal, relive prior sexual acts, visualize fantasies, and focus attention during masturbatory manipulation when alone.
- To reduce the inhibitions of the child
  - After a child's initial shock, a molester will point out that the children and adults in the pictures are enjoying their mutual sexual activities and that "lots of kids do it; pictures don't lie." The perpetrator can then convince the child that it is normal for children to be sexually active with adults, and their fears are unfounded.
- As an instructional tool
  - Pornography is used literally as a textbook of visual instruction to educate children to perform specific sex acts.
- For barter, trade, or sale
  - Transactions may be for money, pornographic materials, or information about how to gain sexual access to children.
- To blackmail the child
  - "Silence is golden when a child has been abused," according to one molester. In addition to silence, a child may be required to recruit siblings or friends for the molester. Many times children are told that they will be ridiculed, disbelieved, or reprimanded by their parents and police if anyone finds out what has taken place. A pedophile knows how to put a heavy burden on the child to bear the blame if his family is broken up and he's taken away, or his parents break up, etc., if the incident ever becomes public.

The pedophile uses a combination of deception, desensitization, and psychological conditioning to lure potential child victims into a sexual molestation relationship. Before any sexual advances are made, the molester generally befriends the child through the use of rewards such as food, toys, movies, or money. This first step of becoming close to the child is part of an elaborate nurturing process leading to a friendly and trusted relationship between the pedophile, the victim, and often times the parents or guardians of the child. Once the relationship is established, the door to sexual abuse and molestation is open. Most pedophiles do not use force or intimidation, but a long-term approach, to gain the confidence of the child.

The molester has such success with children because he communicates with them at their emotional and psychological level. He plays their games, speaks their language, and even likes their toys. In the course of grooming potential victims, each pedophile develops a somewhat unique modus operandi, leaving behind valuable evidence for investigators. Often the investigation in such cases reveals that the pedophile's victims were approached in a similar way and the process leading to the abuse followed a similar pattern. Such evidence is crucial for successful prosecution of the pedophile at a later trial.

The molestation process follows a typical pattern known as the cycle of victimization. First, adult pornography is casually shown to a target child in an effort to raise the child's curiosity level and provide a sex education of sorts. The child is often surprised and bewildered by the images in men's magazines, but the molester explains that these images demonstrate that this kind of behavior is normal and acceptable.

A number of children testified before the 1986 Attorney General's Commission on Pornography that what their molester showed them was to demonstrate that this was what "all big boys and girls did." Once the molester has used adult pornography to convince the child that sex is acceptable, even enjoyable, for children, more deviant forms of pornography are introduced to further the learning process. Actual or simulated child pornography is shown to convince the child that other children regularly participate in sexual activities with adults or peers. Simulated child pornography includes pictures of youthful-looking adults dressed up and acting as children or computer-generated images of children involved in sexual activity. These images can be real or created out of the imagination of a computer user; either way they have the same devastating effect on the children who see them. Continued exposure to pornography lowers the inhibitions of the child to a point where he allows the molester to kiss and touch him sexually. Eventually, if successful, the seduction process progresses to more explicit activity between the child victim and adult or other children, using the pornography as an instructional tool.

Once the desire is initiated in the child to view pornographic materials and once the pedophile realizes that the child will not tell that they have seen the material, the process of molestation progressed into the next level. The child is now exposed to increasingly more graphic pornography, typically depicting children engaging in sexual acts with each other or with adults. Inevitably, questions about the acts being portrayed would arise to be readily answered by the pedophile. The pedophile would then begin to demonstrate that the sexual acts feel good and aren't wrong for the child to engage in. It is often at this point that the child victim is photographed, innocently at first, but eventually progressing to nudity and sexually explicit types of pictures. The attention garnered on the victim is especially damaging if the child has needs for attention and love that are not being fulfilled by their family or friends. Such children are particularly vulnerable to a pedophile's advances.

CHILD MOLESTATION

According to law enforcement statistics, an estimated 89,000 cases of child sexual abuse were substantiated in 2000. However, the true number of actual child sexual abuse cases is much higher. A telephone survey of 2,000 children between the ages of 10 and 16 revealed that 3.2 percent of girls and 0.6 percent of boys had suffered, at some point in their lives, sexual abuse involving physical contact. If one infers that those statistics can be generalized to the rest of the country, children have experienced (but not reported) levels of victimization that far exceed those reported.[118] Most child molesters are able to molest numerous children before they are caught and have only a three percent (3 percent) chance of being apprehended for their crimes. Statistics show that boys and girls are at nearly equal risk for abuse and almost a quarter will be molested sometime before their 18th birthday; however, less than five percent (5 percent) will tell anyone. The overwhelming majority of child victims are abused by someone they know, or a family member. In general, most molestations are perpetrated by adolescent males, but older pedophiles, though fewer in number, molest in greater numbers and with greater frequency.

Child molestation or exploitation can be defined as any sexual behavior or activity that is abusive or nonconsensual toward a child or sexual behavior that is specifically prohibited by state or federal law. Various states have differing definitions and age limits in their statutory rape laws and concerning the age at which a person can voluntarily consent to sexual relations. Some states define a specific age, such as 16, to enumerate the point at which a person can voluntarily consent to sex. Others include an age range difference, such as three years, up to a certain age where a person can consent to sex. For example, a 16-year-old could consent to sex with an 18-year-old but not anyone over the age of 19. While statutory offenses comprise a substantial portion of sexual offenses, largely unreported, the more important area concerns the molestation and exploitation of children by adults and strangers. Fondling, oral sex, simulated or actual intercourse, exhibitionism, taking sexually explicit pictures of children, showing sexually explicit material to children or having sex in front of a child are all considered child sexual abuse. In such cases, the sexual contact is between a child that cannot voluntarily consent to sex and someone in a position of power or trust. The sexual relations are concealed by the abuser through denial, secrecy, and threats to the child. Such cases are the primary focus of this show.

In a stunning study, Abel et al.[119] recruited and interviewed 561 nonincarcerated pedophiles and child molesters. Their findings revealed:

- A total of 291,737 "paraphilic acts" were committed against 195,407 victims under the age of 18.

- The five most frequently reported paraphilic acts involved criminal conduct:
  - Nonincestuous child molestation with a female victim (224 of the 561 subjects reported 5,197 acts against 4,435 victims).
  - Nonincestuous child molestation with a male victim (153 of the 561 subjects reported 43,100 acts against 22,981 victims).
  - Incest with a female victim (159 of the 561 subjects reported 12,927 acts against 286 victims).
  - Incest with a male victim (44 of the 561 subjects reported 2,741 acts against 75 victims).
  - Rape (126 of the 561 subjects reported 907 acts against 882 victims).

The remaining 16 categories included a wide range of paraphilias, which may or may not have involved coercion. The first five categories included a total of 64,872 acts. The total number of subjects and victims cannot be determined since the categories are overlapping (i.e., many subjects reported multiple paraphilias and hence were recorded in multiple categories). This study and other estimates based on victimization studies and self-report crime studies paint a much darker picture of the true extent of sexual assault and child molestation in the United States.

The Problem of Child Sexual Abuse

David Finkelhor developed a four-part model that enunciates how a sex offense occurs between an offender and a child victim. He argues that each part must occur for an offense to take place.

1. *A potential offender must have some motivation to sexually abuse a child.* The potential offender must feel some form of emotional congruence with the child, sexual arousal with the child must be a potential source of gratification, and alternative sources of gratification must be unavailable or less satisfying.

2. *Any internal inhibitions against acting on the motivation to engage in sexual assault must be overcome.* For example, alcohol or drugs may be used in order to lower inhibitions against sexual offending. This may be combined with the knowledge that society often shows greater tolerance toward those who commit crimes while under the influence of substances.

3. *Any external impediments to acting on the impulse to abuse must be overcome.* Inadequate care or supervision by a parent or guardian can provide an opportunity for an offender to act.

4. *Avoidance or resistance by the child must be overcome.* This may involve enticing an emotionally deprived child into accepting inappropriate attention, or overt coercion to achieve domination of the relatively powerless child.

A voyeur or exhibitionist is motivated by a sexual desire for exhibitionist behavior towards children, perhaps as a preliminary step to approaching children or as part of some fantasy. Care or supervision by a guardian is overcome through the exhibitionist exposing themselves to children with their parents or in the presence of other children. There is little, if any, need to overcome resistance as is often the case, the sexual stimulation comes from the reactions of the children involved. In contrast, the incest, molestation, and rape offenders achieve their goals through different mechanisms. The incest offender is motivated by sexual desires and uses the already established power relationship to offend within their own family. These offenders reduce inhibitions through alcohol or drugs frequently; in fact, most offenses between a parent or guardian and their child occur while under the influence of a substance. Additionally, incest offenders victimize children while capable guardians are out of the house, discreetly at night, or when the child is vulnerable. Resistance by the child is overcome through coercion, lying, or through extra attention, leading the child victim into submitting and even welcoming some sexual advances. However, the relationship between the offender and victim is always based on power and control and not voluntary or consensual relations, when the victim is under the age of consent.

Offenders typically select their victims in one of two ways: preselection involving a certain type of child, or a child that they know or through opportunity. Each of these types of offenders has different characteristics discussed previously. Investigators should recognize the differences between a situational child molester and a pedophile. A situational child molester is generally a socially inadequate, low self-esteem, inhibited and introverted individual. They frequently have a substance abuse problem and will deny any involvement in the molestation. There are numerous categorizations of child molesters, but there are four generally recognized types. The first is the *regressed* child molester. This subtype usually leads the most stable life, preferring female victims. Oral and vaginal intercourse is their goal. They tend to always keep a "stable" of potential victims in various stages of seduction. The second type is the *morally indiscriminate* child molester, who frequently exhibits multiple paraphilias and a desire to experiment sexually. They frequently interact with others who share similar desires and will network in attempts to find victims. The third type is the *inadequate* child molester. Their sexual desires vary, but always revolve around a perceived inadequacy in their lives or their inability to mesh socially with other adults. These offenders can progress into serial killers, substituting child murder for the sexual aspect of their offenses. The molestation, in many cases, is driven by a need to "get even" with some perceived injustice experienced by the molester. Finally, the *sexually indiscriminate* molester does not necessarily specialize in a certain type of sex or sexual partner, but will try anything and everything. The difference between this type and the others is the gratuitous use of pornography and the high victim total when eventually apprehended. Table 7.3 depicts the differences among the four types.

TABLE 7.3   Characteristics of the Situational Child Molester

	Regressed	Morally Indiscriminate	Sexually Indiscriminate	Inadequate
Basic characteristics	Poor coping skills	User of people	Sexual experimentation	Social misfit
Motivation	Substitution	Why not?	Boredom	Insecurity and curiosity
Victim criteria	Availability	Vulnerability and opportunity	New and different	Nonthreatening
Method of operation	Coercion, force, younger victims	Lure, force, or manipulation	Involved in existing activity	Exploits size, advantage
Pornography collection	Possible	Sadomasochistic detective magazines	Highly likely, varied	Almost certainly, varied

Source: Deviant and Criminal Sexuality (1993), 2nd edition, NCAVC, FBI Academy.

Pedophiles attracted to teenage boys might have their homes decorated the way a teenage boy would. This might include toys, games, stereos, rock posters, and so on. The homes of some pedophiles have been described as shrines to children or as miniature amusement parks. In addition, virtually every pedophile has access to and a collection of child pornography. Molesters also test and desensitize children by telling dirty jokes, talking about sexual things and engaging in nonsexual physical contact like back rubs, wrestling, hugging, and horseplay. This behavior generally starts long before sexual touching and serves to normalize contact and trust.

Many molesters work just as hard to seduce and manipulate adults as they do to trick children. Most pedophiles think out, far in advance, plans and tactics to use to reduce the likelihood that a child will report the offense. Separate tactics and justifications are used to allay the fears and inquiries voiced by adults. Many have elaborate denial routines and are extremely adept at lying and convincing people that the child is mistaken or has misinterpreted the interactions. Investigators must be extremely adept at interviewing children and adept at working the investigation with the adult guardians, if available. A common presumption is that children will not lie or make up stories about molestation, but several cases in the recent past have demonstrated that pressure by social workers has led some children to make up stories of sexual assault. Investigators must be wary of putting words in the child's mouth and leading them to conclude that they were molested. A common tool is to use anatomically correct dolls to allow children to show exactly what happened. The use of these dolls and other tactics should be done only by a trained investigator familiar with the rule of evidence in these cases and the correct use of investigational tactics when dealing with children.

SEX TOURISM

Sex tourism is a loosely defined practice that encompasses several sexually related practices, some legal in certain countries and some illegal. In many instances, visitors to foreign countries utilize legal brothels and other sexually oriented businesses that are illegal in their home country. In other instances, the visitors use services that are illegal in both countries. Finally, a growing practice is for typically wealthy Westerners to travel specifically to certain countries to procure sexual services of adolescents or to be set up with children for sexual purposes. In sum, sex tourism is the practice of men (there are virtually no known cases of women engaging in this practice) from Western countries visiting developing or third world nations for the purpose of engaging in sexual activity that is illegal in their home country or that they don't want to be discovered committing in their home country. Often, the sexual desires of these tourists are for adolescents, for children, or for a paraphilic or strange sexual encounter. Sex tourism has been growing over the last several decades, with the highest prevalence occurring in Southeast Asian countries, particularly those with long histories of sexually oriented businesses.

The growth of sexual tourism is often attributed to a Western military presence that has increased the demand for sex workers and sexually oriented businesses.

However, recent research shows that many other factors contribute to the sex tourism practice and industry. The sex tourism industry has become an important source of income for many nations, supporting weak economies and aiding in putting money in the hands of governmental officials and law enforcement officials. Thus, eliminating the industry is difficult without the cooperation of the countries where the tourists travel. Without international agreement and implementation of certain standards dictating the way these businesses are owned and operated, it is unlikely that a change in practice will occur. Nonetheless, there have been several attempts made in recent years to change the way that the world views the practice of sexual tourism. Both the United States and the European Union have passed laws making it illegal for citizens to make use of these types of services when underage children are involved. In the future, the elimination of the child sex tourism industry needs to be addressed as well as increased awareness and care for adult sex workers who are forced into this line of work.

Of the 160 pedophiles and sex tourists arrested up to 1994, 25 percent were American, 18 percent German, 14 percent Australian, 12 percent British and 6 percent French. Estimates of the number of children involved in the worldwide sex trade vary. The United Nations Children's Fund (UNICEF) contends that one million children at any one given time are involved in prostitution in Asia alone. End Child Prostitution in Asian Tourism (ECPAT) assesses the value of the prostitution industry to be $5 billion. These appraisals, whether completely accurate or, at least, reflective of educated guesses, bespeak the extent that children are actually affected by sex tourism.[120] Estimates of child prostitutes in South Asia, which are difficult to come by, place the number for Bangladesh at 10,000; India, 400,000–500,000; Pakistan, 40,000; and Sri Lanka, 30,000.[121]

It has been suggested that men are more likely to travel to an Asian nation because they do not speak the same language and therefore all human attributes are obliterated to hide the identity of the girl. Because there can be no verbal communication, the customer does not have to explore the girl's past or even know her name.[122] This situation allows for a completely confidential exchange in which the consumer gets what he paid for and has no connection to the encounter once it is complete.

The Internet is a primary facilitator of the sex tourism industry.[123] It allows for quick and easy access to a number of different destinations and options at a range of prices. These excursions are usually offered in packages in which the men can travel for a desired period of time. For example, in India these trips can be as short as 24–48 hours, during which time sex tourists can experience sexual encounters with a number of different women.[124] In 1999, Philipine Adventure Tours (PAT) of California advertised their tourist package on the Internet. For $1,645, a tourist would receive roundtrip airfare, hotel accommodations and a guided tour of bars where they could purchase sex from prostitutes who were working in bars as entertainers.[125] The Internet allows for men freely to search available destinations and to make choices based on desire and the potential for pleasure. The Internet contributes to the tourism industry and the hidden identity of sex workers through its display of women and children as toys and entertainment. The most dangerous type of person who may retrieve this type of information from the Internet includes pedophiles, who want nothing more than to use and exploit children to fulfill their sexual fantasies and desires.

Although little research exists on how tourists find their way to these hotels and brothels abroad, clearly the Internet has led to an explosion of interest in this area. The process typically begins with the viewing or exchanging of pornography on the World Wide Web, via newsgroups or via ftps and file exchange software. Many sex offenders and pedophiles report on sex rings or clubs that they have encountered on the Internet. The clubs routinely trade pornography. Some also provide services in the way of information and the procurement of sex workers for interested parties willing to pay for their visits. The exchange of information revolves around known hotels where sexual services can be obtained, bars or nightclubs where contacts can be made, or sex clubs and brothels where these people can go for services. The process a sex tourist goes through to be trusted by the club or ring prior to gaining the information they need is unclear. In some cases, the sex club or brothel will advertise in the newsgroups, via e-mail, or even posted directly to the Web (deviant sexual services and sex with children is not commonly advertised or posted). There are reports that child sex rings are shuffling children between pedophiles for sex in these countries and even in the United States. The price for admission to the club or sex ring is often photographs of the potential member engaged in a sexual act with the children.

The Process of Sex Tourism

The sex tourist encounter is rather typical. The sex tourist is usually male, most likely either from Europe or North America. Some of the perpetrators are pedophiles, but most are "respectable" doctors, lawyers, servicemen and teachers—many with children of their own.[126] Sex tourists are generally divided into two groups: preferential abusers and situational abusers. Preferential abusers, the pedophiles, have clear and definite sexual preferences for children, while situational abusers generally have not planned to have commercial sex while abroad, but took the opportunity when it presented itself. Most of these perpetrators tell themselves that there is no abuse or harm occurring to the child because the child has actively "chosen" that "profession." They also assume that because the child has "chosen" prostitution, the child consents to and ultimately benefits from sexual relations with adults, and that commercial sex is a way to help children out of poverty. Many of these perpetrators believe that the victims are inferior people and thus they have little problem with or remorse about exploiting them. Steinman[127] outlines an interview with a sex tourist to Latin America:

> "On this trip, I've had sex with a 14-year-old girl in Mexico and a 15-year-old in Colombia," says a 65-year-old retired Orlando schoolteacher. He talks about his trip, on the condition of anonymity, in a ramshackle casino in downtown Tegucigalpa. For three months this winter, the divorced grandfather traveled Latin America, visiting brothels. He sees nothing wrong with having sex with teens. "I'm helping them financially," he says. "If they don't have sex with me, they may not have enough food. If someone has a problem with me doing this, let UNICEF feed them. I've never paid more than $20 to these young women, and that allows them to eat for a week." Sexual tourists attempt to delude themselves that they commit no wrong by telling themselves that Latin American cultures are less sexually inhibited and sexually freer than Western societies. They rationalize this by

maintaining that "girls in these countries are portrayed as grown up and sexually experienced at 14 already, and that there is no stigma attached to prostitution." Many of these perpetrators enjoy the anonymity of traveling abroad, which releases them from social constraints that they would feel in their home countries. Child sex tourists persuade themselves that in another country, normal social and moral restraints can be discarded, along with the belief that one will not be held responsible for his behavior. It is within these circumstances that child sexual exploitation thrives.

The tour can be self-initiated by the sex tourist with the aid of the Internet and sales brochures. It is common that many of them will hear about certain hotels or bars where such services can be procured, usually through word of mouth or via the Internet. Other tourists utilize the services of a procurer or facilitator. Procurers and facilitators are simply the pimps who provide the services, capital, and resources that make sexual trafficking of children both a feasible and lucrative industry. Some of the procurers are former child prostitutes, who "climbed the ranks" within the industry.[128] Facilitators, while often not directly involved in the child prostitution transaction itself, expedite the victimization process. The facilitator might be a recruiter, a parent who sells his or her child into prostitution, a landlord or motel owner who permits the activity to occur on his or her property, or a sex tour travel agent. These sex tour travel agents publish brochures and guides that cater to sex tourists. The brochures emphasize the youth of prostitutes at these advertised destinations. In 1999, there were over 25 businesses in the United States that offered and arranged sex tours.[129]

Thailand, the Philippines, Sri Lanka, and Taiwan are the countries traditionally connected with child sex tourism, and all have serious child prostitution problems. Prostitution of a massive nature involving children originated in Thailand and the Philippines in the late 1960s, during the Vietnam War. In Thailand, Burmese women and girls as young as 13 are illegally trafficked across the border by recruiters, and sold to brothel owners. In the Philippines, many children are tricked into prostitution after their parents sell them to recruiters with the promise of legitimate work in the city. The Philippine government has calculated the number of child prostitutes in the Philippines at 50,000.[130] During the late 1970s and early 1980s, pedophiles from Europe and North America found a Shangri-La for sexual activity with minors in Thailand and the Philippines. More than half of the sex tourists overall are pedophiles, and approximately one-third of them are North American or European.[131] Currently, tourist agencies actively campaign to entice travelers to visit their countries for sex with "young women." Although agents running these tourist organizations deny that child prostitutes are involved, investigations by reporters illustrate that is untrue. Some agencies go as far as to compose travel guides delineating the laws of countries patrons visit and explain how prosecution for sex tourism in those countries is avoidable. Patrons' willingness to travel to engage in sexual activity with children clearly shows that the child sex industry will continue to thrive, especially if ignored.[132]

As growing international attention has increased public awareness of the prevalence and dangers associated with sex tourism, prosecution against sex tourists and owners of such establishments have also become more prevalent. Many of the recent cases which have been successfully prosecuted have been against older men who engage in child sex tourism. For example, in 1996, Michael Clark, a British citizen, was convicted of inducing child prostitution and sentenced to over 16 years in prison. Clark organized sex tours and provided minor children for the pleasure of sex tourists in the Philippine cities of Olongapo and Angeles. The Philippine court also ruled him to be deported after serving his sentence and he has been barred from ever returning to the Philippines.[133]

In 2002, a businessman out of Dallas, Texas was convicted of having traveled out of the country to engage in sexual conduct with a minor. Nicholas Bredimus traveled to Thailand where he sought the companionship of young girls and boys, photographed himself engaged in sexual conduct with the children, and took explicit photos of young boys. Bredimus was sentenced to $6\frac{1}{2}$ years in prison, a $30,000 fine, and three years of supervised release following his sentence, during which time his access to children and the Internet will be closely monitored.[134] The author had the opportunity to interview Mr. Bredimus prior to his sentencing for these crimes and can offer the following description of the offense.

Mr. Bredimus was a well known and well liked software designer and airline consultant in the Dallas area. The details of his background in sex offenses and how he obtained the knowledge of the sex tourism industry is still sketchy. However, he was able to arrange several visits to Thailand, where he obtained sexual services through a procurer. Mr. Bredimus also obtained fake passports that he used to leave the country from a vacation in Hawaii. On the particular trip that he was convicted for, he left Hawaii, traveled to Japan, and then to Thailand. Once in Thailand he made his way to a border town (on the border with Burma) called Mae Sai, where he arranged for his procurer to rent two adjacent hotel rooms and then asked that young boys aged 10 to 15 be brought to one of the rooms.

The procurer met with a bellman at another hotel known to be a sex tourist location and he helped the procurer round up six boys aged 11 to 14. Each of the boys was paid approximately $22 for their services. He systematically examined each of the boys, rejecting one of them for having a deformed toe, and each boy was ordered to shower prior to being led into the room that Bredimus occupied. In his room, he had set up his laptop, a digital video camera, and had a still digital camera with him. Each boy was led in systematically and ordered to undress. Mr. Bredimus was in his underwear and proceeded to molest the boys while filming each encounter with the video camera on the tripod and taking pictures with the camera. The level of sexual assault increased over the course of the event, with Bredimus eventually inserting his finger into the anus of one of the boys who cried out in anguish. One of the boys left the hotel and alerted the police that a Westerner was in the hotel molesting young boys. The Thai police knocked on the door and eventually had to force their way into the room. They stopped Mr. Bredimus as he was attempting to erase the images on the camera and video camera. The Thai police seized his equipment and arrested him. He was able to bond out for $13,000; incredibly, the Thai police returned his laptop to him, as they were unable to crack the password on the computer.

Mr. Bredimus fled the country with another phony passport, eventually returning to Hawaii. The case would never have come to light had it not been for the work of Fight Against Child Exploitation (FACE), a Thai-based organization that alerted U.S. officials to the crimes. American law enforcement officials then went to Thailand to interview the police and victims, and eventually brought charges against Mr. Bredimus in the U.S. District Court in Dallas. This case is one of the first in the United States where a child sex tourist has been successfully sent to prison. It also demonstrates the extraordinary difficulty in dealing with crimes such as these that occur abroad.

ISSUES IN THE INVESTIGATION OF INTERNET EXPLOITATION, CYBERSTALKING, AND OBSCENITY

Numerous challenges and obstacles exist to effectively enforcing and prosecuting these types of cybercrimes. First, there are numerous, and overlapping, law enforcement initiatives that target these types of crime. There is already a problem: Overlapping effort, overlapping jurisdictions, and a general lack of funding and priority dedicated to these types of crimes are pronounced. Second, the cybercriminal of today is elusive, largely anonymous, and often likely to be operating in a jurisdiction outside of the United States. Finally, there are several evidentiary issues and problems in the prosecution of these types of crimes that make it more difficult to gain a conviction.

Law Enforcement Initiatives

The primary federal agencies that have been combating this type of crime are the FBI, the Customs Service, the Postal Inspection Service, the Department of Justice's Child Exploitation and Obscenity Section (CEOS), and the National Center for Missing and Exploited Children (NCMEC).[135] In 1995, the FBI initiated Innocent Images, which is a proactive, intelligence-driven, multiagency investigative initiative. It serves as the clearinghouse and coordinating body for all FBI investigations that involve child exploitation or child pornography. Within three years, the unit secured 232 convictions. The U.S. Customs Service initiated the Cyber Smuggling Center, which develops leads about cybercrime, and receives and coordinates undercover operations against international child pornography and child sexual exploitation rings. Some of these leads come from the center's Web site, which received almost 6,000 tips between November 1997 and November 1998.[136]

The National Center for Missing and Exploited Children (NCMEC) produced a Cyber Tipline for leads about child sexual exploitation.[137] Mandated by Congress, the Cyber Tipline allows individuals to report on line (and via a toll-free number) incidents of child luring, molestation, pornography, sex tourism, and prostitution. Since March 1998, the Cyber Tipline has received over 8,000 reports of child pornography alone.[138] The Postal Inspection Service has conducted more than 3,500 child exploitation investigations, resulting in the arrest and conviction of over 2,900 child molesters and pornographers.[139] Their investigations of child molesters reveal that these offenders are using computers increasingly, along with the mail, to find potential victims, to communicate with other criminals, and to locate sources of child pornography. In 1998, nearly half of the Service's child exploitation cases involved computers.[140] The undercover operations include the placement of contact advertisements in sexually oriented publications, written contact and correspondence with subjects of investigations, development of confidential sources, and more recently, undercover contact with suspects via the Internet. The Child Exploitation and Obscenity Section of the Justice Department (CEOS) has taken an active role in training federal prosecutors to handle child crime cases that were once mainly handled by local jurisdictions. The section has sponsored several training seminars for federal prosecutors on the issues of child pornography and child exploitation. In addition to these operations, many law enforcement agencies of the federal government have begun to seek partnerships with corporations and local law enforcement to target cybercrime. These partnerships are frequently called electronic crime task forces, and seek to coordinate efforts and eliminate overlap.

Overlapping Jurisdictions and Duplication of Effort

The government currently has numerous operations dedicated to child pornography and additional units and operations targeting obscenity in general.[141] As is the case with other areas of law enforcement, a problem exists with overlapping jurisdictional boundaries and duplication of effort between agencies. Two examples cited in a recent report on cybercrime highlight the problems of overlapping effort:[142]

> Some state and local law enforcement agencies also have been frustrated by jurisdictional limitations. In many instances, the cyberstalker may be located in a different city or state than the victim, making it more difficult (and, in some cases, all but impossible) for the local authority to investigate the incident. Even if a law enforcement agency is willing to pursue a case across state lines, it may be difficult to obtain assistance from out-of-state agencies when the conduct is limited to harassing e-mail messages and no actual violence has occurred. A number of matters have been referred to the FBI and/or U.S. Attorney's offices because the victim and suspect were located in different states and the local agency was not able to pursue the investigation.

Cybercriminals can cross national or international boundaries at will via a computer and information and property can be easily transmitted through communications and data networks. As a result, law enforcement agencies are forced to try to work with local officials, foreign governments, and other agencies of the federal government—something that they have been quite reluctant to do in the past. As one report noted, a law enforcement official could secure a search warrant for a computer in the United States and, as a result of the search, remotely access a computer in Canada, which irrespective of the warrant is potentially a crime in Canada. Further, certain cybercrimes that are illegal in this country are perfectly legal in other countries (i.e., gambling, prostitution, and underage sexual relations). As a result, Congress has passed some laws that make certain offenses a crime regardless of whether they are legal in the host country.

Identification of Suspects

We all tend to enjoy the feeling of anonymity that the Internet provides, allowing us to conduct business and communicate without fear of "somebody listening" to our personal communications. Several Web services offer anonymous e-mail and Web accounts.

Further, it is quite difficult to trace some communications over the Net, especially with the availability of access on numerous college campuses and Internet cafes. Further, many criminals assume the identity of someone else to conduct their crimes on line, theft of e-mail addresses and hacking into someone else's computer to conduct business (making that computer a zombie). Another service provided by some ISPs are mail servers that purposefully strip identifying information and transport headers from electronic mail. By forwarding mails through several of these services serially, cybercriminals can make the message almost completely anonymous. The sending of anonymous communications is thus relatively easy for the criminal and makes it difficult for law enforcement to identify the suspect responsible for the crime.

Issues with Evidence and Detection

The problems of evidentiary collection and analysis are fully discussed in Chapters 11 and 12; however, a few problems in this area deserve mention. As you are aware, computer data is easily destroyed, deleted, or modified. The discussion of the morphing of images and the purposeful alteration of material has already reached the Supreme Court. Further, the technical capability to collect, preserve, and analyze such evidence is not widely distributed in the law enforcement community. Finally, the fact that people can use their computers to conduct both lawful and unlawful activities or to store both contraband and legally possessed material presents another significant issue.[143] Termed commingling, one computer can be used in multiple fashion, by multiple users, and be connected to multiple other machines. As such, investigations would naturally have to cross boundaries, invade computers that were not necessarily involved in the criminal act, and involve people who might be upset at the intrusiveness of the investigation.

Enforcement of the laws against child pornography often leads law enforcement officials to use sting operations over the Internet to catch pedophiles and find child pornography. As such, issues of entrapment have been raised by civil rights groups. In one case, postal inspectors posed as an organization that dealt in sexual freedom and hedonism. They seized several mail lists of individuals in raids of pornography distributors. Then they sent out a sexual attitude questionnaire and a membership application to people on the mail list. The suspect completed and mailed in the sexual survey with his membership fee, noting that he would like to receive additional material and that he was interested in sexual depictions of preteenagers. He was then mailed another survey and a list of "pen pals" who shared his sexual interests. The suspect began corresponding with one of these pen pals, an undercover postal inspector. Over a period of 27 months, the suspect received "two sexual attitude surveys, seven letters measuring his appetite for child pornography, and two sex catalogues."[144] He was assured in the mailings that the materials were completely legal. Over the course of the investigation, he corresponded eight times with the inspectors and eventually ordered the magazine "Boys Who Love Boys" from a Postal Service catalogue and a set of sexually explicit photographs of young boys from a Customs Service brochure. Upon verifying that the man had received the magazine, postal inspectors searched his home, finding the illicit magazine, and arrested him for receiving it through the mail in violation of federal law. At trial, man raised two defenses. First, he argued that he had been entrapped as a matter of law, but the court found sufficient evidence of predisposition to submit the issue to the jury. Second, he asserted that the government's conduct was outrageous, thus violating his due process rights. The jury rejected his defenses and found him guilty of knowingly receiving through the mail sexually explicit material depicting a minor. He appealed his conviction to the Eighth Circuit, which affirmed the trial court, holding that the government's actions did not constitute entrapment or outrageous governmental conduct, despite the government's lack of reasonable suspicion to target the man as a predisposed consumer.[145]

S U M M A R Y

This chapter reviewed the nature and dynamics of exploitation, stalking, and obscenity on the World Wide Web. A variety of victimizations can occur on line, many that are similar to their noncyberspace counterparts. In particular, the nature of the victimizations included threats, obscene comments and intimations, and exposure to obscene and threatening materials, including pictures and other media. Most often, children and women are the primary targets of those who would commit cyberstalking and exploitation over the Internet. Young people report relatively high rates of victimization while on line and many youths report exposure to sexually oriented and obscene material that they did not wish to view. Most commonly, white males between the ages of 18 and 35 make up the majority of the offenders. Similar to most criminal victimizations, the victim and the offender had some type of prior relationship before the stalking or exploitation occurred. However, the percentage of stranger-on-stranger victimizations on line was higher. Children are most commonly victimized on line through unwanted exposure to sexually related material, sexual solicitations and approaches, harassment, and other distressing incidents. The rates of these types of offenses is larger than most people would think. Children rarely report such incidents to their parents or other authorities.

The laws and legislation targeting on line stalking, exploitation, and obscenity are in their infancy, with many of these laws being challenged in the court system. The Supreme Court of the United States has had the opportunity to hear several cases regarding cybercrime laws. Many of the same issues involving noncybercrimes are being heard by the court. Many of the laws were overturned for being too vague and sweeping with too broad of a stroke. The federal government has responded with the passage of new laws and refinements of the old laws in an attempt to regulate and control content on the Internet, particularly the access of children to objectionable content. These types of crimes also present unique difficulties for law enforcement, including lack of expertise, lack of resources, and difficulty in tracking and prosecuting offenders. Cyberspace offers greater anonymity for offenders and permits offending to cross state and international boundaries, making prosecution increasingly difficult. In the future, local law enforcement agencies are likely to see increased reports of cyberrelated cases of stalking, exploitation, and exposure to unwanted materials.

REVIEW QUESTIONS

1. What are the various types of exploitation that can occur over the Internet?
2. What are the characteristics of the typical victims of Internet exploitation crimes?
3. What are the characteristics of the typical perpetrators of Internet exploitation crimes?
4. How common is it to become the victim of an Internet-involved crime in the area of exploitation or stalking?
5. What is cyberstalking?
6. What types of offenses can occur that could be defined as cyberstalking?
7. What are the primary types or categories of stalkers?
8. What are the primary federal laws that target Internet exploitation?
9. What are the major Supreme Court cases on cyber exploitation?
10. How prevalent is child pornography on the Internet?
11. How do pedophiles and other child exploiters use the Internet to commit their crimes?
12. What role does child pornography play in child molestation?
13. What is sex tourism?
14. What are the roles of the various law enforcement agencies in the area of cyber exploitation?
15. What are the primary challenges that law enforcement agencies face in investigating cyber exploitation?

ENDNOTES

1. Office for Victims of Crime (2001). *Internet Crimes Against Children.* Washington, DC: U.S. Department of Justice.
2. Youth Advocate Program International (1998). "Children for Sale: Youth Involved in Prostitution, Pornography and Sex Trafficking." *Youth Advocate Program International Report Vol. 3, No. 2, Summer.* Available on line: *http://www.yapi.org*
3. *Ibid.*
4. Office for Victims of Crime. (2001). *Internet Crimes Against Children.* Washington, DC: U.S. Department of Justice.
5. UNICEF (2001). *Profiting from Abuse: An investigation into the sexual exploitation of our children.* United Nations. Available on line: *http://www.unicef.org/publications/index_5623.html.*
6. *Ibid.*
7. *Ibid.*
8. FINKELHOR, DAVID, KIMBERLY J. MITCHELL, and JANIS WOLAK (2000). *Online Victimization: A Report on the Nation's Youth.* Washington, DC: National Center for Missing and Exploited Children.
9. *Ibid.* at x.
10. *Ibid.* at ix.
11. *Ibid.,* p. 21.
12. Office of Victims of Crime (2002). Strengthening Anti-Stalking Laws. Washington, DC: National Institute of Justice. NCJ 189192.
13. *Ibid.*
14. *Ibid.*
15. *Ibid.*
16. Under California law, a person commits stalking if he or she "willfully, maliciously, and repeatedly follows or harasses another person and . . . makes a credible threat with the

intent to place that person in reasonable fear for his or her safety, or the safety of his or her immediate family." The term "credible threat" includes "that performed through the use of an electronic communication device, or a threat implied by a pattern of conduct or a combination of verbal, written, or electronically communicated statements." "Electronic communication device" includes "telephones, cellular phones, computers, video recorders, fax machines, or pagers." Office of Victims of Crime (2002). Strengthening Anti-Stalking Laws. Washington, DC: National Institute of Justice. NCJ 189192.

17. Office of Victims of Crime (2002). National Victim Assistance Academy. Washington, DC: Office of Justice Programs. Available on line: *http://www.ojp.usdoj.gov/ovc/assist/nvaa2002/chapter22_2sup.html*

18. MELOY, J.R. (1998). *In* MELOY, J.R. (1998). *The Psychology of Stalking: Clinical and Forensic Perspectives.* San Diego, CA: Academic Press.

19. Office of Victims of Crime (2002). National Victim Assistance Academy. Washington, DC: Office of Justice Programs. Available on line: *http://www.ojp.usdoj.gov/ovc/assist/nvaa2002/chapter22_2sup.html*

20. PETHERICK, WAYNE (2003). *Cyber-Stalking: Obsessional Pursuit and the Digital Criminal.* Court TV Crime Library. Available on line: *http://www.crimelibrary.com/criminal_mind/psychology/cyberstalking/1.html*

21. Office of Victims of Crime (2002). National Victim Assistance Academy. Washington, DC: Office of Justice Programs. Available on line: *http://www.ojp.usdoj.gov/ovc/assist/nvaa2002/chapter22_2sup.html*

22. *Ibid.*

23. *Ibid.*

24. *http://www.mcafee.com/anti-virus/parents/contributors.asp*

25. PETHERICK, WAYNE (2003). *Cyber-Stalking: Obsessional Pursuit and the Digital Criminal.* Court TV Crime Library. Available on line: *http://www.crimelibrary.com/criminal_mind/psychology/cyberstalking/1.html*

26. Office of Victims of Crime (2002). National Victim Assistance Academy. Washington, DC: Office of Justice Programs. Available on line: *http://www.ojp.usdoj.gov/ovc/assist/nvaa2002/chapter22_2sup.html*

27. Attorney General to the Vice President (1999). *1999 Report on Cyberstalking: A New Challenge for Law Enforcement and Industry.* Available on line: *http://www.usdoj.gov/criminal/cybercrime/cyberstalking.htm*

28. TJADEN, P., and N. THEONNES (1998). *Stalking in America: Findings from the National Violence Against Women Survey.* Washington, DC: U.S. Department of Justice, National Institute of Justice; Office of Victims of Crime (2002). National Victim Assistance Academy. Washington, DC: Office of Justice Programs. Available on line: *http://www.ojp.usdoj.gov/ovc/assist/nvaa2002/chapter22_2sup.html*

29. *Ibid.*

30. *Ibid.*

31. See, e.g., ZONA, M.A., K.K. SHARMA, and M.D. LANE (1993). "A Comparative Study of Erotomanic and Obsessional Subjects in a Forensic Sample." *Journal of Forensic Sciences,* 38, p. 894–903; GEBERTH, V.J. (1992). "Stalkers." *Law and Order,* October, 138–143; J.A. WRIGHT, A.G. BURGESS, A.W. BURGESS, A.T. LASZLO, G.O. MCCRARY, and J.E. DOUGLAS (1996). "A Typology of Interpersonal Stalking." *Journal of Interpersonal Violence,* 11 (4) 487–503; M.A. ZONA, R.E. PALAREA, and J.C. LANE (1998). "Psychiatric Diagnosis and the Offender–Victim Typology of Stalking." *In* MELOY, J.R. (1998). *The Psychology of Stalking: Clinical and Forensic Perspectives.* San Diego, CA: Academic Press; P.E. MULLEN (1997).

"Erotomanias: (Pathologies of Love) and Stalking." *Directions in Mental Health Counselling,* 7 (3), p. 3–15; and WAYNE PETHERICK (2003). *Cyber-Stalking: Obsessional Pursuit and the Digital Criminal.* Court TV Crime Library. Available on line: *http://www.crimelibrary.com/ criminal_mind/psychology/cyberstalking/1.html*; Office of Victims of Crime (2002). National Victim Assistance Academy. Washington, DC: Office of Justice Programs. Available on line: *http://www.ojp.usdoj.gov/ovc/assist/nvaa2002/chapter22_2sup.html*

32. Office of Victims of Crime (2002). National Victim Assistance Academy. Washington, DC: Office of Justice Programs. Available on line: *http://www.ojp.usdoj.gov/ovc/assist/ nvaa2002/chapter22_2sup.html*

33. *Ibid.*

34. Attorney General to the Vice President (1999). *1999 Report on Cyberstalking: A New Challenge for Law Enforcement and Industry.* Available on line: *http://www.usdoj.gov/ criminal/cybercrime/cyberstalking.htm*

35. *Ibid.*

36. *Ibid.*

37. 18 U.S.C. 875(c).

38. 47 U.S.C. 223.

39. 18 U.S.C. 2261A.

40. Computer Crime and Intellectual Property Section (CCIPS) (2000). *The Electronic Frontier: The Challenge of Unlawful Conduct Involving the Use of the Internet: A Report of the President's Working Group on Unlawful Conduct on the Internet.* Washington, DC: Department of Justice. Available on line: *http://www.usdoj.gov/criminal/cybercrime/ unlawful.htm*

41. Attorney General to the Vice President (1999). *1999 Report on Cyberstalking: A New Challenge for Law Enforcement and Industry.* Available on line: *http://www.usdoj.gov/ criminal/cybercrime/cyberstalking.htm*

42. *Miller* v. *California,* 413 U.S. 15, held that (1) obscene material was not protected by the First Amendment; (2) the proper First Amendment standards to be applied by the states in determining whether particular material was obscene and subject to regulation, were (a) whether the average person, applying contemporary community standards, would find that the work, taken as a whole, appealed to the prurient interest, (b) whether the work depicted or described, in a patently offensive way, sexual conduct specifically defined by the applicable state law, as written or authoritatively construed, and (c) whether the work, taken as a whole, lacked serious literary, artistic, political, or scientific value; (3) there was no requirement that the material must be shown to be "utterly without redeeming social value"; (4) the requirement that state law, as written or construed, must specifically define the sexual conduct as to which depiction or description was proscribed, provided fair notice as to what public and commercial activities would bring prosecution, and (5) obscenity was to be determined by applying "contemporary community standards," not "national standards"— there thus having been no constitutional error in instructing the jury in the instant case to apply state community standards.

43. Public Law 105-314: The Child Protection and Sexual Predator Punishment Act of 1998, October 30, 1998.

44. (Child Abuse Act), 18 U.S.C. 2423(b).

45. 18 U.S.C. § 2423 (b) Travel with intent to engage in illicit sexual conduct. A person who travels in interstate commerce or travels into the United States, or a United States citizen or an alien admitted for permanent residence in the United States who travels in foreign commerce, for the purpose of engaging in any illicit sexual conduct with another person

shall be fined under this title or imprisoned not more than 30 years, or both. (c) Engaging in illicit sexual conduct in foreign places. Any United States citizen or alien admitted for permanent residence who travels in foreign commerce, and engages in any illicit sexual conduct with another person shall be fined under this title or imprisoned not more than 30 years, or both.

46. 18 U.S.C. § 2260.
47. Title 18 Part I, Chapter 110, Section 2252.
48. Child Pornography Prevention Act 18 U.S.C. § 2252A.

  (a) Any person who

    (1) knowingly mails, or transports or ships in interstate or foreign commerce by any means, including by computer, any child pornography;

    (2) knowingly receives or distributes

      (A) any child pornography that has been mailed, or shipped or transported in interstate or foreign commerce by any means, including by computer; or

      (B) any material that contains child pornography that has been mailed, or shipped or transported in interstate or foreign commerce by any means, including by computer;

    (3) knowingly reproduces any child pornography for distribution through the mails, or in interstate or foreign commerce by any means, including by computer;

    (4) either

      (A) in the special maritime and territorial jurisdiction of the United States, or on any land or building owned by, leased to, or otherwise used by or under the control of the United States Government, or in the Indian country, knowingly sells or possesses with the intent to sell any child pornography; or

      (B) knowingly sells or possesses with the intent to sell any child pornography that has been mailed, or shipped or transported in interstate or foreign commerce by any means, including by computer, or that was produced using materials that have been mailed, or shipped or transported in interstate or foreign commerce by any means, including by computer; or

    (5) either

      (A) in the special maritime and territorial jurisdiction of the United States, or on any land or building owned by, leased to, or otherwise used by or under the control of the United States Government, or in the Indian country, knowingly possesses any book, magazine, periodical, film, videotape, computer disk, or any other material that contains an image of child pornography; or

      (B) knowingly possesses any book, magazine, periodical, film, videotape, computer disk, or any other material that contains an image of child pornography that has been mailed, or shipped or transported in interstate or foreign commerce by any means, including by computer, or that was produced using materials that have been mailed, or shipped or transported in interstate or foreign commerce by any means, including by computer, shall be punished as provided in subsection (b).

  (b)

    (1) Whoever violates, or attempts or conspires to violate, paragraphs (1), (2), (3), or (4) of subsection (a) shall be fined under this title or imprisoned not more than 15 years, or both, but, if such person has a prior conviction under this chapter, chapter 109A, or chapter 117, or under the laws of any State relating to aggravated sex-

ual abuse, sexual abuse, or abusive sexual conduct involving a minor or ward, or the production, possession, receipt, mailing, sale, distribution, shipment, or transportation of child pornography, such person shall be fined under this title and imprisoned for not less than 5 years nor more than 30 years.

(2) Whoever violates, or attempts or conspires to violate, subsection (a)(5) shall be fined under this title or imprisoned not more than 5 years, or both, but, if such person has a prior conviction under this chapter, chapter 109A, or chapter 117, or under the laws of any State relating to aggravated sexual abuse, sexual abuse, or abusive sexual conduct involving a minor or ward, or the production, possession, receipt, mailing, sale, distribution, shipment, or transportation of child pornography, such person shall be fined under this title and imprisoned for not less than 2 years nor more than 10 years.

(c) It shall be an affirmative defense to a charge of violating paragraphs (1), (2), (3), or (4) of subsection (a) that

(1) the alleged child pornography was produced using an actual person or persons engaging in sexually explicit conduct;

(2) each such person was an adult at the time the material was produced; and

(3) the defendant did not advertise, promote, present, describe, or distribute the material in such a manner as to convey the impression that it is or contains a visual depiction of a minor engaging in sexually explicit conduct.

(d) Affirmative Defense. It shall be an affirmative defense to a charge of violating subsection (a)(5) that the defendant

(1) possessed less than three images of child pornography; and

(2) promptly and in good faith, and without retaining or allowing any person, other than a law enforcement agency, to access any image or copy thereof

(A) took reasonable steps to destroy each such image; or

(B) reported the matter to a law enforcement agency and afforded that agency access to each such image.

49. 18 U.S.C. § 2251; 18 U.S.C. § 2256.
50. 18 U.S.C. § 2422.
51. 18 U.S.C. § 2423.
52. 18 U.S.C. § 2425.
53. 18 U.S.C. § 2251.
54. 18 U.S.C. § 2251 (b).
55. 18 U.S.C. § 2251(c).
56. 18 U.S.C. § 2251 (d).
57. 18 U.S.C. § 2252.
58. 18 U.S.C. § 2252 (c).
59. 18 U.S.C. § § 1301, 1302.
60. 18 U.S.C. § 2425.
61. *Ibid.*
62. 18 U.S.C. § 1470.
63. 18 U.S.C. § 2427.
64. An attempt provision was added to 18 U.S.C. 2422(a), Coercion and Enticement and 18 U.S.C. 2421, Transportation generally.
65. The Act clarifies that in 18 U.S.C. 2422(b), Coercion and enticement of a minor, coercion can be through use of the mail, or any facility of interstate or foreign commerce, and increases the maximum sentence to 15 years.

66. The Act amends 18 U.S.C. § § 2251(a) and (b), Production of Child Pornography by expanding the jurisdictional reach of the federal child pornography production statutes. The existing statute required the knowing transportation, transmission or distribution of the child pornography. The amendment creates a jurisdictional element similar to the possession, receipt, and transmission statutes which are violated if the individual, e.g., possesses child pornography that was made with materials (e.g., the paper, the computer, the diskettes, the camera) that had been transported in interstate or foreign commerce. The amendment thus increases the possibility of federal prosecution for the direct abuse of the child in the production of child pornography.

67. The Act increased the maximum statutory penalty for the following offenses: 18 U.S.C. § 2422(a) [from 5 to 10 years], 18 U.S.C. § 2422(b) [from 10 to 15 years)], 18 U.S.C. § 2423(a) [from 10 to 15 years], and 18 U.S.C. § 2423(b) [from 10 to 15 years]. In addition, an individual convicted of 18 U.S.C. § 2244 involving a victim under the age of 12 can receive double the maximum statutory penalty, under the new Section 2244(c).

68. Death Penalty. If a minor under the age 14 dies as a result of the commission of an offense under 18 U.S.C. § § 2251, 2422, or 2423, the defendant may receive the death penalty under a new provision, 18 U.S.C. § 3559(d), Death or Imprisonment for Crimes Against Children This provision was added, in part, to increase penalties for "snuff" films involving minors.

69. Criminal forfeiture, under Section 2253, and civil forfeiture, under Section 2254, are now available for offenses under 18 U.S.C. § § 2251, 2251A, 2252, 2252A, 2260, 2421, 2422, and 2423. Civil remedies, under Section 2255, are now available for offenses under the aforementioned statutes and Sections 2241(c), 2242, and 2243. See below under "Forfeiture Provisions." The forfeiture provisions should provide incentives for increased investigative work by local, state, and federal law enforcement in all cases involving child pornography, luring and transportation of minors, and trafficking of women and minors for prostitution cases. The civil remedy provisions may be useful in providing relief for victims.

70. The Protection of Children from Sexual Predators Act amends the Victims of Child Abuse Act of 1990 (42 U.S.C. 13001 et seq.) to require on line service providers to report evidence of child pornography offenses. The measure also amends 18 U.S.C. § 2702(b) of the Electronic Communications Privacy Act of 1986 to create an exception to the general statutory bar against a public provider's voluntary disclosure of customer communications to third parties.

71. 521 U.S. 844 (1997).

72. Title 47 U. S. C. A. § 223(a)(1)(B)(ii).

73. Title 47 U. S. C. A. § 223(d).

74. 535 U.S. 234 (2002).

75. 18 U.S.C. § 2256.

76. 535 U.S. 564 (2002).

77. 47 U.S.C. § 231(a)(1).

78. *Miller* v. *California,* 413 U.S. 15 where obscene material is judged based on: (a) whether "the average person, applying contemporary community standards" would find that the work, taken as a whole, appeals to the prurient interest, (b) whether the work depicts or describes, in a patently offensive way, sexual conduct specifically defined by the applicable state law, and (c) whether the work, taken as a whole, lacks serious literary, artistic, political, or scientific value.

79. No. 02-361 (2003).

80. Public Law No: 108-21. The PROTECT Act Prohibits: (1) making a visual depiction that is a digital image, computer image, or computer-generated image of, or that is indistinguishable from an image of, a minor engaging in specified sexually explicit conduct; (2) knowingly advertising, promoting, presenting, distributing, or soliciting through the mails

or in commerce, including by computer, any material that is or contains an obscene visual depiction of a minor engaging in sexually explicit conduct or a visual depiction of an actual minor engaging in such conduct; (3) knowingly distributing, offering, sending, or providing to a minor any such visual depiction using the mails or commerce, including by computer, for purposes of inducing or persuading a minor to participate in an illegal act; and (4) knowingly producing, distributing, receiving, or possessing with intent to distribute a visual depiction of any kind, including a drawing, cartoon, sculpture, or painting, that, under specified circumstances, depicts a minor engaging in sexually explicit conduct and is obscene, or depicts an image that is or appears to be of a minor engaging in such conduct and such depiction lacks serious literary, artistic, political, or scientific value. Allows as an affirmative defense to the charge of virtual child pornography only that: (1) the alleged pornography was produced using only actual persons all of whom were adults; or (2) the alleged pornography was not produced using any actual minors.

81. OSANKA, FRANKLIN M. and SARA LEE JOHANN (1989). *Sourcebook on Pornography.* Lexington, MA: Lexington Books.

82. REISMAN, JUDITH A. (1994). Child Pornography in Erotic Magazines, Social Awareness, and Self-Censorship. pp. 313–326 in *Media, Children, and the Family: Social Scientific, Psychodynamic, and Clinical Perspectives.* DOLF ZILLMAN, JENNINGS BRYANT, and ALTHEA C. HUSTON, eds. Hillsdale, NJ: Lawrence Erlbaum and Associates, Publishers.

83. *Ibid.*

84. *Ibid.*

85. HENLEY, JOHN (1996). "The Observer Campaign to Clean up the Internet: Hackers Called in as Cybercops to Drive Out Porn." *Observer,* Sept. 1, 1996.

86. OSANKA, FRANKLIN M. and SARA LEE JOHANN (1989). *Sourcebook on Pornography.* Lexington, MA: Lexington Books.

87. SCHUIJER, JAN and BENJAMIN ROSSEN (1992). "The Trade in Child Pornography." *Issues in Child Abuse Accusations* 4, 2: 55–107.

88. SEVEL, JAMES (1999). U.S. Customs Service Agent, Cyber Smuggling Center. Personal interview.

89. LANNING, KENNETH V. and ANN W. BURGESS (1989). "Child Pornography and Sex Rings." pp. 235–258 in *Pornography: Research Advances and Policy Considerations.* DOLF ZILLMAN and JENNINGS BRYANT, eds. Hillsdale, NJ: Lawrence Erlbaum and Associates, Publishers.

90. *Ibid.*

91. CAMPAGNA, DANIELS S. and DONALD L. POFFENBERGER (1988). *The Sexual Trafficking in Children: An Investigation of the Child Sex Trade.* Dover, MA: Auburn House Publishing.

92. *Ibid.;* LANNING, KENNETH V. and ANN W. BURGESS (1989). "Child Pornography and Sex Rings." pp. 235–258 in *Pornography: Research Advances and Policy Considerations.* DOLF ZILLMAN and JENNINGS BRYANT, eds. Hillsdale, NJ: Lawrence Erlbaum and Associates, Publishers.

93. *Ibid.*

94. CAMPAGNA, DANIELS S. and DONALD L. POFFENBERGER (1988). *The Sexual Trafficking in Children: An Investigation of the Child Sex Trade.* Dover, MA: Auburn House Publishing.

95. *Ibid.*

96. DURKIN, KEITH F. (1997). "Misuse of the Internet by Pedophiles: Implications for Law Enforcement and Probation Practice." *Federal Probation* 61 (3): 14–18.

97. *Ibid.*

98. LANNING, KENNETH V. and ANN W. BURGESS (1989). "Child Pornography and Sex Rings." pp. 235–258 in *Pornography: Research Advances and Policy Considerations.* DOLF ZILLMAN and JENNINGS BRYANT, eds. Hillsdale, NJ: Lawrence Erlbaum and Associates, Publishers.

99. SEVEL, JAMES (1999). U.S. Customs Service Agent, Cyber Smuggling Center. Personal interview.

100. U.S. Attorney General's Office (1986). *Final Report of the Attorney General's Commission on Pornography.* Nashville, TN: Rutledge Hill Press.

101. *Ibid.*

102. *Ibid.*

103. *Ibid.*

104. LANNING, KENNETH V. and ANN W. BURGESS (1989). "Child Pornography and Sex Rings." pp. 235–258 in *Pornography: Research Advances and Policy Considerations.* DOLF ZILLMAN and JENNINGS BRYANT, eds. Hillsdale, NJ: Lawrence Erlbaum and Associates, Publishers.

105. SEVEL, JAMES (1999). U.S. Customs Service Agent, Cyber Smuggling Center. Personal interview.

106. CLINE, VICTOR B. (1994). "Pornography Effects: Empirical and Clinical Evidence." pp. 229–248 in *Media, Children, and the Family: Social Scientific, Psychodynamic, and Clinical Perspectives.* DOLF ZILLMAN, JENNINGS BRYANT, and ALTHEA C. HUSTON, eds. Hillsdale, NJ: Lawrence Erlbaum and Associates, Publishers; LYONS, JOHN S., RACHEL L. ANDERSON, and DAVID B. LARSON (1994). "A Systematic Review of the Effects of Aggressive and Nonaggressive Pornography." pp. 271–312 in *Media, Children, and the Family: Social Scientific, Psychodynamic, and Clinical Perspectives.* DOLF ZILLMAN, JENNINGS BRYANT, and ALTHEA C. HUSTON, eds. Hillsdale, NJ: Lawrence Erlbaum and Associates, Publishers; MALAMUTH, NEIL M. and EDWARD DONNERSTEIN eds. (1984). *Pornography and Sexual Aggression.* Orlando, FL: Academic Press; MARSHALL, W.L. (1989). "Pornography and Sex Offenses." pp. 185–214 in *Pornography: Research Advances and Policy Considerations.* DOLF ZILLMAN and JENNINGS BRYANT, eds. Hillsdale, NJ: Lawrence Erlbaum and Associates, Publishers; OSANKA, FRANKLIN M. and SARA LEE JOHANN (1989). *Sourcebook on Pornography.* Lexington, MA: Lexington Books; U.S. Attorney General's Office (1986). *Final Report of the Attorney General's Commission on Pornography.* Nashville, TN: Rutledge Hill Press.

107. SHOWERS, ROBERT (1994). "Research, Public Policy, and Law: Combination for Change." pp. 327–339 in *Media, Children, and the Family: Social Scientific, Psychodynamic, and Clinical Perspectives.* DOLF ZILLMAN, JENNINGS BRYANT, and ALTHEA C. HUSTON, eds. Hillsdale, NJ: Lawrence Erlbaum and Associates, Publishers.

108. *Ibid.*

109. *Ibid.*

110. CLINE, VICTOR B. (1994). "Pornography Effects: Empirical and Clinical Evidence." pp. 229–248 in *Media, Children, and the Family: Social Scientific, Psychodynamic, and Clinical Perspectives.* DOLF ZILLMAN, JENNINGS BRYANT, and ALTHEA C. HUSTON, eds. Hillsdale, NJ: Lawrence Erlbaum and Associates, Publishers; LYONS, JOHN S., RACHEL L. ANDERSON, and DAVID B. LARSON (1994). "A Systematic Review of the Effects of Aggressive and Nonaggressive Pornography." pp. 271–312 in *Media, Children, and the Family: Social Scientific, Psychodynamic, and Clinical Perspectives.* DOLF ZILLMAN, JENNINGS BRYANT, and ALTHEA C. HUSTON, eds. Hillsdale, NJ: Lawrence Erlbaum and Associates, Publishers; MARSHALL, W.L. (1989). "Pornography and Sex Offenses." pp. 185–214 in *Pornography: Research Advances and Policy Considerations.* DOLF ZILLMAN and JENNINGS BRYANT, eds. Hillsdale, NJ: Lawrence Erlbaum and Associates, Publishers; OSANKA, FRANKLIN M. and SARA LEE JOHANN (1989). *Sourcebook on Pornography.* Lexington, MA: Lexington Books; SHOWERS, ROBERT (1994). "Research, Public Policy, and Law: Combination for Change." pp. 327–339 in *Media, Children, and the Family: Social Scientific, Psychodynamic, and*

Clinical Perspectives. DOLF ZILLMAN, JENNINGS BRYANT, and ALTHEA C. HUSTON, eds. Hillsdale, NJ: Lawrence Erlbaum and Associates, Publishers.

111. CLINE, VICTOR B. (1994). "Pornography Effects: Empirical and Clinical Evidence." pp. 229–248 in *Media, Children, and the Family: Social Scientific, Psychodynamic, and Clinical Perspectives.* DOLF ZILLMAN, JENNINGS BRYANT, and ALTHEA C. HUSTON, eds. Hillsdale, NJ: Lawrence Erlbaum and Associates, Publishers; LYONS, JOHN S., RACHEL L. ANDERSON, and DAVID B. LARSON (1994). "A Systematic Review of the Effects of Aggressive and Nonaggressive Pornography." pp. 271–312 in *Media, Children, and the Family: Social Scientific, Psychodynamic, and Clinical Perspectives.* DOLF ZILLMAN, JENNINGS BRYANT, and ALTHEA C. HUSTON, eds. Hillsdale, NJ: Lawrence Erlbaum and Associates, Publishers; MARSHALL, W.L. (1989). "Pornography and Sex Offenses." pp. 185–214 in *Pornography: Research Advances and Policy Considerations.* DOLF ZILLMAN and JENNINGS BRYANT, eds. Hillsdale, NJ: Lawrence Erlbaum and Associates, Publishers.

112. *Ibid.*

113. MARSHALL, W.L. (1989). "Pornography and Sex Offenses." pp. 185–214 in *Pornography: Research Advances and Policy Considerations.* DOLF ZILLMAN and JENNINGS BRYANT, eds. Hillsdale, NJ: Lawrence Erlbaum and Associates, Publishers.

114. CLINE, VICTOR B. (1994). "Pornography Effects: Empirical and Clinical Evidence." pp. 229–248 in *Media, Children, and the Family: Social Scientific, Psychodynamic, and Clinical Perspectives.* DOLF ZILLMAN, JENNINGS BRYANT, and ALTHEA C. HUSTON, eds. Hillsdale, NJ: Lawrence Erlbaum and Associates, Publishers; LYONS, JOHN S., RACHEL L. ANDERSON, and DAVID B. LARSON (1994). "A Systematic Review of the Effects of Aggressive and Nonaggressive Pornography." pp. 271–312 in *Media, Children, and the Family: Social Scientific, Psychodynamic, and Clinical Perspectives.* DOLF ZILLMAN, JENNINGS BRYANT, and ALTHEA C. HUSTON, eds. Hillsdale, NJ: Lawrence Erlbaum and Associates, Publishers; MARSHALL, W.L. (1989). "Pornography and Sex Offenses." pp. 185–214 in *Pornography: Research Advances and Policy Considerations.* DOLF ZILLMAN and JENNINGS BRYANT, eds. Hillsdale, NJ: Lawrence Erlbaum and Associates, Publishers.

115. MARSHALL, W.L. (1989). "Pornography and Sex Offenses." pp. 185–214 in *Pornography: Research Advances and Policy Considerations.* DOLF ZILLMAN and JENNINGS BRYANT, eds. Hillsdale, NJ: Lawrence Erlbaum and Associates, Publishers.

116. CLINE, VICTOR B. (1996). Testimony on Child Pornography Prevention. U.S. Senate Judiciary Committee Hearing on S 1237, "Child Pornography Prevention Act of 1995," 10 AM, Rm 226, Dirksen Senate Office Bldg., June 4, 1996.

117. *Ibid.*

118. PRENTKY, ROBERT A., RAYMOND A. KNIGHT, and AUSTIN F.S. LEE (1997). *Child Sexual Molestation: Research Issues.* Washington, DC: National Institute of Justice.

119. ABEL, G.G., J.V. BECKER, M.S. MITTELMAN, J. CUNNINGHAM-RATHNER, J.L. ROULEAU, and W.D. MURPHY (1987). "Self-Reported Sex Crimes of Nonincarcerated Paraphilics," *Journal of Interpersonal Violence 2:*3–25.

120. GIORDANELLA, HEATHER C. 1998. "Comment: Status of 2423(B): Prosecuting United States Nationals for Sexually Exploiting Children in Foreign Countries." *Temple International and Comparative Law Journal* 12 Temp. Int'l & Comp. L.J. 133.

121. RAO, NINA (1999). "Sex Tourism in South Asia." *International Journal of Contemporary Hospitality Management 11:*96–99, University Press.

122. *Ibid.*

123. JEFFREYS, SHEILA (1999). "Globalizing Sexual Exploitation: Sex Tourism and the Traffic in Women." *Leisure Studies 18:*179–196.

124. RAO, NINA (1999). "Sex Tourism in South Asia." *International Journal of Contemporary Hospitality Management 11*:96–99, University Press.

125. Captive Daughters (1999). "Sex Tours—A Learning Model." Retrieved from *http://www.captivedaughters.org/ByandAboutCD/CDdocuments/cdfactsheet1.htm*

126. STEINMAN, KATHY J. (2002). "Sex Tourism and the Child: Latin America's and the United States' Failure to Prosecute Sex Tourists." *Hastings Women's Law Journal* 13 Hastings Women's L.J. 53.

127. *Ibid.*

128. *Ibid.*

129. *Ibid.*

130. BEVILACQUA, ELIZABETH (1998). "Note: Child Sex Tourism and Child Prostitution in Asia: What Can Be Done to Protect the Rights of Children Abroad Under International Law?" *ILSA Journal of International & Comparative Law* 5 ILSA J Int'l & Comp L 171.

131. *Ibid.*

132. GIORDANELLA, HEATHER C. (1998). "Comment: Status of 2423(B): Prosecuting United States Nationals for Sexually Exploiting Children in Foreign Countries." *Temple International and Comparative Law Journal* 12 Temp. Int'l & Comp. L.J. 133.

133. ABBUGAO, MARTIN. (Oct. 1996). "Briton Child-Sex Tour Organiser Jailed for 16 Years." *Agence France Presse.* Retrieved from *http://www.vachss.com/help_text/archive/sex_tourism_briton_jailed.htm*

134. Associated Press. (Nov. 2002). "Businessman Sentenced on Sexual Abuse Charge." Retrieved from *http://www.vachss.com/help_text/a2/n_bredimus.com*

135. Computer Crime and Intellectual Property Section (CCIPS) (2000). *The Electronic Frontier: The Challenge of Unlawful Conduct Involving the Use of the Internet: A Report of the President's Working Group on Unlawful Conduct on the Internet.* Washington, DC: Department of Justice. Available on line: *http://www.usdoj.gov/criminal/cybercrime/unlawful.htm*

136. *Ibid.*

137. *www.cybertipline.com*

138. Computer Crime and Intellectual Property Section (CCIPS) (2000). *The Electronic Frontier: The Challenge of Unlawful Conduct Involving the Use of the Internet: A Report of the President's Working Group on Unlawful Conduct on the Internet.* Washington, DC: Department of Justice. Available on line: *http://www.usdoj.gov/criminal/cybercrime/unlawful.htm*

139. *Ibid.*

140. *Ibid.*

141. *http://www.usdoj.gov/criminal/ceos/obscenity.htm*

142. Computer Crime and Intellectual Property Section (CCIPS) (2000). *The Electronic Frontier: The Challenge of Unlawful Conduct Involving the Use of the Internet: A Report of the President's Working Group on Unlawful Conduct on the Internet.* Washington, DC: Department of Justice. Available on line: *http://www.usdoj.gov/criminal/cybercrime/unlawful.htm*

143. *Ibid.*

144. PEREZ, CYNTHIA (1999). "*United States v. Jacobson:* Are Child Pornography Stings Creative Law Enforcement or Entrapment?" 46 *U. Miami L. Rev.* 235.

145. *Ibid.*

Chapter 8

Anarchy and Hate on the World Wide Web

Chapter Objectives

After completing this chapter, you should be able to:

- Legally define a hate crime and describe how white supremacist groups use the Internet to spread their message of hate.
- Explain the relationship between left-wing groups and "special interest or single-issue extremist" groups.
- Describe ALF and ELF, and provide examples of each groups' recent terrorist activities in the United States.
- Describe some of the techniques that right-wing hate groups use to spread their propaganda.
- Discuss the primary issues associated with the USA PATRIOT Act, and list the four traditional tools of surveillance that have been expanded within the act.
- Explain the conflicting roles and activities observed within law enforcement pertaining to investigation versus intelligence gathering.

INTRODUCTION

The rise of the Internet over the last decade has paralleled some of the greatest milestones in communications history. Along with such great strides in bringing the world together has also come the frightening aspect of accessing information and propaganda that tests the very limits of the U.S. Constitution. With just a few keystrokes, an individual can have access to all forms of pornography, bomb-making instructions and poison recipes, and a plethora of extremist ideologies expressing everything from radical religious cults to clandestine organized crime groups. The Internet makes it now possible to view all sorts of material heretofore not easily found in the public venue. Many visitors to radical Web sites are shocked by not only the vast quantity of sexually oriented material, but also the open advocacy of violence against specific groups of people. One of the more interesting multimedia promotions that are found on the Internet arises from the ashes of Nazism and the far right.

DIGITAL HATE

Right-wing extremism represents a movement that promotes whites, especially Northern Europeans and their descendants, as intellectually and morally superior to other races.[1] It is not coincidental that as these groups have grown in strength, so have the number of reported hate crimes. Hate crimes and hate incidents are major issues for all Americans because of their unique impact on victims as well as the community. Hate crimes are often very brutal or injurious, and victims are not only hurt physically, but emotionally traumatized and terrified. Others in the community that share the same victim's characteristic may also feel victimized and vulnerable, posing a potential escalation in an attempt to retaliate for the original offense.

In the past, police officers have not been adequately trained to handle such incidents, treating them as routine assaults or vandalism. However, with new federal legislation has come the development of the National Institutes Against Hate, located at the Simon Wiesenthal Center in Los Angeles. The institute provides training for teams of criminal justice professionals from the same jurisdiction to combat hate crimes. Their goal is to provide new strategic approaches to combating hate crimes based on a new understanding of the unique elements that differentiate them from other acts. The center has been highly successful, training over 500 participants and providing an ongoing support center for follow-up communication, program evaluation and professional development via Web site updates and video-conferences.[2]

Legal definitions of hate crimes vary. The federal definition of hate crimes addresses civil rights violations under 18 U.S.C. Section 245. A hate crime is a criminal offense committed against persons, property or society that is motivated, in whole or in part, by an offender's bias against an individual's or a group's perceived race, religion, ethnic/national origin, gender, age, disability or sexual orientation.[3] Most states have a hate crime statute that provides enhanced penalties for crimes in which victims are selected because of perpetrator's bias against a victim's perceived race, religion or ethnicity. Some states also classify as hate crimes those in which a victim is selected based on a perception of his/her sexual orientation, gender or disability. In some states, the passage of a hate crime statute has been very controversial as politicians have debated the constitutionality of enhanced penalties based on a suspect's association with an extremist group, or the inclusion of homosexuality as a protected class.

White Supremacy, Hate, and the Internet

Many white supremacist groups have used the Internet to recruit potential new members and spread their message of hate. Over 1,500 Web sites can be identified and attributed to extremist organizations that incite racial hatred and religious intolerance, as well as terrorism and bomb making (see Box 8.1). More disturbing is the effort directed by many of these groups to attract young people into their ranks. Based in part on links to other social youth movements involving music and dress (e.g., skinheads, black cults, heavy metal music), aggressive recruitment on college campuses and the development of Internet Web pages designed to attract young people are now quite common. In addition, white-power rock concerts are often sponsored by extremist groups such as the National Alliance and the World Church of the Creator. These concerts provide face-to-face opportunities for meeting and recruitment.

White supremacist groups have also created sophisticated computer games aimed at attracting teenagers. *Ethnic Cleansing,* the most high-tech game of its kind, encourages players to kill blacks, Jews, and Hispanics as they run through urban ghettos and subway environments. In the game, players can dress in Ku Klux Klan robes and carry a noose. Every time a black enemy is shot, he emits a monkey-like squeal, while Jewish characters shout "Oy vey!" when they are killed.[4] Quite predictably, the game has spurred significant controversy between the media and game developers versus censor advocates. Very little can be done to ban the game since many other video games are designed to allow enthusiasts to create new levels and characters, while free software tools enable programmers to build new platforms.

These types of games and directed recruitment efforts have been effective tools in swelling the ranks of some extremist organizations.[5] According to one skinhead source, young people represent the future: "They are the front-line warriors in the battle for white supremacy."[6]

BOX 8.1   Resistance Records

Resistance Records is a racist recording label and Internet site that is part of the National Alliance. The National Alliance is a right-wing white supremacist organization founded by the author of the Turner Diaries, William Pierce. The National Alliance is one of the largest and most well known racist organizations and has gone to great lengths to utilize the Internet. Resistance Records is constructed to appeal to the youth of America. The violent music and games on the site not only attract racist teens, but the mainstream punk/alternative crowd. The racist propaganda portrayed on the site and in the music and games will have some effect on the beliefs of the individuals who frequent the site at *www.resistance.com.*

TERRORIST EXTREMISTS FROM THE LEFT

The far right is not the only set of terrorists that pose a threat domestically. The traditional left-wing extremist were replaced in the 1990s by the right wing as the most dangerous domestic terrorists, but subgroups of the left have developed which are potentially just as dangerous as the right and arguably more economically destructive.[7] A resurgence of anarchist groups, including those associated with Anarchist International, have dramatically increased since September 11, 2001. Most of these groups are relatively small and confine their activities to "rallies" against what they see as incursions of the government into the individual rights of people. Several "Black Bloc" rallies in protest of the USA PATRIOT Act and the increased security associated with terrorism prevention have be observed in several cities. However, unlike the anarchist groups of the 1960s (e.g., Weather Underground, Symbionese Liberation Army), there have been few violent acts attributed to these newly formed groups.

Those aspiring to extreme left movements are best observed in the modern eco-terrorists.[8] The FBI defines eco-terrorism as the use or threatened use of violence of a criminal nature against innocent victims or property by an environmentally oriented national group for environmental–political reasons, or aimed at an audience beyond the target, often of a symbolic nature.[9]

While these groups are definitely liberal and considered left-wing extremists, they are most often referred to as "special-interest or single-issue extremists."[10] Special-interest extremists are seen as different from traditional right- and left-wing extremists because they are not trying to effect a more widespread political change, but seek to resolve specific issues. These issues include animal rights and environmentalism on the left, and pro-life, anti-gay, and anti-genetic on the right.[11] In attempting to understand these groups, it is important not to be clouded by the political rhetoric of the left or the right. These groups attempt to change one aspect of the social or political arena through terrorism.[12]

Many special interest groups try to claim that they are not terrorist groups because they do not harm any animal, human or nonhuman, by their actions. Unfortunately, they often enjoy a sympathetic reception by many liberal affluent Americans unaware of the true actions of these groups. While in the United States to date, no murders have been directly attributed to environmental activists, they have used intimidation tactics on those they see as enemies and have caused millions of dollars in damage. The FBI estimates that the Animal Liberation Front—ALF, and the Earth Liberation Front—ELF, have committed more than 600 criminal acts in the United States since 1996, which has resulted in damages that exceeded $43 million.[13] Unfortunately, other single-issue groups like those associated with the anti-abortion movement have been very violent, having been responsible for the murder of numerous doctors and nurses that perform such operations.

Contrary to the claims of their partisans that eco-groups are not terrorists because they have not killed or injured any living being, making their acts mere vandalism and not terrorism, their use of arson and pipe bombs challenges their claims of innocence. It is also obvious that their intent is to influence policy by intimidation and coercion.[14]

Moreover, subcommittee Chairman Rep. Scott McInnis (R-Colorado) claims that "these are hardened criminals. They are dangerous, they are well-funded, they are savvy, sophisticated and stealthy, and if their violence continues to escalate, it is only a matter of time before their parade of terror results in a lost human life."[15] The loss of human life has already happened abroad, with the murder of Dutch politician Pym Fortuyn by an animal rights extremist.[16]

ELF and ALF

The Animal Liberation Front (ALF) and The Environmental Liberation Front (ELF) are arguably the most central and active groups of liberal activism today. The ALF, established in Great Britain in the mid-1970s, is a loosely organized movement committed to ending the abuse and exploitation of animals. The American branch of the ALF began its operations in the late 1970s. Similar to the right wing's leaderless resistance, individuals become members of ALF simply by engaging in "direct action" against those who utilize animals for research or economic gain. Direct action is generally defined by the group as criminal activity, which is aimed at causing economic loss or destroying company operations. The ALF activists have engaged in a steadily growing campaign of illegal activity against fur companies, mink farms, restaurants, and animal research centers.[17]

ELF emerged from a group called Earth First! This group developed in Arizona in 1980 after a series of acts of sabotage over the prior decade. Some of the first actions taken were in the early 1970s by University of Arizona students known as "The Eco-Raiders," who protested the spread of the city into the Sonoran Desert by vandalizing construction sites. In 1975, a fictional account of ecological saboteurs who chopped down billboards and plotted to blow up Glen Canyon Dam, called the "The Monkey Wrench Gang," was published by Edward Abbey. Further, two homes built in the Tucson Mountains were knocked down by a hot-wired bulldozer in 1977. Subsequent acts, such as those performed by saboteurs who sawed through the supporting poles of four billboards just south of Tucson in 1979, toppling them, seemed to have been inspired by "The Monkey Wrench Gang."[18]

It was in 1980 that five radicals lead by Tucson resident Dave Foreman created Earth First! and began a nine-year campaign of civil disobedience and monkey-wrenching (a term used to describe vandalism against active construction and lumbering locations). This was the group who started the practice of "tree spiking," or the insertion of metal or ceramic spikes in trees designed to damage saws and potentially injure workers.[19] The acts of tree spiking are exceedingly dangerous, as chainsaws buck back, often uncontrollably, against the user. In 1992 dissatisfied members who did not wish to abandon illegal actions when others wanted to mainstream Earth First! founded the Earth Liberation Front in Brighton, England. This group has gone on to claim responsibility for dozens of acts of eco-terrorism throughout the United States, starting in 1996. One of the more infamous examples of their acts was the $12 million in damages created when they set fire to a Vail, Colorado ski lodge in 1998.[20]

ELF and ALF are similar groups committing similar acts, the difference being that one focuses on the environment and the other animal rights. Members of these groups consistently use improvised incendiary devices equipped with crude but effective timing mechanisms.[21] While the ALF/ELF are the driving force for the liberal/environmental terrorist groups, there are other attached groups that also commit illegal activities, as well as the groups that are legitimate and nonviolent.

As we stated in the preceding chapter, cyberterrorism is an issue that has gained much attention in recent years. This type of terrorism is seen as unlawful attacks or threats of attacks on computers, networks and the information stored therein for the propose of intimidation or coercion of a government or its people for the furtherance of a political or social goal.[22] Many officials fear that domestic terrorist groups will crack into important systems and create severe damage or steal classified information.

While the government has responded to this threat with the development of new legislation to combat this threat, such as the Cyberterrorism Preparedness Act of 2002, and parts of the USA PATRIOT Act, the Internet poses a much more serious and widespread issue in its ability to unite people and spread information.[23]

DOMESTIC TERRORISTS IN CYBERSPACE

The domestic terrorist groups that pose a threat in the United States are strongly entrenched in cyberspace. Neo-Nazis, animal rights groups, militias, Black Blocs, and hate mongers all have not only Web sites, but clubs, posting boards, news groups and all other types of Internet communities.

The danger the Internet posses with domestic terrorist groups is that it allows for a level of communication between separate groups that traditionally has not occurred. Also, it allows for wider recruitment. For instance, Neo-Nazi skinheads around the world can talk in chat rooms, and right-wing groups that in the past would not have interacted in the outside world, find camaraderie in cyberspace. This camaraderie will eventually solidify and pass out into the real world, where it will pose a threat of a larger, more united group. People who would never have gone to a skinhead rally or a PETA demonstration now feel free to explore the Web sites of these groups and participate in their chatrooms in anonymity. Unfortunately, once they have become involved in these on line communities, they are more likely to bring their participation out of cyberspace. These Internet sites pose many potential areas for concern.

Dehumanize, Desensitize, and Demonize

Several Web sites use images, music, games, and the like to spread their propaganda. By using these types of paraphernalia the groups can appeal to people who do not necessarily share their particular beliefs. Once a person is exposed to these ideas for a long enough time they begin to seem normal.

One of the more effective and therefore more dangerous techniques these sites use to dehumanize the "enemy" or desensitize the consumer toward violence are computer games that are filled with extremist beliefs. This new trend of racist, hate-filled computer games has gained much attention and concern. It is believed that exposure to the racist propaganda in the games coming into the mind under the cover of the action will serve to desensitize individuals to the horrors of hate that these groups preach. This follows from the idea that the youth of America have become desensitized to violence, from more acceptable games, movies, and television. While the violence prevalent in modern media doesn't necessarily lead to violence by the consumer, it does seem that people are not as affected by the sight of true violence as they once were. This means that young people who play these games are not necessarily going to commit acts of hate and violence directly, but they may become less outraged when these acts occur in their own community. Vigilance and outrage against such acts of hate are necessary to eliminate these types of behavior in our communities.

As stated earlier, Resistance Records[24] has released one of the most advanced of these games. The game was released featuring an altered picture similar to the popular video game *Doom*. However, rather than killing monsters and other creatures, gamers kill ethnic minorities and Jews. *Ethnic Cleansing* was released on Martin Luther King Day with the slogan "Celebrate Martin Luther King Day with a Virtual Race War." The players can choose from KKK or Neo-Nazi skinhead attire, roam the streets of New York murdering the "subhumans," i.e., nonwhites, and their Jewish masters. The New York of the game has been destroyed by gangs of the subhumans who work under the control of the great Jewish conspiracy. This game shows a world that has fallen to the extreme right's worse fear: the Jewish conspiracy. At the end of the game the player encounters the "end boss," who is characterized as Ariel Sharon. When he is defeated and dying, his last words are "Filthy White dog, you have destroyed thousands of years of planning."[25] This characterization further leads to demonizing the Jewish race, by showing them as "masters" who have been plotting for "thousands of years" to destroy the whites.

While this is not the first, and certainly not the only, racist game available, it is the most advanced. It was created using an open-source game program that allows for almost anyone to create a game simply by plugging in their ideas. In this manner, a person can take an existing game code and modify it to reflect the characters, backgrounds, sounds, and environment that the designer wants. By creating these highly interactive and attractive games, hate groups can spread their racist messages to thousands of unsuspecting players.[26] The importance of these more advanced games is that they have the ability to attract the serious gamer, someone who is not a racist, and not just the individuals who are already part of the racist right.

Resistance Records is a well known racist music distributor. Music of different genres, but especially the punk/alternative types, are accessible through this company. Just like racist games, this type of music attracts people who are not active or even fringe racists. Exposure to racist propaganda and music again serves to dehumanize, desensitize, and demonize specific acts of violence against individuals based on race, ethnicity, or lifestyle.

Internet Cartoons

Besides computer games and music, many sites use cartoons to spread their ideas. One of the most widely distributed cartoons of the right is *Jew Rats*.[27] This is a computer program that consists of 14 cartoons that depict Jews as humanoid rats and African-

Americans with highly exaggerated features. The depiction of nonwhite individuals in this manner further, yet subtly, dehumanizes the target race or ethnicity because their features are depicted in unattractive ways, as opposed to those caricatures that represent the Aryan ideal. The cartoons in *Jew Rats* depict many aspects of the Jewish Conspiracy put forth by the extreme right. The cartoons also show the Anti-Defamation League and the NAACP as puppets of the Jewish Conspiracy, and thus set on the destruction of the white race. This type of propaganda is used to counteract and undermine the effect that these groups have in opposition to the racist right's doctrine. On most of the cartoon pages, there are links to propaganda and articles with such names as Jewish Communism, Jew Business Thugs, and Who really brought the slaves to America? These articles offer names of famous people who are the true "enemies" of the white race, as well as further explaining the beliefs that the racist right holds dear. *Jew Rats* not only dehumanizes nonwhites, but also helps in demonizing the Jews by extolling the beliefs of the Jewish Conspiracy.

It is easy to find examples of hate propaganda, games, and cartoons of the extreme right on the Internet. Unlike radical environmentalism, racism is not considered hip or even politically correct. All racists are seen as evil or bad even when they are nonviolent and do not participate in hate crimes or other violent actions. On the other hand, even the environmentalists who commit criminal acts tend to be romanticized and seen as righteous. There is a tendency to paint liberal extremists as Robin Hood types. While there are no hordes of violent cartoons, songs, and the like, the environmental and animal rights activist (ELF and ALF) sites do employ propaganda-filled images. Unfortunately, they do not possess the same negative image and social stigma associated with overt racism and bigotry. The propaganda of People for the Ethical Treatment of Animals (PETA)[28] and other noncriminal groups instill the ideas of resistance that can later lead to more extreme activism.

On PETA's homepage there is an Internet link that is aimed directly at young people. The Web page has a graphic icon depicting a scissors cutting a Mastercard in half with the message, "Cut up Mom and Dad's Mastercard!" It is obvious that this graphic is designed to gain attention and to promote action, even though the page linked has the following statement:

> **Take Charge: Tell Your Parents That Their MasterCard Buys Big Top Abuse!** Do your mom and dad have MasterCards? Get them a pair of scissors—stat! MasterCard has teamed up with big-time animal bully Ringling Brothers and Barnum & Bailey Circus to give people who have MasterCards low-priced circus tickets. PETA has asked them to stop, but they won't budge.

The first thing a person sees is an order to cut up someone's credit cards. Just because the message within the link says to ask permission and persuade the owner of the card to cut it up, most people never take the time to follow the link.

A liberal mainstream site that is youth oriented is PETA 2.[29] PETA 2 appeals directly to teenagers with youth-oriented graphics that purport the ideas of resistance and revolution. There are numerous graphics on the PETA Web site that encourage violence in the name of protecting the animals. One graphic in particular depicts a bloody knife in a hand holding books and asks the viewer to "question authority" (*http://peta2.com/*). Other graphics blend pop culture icons with messages that it is all right to use violence to change the world. News on popular actors or bands who are vegetarians or environmentalists is also offered. This site and the propaganda it conveys opens the door and motivates people to go on to more active resistance by employing the same desensitizing and dehumanizing effect as the right's propaganda, yet it is more universally seen as legitimate. Any racist, antigay or even prolife sites are seen as "criminal" in their own right even if they do not extol the righteousness of violence, while the left can be considered mainstream when they do not laud violence.

STORAGE AND DISSEMINATION OF INFORMATION

The ability of the Internet to store information and make it available to everyone is obvious. So it is little wonder that extremists, just as everyone else, utilize this ability. Many racist sites archive the sermons of different preachers, whether Christian Identity or other, that exemplify the beliefs that these groups hold paramount. For instance, anyone can find and download for free all of the sermons of Wesley Swift (one of the most influential right-wing extremists in our history and a primary developer of Christian Identity). In addition, there are sites that have on line copies of the *Protocols of Zion* as well as the *Turner Diaries,* and other racist books. The latter book (*Turner Diaries*) was found in the automobile of Timothy McVeigh as he was arrested after the bombing of the Alfred P. Murrah Federal Building in Oklahoma City, Oklahoma in 1995. Before the age of the Internet, racists could only find these manuscripts at swap meets or meetings. Now even nonracists are likely to find these manuscripts on the Internet. A simple Google search reveals sites and locations dedicated to hate and bigotry.

On the anarchist and left-oriented sites, such information as how animals are treated by certain organizations or groups or the merit of the vegan diet are easily available. People for the Ethical Treatment of Animals (PETA) even offers vegan starter packages free of charge to anyone who wishes one. Moreover, the sites offer advice and help on performing "legitimate" activist actions. PETA offers information on organizing demonstrations and spreading their message to anyone who is interested.

The Internet also allows groups to put their credos or mission statements where millions of people who would not have had the chance to see them before can now read them at the click of a mouse. One such credo that has found a home on the Web is that of the ALF[30]:

> Because ALF actions are against the law, activists work anonymously, either in small groups or individually, and do not have any centralized organization or coordination.
> The ALF guidelines are:
>
> 1. TO liberate animals from places of abuse, i.e., laboratories, factory farms, fur farms, etc, and place them in good homes where they may live out their natural lives, free from suffering.
> 2. TO inflict economic damage to those who profit from the misery and exploitation of animals.

3. TO reveal the horror and atrocities committed against animals behind locked doors, by performing nonviolent actions and liberations.

4. TO take all necessary precautions against harming any animal, human and nonhuman.[31]

The Internet also offers blueprints for violent criminal acts. For instance, along with the ALF mission statement above are the following instructions for how to send in information on any actions individuals perform against the "enemy."

> If you are a member of an active A.L.F. cell, send us any clippings, or your own report, with date, time, place, and a few details about the action. Send your reports on plain paper, using block capital letters, or a public typewriter that many people have access to. Wear gloves at all times so your fingerprints are not on the paper, envelope, or stamp. Do not give your address, and don't lick the stamp or envelope; wet it with a sponge. Remember, you should expect that all of our mail and any other support groups' mail is opened and read by the authorities.

Many of the sites also publish newsletters that glorify the beliefs and activities of the group. Newsletters offer articles, propaganda, letters, and more in one place with easy access. The Internet then allows many diverse people to take advantage of the product. Box 8.2[32] offers an example of the features offered in one such newsletter.

More dangerous are the sites that offer directions for bombs or other devices. The ELF site offers a large link on their home page to directions for the incendiary devices that are the eco-terrorist's trademark.[33] Many bombings in the recent past have been committed by people who obtained the plans for the device off the Internet. In fact, complete directions for building an incendiary torch revealing the same type of ignition device used in the arson of a Vale, Colorado ski resort were found on the ELF site.

Other sites, such as developed on Ka-Fucking-Boom.com provide detailed instructions on bomb making and ignition devices. While these Web sites are *not* asso-

---

BOX 8.2   Newletter Feature for "Green Anarchy"

Green Anarchy #13

(Summer '03) is out now!

Issue #13 features:

"Youth Liberation: Burn the Schools and Destroy the Media", "The Rising of the Barbarians", "Between Analysis and Vision: Moving Beyond the Theory–Practice Dichotomy", "A Quest Among the Bewildered", "Thoughts on the City", "On the Sabotage of the Fine Arts", "Zero War—Total Liberation", "Decoding the Apocalypse of the Militant Left", "Green Amazon Economics 101", "The Doctor is Sick: Schizophrenia, Anti-Psychiatry, and Anarchism", "News from the Balcony", reprints from the finest of sources, updates from insurrections around the world, direct action reports, state repression and prisoner into (including a Break the Chains Conference Manifesto), reviews, letters, and much, much more! This one is 36 pages (our largest yet!)

ciated directly with a specific group, they provide information that assists them in carrying out their mission of destructiveness and violence.

The home pages of many eco-terror sites have excerpts from letters sent in about individuals' actions and links to even more stories. As seen on the ALF site earlier, they offer descriptions on how to send in the information without being caught. Moreover, all of the sites make sure to tell people that they should not send in any information on acts that have not yet been committed.

Publishing Information on Potential Victims

Many sites also celebrate acts of violence. For example many racist or antigay sites lauded the actions of those who killed Mathew Shepard. One site even claimed in a "memorial" to him that he "got himself killed" due to his "satanic lifestyle" and "will be in hell for all eternity." Another site claims that the convicted murderer of James Byrd is an "American Hero."[34]

While this praise of past actions is dangerous and deplorable, the most dangerous actions of these Web sites are when they place specific information about individuals on their sites. The most famous instance of this was the Nuremberg Files case.[35] The original Nuremberg Files offered extensive personal information about abortion providers such as pictures, work and home addresses, phone numbers, license plates, Social Security numbers, names and birth dates of spouses and children. People are also asked to send in any information they have from pictures to videos on "the abortionist, their car, their house, friends, and anything else of interest." The site claimed that any information gathered would be used to prosecute abortion providers once abortion becomes illegal, just as Nazi leaders were prosecuted after the Second World War. The 9th Circuit Court upheld the concept that this site was being used for a much more violent purpose, and awarded the plaintiffs $107 million in damages.

The list of abortion providers read like a list of targets for assassination. Names in plain black lettering were still "working"; those in gray letters were "wounded"; and those names that were "Str[uck]through" indicated doctors who had become "fatalit[ies]." The site was actually a list of people targeted for assassination. Within hours of the murder of Dr. Barnett Slepian in Amherst, New York in 1998, his name was struck through, indicating that he had become a "fatality."[36]

The court found that the site's language and the strikethrough on the murdered person's names constituted a threat to others on the list. District Judge Robert Jones called certain language on the site "blatant and illegal communication of true threats to kill."[37] While the original site, with all of its trappings is gone, many sites today host the Nuremberg files, just without listing the slain.

A similar site is the SHAC Web site[38] (see Box 8.3). This site offers a map of the United States that can be clicked on to find information on those individuals or companies committing "crimes" against animals anywhere. Clicking over a specific area gives a list of all "offenders" in that area. It has the names, addresses, phone numbers and e-mail addresses of companies that do business with Huntingdon as well as some names of executives or other employees. The homes and/or cars of some of the people whose

---

BOX 8.3   "Letters to the Editor" Invoking Action against the Huntingdon Life Sciences Corporation

Stop Huntingdon Animal Cruelty (SHAC)

The focus of SHAC is on Huntingdon Life Sciences, a firm that is involved in pharmaceutical testing. The smaller focus of the group may make them the most effective of the radical environmental and animal rights groups. The SHAC Web site reports on the actions of its supporters. For instance, the Web site publishes the letters sent in by activists. The following are just two of the letters that are published on the site with personal information x'd out.

Received from Canadian activists:

CANADA JOINS THE FIGHT TO SMASH HLS!
On July 28, 2003, about 25 Canadian activists joined in the fight to shut down HLS. Gathering in a major park in downtown Montreal, activists made speeches and handed out leaflets to hundreds of onlookers before taking over the street and marching to the offices of Sumitomo Canada.

Once there, activists attempted to enter the building and had a rousing protest, complete with spray painted anti-HLS slogans and strategically placed stickers. Everyone entering and exiting the building was treated to a crash course on the atrocities supported by their neighbours in the Sumitomo suite. A whole slew of newspeople were educated as well, and the demo appeared on the 6 o'clock news of two major T.V. stations. The demonstration ended with a reminder to Sumitomo that until it severs all ties with HLS—
"We will be back!"

Received anonymously:

WAKE UP CHIRON SCUM!
We couldn't sleep on Tuesday night, so we decided to go see what one of our local Chiron scum was up to at 2:30 am. We knocked and knocked on the door of Linda Short (27 xxxx Ave. xxxxxxx, CA, xxx-xxx-xxxx) but she didn't answer. Go figure, she must have been fast asleep. We were really curious to know for sure, so we decided to use our trusty bullhorns to make sure she knew we we were outside anxiously awaiting her. We finally got the hint that she wasn't going to come out to visit with us, but our curiosity as to what she was up to got the best of us, so we decided to give her a call or two or three . . .

Chiron when are you going to get it? Wake up and realize that we have tons of energy and we are determined. We know where you live and we're finding out more and more personal information about you every day. Ask yourself if can you take it. Stop doing business with Huntingdon Life Sciences![27]

---

names have been listed by SHAC have been vandalized. These people have also faced demonstrations outside their homes at all times of the day and night, received harassing telephone calls or e-mails and in some extreme cases have been physically attacked.[39]

Unlike the Nuremberg Files, this site seems to understand what is and is not allowed under freedom of speech (for more on freedom of speech, see Box 8.4).[40] SHAC

BOX 8.4   Freedom of Speech

The only lawful limitations on speech are as follows:

Obscenity. Obscenity is speech that (1) the average person, applying contemporary community standards, would find, taken as a whole, to appeal to the prurient interest; (2) depicts or describes in a patently offensive manner specifically defined sexual conduct; and (3) lacks as a whole serious literary, artistic, political or scientific value.

Fighting words. Speech likely to provoke an average listener to retaliation, and thereby cause a breach of peace.

Commercial speech. The government can ban deceptive or illegal commercial speech; any other regulation must be supported by a substantial interest to be achieved by restrictions, regulations in proportion to that interest, and a limitation on expression carefully designed to achieve the state's goal.

Incitement ("clear and present danger"). Speech that is intended and likely to incite "imminent lawless action," or where the speech presents a "clear and present danger" to the security of the nation.

Time, place, and manner. Content-neutral regulation of the time, place, or manner of speech that does not interfere with the message being delivered and leaves open adequate alternative channels of communication is permissible.

Libel/slander. Speech that is not only false but that the speaker was negligent to some degree in using. The level of negligence is raised to "actual malice" (knowing or reckless disregard for the truth of the statement) for all statements made about public figures.

It is widely acknowledged that the Internet poses challenges to traditional law, but many people have tried to impose regulation. Most of these regulations have fallen to the First Amendment. The Communications Decency Act and the Child Online Protection Act are both congressional acts that tried to place limits on any information that is considered harmful to children, that were held unconstitutional.

Another issue of First Amendment rights was the case against Yahoo in the French courts. Yahoo was found in violation of French law because they hosted Nazi paraphernalia in their on-line auctions. An American judge ruled that the French decision could not be enforced in U.S. courts because the First Amendment protects American companies from foreign laws that are more restrictive. The site that hosted the controversial material was on the American Yahoo server and they can not regulate where people are when they view the sites. The French Yahoo site had always conformed to the French laws.

So the open nature of the Internet and the First Amendment make regulations hard to implement. Many of the sites walk a fine line, but with care all sites, extremist or not, can continue to operate if they are careful to remain within constitutional protections.

has faced multiple lawsuits, but they have always prevailed. Their knowledge of the law can best be seen in the following disclaimer that is linked to many places within the site:

> The SHAC USA Web site and eNewsletter, its hosts, designers, contributors, and sponsors, are not responsible for actions on the part of any individual which prove defamatory, injurious or prejudicial to the individuals or entities named herein, their families, or acquaintances. This publication is provided for informational purposes only, and is not intended to incite any criminal action on the part of its readers, visitors, or recipients.[41]

Fundraising

Fundraising has also been helped by the Internet. The fact that millions of people are potentially exposed to numerous sites means that more potential donors will be reached than ever before. Many of the sites have information on how to send in donations. Some sites, like PETA, even allow for secure on line credit card donations.

Besides donations, these groups also earn money through the selling of merchandise. For example, Resistance Records sells *Ethnic Cleansing* at $14.88. Other than the games and of course the music they release, they have a large on line catalog of clothing, bumper stickers and all other types of racist paraphernalia. Another source of income is through selling sermons, articles or racists books on their sites. While if a person looks long enough they can find free downloads of Wesley Swift's sermons, many more sites only offer them as mail-ordered hard copies. Somone can order a hard copy of lots of different types of works off these sites.

An example of a right-wing group that employs the Internet's fundraising ability is Kingdom Identity Church,[42] which offers many different products. To begin with, they offer an "American Institute of Theology Bible Course," which is a 12-lesson plan that costs $100 and upon completion gives the student a "Certificate in Christian Education." Moreover, they have audio- and video-tape catalogues. The audiotapes, which are of sermons or lessons, are offered for a suggested donation of $3.50 per cassette. Similarly the videotapes which are proclaimed to be "professionally produced documentaries of our Christian Israelite heritage" have a suggested donation of $22. These are only an example of the products that this site sells, or more accurately, offers in exchange for donations. The only limit to the money-making abilities of these sites in the imagination of the site designer.

TERRORISM, INTELLIGENCE GATHERING AND THE USA PATRIOT ACT

One of the most controversial topics in America today focuses squarely on the emergence of domestic groups that express radical and extremist political thoughts on the Internet. Are these groups free to express their political opinions under the protection of the First Amendment without scrutiny or monitoring by law enforcement agencies? Certainly, the existence of controversial and inflammatory material on the Web has been safeguarded, including most forms of pornography and hate speech (refer to Chapter 7 for a discussion of the law and legislation surrounding this issue). This discussion focuses more on the role of the police to collect and analyze information (or intelligence) on groups expressing radical thoughts and ideas through their Web sites. Do the police have an inherent duty to collect information on individuals involved in the development of these types of Web sites in an effort to thwart or prevent violent crimes and terrorist attacks? Nowhere are these questions more openly evoked than in the passage of the new USA PATRIOT Act, and it is within this environment that we shall discuss the issues of privacy, freedom of speech and expression, and the right of society to be secure from future attacks.

A Short History of Intelligence in the United States

The framework for U.S. intelligence was created in a different time to deal with different problems other than terrorism. The National Security Act of 1947, which established the Central Intelligence Agency (CIA), envisioned the enemy of the United States to be nation-states such as the Soviet Union, China, and North Korea. The result was organizations and authority based on distinctions between domestic versus foreign threats, law enforcement versus national security concerns, and peacetime versus wartime.[43] The Federal Bureau of Investigation (FBI) was given responsibility for domestic intelligence and the CIA, the National Security Administration (NSA), and the Defense Intelligence Agency (DIA) were given primary responsibility for foreign intelligence outside the United States. During the politically active periods of the Vietnam War and Watergate, the roles between foreign and domestic intelligence agencies were further delineated and separated by executive and legislative initiatives (among these can be included the Privacy Act, the Freedom of Information Act, and the Attorney General Guidelines of Levi and Smith).

Domestic Intelligence and Policing

Law enforcement's primary focus was to collect evidence after a crime was committed in order to support prosecution in a court trial. This process is commonly called investigation and is reactive in nature. Previous to the passage of the USA PATRIOT Act, police intelligence activity had to focus on the development of probable cause that would justify other law enforcement and prosecutorial activities. In most incidents, a subject had actually to break the law or threaten to break established law before the FBI or other police agencies could utilize intelligence operations. The frustrating predicament in which the law enforcement community found itself was that law enforcement agencies could not act without probable cause, but at the same time were prevented from engaging in the activity from which that probable cause could originate.[44] The most critical point pertinent to the functions of domestic intelligence concerned the protection of civil liberties and constitutional rights of individual citizens, such as those that develop political inflammatory and radical Internet sites. The primary purpose of law enforcement is to protect the rights of all citizens through the objective enforcement of the law. This goal is seriously thwarted, as some question the ethical validity of covert intelligence operations against its own citizens. Such activities are violative of constitutional safeguards inherent in our democracy and could culminate in the formation of a police state.

Conflicting Roles

In contrast to the FBI and other police organizations, the CIA collects and analyzes information regarding national security in order to warn our government before an act occurs. The CIA is relegated to working *outside* the United States; agents have no arrest powers, and their activities are proactive in nature. The two roles of domestic versus foreign intelligence gathering and analysis are directly competitive in function. The FBI and other police agencies are restricted in sharing information with the CIA so as not to compromise future court action or abridge the civil liberties of U.S. citizens. Similarly, the CIA is reluctant to give information to the FBI (or other law enforcement agencies) for fear of having sources and methods of acquiring information being revealed in court.[45] Note the difference between investigation and intelligence in Box 8.5.

Defining Intelligence

Intelligence can be defined as information, which has been identified as relevant, collected, verified, and interpreted within the context of specific objectives. This necessarily includes that the information has been analyzed, classified, and distributed to policy makers who utilize this information towards the betterment of the country or the community.[46] Historically, the missing dimension in quality intelligence has been analysis. The transformation of raw data, whether acquired through human, technical, or open sources, must be collated, scrutinized and processed accurately and in a timely manner. The ultimate goal of this analytic process is a finished product more intelligible, accurate and usable than the data and information drawn upon to prepare it.[47] Placing this discussion in perspective, information collected by the FBI and other police agencies on individuals within groups that develop radical Web sites when no crime has been reported becomes intelligence data.

BOX 8.5   The Differences between Investigation and Intelligence

- *Investigation*
    - Reactive; occurs after the event or incident
    - Reports are generally open
    - Sources are generally known and open
    - Arrests are made based on evidence and facts
- *Intelligence*
    - Proactive; information gathered before the event
    - Reports are almost always closed
    - Sources are confidential and closed
    - Arrests are rarely made

U.S. Intelligence Weaknesses

In the aftermath of September 11, 2001, several studies were conducted to assess short-comings that may exist in our nation's ability to collect and analyze important intelligence information on terrorist groups. Several weaknesses were identified in counterterrorism efforts led by the FBI, CIA, and the National Security Agency. These included communication problems among agencies, a shortage of linguists, and a failure by these agencies to correctly analyze relevant intelligence information to potential terrorist threats. Several of the issues identified as potential problems existing within the U.S. intelligence community included: (1) a failure to place an emphasis on traditional human intelligence gathering and analysis, relying too much on technology tools such as spy satellites and expert system programs to gain intelligence advantages; (2) a failure to provide timely, accurate and specific intelligence information to law enforcement agencies and U.S. policy makers; (3) an overly bureaucratic and decentralized structure (particularly within the FBI) that hindered counterterrorism efforts and the efficient use of intelligence information; (4) outdated and obsolete computer systems that were not compatible with other systems and unable to provide accurate and timely sharing of critical information nationally; and (5) overly restrictive guidelines and laws that hindered the effective use of informants and the general collection of intelligence information.[48]

These problems are particularly distressing, considering the effort to combat terrorism. The organized, clandestine and destructive activities of terrorist groups uniquely confound both the gathering and analysis of intelligence information. Complicating this matter is the inability of policy makers to place the acts of terrorism within the scope of one jurisdiction. Are acts of terrorism crimes to be investigated by the FBI, or are they threats to our national security that fall within the purview of our military and national security agencies?

THE USA PATRIOT ACT

In an effort to clarify and improve these conditions, and provide sweeping new powers to both domestic law enforcement and traditional intelligence agencies, President George W. Bush signed into law the USA PATRIOT Act on October 26, 2001. The USA PATRIOT Act (**P**rovide **A**ppropriate **T**ools **R**equired to **I**ntercept and **O**bstruct **T**errorism) changed over 15 different statutes with little or no external review. The law addressed not only terrorism and intelligence issues, but also focused on more traditional money laundering, computer abuse and crime, immigration processes, and fraud. However, the most substantial part of the act is that it expanded all four traditional tools of surveillance used by law enforcement with significantly reduced checks and balances:

- *Wiretaps:* The surreptitious eavesdropping on a third-party conversation by wire, oral, or electronic communication. Usually conducted with a microphone receiver ("bug") on a telephone device; requires both a search warrant and a court order.
- *Search warrants:* A legal document signed by a judge directing police officers to search a specific area for a specific person or item of evidence/contraband.

The document must be based on probable cause that a crime has occurred or is about to occur.

- *Pen/trap and trace orders:* Telephone call set-up information only is intercepted without individual communications. A "pen register" provides the law enforcement agency access to the numbers dialed from a subject's phone, while a "trap and trace" provides the incoming numbers to the subject's phone (like Caller ID).

- *Court orders and subpoenas:* A court document signed by a judge that instructs the police to perform a specific task. A subpoena is a court order that commands a person to appear in court at a specified date and time to testify.

Law enforcement and intelligence agencies can now more easily and more surreptitiously monitor the Web surfing and communication of individuals using the Internet, conduct nationwide roving wiretaps on cell and line telephones, and build profiles on the reading habits of people visiting public libraries. Under the act, police can now force ISPs (Internet Service Providers—such as America Online, AT&T Worldnet, and Prodigy) to "voluntarily" hand over information on customer profiles and Web-surfing habits *without* a warrant or court order. This has a dramatic potential impact on the various radical groups and Web sites discussed here. Not only do the police have the legal right to monitor politically and socially extreme Web sites, but the ability to monitor those individuals that visit such Web sites!

Constitutional Rights and the USA PATRIOT Act

The expanded scope and breadth of the act has raised concerns from a variety of sources.[49] Most agree that intelligence gathering and analysis has to improve in order to prevent future domestic and international terrorist attacks. However, some argue that the USA PATRIOT Act may well go too far. The act increases information sharing between domestic law enforcement departments and traditional intelligence agencies such as the FBI and CIA. In such a state, the line between intelligence gathering and public law enforcement becomes blurred. Critics are quick to point out the civil rights abuses that have occurred in the past whenever police agencies have become too involved in intelligence gathering. Most major cities, including New York, Chicago, Denver, and Los Angeles, have had relatively recent litigation aimed at limiting the role of the police in this function. The arguments focus on the collection of irrelevant private information of individuals (including Web-surfing habits and sexual orientation) to the profiling of individuals in minority communities. In one case, an intelligence officer in Portland, Oregon developed boxes of information on over 500 community groups and over 3000 well known citizens of the city and stored them at his own residence. Over 20 years of police intelligence records were discovered by family members several years after the officer died. The dusty reports and pictures not only focused on private meetings and information on local politicians, but revealed that the officer had himself been an active member of the John Birch Society, a right-wing organization often under scrutiny by governmental intelligence agencies.[50] Some argue that the expanded role of police in intelligence gathering under the act will only provide a significant threat to the personal and civil liberties of all Americans and do very little to thwart terrorism.[51]

SUMMARY

To date, nothing has been court tested and several appeals to the USA PATRIOT Act are working their way through Congress.[52] With the passing of the Homeland Security Act in late 2002, it became clear that police will at least maintain a significantly new role in the fight against terrorism involving intelligence gathering, particularly using the Internet. This new role must be accompanied by vastly new training for law enforcement officers, defining the tactical, operational, and legal limits involving intelligence gathering and analysis.

The Internet offers people the ability to participate in or be exposed to all sorts of questionable material. Some of this includes politically and socially extreme Web sites developed by hate mongers, bigots, racists, and radicals. These can be experienced in the privacy of one's own home, no matter where they live. A person can download information, order products, or communicate with others without ever having to leave their home. Moreover, using the computer to explore and chat gives a person a feeling of anonymity that allows them to do or participate in things they never would in the real world. Most certainly, the freedom offered by the Internet allows for a continuation of extremist goals by reaching a wider audience and provides a means for easy excess to information, no matter how distasteful.

REVIEW QUESTIONS

1. Legally define "hate crime," and explain why hate crime legislation have been so controversial in the United States.
2. What is *Ethnic Cleansing*, and why is it so controversial?
3. What are ELF and ALF? Explain their similarities and differences.
4. What are the primary purposes of right-wing hate Web sites that use images, music, games and the like to spread their propaganda?
5. What are the "Nuremberg Files," and why were they important in setting legal precedence relating to communication on the Internet?
6. Explain and discuss the inherent conflicts associated with the police as intelligence gatherers.
7. List and discuss some of the weaknesses associated with U.S. intelligence in the aftermath of September 11, 2001.
8. What is the USA PATRIOT Act, and what are the four traditional tools of surveillance expanded with the act?

ENDNOTES

1. *The New Lexicon of Hate: The Changing Tactics, Language and Symbols of America's Extremists* (Los Angeles: Simon Wiesenthal Center, 1999).

2. For more information, visit the Nation Institutes Against Hate Crimes Web site: *http://www.wiesenthal.com*

3. *Responding to Hate Crimes: A Police Officer's Guide to Investigation and Prevention* (Washington, D.C.: U.S. Department of Justice and IACP, 1999).

4. GODINEZ, VICTOR. "Hate Group Wooing Teens by Making a Game Out of Racism," *Dallas Morning News,* March 14, 2002, p. 2A.

5. TAYLOR, R.W., E.J. FRITSCH, and T.J. CAETI. *Juvenile Justice: Policies, Programs, and Practices* (New York: Glencoe/McGraw-Hill Publishers, 2002), pp. 518–520.

6. An interview with leader of the Texas Militia in Dallas, Texas (January, 2000) reflecting many of the sentiments expressed by Tom Metzger, a leader of the White Aryan Resistance (WAR).

7. JARBOE, JAMES F. (Feb. 12, 2002). Domestic Terrorism Section Chief, Federal Bureau of Investigation. "The Threat of Eco-Terrorism." Speech before the House of Resources Committee, Subcommittee on Forests and Forest Health.

8. *Ibid.*

9. FREEH, LOUIS J. (May 10, 2001). Director, Federal Bureau of Investigation. "Threat of Terrorism to the United States." Speech before U.S. Senate, Committees on Appropriations, Armed Services, and Select Committee on Intelligence.

10. SMITH, BRENT L. (1994). *Terrorism in America: Pipe Bombs and Pipe Dreams* (Albany, New York: State University of New York Press), p. 125.

11. LOUIS J. FREEH.

12. BRENT L. SMITH.

13. JAMES F. JARBOE.

14. Center for the Defense of Free Enterprise (CDFE). "Ecoterrorism." *www.cdfe.org/ecoterror.hml*

15. SCHABNER, DEAN (Feb. 26, 2002). "New Front on Ecoterror? Some Want to Target High-Profile Activists in Battle on Ecoterror." ABCNews.com. *http://abcnews.go.com/sections/us/DailyNews/ecoterror_support020226.html*

16. CDFE, "Ecoterrorism."

17. JAMES F. JARBOE

18. Off-Road.com. "A Short History of Ecoterrorism." *http://www.off-road.com/land/ecoterrorism_history.html* (viewed July 2003).

19. JAMES F. JARBOE.

20. Off-Road.com.

21. JAMES F. JARBOE.

22. KIM AYLWARD, et al. (2003). "Cyberterrorism." *http://www.cob.vt.edu/accounting/faculty/belanger/sec/article5.ppt* (viewed July 2003).

23. KIM AYLWARD.

24. Resistance Records. *http://www.resistance.com/* (viewed July 2003).

25. Anti-Defamation League (ADL). "Racist Groups Using Computer Gaming to Promote Violence Against Blacks, Latinos and Jews." *http://www.adl.org/videogames/default.asp* (viewed July 2003).

26. Anti-Defamation League (ADL). "Creating a Racist Computer Game—A Relatively Simple Task." *http://www.adl.org/videogames/game_creating.asp* (viewed July 2003).

27. "Jew Rats." *http://www.nsec-88.org/ruzne/jew_rats/jew-rats.zip* (downloaded July 2003).

28. People for the Ethical Treatment of Animals (PETA). *peta.org* (viewed July 2003).

29. PETA 2. *peta2.com* (viewed July 2003).

30. The Animal Liberation Front (ALF). *Animalliberationfront.org* (viewed July 2003).

31. *Ibid.*

32. Green Anarchy. *greenanarchy.org* (viewed July 2003).

33. Earth Liberation Front (ELF). *www.earthliberationfront.com* (viewed July 2003).

34. ADL. "Poisoning the Web: Hatred Online, Internet Bigotry, Extremism and Violence." *http://www.adl.org/poisoning_web/introduction.asp* (viewed July 2003).

35. See *Planned Parenthood* v. *American Coalition of Life Activists,* 41F. Supp 2nd, 1130 (D. OR 1999). This is a landmark First Amendment case involving a $107 million dollar award against antiabortion activists that branded abortion doctors as "murderers" and then crossed out their name when they were killed.

36. ADL. *Poisoning the Web.*

37. SCHABNER, DEAN (May 5, 2003). "Interactive Ecoterror? Animal Rights Group Provides Target List in Anti-Lab Campaign." ABCNews.com. *http://abcnews.go.com/sections/us/ SciTech/ecoterror030505.html* (viewed July 2003).

38. Stop Huntingdon Animal Cruelty (SHAC). shacusa.org (viewed July 2003).

39. DEAN SCHABNER (May 5, 2003).

40. Electronic Privacy Information Center. "Free Speech." *http://www.epic.org/free_speech/* (viewed July 2003).

41. *shacusa.org.*

42. Kingdom Identity Church. *http://www.kingidentity.com/*

43. DEUTSCH, J. and J.H. SMITH, "Smarter Intelligence." *Foreign Policy, 128* (2002), pp. 64–69.

44. MOTLEY, J.B. *U.S. Strategy to Counter Domestic Political Terrorism.* Washington, DC: National Security Affairs Monograph Series, 2 (1983), pp. 62–70.

45. TAYLOR, ROBERT W. "Terrorism and Intelligence." *Defense Analysis, 3* (1987), pp. 165–175.

46. MCCARTHEY, S.P. *The Function of Intelligence in Crisis Management* (Burlington, VT: Ashgate Publishing, 1998).

47. GODSON, R. ed. *Intelligence Requirements for the 1980s: Elements of Intelligence,* revised edition. Washington, DC: National Strategy Information Center, 1983.

48. Summary of Classified Report to the U.S. Congress, House of Representatives Intelligence Subcommittee. *Report on Intelligence Gathering and Analysis pre September 11, 2001.* July 16, 2002.

49. Electronic Frontier Foundation. "EFF Analysis of the Provisions of the USA PATRIOT Act." October 31, 2001. See: *www.eff.org/Privacy/Surveillance/Terrorism_militias/ 20011031_eff_usa_patriot_analysis.html*

50. "Terrorism Forces Renewed," *The Portland Observer,* September 25, 2002, p. 1.

51. *Ibid.*

52. See *Title II: Uniting and Strengthening America Act of 2002—The USA Act.* A bill sponsored by Senator Patrick Leahy.

Chapter 9

Digital Laws and Legislation

Chapter Objectives

After completing this chapter, you should be able to:

- Explain the intent and fundamental concepts of search and seizure law as it applies to digital crime.
- Identify situations where search and seizure is possible without a warrant and describe its limits.
- Describe the federal statutes that govern electronic surveillance in communications networks.
- Discuss the issues presented regarding the admission of digital evidence at trial.
- Identify and discuss the significant U.S. Supreme Court cases focusing on digital crime and evidence.

INTRODUCTION

In this chapter, law and legislation as it applies to the collection of evidence and prosecution of digital crime will be discussed. First, search and seizure law for digital evidence will be analyzed, including searches with warrants and numerous searches without warrants. Second, the major federal statutes governing the collection of digital evidence, especially electronic surveillance law, will be covered along with federal criminal statutes which forbid certain types of computer crime. Third, issues related to the admission of digital evidence at trial, including authentication and hearsay, will be reviewed. Fourth, significant U.S. Supreme Court cases in the area of digital crime will be highlighted.

SEARCH AND SEIZURE LAW FOR DIGITAL EVIDENCE

Our current body of search law is the ongoing product of the interaction of legislation, case law, and constitutional law. Most of the search law discussed in this section applies to searches and seizures overall, not just those involving digital crimes and evidence. In fact, much search and seizure law has failed to keep up with the changes brought about by increases in digital crimes and the increasing need to collect digital evidence.

The Fourth Amendment states:

> The right of the people to be secure in their persons, houses, papers, and effects, against unreasonable searches and seizures, shall not be violated, and no warrants shall issue, but upon probable cause, supported by oath or affirmation, and particularly describing the place to be searched, and the persons or things to be seized.

As simple as this language may be, numerous questions may be raised by the specific details occurring in searches and seizures of digital evidence. In general, questions focus on whether or not an activity is a "search" and whether a search is "reasonable." The best way to ensure that a search is not "unreasonable" is to seek and obtain a warrant from a neutral, detached magistrate. In *Johnson* v. *United States,*[1] the U.S. Supreme Court stated:

> The point of the Fourth Amendment, which often is not grasped by zealous officers, is not that it denies law enforcement the support of the usual inferences which reasonable men draw from evidence. Its protection consists in requiring that those inferences be drawn by a neutral and detached magistrate instead of being judged by the officer engaged in the often competitive enterprise of ferreting out crime.

The key to understanding search and seizure law is to remember the point is not to protect criminals; the point is to enforce a reasonable person's expectation of privacy. Criminals entering their home with the police chasing them do not receive sanctuary. Similarly, a guilty desire to hide something does not necessarily create a reasonable expectation of privacy. The Fourth Amendment protects persons evidencing an expectation of privacy; however, society must be willing to recognize that expectation as reasonable.[2]

A seizure of property occurs when there is some meaningful interference with an individual's possessory interests in that property.[3] In relation to property, a seized item deprives an owner of its use. On the other hand, a search is an attempt by law enforcement officers to obtain evidence. By definition, a search intrudes into a person's reasonable expectation of privacy.[4] Therefore, a search occurs, in a constitutional sense, any time there is a governmental intrusion into a person's reasonable expectation of privacy. An act as simple as opening a notebook and reading the contents in a suspect's living room changes the character of the interaction from simple observation to a search.[5] However, just because the police intrude into a person's reasonable expectation of privacy does not mean that the intrusion is unlawful. There are several mechanisms available to the police in which they can lawfully search a person or property and thus lawfully intrude into a person's reasonable expectation of privacy. In the following sections, these mechanisms will be discussed, including searches with warrants and searches without warrants.

Searches with Warrants

In order to obtain a search warrant, a law enforcement officer must show probable cause by reasonably establishing:

1. A crime has been committed.
2. Evidence of the crime exists.
3. The evidence presently exists in the place to be searched.

Further, the law enforcement officer must particularly describe the place to be searched and the evidence to be seized. Specific evidence of a specific crime must be named. General evidence facilitating a criminal act may be described by function. The investigator can search anywhere the named item(s) can be found. The judicial officer issuing the search warrant must be legally authorized to issue search warrants. Different jurisdictions empower different officers with this authority. Local policies and procedures should specify who has the power to issue search warrants. Furthermore, the judicial officer issuing the search warrant must have jurisdiction over the area to be searched.

Jurisdiction "is the power of the court to decide a matter in controversy and presupposes the existence of a duly constituted court with control over the subject matter and the parties."[6] When a transaction crosses state boundaries, typical in digital crime cases, jurisdictional issues may arise. A search warrant is only valid within the jurisdiction of the magistrate signing it. The degree of activity projected into a geographic area determines whether the doctrine of personal jurisdiction applies. If a criminal actor actively engages a victim, the local court may exercise personal jurisdiction over the actor. If the criminal actor simply provides information from a Web site, the victim's local court may not have grounds to exercise personal jurisdiction; however, local investigators are by no means ever prevented from engaging the assistance of remote law enforcement or courts to further an investigation.[7]

The remedy for a flawed search is most frequently suppression of the evidence obtained during the trial. This means that even the most clear-cut and self-evident material can be ruled inadmissible at trial. Some violations of statute may incur civil liability for the investigator, the investigator's department, or parent jurisdiction. An improper search and seizure is eligible for civil suit under 42 U.S.C. §1983. The current implementation of the exclusionary rule is defined in *Mapp* v. *Ohio* (1961). The sole purpose of the exclusionary rule is to curb police abuse of civil rights. There is no common law expectation of the suppression of evidence improperly obtained. To invoke the exclusionary rule, the defendant must have standing; that is, the defendant must be the one whose rights were violated by the search.

The good faith doctrine provides one possible defense to accusations of a flawed search. If the investigator has a reasonable, bona fide (good faith) belief that the search conducted is based on a valid warrant, but that warrant is in actuality unsupported by probable cause, the fruits of the search are admissible. The reasoning behind the exclusionary rule is to deter police from misconduct, not to remedy violations of rights.[8] The exclusionary rule applies not only to evidence improperly obtained, but to evidence discovered using the improperly obtained evidence (i.e., derivative evidence). This is known as the fruit of the poisonous tree doctrine. Again, the rationale is to discourage the violation of citizens' rights by not rewarding such behavior.

There are two other defenses to the exclusionary rule that are related to one another. First, an independent source of the same information can redeem the evidence tainted by illegal search. Thus, if an illegal search—a forensic fishing expedition—reveals child pornography, the investigator may seek independent indication of the suspect's involvement in child pornography. A posting from a pedophile Web site may indicate the presence of evidence, but remain completely independent of the tainted source. Another potential defense is that the tainted evidence may lead to a short-cut, but would otherwise have been obtained (known as the inevitable discovery doctrine). For example, a coerced confession of possession of child pornography without a lawyer present would be suppressed, but a search warrant which was issued prior to the coerced confession could show the inevitable discovery of the materials. Since the materials would have been discovered if the process had continued, an illegal search does not immunize the evidence to discovery.

Searches Without Warrants

Numerous exceptions exist to the general rule that searches must be conducted pursuant to a warrant. In fact, most searches conducted by the police do not involve a warrant (known as warrantless searches). Although numerous established exceptions to the warrant requirement exist and will be discussed in this section, it is best to be cautious in applying real-world analogies to the electronic world. Even if an officer believes they have a legitimate exception to the warrant requirement, it may still be worth stopping and seeking a warrant. Furthermore, the level of analysis required to obtain digital evidence can rarely be justified without a warrant; however, it may be appropriate to seize potential evidence to preserve it, while awaiting a warrant for the analysis. This section will discuss several warrantless searches.

Stop and Frisk

A law enforcement officer has the right to self-protection during a brief interview by conducting a frisk of a citizen for weapons. A frisk is limited to a patdown of the outer clothing of the individual and can occur based on reasonable suspicion. Although it is possible to identify potential sources of digital evidence during the interview (e.g., a personal data assistant—PDA—or cellular phone), there is no clear justification, under the stop and frisk doctrine, to analyze such a device based on the logic of a stop and frisk (which basically only allows officers to look for weapons). However, if probable cause exists to believe evidence of a crime exists in the device, then further analysis should wait, pending a warrant.

A stop and frisk may be combined with other exceptions to examine content. For example, the plain view doctrine can be used in association with data displayed by the device. Perhaps more useful is a trend in lower court cases allowing the preservation of perishable data under the exigent circumstances doctrine.[9] Warrantless searches of cellular phones and pagers have been allowed due to the possibility of incoming calls deleting evidence.

Consent Search

When attempting to collect digital evidence without a warrant, consent searches are the most commonly used searches conducted by law enforcement. An officer can ask a citizen to consent (i.e., give permission) to a search of their person or property. Valid consent to search allows officers to search for any item within the scope of that consent. The courts apply a "totality of the circumstances" test to ensure that the consent was intelligently granted and free of coercion. Further, a suspect may revoke consent at any time, even during the search. The scope of the search is directly related to the consent given. Again, the totality of the circumstances will dictate the court's acceptance of searches that seem to exceed the scope of the consent.

An additional concern with consent searches is that the person giving consent must be legally capable of doing so. Briefly, these are: persons with equal property rights (e.g., spouses, co-owners, or other employees using the same equipment); hosts during brief stays of a house guest; employers, when it is clear by contract or policy; custodians of children (school officials, parents, etc.); or persons lawfully borrowing the property with access to the areas to be searched.[10] Some relationships have been defined by the courts to preclude legal consent. These include: a spouse or co-owner specifically precluded from an area with reasonable precautions to prevent entry; a landlord (including hotel managers); an employer reserving an area for the exclusive and private use of an employee; or the host of a long-term guest with exclusive or private control over an area.[11]

Even if physical access to a space is granted, that does not come with the assumption of access to protected data. For example, if one spouse takes precautions to keep the other from using a computer (like a password or placing the computer in a separate room and denying access), or if a laptop is in the personal possession of a guest—even if left in an otherwise searchable room—a search of the data contained therein cannot be based on consent.[12]

Exigent Circumstances

The exigent circumstances doctrine allows law enforcement officers to search and/or seize evidence without a warrant if they have probable cause and there is some pressing need (i.e., exigent circumstance) to preserve evidence that is in danger of being destroyed or corrupted. The nature of digital evidence makes it subject to quick disposal and easy corruption. Encryption is another concern in making evidence unusable by an investigator. Once data is encrypted, the key can be almost instantaneously destroyed. The suspect may have another copy of the key somewhere nearby, but the location may be unknown to investigators. These very real dangers may justify warrantless searches under the proper conditions, but the burden of proving exigent circumstances falls on law enforcement.

Unless the computer, device or network cannot be secured, it is unlikely that exigency will allow analysis; it will just allow for the seizure of the items. For example, the mobility of laptop computers makes them analogous to a vehicle. Investigators may seize the laptop without a warrant to prevent it from being taken out of their control, but it would require truly unusual circumstances to justify searching the contents without a warrant.

Search Incident to Arrest

The Supreme Court has ruled that officers are allowed to search the person arrested for any weapons or for any evidence on the arrestee's person in order to prevent its concealment or destruction. Further, officers may also search areas within the arrestee's immediate control for the same purpose.[13] Like the stop and frisk, this exception could yield the physical container of evidence (e.g., PDA or cell phone), but would not justify analysis of the contents without exigent circumstances (e.g., batteries dying or new calls replacing numbers in memory).

Plain View

The plain view doctrine allows an officer lawfully to seize an item as long as certain requirements are met. In order to seize an item under the plain view doctrine, an officer must (1) see the item, (2) be legally present in the area from which the item is viewed, and (3) immediately recognize that the item is subject to seizure. If these three requirements are met, then an officer can seize the item(s) under the plain view doctrine. Since the officer is not conducting a search (i.e., the item is in plain view and thus there is no governmental intrusion into a person's reasonable expectation of privacy), the criminal nature of the item to be seized or observed must be immediately apparent to the officer (e.g., child pornography).[14]

Each of these requirements apply to the discovery and seizure of digital evidence, but it is possible that upon closer examination evidence not covered by a warrant will be discovered in plain view. For example, a search warrant may allow an investigator to search a hard drive for evidence of fraud. While the investigator is conducting the analysis, the officer discovers child pornography on the hard drive. The child pornography can be seized under the plain view doctrine since the three requirements discussed above have been met. As it applies to digital evidence, Orton states that it is important for investigators to not change the focus of their examination as a result of discovering a plain view item. As an example, Orton states:

> [I]f a search protocol calls for examining all files sequentially on a computer, then every file may be examined . . . [I]f the search . . . calls for a key word search and an

examination of the directory and file structure, but not the examination of each individual file, then the discovery of a possibly incriminating file name does not justify the opening of that file.[15]

If evidence is discovered in plain view while conducting another analysis, it is best to stop the analysis and seek a warrant based on the plain view evidence.

The Supreme Court has examined the use of technology to achieve the "simple observation" contemplated by the plain view doctrine. In *Kyllo* v. *United States,* the U.S. Supreme Court stated:

> Where, as here, the Government uses a device that is not in general public use, to explore details of a private home that would previously have been unknowable without physical intrusion, the surveillance is a Fourth Amendment "search," and is presumptively unreasonable without a warrant.[16]

This decision does not preclude technology in general use by the public. The decision allows technology not contemplated by the framers of the Constitution, but in common use, to define an expectation of privacy.

Border Searches

In order to protect the government's ability to monitor contraband and other property that may enter the United States illegally, the courts have recognized the need to allow for border searches that are more intrusive than would be allowed in other locations. In at least one case, the court allowed a warrantless search of a computer disk for contraband computer files because the search was classified as a border search. In *United States* v. *Roberts,* Customs agents believed that William Roberts was in possession of computerized images of child pornography. He was scheduled to travel from Houston to Paris on a particular day. On the day of the flight, the agents set up an inspection area in the jetway of the Houston airport with the purpose of searching Roberts. After Roberts arrived at the inspection area, he was told by agents that they were searching for "currency" and "high technology and other data" that could not be exported legally. The agents searched Robert's property and found a laptop computer and six Zip diskettes. Roberts then gave the agents consent to search the diskettes and several thousand images of child pornography were located. The Fifth Circuit Court of Appeals upheld the search.[17]

Searches by Private Citizens

Given that the Fourth Amendment only restricts the activities of government officials, the silver platter doctrine allows evidence collected by members of the public and presented to law enforcement to be admitted as evidence. Evidence presented to investigators "on a silver platter" is admissible as evidence at trial. For example, if a computer technician discovers contraband, investigators could use the contraband as a basis for further searches or as evidence in and of itself. In one case, the Court allowed a warrantless examination by law enforcement of the contents of a container already opened by a private company hired to transport the container. The scope of the search is limited to the scope employed by the private party. However, the fruits of a limited search may be used to obtain a warrant for a more complete search.[18]

FEDERAL STATUTES

Search and seizure law has developed incrementally as Congress and the courts have struggled to come to grips with criminal activity involving electronic communication. Because of this incremental development, the laws have built upon past concepts rather than attempting comprehensively to address the rapidly changing world of digital communication. This section discusses significant federal statutes that assist law enforcement in obtaining and seizing evidence related to digital crime. Most of the laws discussed were created for other purposes besides finding evidence of digital crime, but the laws have been adapted to include such actions by law enforcement. The focus of this section will be on federal statutes. It is important to note that states have laws that govern similar practices by law enforcement. Some state laws may place more restrictions on law enforcement than is required by federal statutes. For example, an exception to the wiretap statute discussed below is consent of one of the parties involved. This exception applies if the law enforcement officer is one of the parties communicating or has obtained prior consent from such a person. The exception authorizes the interception of communications when one of the parties to the communication consents to the interception. However, some states forbid the interception of communications unless all parties consent.[19] The federal laws governing electronic surveillance in communication networks as well as significant federal criminal statutes will be discussed in this section.

Criminal investigations involving digital crime frequently require electronic surveillance. As it applies to computer crimes, agents may want to monitor a hacker, a suspect's e-mail correspondence, or an individual sending or receiving child pornography via the Internet. Two federal statutes govern the practice of electronic surveillance in criminal investigations: Title III of the Omnibus Crime Control and Safe Streets Act of 1968, and the Pen Registers and Trap and Trace Devices chapter of Title 18. These statutes do not apply exclusively to criminal investigations involving computers, but more generically to traditional forms of electronic surveillance such as wiretapping a suspect's telephone. In general, the pen/trap statute regulates the collection of addressing and other noncontent information for wire and electronic communications. Title III governs the collection of actual content of wire and electronic communications.[20] As it applies to the Internet and e-mail, the pen/trap statute allows the government to obtain the addressing information of Internet communications much as it would allow the government to obtain phone numbers for traditional phone calls. However, reading an Internet or e-mail communication requires compliance with Title III.

The Pen/Trap Statute 18 U.S.C. §3121-27

The pen/trace statute regulates the collection of addressing information from wire communications. The statute takes its name from the now-obsolete physical devices attached to phone wires to perform this function. A pen register records outgoing numbers dialed from a phone. A trap and trace device records this information from incoming calls, similar to Caller ID. The pen/trap statute allows the government to apply for a court order authorizing the installation of a pen register or trap and trace device so long as the information likely to be obtained is relevant to an ongoing criminal investigation.[21] This statute has been applied to include computer network communications, not just telephone communications (e.g., an Internet user account, an e-mail account, or an IP address). To obtain a court order for a pen/trap device, applicants must identify themselves, identify the agency conducting the investigation, and must certify their belief that the information likely to be obtained is relevant to an ongoing criminal investigation.[22] The court can authorize the installation and use of a pen/trap device anywhere in the United States. The order may authorize the use of a pen/trap device for up to 60 days, and may be extended for additional 60 day periods.[23] Pen/trap devices are used more frequently by law enforcement than wiretaps.

The Wiretap Statute (Title III) 18 U.S.C. §2510-22

Title III regulates the collection of communication content. It was passed under Title III of the Omnibus Crime Control and Safe Streets Act of 1968 and provides the statutory framework that governs real-time electronic surveillance of the contents of communications (e.g., listening in on a phone conversation). The statute prohibits a third party (such as the government) who is not a participating party to the communication from intercepting private communications between the parties using an "electronic, mechanical, or other device" unless one of several statutory exceptions applies.[24] In other words, communication content intercepted from a wire communication may not be used in court unless an exception applies. Title III contains dozens of exceptions, but seven exceptions apply the most frequently in computer crime cases.

   1)   *Interception pursuant to a Title III court order (wire tap order)* Title III permits law enforcement to intercept wire and electronic communications pursuant to a court order under 18 U.S.C. §2518. Approval from Department of Justice administration is required for the application. A United States District Court or Court of Appeals judge must then approve of the application. When authorized, a Title III order permits law enforcement to intercept communications for up to 30 days.[25] Wire tap orders carry more stringent standards than an application for a federal search warrant, with an annual reporting requirement by the Administrative Office of the United States Courts (AOUSC). This reporting requirement and explicit processes to minimize intrusion into subjects' privacy raises the procedural burden beyond that of a search warrant.

   2)   *The consent exception [§2511 (2)(c)-(d)]* This exception applies if the law enforcement officer is one of the parties communicating or has obtained prior consent from such a person. The exception authorizes the interception of communications when one of the parties to the communication consents to the interception. Some states forbid the interception of communications unless all parties consent.[26]

   3)   *The provider exception [§2511 (2)(a)(i)]* Employees or agents of communications service providers may intercept and disclose communication to protect the

providers' rights or property. For example, system administrators of computer networks generally may monitor hackers intruding into their networks and then disclose the fruits of monitoring to law enforcement without violating Title III. This privilege belongs to the provider alone, however, and cannot be exercised by law enforcement. Once the provider has communicated with law enforcement, the computer trespasser exception may provide a basis for monitoring by law enforcement.[27]

4) *The computer trespasser exception [§2511 (2)(i)]* This exception allows victims of computer attacks to authorize law enforcement to intercept wire or electronic communications of a computer trespasser. In order to use this exception, the owner or operator of the computer must authorize the interception, the person who intercepts the communications must be lawfully engaged in an investigation, the person who intercepts the communications must believe that the content of the intercepted communication will be relevant to the investigation, and the interception should not acquire any communications other than those transmitted to or from the computer trespasser.[28]

5) *The extension telephone exception [§2510 (5)(a)]* This exception was originally designed to allow businesses to monitor by way of an extension telephone the performance of their employees who spoke on the phone to customers. Today, routine taping of all telephone calls made to and from a police station may fall within this exception as well.[29]

6) *The inadvertently obtained criminal evidence exception [§2511 (3)(b)(iv)]* Communication unintentionally obtained by the provider which appears to relate to a crime can be released to a law enforcement agency. For example, a provider could report evidence of a fraud scheme to law enforcement if the provider inadvertently obtained such evidence.[30]

7) *The accessible to the public exception [§2511 (2)(g)(i)]* Intercepting unscrambled or unencrypted communication broadcast over public frequencies does not violate the wire tap statute. In addition, the language of this statute appears to permit the interception of an electronic communication that has been posted to a public bulletin board, a public chat room, or a Usenet newsgroup.[31]

Electronic Communications Privacy Act (ECPA) 18 U.S.C. §§2701-11

The ECPA is an unusually complicated statute. It regulates how the government can obtain stored account information from network service providers such as ISPs. Whenever officers seek stored email, account records, or subscriber information from a network service provider, they must comply with the ECPA. The stored communication portion of the ECPA creates statutory privacy rights for customers and subscribers of computer network service providers.[32] The wire communication portion of the ECPA affirms a higher level of protection for communication in transit. This recognizes the fact that electronic communication follows a store-and-wait model rather than a direct exchange model like the telephone system, but affirms a citizen's expectation of privacy in communication. However, once the purpose of communication is achieved (i.e., the recipient reads or receives it), it enjoys the lesser protection of any stored document. To achieve a functional distinction between these points, the ECPA creates two categories of computer service.

- *Electronic Communication Service (ECS):* An ECS provider is a company holding an electronic message in transit (e.g., an unopened e-mail on a mail server).
- *Remote Computing Service (RCS):* An RCS provider is a company that holds or processes the data of a customer (e.g., saving an e-mail that has already been read makes the server's owner an RCS. An RCS can also be any form of data warehousing).

Information to be obtained under ECPA must be specified as one of three categories. Each category enjoys progressively greater protection through procedural burdens on the investigator.

1. Basic subscriber information [§2703 (c)(1)(C)]:
    - Name
    - Address
    - Local and long distance telephone toll billing records
    - Telephone number or other subscriber number or identity
    - Length of service and types of service

2. Records or logs pertaining to a subscriber [§2703 (c)(1)(A)-(B)]:
    - The contents of any relevant logs
    - All basic subscriber information
    - Cell site data for calls made
    - Destinations of outgoing e-mail
    - Any other noncontent records

3. Contents of communication [§2510 (8)]

Each category of information above requires a progressively greater showing of cause to obtain. The ECPA also defines five types of instruments that may be required to obtain such information: subpoena, subpoena with prior notice to service user, §2703(d) order, §2703(d) order with prior notice to service user, and search warrant.

1) Investigators can subpoena basic subscriber information. The legal requirements that must be met before issuing a subpoena are not stringent.[33]

2) Investigators can subpoena opened e-mail (and other stored electronic or wire communications in electronic storage more than 180 days) from a provider if they comply with the notice provisions required by the ECPA. The notice provisions are satisfied by giving the customer prior notice of the disclosure. The notice can be delayed for 90 days if there is reason to believe that notification of a subpoena will have an adverse result (e.g., jeopardize a pending investigation or endanger the safety of someone).[34]

3)   Agents need a §2703(d) court order to obtain most account logs and most transactional records. In other words, all relevant records (except the contents of communications) held by providers of electronic communications services and remote computing services can be obtained with a §2703(d) order.[35]

4)   Investigators can obtain everything in an account except for unopened e-mail or voicemail stored with a provider for 180 days or less using a §2703(d) order combined with the prior notice provisions discussed above.[36]

5)   Investigators can obtain the full contents of an account with a search warrant. ECPA does not require the government to notify the customer when it obtains information from a provider using a search warrant.[37]

It is also possible under certain circumstances for the service provider to voluntarily disclose account information to law enforcement. Nonpublic providers may disclose both contents and other records relating to stored communications. The ECPA imposes significant restrictions on voluntary disclosures by public providers, but exceptions do exist to the restrictions.[38]

USA PATRIOT Act

The USA PATRIOT Act was passed in the aftermath of the 9/11 attacks. This treatment only considers the domestic provisions of the act. The PATRIOT Act is discussed further in Chapter 8. The foreign provisions can be applied to foreign operatives in the United States, but will generally not be applicable to domestic law enforcement. The act primarily updates and enhances surveillance procedures while maintaining the established distinction between content and routing information. The PATRIOT Act also:

- Permits the seizure of voicemail messages older than 180 days with a §2703 order (§209)
- Permits the seizure of voicemail messages less than 180 days old with a search warrant (§209)
- Expands the definition of "basic subscriber information" to include a more detailed length of service use, type of service use, dynamic IP assigned, and means and source of payment (§210)
- Permits emergency disclosure by public service providers to protect life and limb or regarding terrorism offenses (§212 & §505)
- Permits delay of required notice of the execution of a warrant if notice may produce an adverse result (§213)
- Makes warrants and pen/trace orders national (§216 & §220)

Contrary to popular opinion, the USA PATRIOT Act does not change any of the procedural burdens previously placed on investigators when seeking information. From the highest burden to lowest, these are shown in the table on page 254.

Instrument	Procedural Burden
Title III interception order	Probable cause standard with explicit minimization and reporting
F.R.C.P. Rule 41 search warrant authorizing the search of physical premises and physical items or ECPA search warrant authorizing search of "in-transit" data held by an ECS for less than 180 days	Probable cause standard
ECPA §2703(d) order or ECPA §2703(d) order with notice	Specific and articulable facts showing reasonable grounds to believe that the records are relevant and material to an ongoing criminal investigation
Pen register and trap-and-trace device order	Relevant to a criminal investigation
Subpoena with notice, ECPA §2703(b)(1)(B)	Filed with the court
Subpoena with delayed notice, ECPA §2705	Notice may be delayed in successive 90-day periods "upon the written certification of a supervisory official that there is reason to believe that notification of the existence of the subpoena may have an adverse result."

Communication Assistance for Law Enforcement Act

The Communication Assistance for Law Enforcement Act (CALEA) was signed into law in 1994. Although telecommunications companies have been required, since 1970, to cooperate with law enforcement in conducting lawfully authorized electronic surveillance (e.g., wiretaps), CALEA requires telecommunications companies to modify the design of their equipment, facilities, and services to ensure that lawfully authorized electronic surveillance can actually be performed by law enforcement personnel.

Federal Criminal Statutes

There are also several federal criminal statutes that focus on computer crime. Three significant statutes will be discussed in this section, including the Consumer Fraud and Abuse Act, the Economic Espionage Act, and the Copyright Act.

The Consumer Fraud and Abuse Act

The Computer Fraud and Abuse Act was originally passed in 1984.[39] It was later amended in 1986, 1994, and 1996. It is the primary federal statute targeting unauthorized computer use, primarily focusing on unauthorized access and theft of information from computers. It covers a broad range of acts and protects a broad range of computers that facilitate interstate and international commerce and communications. After several amendments, the act basically covers any computer connected to the Internet. For example, the act makes it a crime to access a computer without authority to obtain financial information from a financial institution or any information in possession of the government. Furthermore, another section of the act makes it a crime for anyone to cause the transmission of a computer program, information, code, or command that results in unauthorized damage to a protected computer.[40] Criminal actions covered by the Computer Fraud and Abuse Act include access to and transmission of government classified information, access to computers used in interstate commerce, intentional access of a government nonpublic computer, knowingly accessing and intentionally causing damage to a protected computer, and intentionally accessing a computer without authorization and causing damage.[41]

The Economic Espionage Act

The Economic Espionage Act was enacted in 1996. The primary purpose of the Economic Espionage Act is to impose criminal penalties on the theft of trade secrets. The trade secrets may be stored either physically or electronically. In order to be defined as a trade secret, the property must be economically valuable and the owner must take measures to protect it. In addition, in order to be covered by the act, the person who is stealing the trade secret must know that the theft will result in economic loss to the owner and a benefit to another person.[42] This act applies anywhere in the world as long as a U.S. citizen or company is the perpetrator. A recent alleged violation of this act occurred when a software engineer for Cisco Systems took a job with a competitor. The engineer was arrested for taking voice-over and optical network software designs contained on a CD from Cisco Systems.[43]

The Copyright Act

Copyright infringement has become a significant focus for law enforcement with the increased use of computers and the internet. Copyrightable property includes literary works, musical works, dramatic works, pantomimes and choreographic works, pictorial and graphic works, motion pictures and audiovisual works, sound recordings, and architectural works. Copyright infringement as it applies to computers typically involves software piracy but has recently focused on downloading music and video files. The primary criminal statute protecting copyrighted works is Title 17 U.S.C. §506(a). This act makes it against the law to willfully infringe upon a copyright for commercial advantage or private financial gain.

ADMITTING EVIDENCE AT TRIAL

In this section, issues related to admitting computer records and other digital evidence into trial will be discussed. Much of the discussion will focus on the Federal Rules of Evidence. Most federal courts that have evaluated the admissibility of computer records have focused on computer records as potential hearsay.[44] The courts have typically admitted computer records upon a showing that the records fall within the business records exception to the Federal Rules of Evidence 803 (6).

However, the evidentiary issues raised by the admission of computer records really depends on what type of computer records are being admitted as evidence. Computer records that contain text can typically be divided into two categories: computer-generated records and computer-stored records.[45] The difference depends on whether a person or machine created the record. Computer-stored records include documents that have been created by a person. Examples of such records that may be admitted as evidence include word processing files, e-mail messages, and chat room messages. In comparison, computer-generated records contain output from computer programs that have not been manipulated by a person. Such computer-generated records include log-in records from Internet service providers, telephone records, and ATM receipts.[46] The evidentiary issues are typically different for these two types of records. For computer-stored records the evidentiary issue involves a question of whether a person's out-of-court statement was truthful and accurate. In other words, using computer-stored records as evidence brings up the issue of hearsay. However, when the evidence involves computer-generated records, the question becomes whether the computer program that generated the record was functioning properly. This is a question of authenticity, not hearsay.

Therefore, the admission of computer records as evidence usually involves two issues. First, the government needs to establish that the computer records are authentic. Second, if the records involve computer-stored records created by a person, then the government must demonstrate that the person-generated records are not inadmissible hearsay.[47] The issues of authentication, hearsay, as well as the best evidence rule will be discussed in further detail.

Authentication

Before the government or a defendant can move for the admission of a computer record as evidence, the authenticity of the record must be proven first. The government must offer evidence "sufficient to support a finding that the computer record or other evidence in question is what its proponent claims."[48] In authenticating computer records, the witness must have first-hand knowledge of the relevant facts to which he or she testifies.[49]

Challenges to the authenticity of computer records often take one of three forms. First, parties may challenge the authenticity of both computer-generated and computer-stored records by questioning whether the records were altered, manipulated, or damaged after they were created. In challenging the admission of computer records, opposing counsel frequently alleges that computer records lack authenticity because they were tampered with or changed after they were created. Generally, the courts are skeptical of unsupported claims that computer records have been altered. Therefore, the mere possibility of tampering does not affect the authenticity of a computer record: Specific evidence that tampering occurred must be presented.[50]

Second, parties may question the authenticity of computer-generated records by challenging the reliability of the computer program that generated the records. The opposing counsel makes the argument that the computer-generated record may not be authentic because the program that creates the record contains serious programming errors. Often, the reliability of a computer program can be established by showing that users of the program rely on it on a regular basis during their ordinary course of business.[51]

Third, parties may challenge the authenticity of computer-stored records by questioning the identity of their author. Although handwritten records may be penned in a distinctive handwriting style, computer-stored records do not necessarily identify their author. For example, technology allows users to send effectively anonymous e-mails and chat rooms allow users to communicate without using their real names. Defendants frequently challenge the admission of computer-stored records of this nature by arguing that they are not the authors of the material. The key to establishing authorship of computer-stored records typically involves the use of circumstantial evidence.[52]

Hearsay

The hearsay rule exists to prevent unreliable out-of-court statements by people from influencing the outcomes of trials. Therefore, rules of evidence require that individuals making statements be placed on the stand and subjected to cross-examination. When a computer record contains the assertions of a person, the record can contain hearsay.[53] Before a court will admit the records, the court must establish that the statements contained in the record were made in circumstances that tend to ensure their trustworthiness. In order to accomplish this, the government typically fits the record within a hearsay exception such as the business records exception. The business record exception is the most common hearsay exception applied to computer records [Federal Rules of Evidence 803 (6)]. It states:

> *Records of regularly conducted activity.* A memorandum, report, record, or data compilation, in any form, or acts, events, conditions, opinions, or diagnoses, made at or near the time by, or from information transmitted by, a person with knowledge, if kept in the course of a regularly conducted business activity, and if it was the regular practice of that business activity to make the memorandum, report, record, or data compilation, all as shown by the testimony of the custodian or other qualified witness, unless the source of information or the method of circumstances of preparation indicate lack of trustworthiness. The term "business" as used in this paragraph includes business, institution, association, profession, occupation, and calling of every kind, whether or not conducted for profit.[54]

In applying this principle, courts have generally indicated that computer records can be admitted as business records if they are kept following a routine procedure to ensure their accuracy.[55] The hearsay rule is discussed further in Chapter 11.

The Best Evidence Rule

The authentication requirement and the hearsay rule are typically the two biggest issues encountered by prosecutors when seeking the admission of computer records as evidence at trial. Another issue that sometimes comes up is known as the best evidence rule. The best evidence rule states that to prove the content of a writing, recording, or photograph, the "original" writing, recording, or photograph is ordinarily required.[56] Prosecutors sometimes are concerned that a printout of a computer-stored electronic file may not be an "original" for the purpose of the best evidence rule.[57] The original file is a collection of 0s and 1s, while the printout is a result of manipulating the original file. However, the Federal Rules of Evidence have expressly addressed this issue. Federal Rules of Evidence 1003 states that "if data are stored in a computer or similar device, any printout or other output readable by sight, shown to reflect the data accurately, is an "original."[58] Therefore, an accurate printout of computer data always satisfies the best evidence rule.[59]

SIGNIFICANT COURT CASES

In *Katz* v. *United States* (1967),[60] Katz made a phone call from a public phone booth. Federal agents placed a listening device in the phone booth but did not tap the line. They obtained incriminating evidence. Katz appealed. The government contended that the phone booth was a public place. The Court concluded that the Fourth Amendment protects persons evidencing an expectation of privacy; however, society must be willing to recognize that expectation as reasonable.

Perhaps most important for future electronic search and seizure law, the case hinged on the interception of communication content. In attempting to create a "technological workaround" to bypass statutory protections on telephone content (see Title III, discussed previously), the Court defined that the functional equivalent of an impermissible intrusion is an impermissible intrusion regardless of the actual route employed by the technology. Thus, constitutional protections apply to persons and expectations, not to physical locations or actual techniques. The functional presence of officers in a "private" space violates the reasonable expectation of privacy protected by the Fourth Amendment.

In *Florida* v. *Riley* (1989),[61] the Court allowed the use of aerial surveillance of arguably "private" spaces. It has long been established that police can observe private property from a public space; this is not considered a search. Thus evidence observed in an open field (even if it is on private property) carries no reasonable expectation of privacy. Technology has changed the vantage point of police observation. In *Florida* v. *Riley,* the Court decided that the government may use the "high place" of otherwise legal flight to observe illegal activity. This ruling opened observation flights over suspected marijuana fields. Perhaps most significantly, this ruling allowed a fundamental change in the notion of privacy that recognized changing technology.

Thus, the reasonable expectation of privacy is not static; it must adapt to technology beyond the intentions of the framers of the Constitution. The implications for electronic search and seizure are broad. The home, once the bastion of privacy rights, may contain a Web server with illicit materials. Viewing those materials does not constitute a search. Law enforcement officers may use a tool like a Web-based search engine and "invade" the Web server without violating a reasonable expectation of privacy.

Although searches usually implicate the Fourth Amendment, there is a precedent for First Amendment implications as well. In *Zurcher* v. *Stanford Daily* (1978),[62] police sought photographs of a student riot taken by a *Stanford Daily* photographer. In addition to defining search law, a relatively obscure circumstance was observed. The legitimate interest of the police in searching does not automatically override the substantial deference given to the press. The principles derived from the *Zurcher* case include:

1. A search is not unreasonable if items sought are not in the possession of the suspected criminal. The items sought must be reasonably expected at the place searched.

2. The search should not interfere with the execution of actions privileged by the First Amendment, particularly freedom of the press.

This principle was applied to computer search and seizure in the *Steve Jackson Games* (1993) case.[63] Federal agents tracking the theft of an electronic document related to the 911 system traced the document to an electronic bulletin board system maintained by Steve Jackson Games. Players of a conspiracy-paranoia game called *Illumination* exchanged messages about the game and sometimes about real life. Steve Jackson Games also used the system for internal development, e-mail, and newsletters. The Secret Service seized the entire physical system under a search warrant and did not return it for years. The company lost a substantial amount of business and customers and eventually claimed tens of thousands of dollars in damages. More fundamentally, the seizure unnecessarily deprived the company and gamers of a platform for speech and association.

SUMMARY

In this chapter, law and legislation as it applies to the collection of evidence and prosecution of digital crime were discussed. The different types of searches available to investigators searching for digital evidence were analyzed, including searches with and without warrants. The major federal statutes governing the collection of digital evidence were reviewed. Many of these statutes focused on electronic surveillance of communications networks. Issues related to the admission of digital evidence at trial, including authentication, hearsay, and the best evidence rule were reviewed as well. In addition, several significant U.S. Supreme Court cases that affect the investigation and prosecution of digital crime were discussed.

REVIEW QUESTIONS

1. What types of warrantless searches can be conducted by investigators collecting digital evidence?
2. What are the major exceptions to the wiretap statute?
3. What are the major requirements established by the Electronic Communication Privacy Act?
4. What issues arise during the admission of digital evidence at trial?

ENDNOTES

1. *Johnson* v. *United States,* 333 U.S. 10 (1948).
2. *Katz* v. *United States,* 389 U.S. 347 (1967).
3. *United States* v. *Jacobsen,* 466 U.S. 109 (1984).
4. *Ibid.*
5. *Arizona* v. *Hicks,* 480 U.S. 321 (1987).
6. BLACK, H.C., J.R. NOLAN, and J.M. NOLAN-HALEY. *Black's Law Dictionary,* 6th ed. (St. Paul, MN: West, 1990).
7. CASEY, E. *Digital Evidence and Computer Crime: Forensic Science, Computers and the Internet* (San Diego, CA: Academic Press, 2000).
8. *United States* v. *Leon,* 468 U.S. 897 (1984).
9. *United States* v. *David,* 756 F.Supp. 1385 (D. Nev. 1991); *United States* v. *Romero-Garcia,* 168 F.3d 502 (9th Cir. 1999).
10. FERDICO, J.N. *Criminal Procedure for the Criminal Justice Professional,* 7th ed. (New York: Wadsworth, 1999).
11. *Ibid.*
12. IVAN ORTON, "The Investigation and Prosecution of a Cybercrime." *In* RALPH D. CLIFFORD (ed.), *Cybercrime: The Investigation, Prosecution, and Defense of a Computer-Related Crime* (pp. 71–121). (Durham, NC: Carolina Academic Press, 2001); *Trulok* v. *Freeh,* 275 F.3d 391 (4th Cir. 2001).
13. *Chimel* v. *California,* 395 U.S. 752 (1969).
14. *Arizona* v. *Hicks,* 480 U.S. 321 (1987).
15. ORTON, IVAN. "The Investigation and Prosecution of a Cybercrime." *In* RALPH D. CLIFFORD (ed.), *Cybercrime: The Investigation, Prosecution, and Defense of a Computer-Related Crime* (pp. 71–121). (Durham, NC: Carolina Academic Press, 2001), pp. 91–92; *Trulok* v. *Freeh,* 275 F.3d 391 (4th Cir. 2001).
16. *Kyllo* v. *United States,* 533 U.S. 27 (2001).
17. *United States* v. *Roberts,* 274 F.3d 1007 (5th Cir. 2001); U.S. Department of Justice, *Searching and Seizing Computers and Obtaining Electronic Evidence in Criminal Investigations* (Washington, DC: U.S. Department of Justice, 2002).
18. U.S. Department of Justice. *Searching and Seizing Computers and Obtaining Electronic Evidence in Criminal Investigations* (Washington, DC: U.S. Department of Justice, 2002).
19. *Ibid.*
20. *Ibid.*
21. 18 U.S.C. 3122(b)(2).
22. U.S. Department of Justice. *Searching and Seizing Computers and Obtaining Electronic Evidence in Criminal Investigations* (Washington, DC: U.S. Department of Justice, 2002).
23. *Ibid.*
24. *Ibid.*
25. *Ibid.*
26. *Ibid.*
27. *Ibid.*
28. *Ibid.*
29. *Ibid.*
30. *Ibid.*
31. *Ibid.*
32. *Ibid.*

33. *Ibid.*
34. *Ibid.*
35. *Ibid.*
36. *Ibid.*
37. *Ibid.*
38. *Ibid.*
39. 18 U.S.C. §1030.
40. *The Electronic Frontier: The Challenge of Unlawful Conduct Involving the Use of the Internet* (A Report of the President's Working Group on Unlawful Conduct on the Internet, 2000).
41. HILLER, JANINE S. and RONNIE COHEN. *Internet Law and Policy* (Upper Saddle River, NJ: Prentice Hall, 2002).
42. *Ibid.*
43. *Ibid.*
44. KERR, ORIN S. *Computer Records and the Federal Rules of Evidence* (Washington, DC: U.S. Department of Justice, 2001).
45. *Ibid.*
46. *Ibid.*
47. *Ibid.*
48. Federal Rules of Evidence 901 (a).
49. KERR, ORIN S. *Computer Records and the Federal Rules of Evidence* (Washington, DC: U.S. Department of Justice, 2001).
50. *Ibid.*
51. *Ibid.*
52. *Ibid.*
53. *Ibid.*
54. Federal Rules of Evidence 803 (6).
55. KERR, ORIN S. *Computer Records and the Federal Rules of Evidence* (Washington, DC: U.S. Department of Justice, 2001).
56. Federal Rules of Evidence 1002.
57. KERR, ORIN S. *Computer Records and the Federal Rules of Evidence* (Washington, DC: U.S. Department of Justice, 2001).
58. Federal Rules of Evidence 1003.
59. KERR, ORIN S. *Computer Records and the Federal Rules of Evidence* (Washington, DC: U.S. Department of Justice, 2001).
60. *Katz* v. *United States,* 389 U.S. 347 (1967).
61. *Florida* v. *Riley,* 488 U.S. 445 (1989).
62. *Zurcher* v. *Stanford Daily,* 436 U.S. 547 (1978).
63. *Steve Jackson Games, Inc.* v. *Secret Service,* 816 F. Supp. 432, 440, 443 (W.D. Tex. 1993).

Chapter 10

![gray divider bar]

Law Enforcement Roles and Responses

Chapter Objectives

After completing this chapter, you should be able to:

- Provide an overview of the roles and responses of federal law enforcement agencies concerning digital crimes.
- Describe local law enforcement responses to computer crime.
- Identify the factors that have limited local law enforcement efforts against digital crime.
- Highlight the need for interagency cooperation in the detection and apprehension of digital criminals.

INTRODUCTION

The recent emergence of computer technologies and the growing threats created by digital criminals and terrorists have worked to produce a wide array of new challenges for law enforcement officials charged with protecting individuals, private businesses, and governments from these threats. In response, political leaders and police administrators have increasingly recognized the need to emphasize new priorities and foster new and innovative organizational strategies designed to counter the advent and continued growth of computer crimes.

This chapter begins with an overview of federal roles and responses as they relate to computer crimes. The discussion focuses on the responses and organizational initiatives recently enacted by eight prominent federal law enforcement agencies, as well as the anticipated role of the newly formed Department of Homeland Security in these efforts. The chapter continues with a description of the ways in which local law enforcement agencies have joined the fight against computer crime. This section emphasizes the need to strengthen the capabilities of local agencies by identifying several factors that have thus far limited local law enforcement efforts. The chapter concludes by noting the need for interagency collaboration and cooperation in the battle to thwart digital criminals.

FEDERAL ROLES AND RESPONSES

For the most part, federal agencies have spearheaded law enforcement efforts against computer crime because these agencies possess the technical expertise and political clout to garner significant financial and operational resources at the national level. These agencies have increasingly reorganized in an effort to channel resources directly at preventing digital crimes and apprehending computer criminals, including the creation of special sections within these organizations, the recruitment of new personnel who possess specialized technical expertise in this area, and the creation of new collaborative units that combine the resources of multiple agencies.

The Secret Service

The United States Secret Service was created in 1865 to serve a dual purpose: to provide protective services to the President and other Cabinet members, and to safeguard the nation's financial payment system against fraud and counterfeit financial instruments. The agency's responsibilities have increased tremendously as a result of the revolution in computerized information systems and the growth of the Internet as a vehicle for financial transactions.

For example, the ever-increasing sophistication of computerized reproduction capabilities has expanded the potential for the production of counterfeit financial instruments. In addition, the development of Internet communications has facilitated the rapid communication of encrypted messages and financial fraud schemes using phony debit and credit card transactions and electronic funds transfers (EFTs). Finally, the agency's protection responsibilities in terms of special events has grown to include the safeguarding of computerized telecommunications and power systems integral to these events. The convergence of these related factors has thrust the Secret Service into the role of the federal government's primary law enforcement weapon against computer and cybercrime.[1]

The Secret Service's Financial Crimes Division is the agency's primary tool in the fight against computer crime. The division's main responsibilities include the enforcement of three high-profile computer related crimes. First, the division is charged with identifying and investigating financial institution fraud (FIF). Since 1990, the Secret Service has been granted concurrent jurisdiction with the Department of Justice to investigate fraud committed against financial institutions such as banks and savings and loans. Primary

FIF schemes include the creation of counterfeit financial instruments (primarily cash) through desktop publishing systems. Recent Secret Service investigations have pointed to large increases in the production of counterfeit corporate checks and negotiable instruments that have paralleled the advent of sophisticated desktop publishing systems and copying technologies. Title 18, Section 514 of the U.S. Federal Code was enacted in 1996 in order to stem the growing tide of phony cash and checks in circulation.[2]

Second, the Secret Service has primary jurisdiction in cases involving access device fraud. Access device fraud falls under Title 18, Section 1029 of the U.S. Federal Code (the "credit card statute") and involves the fraudulent use of credit card numbers, personal identification numbers (PINs), and computer passwords. In addition to these access device frauds, the Secret Service has increasingly investigated the theft of computer codes located within cellular phones that are used to track billing information. The Secret Service estimates that losses resulting from access fraud cases run into the billions; the agency arrested over 2,400 individuals for access fraud crimes in 1996 alone.[3]

Third, the Secret Service has primary jurisdiction in the investigation of general computer fraud relating to computers and computer systems of "federal interest." These computers can be used as instruments of crime through hacking or other means, as well as tools to produce fraudulent negotiable instruments or store private account information. The Secret Service has recently trained over 100 agents in computer forensics designed to detect and investigate these crimes through the agency's Electronic Crimes Special Agent program (ECSAP).[4]

The Financial Crimes Division houses the Electronic Crimes Branch, specializing in detecting and investigating credit card and other access device fraud. The Electronic Crimes Branch provides computer equipment and technical assistance to special agents concerning lab analysis of computer-related evidence and storage equipment, the seizure of computerized evidence, and the administrative management of all computer-related investigations.[5]

In recognition of the Secret Service's primary role in combating computer and cybercrime and the need for interagency cooperation, provisions of the USA PATRIOT Act (2000) point to the development of a "network" of task forces that span federal jurisdictions. These task forces include federal, state and local law enforcement agency personnel, and have been primarily aimed at addressing the increasingly global nature of computerized financial fraud. Specific task forces have included the Metro Alien Task Force, the West African (Nigerian) Task Force, and the Asian Organized Crime Task Force.[6]

The Department of Justice

The United States Department of Justice (DOJ) was established in 1870. The organization is headed by the chief law enforcement officer of the federal government—the Attorney General. The Attorney General represents the United States in legal matters generally and gives advice and opinions regarding matters of jurisprudence to the President. In cases of extreme importance, the Attorney General may appear before the

United States Supreme Court as the federal government's representative attorney. Under the Attorney General is a vast array of sections and organizational subunits designed to oversee the administration of justice on the federal level. These agencies include: (1) The U.S. Attorney's Office, representing the federal government in court and prosecuting federal suspects; (2) the major federal investigative agencies, including the Federal Bureau of Investigation (FBI), the Drug Enforcement Administration (DEA), and the Bureau of Alcohol, Tobacco, and Firearms (ATF); (3) the Immigration and Naturalization Service; (4) the United States Marshals Service; and (5) the U.S. Bureau of Prisons.[7]

The DOJ has stepped up efforts to respond to the legal threats posed by cyber-criminals. The cornerstone of these efforts is the Criminal Division's Computer Crime and Intellectual Property Section (CCIPS). CCIPS began as the Computer Crime Unit of DOJ in 1991. This unit primarily prosecuted violations of the Federal Code covered by Title 18, Section 1030 of the Computer Fraud and Abuse Act. The scope of DOJ jurisdiction in such crimes was expanded with the enactment of the National Information and Infrastructure Protection Act of 1996. In accordance with this act, as well as the DOJ's recognition of the need to increase prosecutorial resources aimed at combating computer crimes, the department elevated the unit to section status in 1996 and adopted the moniker CCIPS.[8]

Currently, the section employs 32 attorneys who focus solely on legal issues raised by computer and intellectual property crimes. CCIPS attorneys specialize in prosecuting crimes related to encryption, e-commerce, intellectual property crimes, electronic privacy laws, computer hacker investigations, and search and seizure cases involving computers. Members of the CCIPS section advise federal prosecutors on computer crimes cases, and CCIPS attorneys normally take the lead in litigating computer and intellectual property crimes on behalf of the federal government. In addition, CCIPS staff members comment on the legality of proposed computer crime legislation that is designed to mitigate computer crime threats. CCIPS works in close collaboration with the U.S. Attorney's Office in the prosecution of computer crimes. Assistant U.S. Attorneys are designated as Computer and Telecommunications Coordinators. These coordinators obtain specialized training from CCIPS, and they are able to utilize the latest technology in investigating and prosecuting cases.[9]

While CCIPS primarily operates as a prosecutorial arm of the department, the section has also attempted to remedy the growing need for training and interagency cooperation. CCIPS attorneys conduct hundreds of training seminars every year for other federal attorneys in an effort to educate those prosecutors outside of the section in regard to relevant legislation and effective prosecutorial strategies for cases involving computer crime. In addition, CCIPS attorneys act as chairs to the National Cybercrime Training Partnership (NCTP), which is a consortium designed to integrate local, state, and federal prosecutorial efforts regarding "info-tech" crimes. In 2000, the section hosted the prominent "Cybercrime Summit: A Law Enforcement/ Information Technology Dialogue on Prevention, Detection, Investigation, and Cooperation," in which then-acting Attorney General Janet Reno outlined the government's primary goals in the prosecution of computer crimes. On the international front, CCIPS attorneys chair the G-8 subgroup on high-tech crime.[10]

Finally, the DOJ has begun to increase efforts in the detection and prosecution of computer hacking crimes. In 2001 the department expanded the highly successful Computer Hacking and Intellectual Property Unit (CHIP). CHIP is the department's latest effort toward establishing ongoing relationships with local private sector high-tech communities. If successful, CHIPS would not only augment existing CCIPS and U.S. Attorney's prosecutions, but also provide inroads in accomplishing the much sought-after goal of public–private partnerships in the battle against computer crime.[11]

The Federal Bureau of Investigation

The Federal Bureau of Investigation (FBI) was established in 1908 as the investigative branch of the U.S. Department of Justice. The FBI carries a broad mandate that authorizes the organization to investigate any federal crime that has not been specifically designated to another federal agency. These broad legal areas can include civil rights crimes, counterterrorism, foreign counterintelligence, violent federal crimes, organized crime and drugs, and financial crimes. The FBI employs over 11,000 Special Agents who operate out of the Washington, D.C. headquarters, 56 field offices, and over 400 satellite offices globally. The bureau's role in fighting computer crime is twofold: (1) The FBI investigates domestic criminal acts that involve computers, such as Internet fraud, hacking, the transmission of obscene material across state lines, or computer-related financial crimes against banks and other financial institutions; and (2) The FBI and other federal agencies collaborate in protecting the nation's largely computerized critical infrastructure system.[12]

The bureau's Cyber Division works in tandem with the Criminal Investigative Division in the investigation of domestic threats generated by computer-related crimes. The FBI currently operates three computer forensic laboratories nationwide. The bureau's Computer Analysis Response Team (CART) employs 150 forensic examiners who primarily investigate computer hacking crimes against government systems. The FBI caseload for "computer intrusions" doubled to over 1,100 cases from 1998 to 2000.[13] In addition, the bureau has partnered with the National White-Collar Crime Center (NW3C) to operate the Internet Fraud Complaint Center (IFCC). The IFCC provides victims of Internet fraud a mechanism to report suspicious on line activities. The IFCC also provides other federal agencies a "central repository for complaints related to Internet fraud." The goal of the IFCC is to identify wider Internet fraud patterns and trends to aid in the enforcement of these crimes.[14]

In addition to its role in fighting domestically generated computer crimes, the Bureau has collaborated with the U.S. Department of Justice (DOJ) to form the National Infrastructure Protection Center (NIPC). NIPC was created on the recommendation of the President's Commission on Critical Infrastructure Protection (1998), which highlighted the role of federal agencies in protecting critical computer systems against terrorist activities. NIPC is aimed not only at providing an avenue toward public agency collaboration, but is intended to strengthen public and private sector security partnerships. Clearly, both the public and private sectors have a role to play in protecting computerized critical infrastructures.[15] The federal government owns and operates many of these critical infrastructure systems; these law enforcement agencies would be the primary responders in the event of a national crisis. Likewise, the private sector currently operates the vast majority of these systems, and private sector employees often have the greatest expertise in identifying and solving technical problems. NIPC's "InfraGard," a pilot project designed to facilitate the exchange of information among academic institutions, the business community, and the FBI, serves as a prime example of the FBI's agenda for partnerships and interagency collaboration in the fight against cybercrimes.[16]

The National Security Agency

The National Security Agency bills itself as the nation's pre-eminent "cryptologic organization." In more familiar language, the NSA is primarily responsible for designing and maintaining computerized coding systems designed to protect the integrity of United States information systems.[17] In direct relation to these responsibilities, NSA agents are also responsible for detecting and exploiting weaknesses in an adversarial country's computerized secret coding systems. Headquartered in Ft. Meade, MD, the NSA has been providing the nation with "code-breaking" capabilities since these operations began against the Japanese in the Pacific theater of World War II. The NSA's role in providing information system security (INFOSEC) has expanded with the parallel growth in computerized communications technology during the Cold War and the ensuing decades.[18]

The NSA's role in protecting classified computer data demands an eclectic mix of agents who specialize in a wide range of professional fields, including researchers, computer scientists, mathematicians, and engineers. Though much of the work of NSA agents remains secretive in nature, the agency's expertise in the area of information systems has led to a number of collaborative initiatives intended to improve INFOSEC research, knowledge, and expertise through the Federal law enforcement system. For example, the NSA has recently created the INFOSEC Service Center designed to increase research initiatives concerning computer security by the federal government. The NSA has also helped to form the National Computer Security Center (NCSC), which is designed as an avenue to create partnerships among the Federal law enforcement and intelligence communities.[19]

The NSA has also assumed an active role in providing INFOSEC training to both government and private entities through the National INFOSEC Education and Training Program. This program provides training for security specialists, including risk assessment, security design, and information security evaluation. Through these initiatives, NSA aims to provide government agencies and the private sector information system security expertise.[20]

The Federal Trade Commission

The Federal Trade Commission (FTC) was created in 1914 primarily as a way for the government to "trust bust," or apply regulations ensuring a free marketplace for U.S. consumers and business enterprises. In this regard, the FTC enforces antitrust violations that could hamper consumer interests, as well as federal consumer protection laws against fraud, deception, and unfair business practices. The commission's primary enforcement mechanism is the Bureau of Consumer Protection, which is divided into six divisions: (1) enforcement, (2) advertising practices, (3) financial practices, (4) marketing practices, (5) planning and information, and (6) consumer and business education programs.[21]

As the federal government's primary mechanism for protecting consumer markets, the FTC has been forced to apply its traditional enforcement tools in an increasingly computer-related marketplace. Consumers and businesses alike have grown accustomed to the exchange of goods and services through electronic mediums, especially the Internet. Indeed, so-called e-commerce generates over $300 billion in revenue annually, making the Internet economy comparable in size to the energy, automobile, and telecommunications industries. In response to the growth of Internet commerce, the FTC attempts to minimize fraudulent and deceptive business practices that occur on line and educate consumers regarding safe avenues to conduct e-commerce.[22]

The commission has been involved primarily in the enforcement of traditional criminal activities that now often occur on line, including false marketing claims, credit card repair scams, financial pyramid schemes, and fraudulent business opportunity schemes. Since 1994, the FTC has brought 93 federal law enforcement actions against 239 defendants.[23] In addition to these traditional marketplace crimes, the commission has stepped up efforts to combat invasions of consumer privacy that occur on line. The growth of e-commerce has resulted in consumers increasingly providing personal financial and medical information on line, thus expanding the threat that this information could be used fraudulently through theft or other means.

The FTC has developed the Identity Theft Program, designed to provide assistance to local and federal law enforcement agencies attempting to curb the misuse and theft of personal information through on line access. The program aids these agencies in enforcing the Identity Theft and Assumption Deterrence Act of 1998, which is a federal response to the widespread incidence of identity theft in recent years. The act emphasizes that personal information is increasingly used against individuals and businesses to commit fraud on line. Under this act, the FTC was required to create a database of identity theft victim complaints, to provide useful information to consumers and educate them regarding protecting the use of personal information on line, as well as a means to refer victims of identity theft to law enforcement authorities. These mandates resulted in the creation of the *Consumer Sentinel,* which is a centralized database of identity theft complaints used to compile statistics regarding the incidence of identity theft.[24]

The Postal Service

The U.S. Postal Service's widely known primary mission is to provide safe, affordable, and universal mail service to the nation. The nation's mail service delivery agency has also operated one of the country's oldest federal law enforcement agencies—the U.S. Postal Inspection Service—since 1830. Congress empowered the Postal Service to "investigate postal offenses and civil matters relating to the Postal Service." In order to accomplish this task, the U.S. Postal Inspection Service was established to perform "investigative and security functions essential to a stable and sound postal system." Thus, the two main functions of the U.S. Postal Inspection service are to provide businesses with a safe avenue for the exchange of funds and securities, and provide private citizens a safe and secure way in which to transmit correspondence. The Postal Inspection Service employs over 2,000 agents nationwide. These agents investigate and enforce over 200 federal laws covering the illegal and fraudulent use of the U.S. mail service.[25]

In terms of the investigation and prosecution of computer crimes, the U.S. Postal Inspection Service must frequently conduct joint investigations with other federal agencies, primarily because many types of computer crimes involve the use of the mail system to accomplish computer-related fraudulent activities or to transport materials related to computer crimes. In these types of cases, the jurisdiction of the Postal Inspection Service may overlap with that of any number of local or federal agencies, including the U.S. Secret Service, the FBI, and the Department of Justice. The U.S. Postal Service's primary concerns in the area of computer crime are: identity theft, child exploitation and pornography, and electronic crimes.[26]

As detailed elsewhere in this volume, identity theft involves acquiring key pieces of someone's identifying information, including name, address, date of birth, and social security number, in order to impersonate them. Under Title 18, Section 1028 of the U.S. Federal Code, postal inspectors share jurisdiction in these cases because they often involve mail that is stolen in order to obtain the above information. In addition, identity thieves will use computers in order to elicit bogus credit cards and checks from financial institutions through the U.S. mail. In response to these crimes, the U.S. Postal Service has instituted the Mail Theft Reporting System (MTRS). MTRS aims to identify patterns in mail theft across geographic regions, as well as compile statistics relating to mail theft victims and monetary losses. In 2001, postal inspectors arrested 2,217 suspects of credit card and identity theft offenses.[27]

The U.S. Postal Inspection Service is the leading federal agency in combating the production and distribution of child pornography. Increasingly, child pornography crimes have been classified as computer related because they often involve the use of the Internet in production and downloading of pornographic images. Postal inspectors become involved when these computer-generated images are distributed through the U.S. mail. The primary legal vehicle to enforce these crimes used by postal inspectors is Title 18 of the U.S. Federal Code, Sections 1470, 2251, 2252-2254.[28]

In addition, postal inspectors share jurisdiction in any electronic crime that involves the misuse of the U.S. mail. These crimes can include consumer fraud schemes that originate on the Internet through e-mail solicitations, since these crimes often eventually involve use of the U.S. mail in the delivery of fraudulent documents and/or fraudulently obtained currency. Among the most-widely cited of these crimes is the Nigerian advance fee fraud letter and e-mail scam in which Nigerian nationals send letters and e-mails to US citizens. The letters or emails invariably ask the recipient for some kind of fee as a precondition to the transfer of large amounts of money from Nigeria. American citizens have lost over $100 million in these schemes. The Postal Inspection Service has recently joined with the Department of Justice to form an Interagency Law Enforcement Task Force to address the problem.[29]

The Bureau of Customs and Border Protection

The U.S. Bureau of Customs and Border Protection was created in 2003. The agency is the result of a merger of several federal agencies that are entrusted with protecting the integrity of our nation's borders, including the U.S. Customs and Border Patrol, the Immigration and Naturalization Service, and the Animal and Plant Health Inspection Service (APHIS). Traditionally, the U.S. Customs Service enforces all laws related to the regulation of U.S. international trade, including the assessment and collection of duties, excise taxes, and the interdiction of illegal contraband.[30]

Today, the U.S. Customs Service plays a pivotal role in enforcing Internet-related crimes because of the agency's primary responsibilities concerning border protection and the inherently international nature of cyberspace crimes.[31] Agency responsibilities in this area began with the seizing of illegally distributed child pornography materials, a crime that has increasingly involved the use of the Internet. With the expansion of the Child Protection Act of 1984, U.S. Customs was given the authority to investigate cases involving the receipt, transmission, manufacture, or possession of child pornography that is shipped internationally. In 1989, the agency launched its first investigation against computerized child pornography bulletin boards. In response to expanding Internet use in the creation and distribution of child pornography, in 1996 the agency created the U.S. Customs Service International Child Pornography Investigation and Coordination Center (ICPICC). The center is designed to promote interagency cooperation among federal, state and local law enforcement agencies in combating international child pornography rings.[32]

The U.S. Customs Service has recently expanded its enforcement of computer-related crimes with the creation of the Customs Cyber Smuggling Center (3C). In addition to the enforcement of child pornography crimes, the center has enabled U.S. Customs to become involved in the enforcement of a wide variety of cybercrimes, including international money laundering, intellectual property rights violations, and illegal arms trafficking.[33]

The Department of Energy

The U.S. Department of Energy was created in 1977 in order to consolidate existing federal energy programs and activities. The DOE's main responsibilities include the administration of domestic energy production, the promotion of renewable energy resources, and the promotion of energy conservation and efficiency. The department has increasingly relied on computerized technologies to operate and administer the nation's energy-producing infrastructure. The growth in computer crime has created an increasing need to protect these critical infrastructure systems from both domestic and international threats. These threats can involve the introduction of malicious codes designed to interfere with the operation of energy production systems.[34]

In response to these threats, the agency has created the DOE Information Security Server (DOE-IS). The DOE-IS is an advanced Web server that contains tools and documents related to critical infrastructure and energy system security. The server is designed to enhance communications between the DOE and private contractors who use these energy systems so that critical infrastructures can remain protected from cyber attacks.[35] In addition, the DOE collaborates with Computer Incident Advisory Capability (CIAC), an organization that provides computer security expertise in the prevention, detection, and recovery from cyber attacks to critical infrastructures.[36]

The Department of Homeland Security

The preceding section describing the manner in which federal agencies are organized to combat computer crime discussed each agency in separate terms, and characterized the strategies of any single agency as independent and separate from those of the other agencies involved in the fight against computer crime. The attempt to classify these agencies in independent fashion is intended not only to help the reader understand the different roles of each federal agency discussed, but may be viewed as an indication of the historically "piecemeal" nature of law enforcement actions at the federal level. Federal law enforcement agencies have a long history of failing to coordinate and cooperate not only in the relatively recent fight against computer crime, but with regard to a host of more traditional crime problems, including organized crime, the "war on drugs," and more general intelligence gathering operations.

The cost associated with these disjointed federal law enforcement strategies became fatally and critically clear on September 11, 2001, when these domestic agencies collectively failed to detect and prevent the terrorist plot against the World Trade Center and the Pentagon. With the need for federal cooperation becoming abundantly clear in the face of such attacks, President Bush launched an initiative to create a cabinet level department designed to improve information sharing among federal law enforcement agencies, consolidate a host of over 100 federal offices in these departments, and increase interagency coordination in the fight against domestic terror. The recently established Department of Homeland Security (DHS) is the result of these efforts.[37]

DHS has a wide range of organizational components and has subsumed a number of previously discussed federal agencies under the DHS umbrella including: Border and Transportation Security, Emergency Preparedness and Response, Science and Technology, the Coast Guard, the Secret Service, the Citizen and Immigration Service, the Inspector General, and Information Analysis and Infrastructure Protection. The agency now employs over 169,000 federal employees who have been transferred or subsumed from other federal agencies.[38] The Information Analysis and Infrastructure Protection component of DHS is of primary importance in the fight against computer crime. Three initiatives within this section have bolstered federal efforts, including the creation of the National Infrastructure Advisory Council (NIAC), the Protected Critical Infrastructure Information Program (PCII), and the National Cyber Security Division (NCSD).

NIAC's purpose is to enhance public and private partnerships in the protection of information systems for critical infrastructures.[39] The President appoints members to the council from academia, private businesses, and government agencies. The council advises the President on the development of mechanisms to enhance the exchange of security information in the private sector, and to promote periodic risk assessments in order to secure key information systems. PCII provides private sector organizations the opportunity to submit information that is deemed critical to infrastructure protection to the DHS in order to reduce its vulnerability to terror attacks. In this way, federal law enforcement personnel can provide private businesses that are engaged in maintaining critical information databases greater security against external threats, enhancing national security in the process.[40] Likewise, NCSD provides avenues for collaboration both among federal law enforcement agencies and between the public and private sectors. The NCSD's main objectives include conducting an analysis of cyberspace protection systems, issuing alerts concerning impending dangers to those systems, and implementing national level recovery strategies in the event of successful cyber attacks.

STATE AND LOCAL ROLES

As the sections above indicate, the growing danger posed by computer crimes has clearly resulted in an increasing enforcement emphasis at the federal level. Indeed, the current struggle against international terrorist threats—culminating with the September 11th attacks against the World Trade Center and the Pentagon—seems to have galvanized national-level efforts to protect critical computer infrastructures at the federal level. The threats related to computer crimes, however, have also become a growing concern to law enforcement officials at the state and local levels. While federal officials employed by the myriad agencies detailed above seem to have successfully garnered both public and political attention concerning the need for resources aimed at addressing the computer crime problem, law enforcement personnel at the local level continue to encounter a host of issues that have hampered efforts to combat computer crimes effectively within their own jurisdictions. This section will provide an overview regarding what is being done to fight computer crime at the state and local levels of enforcement, with an emphasis on identifying the critical areas of need that have thus far limited efforts to combat computer crime at the local level.

A recent Internet search of state and local level task forces aimed at computer crime enforcement identified 95 such organizations, including 41 local, 22 state-level, 21 county, and ten regional task forces.[41] The number of local, state, county, and regional task forces continues to increase, largely because these agencies have experienced more computer-related criminal activities within their jurisdictions, and citizens and private entities have become increasingly willing to report these activities to local law enforcement departments. For example, a recent survey of local law enforcement computer crime experts found that 80 percent of the respondents indicated a "measurable increase" in the reporting of computer and electronic crimes, especially traditional fraud and theft crimes using computer devices.[42]

The most pressing computer crimes enforced by these agencies appear to be those related to "harmful computer content," especially child pornography and exploitation, threatening communications, and stalking.[43] These types of computer crimes are followed in priority by computer-related frauds (e.g., on-line shopping schemes and electronic funds transfer fraud), other technology-based crimes (e.g., encryption used to hide criminal activities such as drug trafficking), and computer hacking crimes. Higher profile computer crimes, such as threats to critical national infrastructure systems, are rarely handled solely by local and state investigators because they often require federal expertise and resources.[44]

Despite the ever-increasing caseload of computer crimes, there appears to be a lack of recognition and support from upper level management within local police agencies in terms of providing the resources necessary to counter these threats. The majority of these cases receive a low priority at the local level. The fact that computer crime cases have not received the necessary recognition and support from local law enforcement administrators has created several areas in which local level agencies must improve if computer crimes are to be effectively enforced.

Critical Needs at the State and Local Levels of Enforcement

Officers involved in combating computer crime at the local and state level must be supplied with an increase in resources and technology in order to fight computer crime more effectively. These areas can be broadly grouped into four "critical needs": (1) training, (2) equipment, (3) updated criminal codes designed to complement current enforcement efforts, and (4) resources for tapping Federal expertise and equipment related to computer crime enforcement.[45]

The need for training appears to be paramount at the local level. Currently, most local agencies fail to provide any training in computer crime to patrol personnel. This lack of training at the entry level can have severe consequences in regard to prosecuting computer crimes, especially in terms of protecting computer crime scenes and collecting forensic evidence. An untrained patrol officer can easily inadvertently destroy computerized evidence if not trained in protecting such evidence.[46] Related to training needs at the entry level, most local departments do not possess the technical expertise needed to train those officers interested in becoming computer forensic specialists. Often, these officers must obtain specialized training from outside sources such as private industry or the federal government. Some researchers and administrators have cited the need for a national certification program aimed at producing more specially trained computer experts at the local level. Others have noted that the career path for "computer crime specialists" at the local level can often be limited, and career advancement within many local agencies would require reassignment to another priority division.[47]

The need for computer crime training appears to go hand in hand with the procurement of additional resources and equipment. While federal personnel have increasingly used the growing awareness of computer crime at the national level as an avenue for larger equipment expenditures, these dollars have largely failed to trickle down to the local level.[48] The resulting disparity in equipment between federal and local cyber cops can most clearly be seen in the inability of most local agencies to decipher encrypted computer evidence.[49] Surveys of local computer crime experts indicate that for those jurisdictions that currently have computer evidence laboratories, more than

50 percent do not have adequate capabilities to read encrypted evidence. Much of the problem related to lack of equipment can be traced to insufficient funding behind efforts to control computer crime. Many local experts have cited the need to use equipment that has been purchased personally because local departments fail to provide adequate resources from within the organization.[50]

As detailed elsewhere in this text, the explosion in computer technologies and communications has stymied legislative attempts to enact statutes that are current and can be applied to the use of these new technologies. In short, state laws have been largely unable to keep pace with technology. The gap evident between the pace of technological change and the enactment of legal codes has been especially problematic for computer crime specialists and prosecutors at the local level. For example, there are no legal mechanisms designed to allow the enforcement of subpoenas across state lines.[51] In the case of crimes that occur over the Internet, the lack of these mechanisms can effectively halt computer crime investigations at the local level. So too, severe differences exist across jurisdictions in terms of the definition of what constitutes an electronic crime. Some states continue to define many computer crimes as misdemeanor offenses, thereby reducing local law enforcement incentives to increase enforcement resources in this area.[52]

Finally, those officers who are active in the enforcement of computer crimes at the local level have cited a lack of informational resources that would enable them to easily utilize the extensive technical expertise and equipment resources that currently exist at the federal level. Currently, there is no comprehensive source of information containing a list of federal contact persons who could aid local investigators. Such a "guidebook" could include not only a list of prominent federal agents who are experts in the field of computer crime, but also prominent computer forensic laboratories, forensic equipment available for local use, and federally approved equipment manufacturers to aid local agencies who are interesting in upgrading their computer crime resources.[53]

INTERAGENCY COOPERATION AND COLLABORATION

We began this chapter by identifying several federal agencies charged with combating digital crimes, and the various roles these agencies have assumed in the fight against computer crime were presented. The establishment of DHS subsequent to the September 11th attacks highlights the need for interagency cooperation at the federal level. Likewise, the chapter presented the role of local and state agencies as separate from that of the federal agencies. While this method of organization was utilized in order to produce an orderly presentation of material for the reader, the discussion may be viewed as somewhat misleading given the nature of digital crime and the types of collaborative responses that appear to be necessary on the part of the law enforcement community.

As many observers have noted, the emergence of computer crime has been especially unsettling to the law enforcement community because these acts often cross traditional jurisdictional boundaries. The cybercriminal respects no borders. So too, problems related to cybercrime demand attention from a wide variety of groups outside of traditional law enforcement, including consumers, businesses, privacy advocates, and national security interests. Both the public and private sectors have a role to play in fighting cybercrime. For their part, federal agencies must be involved because their agents would be the first responders in the event of major cybercrime events. So too, private industry owns and operates most of the nation's critical computer infrastructures, and these companies tend to employ the most highly trained and qualified individuals in the information technology field.[54] Clearly, the need for collaboration and cooperation across different types of public agencies, as well as between public agencies and private information security specialists, should clearly underscore any discussion concerning the enforcement of computer crime.

The law enforcement community has begun to recognize the importance of building partnerships across public and private domains, as well as between public agencies. Three primary examples of such partnerships include: the FBI's "Operation Cyber Loss," the New York Electronic Crimes Task Force, and the Department of Justice's "Cybercitizen Partnership."

In 2001 the FBI announced the initiation of "Operation Cyber Loss" in conjunction with the Department of Justice. The program is a nationwide investigative task force specifically designed to combat Internet fraud crimes. Operation Cyber Loss is coordinated through the FBI's Internet Fraud Complaint Center (IFCC), and involves investigators from a wide range of federal agencies, including the U.S. Postal Inspectors, the Internal Revenue Service, the U.S. Customs Service, and the U.S. Secret Service. In addition to these federal agencies, the operation has included numerous state and local law enforcement agencies.[55] The operation is mainly concerned with fraud schemes that are multijurisdictional, or those that generate victims around the globe. Thus far, Operation Cyber Loss has exposed schemes affecting over 56,000 individuals, who have collectively lost over $117 million. Specific suspects have been charged in crimes including on line auction fraud, identity theft, and credit card fraud.[56]

The New York Electronic Crimes Task Force (NYECTF) provides an excellent model for collaborative partnerships.[57] The NYECTF was formed in 1995 by the U.S. Secret Service. The Secret Service appears to be uniquely qualified among federal law enforcement agencies to form partnerships with the business community because of the agency's long-standing relationships with companies in the telecommunications, finance, and banking industries. The NYECTF is comprised of 45 federal, state, and local law enforcement agencies, 100 private companies, and six universities. The NYECTF has investigated a wide range of electronic crimes, including child pornography, computer systems intrusions, access device fraud, and identity theft. Since its creation, the NYECTF has prosecuted over 800 suspects.[58]

"Cyber Partnership" is collaboration between the U.S. Department of Justice and computer-related industries. The partnership is multifaceted, and includes the initiation of an education campaign designed to foster computer ethics and public awareness concerning acts that are in violation of electronic crime statutes. In addition, the partnership creates a public–private exchange program, whereby employees from the private sector are familiarized with law enforcement priorities as they relate to computer crimes, and public sector employees are exposed to the technical expertise of personnel working for private information security organizations.[59]

SUMMARY

American law enforcement agencies have assumed a variety of roles and responses to the new and increasing threats posed by computer crimes and terrorism. This chapter has provided an overview of how a number of federal agencies have responded to these threats, including the Secret Service, the Department of Justice, the Federal Bureau of Investigation, the National Security Agency, the Federal Trade Commission, the Postal Service, Customs and Border Protection, and the Department of Energy. These wide-ranging agencies have worked independently to adapt their specialized law enforcement expertise to these new problems. The federal government has increasingly recognized the need for these disparate agencies to collaborate in the fight against computer crime and terror. Moreover, local and state level law enforcement agencies have attempted to assume their own role in enforcing computer crimes. Although a relatively small number of these agencies have responded successfully to these threats through increasing funding and the formation of multiagency task forces, these agencies have largely been limited by several factors, most notably a lack of funds, personnel, and technology.

REVIEW QUESTIONS

1. Which federal law enforcement agency has assumed primary responsibilities in the area of access device fraud, including the fraudulent use of credit card numbers, personal identification numbers, and computer passwords?
2. Which federal agency is responsible for the prosecution of computer fraud and abuse violations through the Computer Crime and Intellectual Property Section (CCIPS)?
3. Which federal agency collaborated with the U.S. Department of Justice to form the National Infrastructure Protection Center (NIPC)?
4. What does NYECTF stand for?

ENDNOTES

1. JACKSON, W. (2003). "E-Crime Squad." *Government Computer News* 22(2).
2. *http://www.ustreas.gov*
3. *Ibid., 2.*
4. *http://www.secretservice.gov*
5. *Ibid., 2.*
6. *Ibid., 2.*
7. *http://www.usdoj.gov*
8. *http://www.usdoj.gov/criminal/cybercrime/ccpolicy*
9. *Ibid., 8.*
10. *http://www.cybercrime.gov*

11. *Ibid.*, 10.

12. *http://www.fbi.gov*

13. BLANK, D.S. (2003). "FBI Plans to Double the Size of Bureau's Cybercrime Team." *Government Computer News* 19(28).

14. *http://www1.ifccfbi.gov*

15. *http://www.nipc.gov*

16. WAIT, P. (2003). "DHS Creates Division for Cybersecurity." *Government Computer News,* June.

17. *http://www.nsa.gov*

18. *Ibid.*, 17.

19. *Ibid.*, 17.

20. *Ibid.*, 17.

21. *http://www.ftc.gov*

22. SWINDLE, O. (1999). "E-Commerce: Tomorrow's Economy—Taxing and Regulation the Old-fashioned Way." Remarks before the Georgia Public Policy Forum, September 11.

23. *Ibid.*, 22.

24. Federal Trade Commission (2002). Seminar: "Attacking Identity Theft Together: Usable Tools for Law Enforcement." Dallas, TX. August 14.

25. *http://www.usps.com*

26. *Ibid.*, 25.

27. *Ibid.*, 25.

28. *Ibid.*, 25.

29. *Ibid.*, 25.

30. *http://www.customs.ustreas.gov*

31. *http://www.cbp.gov*

32. *Ibid.*, 30.

33. DEAN, J. 2000. "Customs Debuts Cybersmuggling Center." *GovExec.Com.,* October 4,

34. *http://www.doe.gov*

35. *http://doe-is.llnl.gov*

36. *http://www.ciac.org*

37. *http://www.dhs.gov*

38. SCARDAVILLE, M. (2002). "Principles for Creating an Effective U.S. Department of Homeland Security." *The Heritage Foundation: Policy, Research, & Analysis,* June 12.

39. *Ibid.*, 37.

40. *Ibid.*, 37.

41. *http://www.ccmostwanted.com*

42. STANBAUGH, H., D.S. BEUPRE, D.J. ICOYE, R. BAKER, W. CASSADAY, and W.P. WILLIAMS (2001). "Electronic Crime Needs Assessment for State and Local Law Enforcement." *National Institute of Justice,* March.

43. *Ibid.*, 38.

44. *Ibid.*, 38.

45. *Ibid.*, 38.

46. *Ibid.*, 38.

47. *Ibid.*, 38.

48. *Ibid.*, 38.

49. *Ibid.*, 38.

50. *Ibid.*, 38.

51. *Ibid.*, 38.

52. *Ibid.*, 38.

53. *Ibid.,* 38.
54. *www.nipc.gov*
55. Kubic, T. (2001). Statement before the House Committee on the Judiciary, Subcommittee on Crime, June 12.
56. *Ibid.,* 51.
57. *http://www.computerworld.com*
58. *Ibid.,* 53.
59. Reno, J. (1999). Press Conference Announcing Formation of "Cyber Partnership," March 15.

Chapter 11

The Investigation of Computer-Related Crime

Chapter Objectives

After completing this chapter, you should be able to:

- Explain and understand the search warrant application process appropriate to electronic evidence at a single-location crime scene.
- Identify hardware and storage devices potentially containing evidence of a crime.
- Explain and understand the legal standards and best current practices for the documentation of a single-location electronic crime scene.
- Explain and describe the best current practices for the collection, preservation, transportation, and storage of electronic evidence.
- Distinguish between single-scene, multiple-scene, and network crimes.
- Be able to communicate an understanding of network architectures and standards relevant to network investigations.
- Identify sources of assistance for multiple-scene and network operations.
- Identify categories of evidence and probable locations of that evidence.
- Broadly outline procedures for preserving and collecting network trace evidence.

INTRODUCTION

This chapter focuses on the current state of the field in computer crime investigations. The personnel available to an investigation will dramatically influence the type and scope of investigations that may be undertaken. Understanding the roles of and skills needed by such personnel is vital to planning appropriate investigations. Although there is no single policy or plan for investigations, this chapter presents an overview of investigations, with special emphasis on the process of the investigation. The chapter breaks investigations into three basic types: single-scene, multiple-scene, and network investigations. Each type of investigation requires different skills from personnel involved. Single-scene investigations require the skills found in trained law enforcement investigators. The skills used in a single-scene investigation form the building blocks of the more complex investigations. Thus, while building on single-scene skills, multiple-scene investigations require additional networking and coordination skills. Coordination of multiple searches at various locations is the realm of an experienced criminal investigator. The networking skills may be provided by a subject matter expert (for example, a computer consultant). Finally, network crimes require the skills of multiple-scene investigators and outside expert assistance. Even the most computer-proficient investigator needs help from the companies that maintain the Internet to track a crime successfully through their servers. However, some degree of preliminary knowledge is required even to know where to start. Techniques for acquiring this type of information are presented in this chapter along with conceptual tools that allow an investigator to communicate with the Internet experts.

INVESTIGATOR ROLES AND RESPONSIBILITIES

The role of computers is growing rapidly in our society; law enforcement has lagged behind. The pervasive use of home computers has added another potential source of evidence to the over 54 million households with computers in the United States.[1] Many large law enforcement agencies have a dedicated electronic crime investigation capacity. Medium-sized agencies may be acquiring their first electronic crime investigation unit or attempting to cross-train detectives from traditional areas. Even the smallest departments encounter electronic crime, but do not have the capacity for a dedicated unit. Thus, the mission of police, from patrol officers to forensic specialists, depends greatly on their department's size and organization. Generally, the role and responsibility of police staff in electronic investigation is the same as their counterparts dealing with physical crime.

First Responders

First responders to a crime scene are often patrol officers. First responders would not normally attempt to complete an electronic search and seizure; however, they do benefit from an awareness of the procedure and, if given even basic training, may be better able to preserve a potential electronic crime scene for specialized investigators. First responders are not dedicated electronic crime investigators. They have many other responsibilities, including safety, security, and basic documentation of an event or scene. Further, patrol officers are often not given the time to conduct in-depth investigations; those are handled by detectives.

A well trained first responder will control the human element of the crime scene first: tending to the injured, isolating suspects, and controlling onlookers. First responders are trained to avoid contaminating a crime scene or destroying physical evidence. As the prevalence of electronic evidence increases, first responders have naturally become aware of the need to protect and preserve it. For example, a recent narcotics investigation turned up valuable evidence in the form of electronic files stored in a personal data assistant (PDA). An alert officer noticed a fleeing suspect throwing the PDA into a nearby bush, and retrieved it. Making first responders aware of potential digital evidence allows them to protect it in the same way they protect physical evidence.

Investigators

Electronic crime investigators are trained law enforcement officers or experienced investigators brought (sometimes unwillingly) into the world of electronic evidence. The basic skills required successfully to organize an investigation, establish the elements of a crime, establish the connection between the suspect and the crime, conceptualize and present the crime, and document the investigation are still needed in electronic crime investigations. In fact, many corporations seek computer investigators and security directors from the ranks of law enforcement rather than technical experts. Investigators must have enough technical skill to gather evidence, comprehend the crime, and communicate effectively with technical experts, but do not need extensive theoretical knowledge or daily experience with computer systems. That is not to say that highly skilled investigators are not desirable.

Forensic Analysts

In physical crime investigations and electronic crime investigations, the complex analysis of evidence is often left to forensic specialists. A detective or crime scene technician would not feel bad about not understanding the intricacies of laboratory DNA analysis. Although computer skills and knowledge are essential to the investigator, the essential skills of an investigator involve collection and preservation of evidence for further analysis. Technical experts conduct this analysis through computer forensic techniques. Special programs and procedures allow forensic specialists to compile evidence and present it to the court. Out of necessity, many computer crime investigators feel compelled to learn these forensic analysis skills. Many investigators become skilled computer forensic examiners, but have to devote a great portion of their time to learning the latest technologies and conducting the analysis instead of conducting their investigations. Forensic analysts provide efficiency through a division of labor and regular practice with their equipment and techniques. It is not uncommon for senior investigators to act as forensic analysts.

Private Police

Private police (usually corporate security or computer security investigators) are hired by corporations to secure the data assets of the corporation. Although they often co-operate with law enforcement, they have a fundamentally different mission. Corporate officers must always consider the good of the corporation. For example, a private computer investigator may be withdrawn from a case if the corporation decides that ex-pending resources on such investigation will not be justified by the results.

Private computer security or investigative consultants are often brought in to re-view security incidents or suspected crimes. A small discrepancy can indicate a sys-tem failure or a major intrusion. In a famous case at the University of California, Cliff Stoll tried to reconcile a trivial accounting error and ended up discovering an attempt at international espionage.[2] It is not always obvious that a crime has been committed without further investigation. Since many crimes are committed by insiders, a security consultant also provides a check to the power of system administrators.[3]

Many corporations keep former police officers on staff to advise them when to call the police and when not to call. Although it is hard for many officers and investi-gators to understand such a decision or even consider it dereliction of a societal duty, many corporations do not want adverse publicity or fear the "seize everything" tactics of law enforcement once a crime is reported. The delays, staff time, and computing re-source down time created by an investigation may cause more financial loss than a break-in. In spite of the potential antagonism between the roles of private police and law enforcement, these groups often work together smoothly. Once a decision is made to report a crime, private police often act as liaisons between investigators and the cor-porate structure, insulating other employees from disruption and facilitating the efforts of investigators. A corporate security director not only will have access to the entire physical premises, but will also be able to issue directives to corporate employees with-out the direct invention of management or company executives.

Subject Matter Experts

Technical expertise has a short shelf life. Many skills that were in great demand two years ago are now virtually obsolete. Using a subject matter expert is one way for an investigator to gain access to detailed knowledge on a highly specialized or uncom-mon topic. Although many investigators feel confident handling a Windows™ system, large, multiuser systems may present unknown challenges and opportunities for mis-takes. Similarly, a complex network with unfamiliar technology may be beyond an in-vestigator's skill level. If an investigator does not feel confident with the technology to be searched or seized, a subject matter expert with experience using that technol-ogy can provide invaluable insight.

A skilled investigator can often successfully conduct analyses on all but the most demanding cases; however, with the staggering complexity of some systems, it is not unreasonable for the investigator to turn to an expert in the system to be examined: its own system administrator. When electronic crime enters the network, investigators are

---

BOX 11.1   Cyber Vigilantism

Cyber vigilantes are not part of the formal investigation process. They are private citizens, not affiliated with law enforcement. There are two basic forms of cyber vigilantes. The first type, Online Neighborhood Watch, simply gathers intelligence and alerts police to unlawful acts. Some organizations, like the CyberAngels, also provide information to victims. The on line watch groups do not take direct action against alleged perpetrators. The second type of cyber vigilantes takes more direct action. In some cases, retaliation simply turns the tables on the supposed offender.

> "[A] notorious spammer, Alan Ralsky, gave an interview in the course of which he mentioned his home in West Bloomfield, Michigan. The interview was posted on Slashdot, the leading geek website, and some enterprising reader found Ralsky's [physical] mail address in a database. Slashdot readers then subscribed him to thousands of catalogues, mailing lists, information requests, etc. The results, according to security expert Bruce Schneier, were devastating: 'Within weeks he was getting hundreds of pounds of junk mail per day and was unable to find his real mail amongst the deluge.'" . . . —John Naughton, "Mailboxing clever," *Manchester Guardian Weekly,* April 30, 2003.

The most extreme examples include so called hack-backs and posting personal information about pedophiles; unsubstantiated reports also indicate direct physical action may be taken against computer intruders. Hack-backs describe a wide range of illegal responses to intrusion attempts. Victim companies may use hostile code or denial of service attacks to disable their attackers. These retaliations may be directed at unwitting, intermediate sites used by attackers. In any case, such direct actions are just as illegal as the attacks that provoke them. Companies and individuals using such tactics are subject to civil and criminal penalties.

Online vigilantes also often pose as underaged girls and boys willing to talk about sex. Generally, it is not a crime to discuss such matters. The crime occurs when the alleged pedophile takes action to meet supposed minors for sexual encounters. Law enforcement stings often use this technique to ensnare pedophiles. Some vigilantes assist law enforcement, but law enforcement officers generally discourage vigilantism. For one thing, individuals acting as "agents of the state" suffer from the same restrictions on entrapment and search as law enforcement officers. Online vigilantes may also commit crimes in their apparent zeal to ensnare pedophiles; many have be charged with possession of child pornography.

Aggressive cyber vigilantes often use public humiliation to punish would-be pedophiles and warn potential victims. They post the names and even physical addresses and pictures of adults discussing sex with vigilantes posing as children. Privacy advocates and attorneys retained by the targets of this form of cyber vigilantism claim that many targets never intended to meet a child for sex, just talk anonymously to someone else about their desires. Other "innocent role-players" claiming to have known they were communicating with adults are also ensnared by vigilantes.

forced to call upon the experts at Internet service providers and corporate information technology (IT) departments. Even the most skilled investigator cannot instantly fathom the processes and data structures of large information systems. Just as the corporate security director becomes the liaison with corporate employees, the system administrator becomes the liaison with corporate data resources. Of course, if the local system administrator is a suspect, this is not appropriate. In such cases, a subject matter expert familiar with that type of system can provide the necessary guidance.

SINGLE-LOCATION CRIME SCENES

Although the gamut of electronic crimes can span the global communication networks and cross many jurisdictions, single-location electronic crime scene search and seizure is the most fundamental skill-set of an electronic crimes investigator. Investigators specializing in other forms of crime possess a set of skills that adapts well to a fairly straightforward single-location electronic crime scene. This is because the single-location crime scene does not involve complex networking or the enormous storage capacity and complexity of network crime scenes.

SEARCH WARRANTS AND ELECTRONIC EVIDENCE

Criminal investigators must establish probable cause in an affidavit in application for a search warrant (also called a "warrant application"). The affidavit must specify that a crime has been committed, evidence of the crime exists, and the evidence presently exists in the place to be searched. Further, the affiant (the investigator applying for the warrant) must particularly describe the evidence to be seized. Specific evidence of a specific crime must be named or general evidence facilitating a criminal act may be described by function. Unless traveling through a network, electronic evidence must be stored in a container or medium. Single-scene crimes, by definition, do not involve networks. Thus, it is often useful to think of the storage medium (i.e., container) when planning a search. Each of the following containers of electronic evidence presents unique challenges and opportunities in the warrant application process.

Computer Systems

If an investigation requires the seizure of an entire computer system, the investigator should decide whether the computer itself is the target of the warrant or if the data on the computer is the target of the warrant. If stolen property is the target of the search, the contraband (i.e., the fruit of the crime) may require specific and particular description. When the data contained on the computer is the target, the magistrate signing the warrant will usually allow the investigator to describe the computer suspected of holding the evidence required by general function. It is fairly easy for a suspect to move information from one physical storage device to another. Even detailed investigations may be outdated by the time the warrant is served. Further, it is often impossible to specify precisely a physical computer when probable cause is established through network investigation; however, network identification or physical, premise location often meet the requirement that a warrant must particularly describe the place or person to be searched (i.e., particularity requirement).

External Storage Media

When data is the target of the search, the warrant should be written to allow seizure of electronic storage media found at the crime scene. Electronic storage devices come in a broad variety of physical sizes, shapes, and storage capacities. It may be impossible precisely to identify the storage medium of electronic evidence in a warrant. In this case, the broad function (i.e., electronic storage device) should be used. The smallness of these devices makes it possible to hide them virtually anywhere; a warrant may have to apply to a broader physical area than the immediate surroundings of a computer system. Common examples include compact disks (data CDs) hidden in the pages of books, data CDs hidden among music CDs (especially if music CDs are home reproductions), and tiny Universal Serial Bus (USB) storage devices hidden near a computer.

Personal Data Devices (PDAs)

PDAs and other data devices are miniature computer systems designed to be highly mobile. They may be found virtually anywhere under the control of a suspect, and may contain data storage comparable to a full-size computer of just a few years ago. Warrant applications should describe the function of the device and person carrying the device rather than trying to specify a physical location. Even though warrants must "particularly describe the place to be searched,"[4] the courts have recognized that must often occur at a time and place determined by the suspect. Warrants for such searches can describe the function of evidence thought to be in the possession of a person.

Other Electronic Devices

Many electronic storage devices do not fit a narrow definition of "computer" and may be excluded as evidence if not properly defined in a search warrant. Examples include, but are not limited to:

1. Telephone answering machines and other electronic telephone equipment (e.g., caller ID boxes)
2. Access control devices such as security smart cards
3. Credit card skimmers and magnetic stripe encoders
4. Personal items such as cellular telephones, digital watches with storage capacity, pagers, calculators with storage, and electronic calendars
5. Digital cameras or digital sound recorders

The range of storage capacity in these different electronic devices ranges from a minute encryption key to a full-motion, DVD™-quality video.

Executing the Search Warrant

Once a warrant is obtained, the details of the search may be finalized. A preliminary plan is often attached to the application for the warrant. If the warrant is signed as written, most of the details will already be in place. The magistrate issuing the warrant may place special conditions on the search; those conditions should be integrated into the plan. For example, a magistrate may not wish to interfere unduly with the First Amendment rights of a disinterested party holding evidence of a crime. The system operator of a Web site hosting discussions may choose not voluntarily to divulge details about users of the Web site. A search warrant may specify that police may seize evidence related to the crime described in the warrant, but may not seize unrelated discussions or interfere with the public forum for discussion found on the Web site. The search strategy would have to include both a way to keep the Web site open and specifically target discussions and logs relevant to the crime. Other considerations in the execution of a warrant include the conditions under which the warrant is to be served and coordination with uniformed officers, or even S.W.A.T. team members.

Priority Concerns

First and foremost, investigators must assess the potential danger to themselves. It is beyond the scope of this book to discuss planning an armed raid with a no-knock warrant versus a full-compliance search; however, officer safety should be a priority regardless of the expected level of compliance of the suspect. Some particular concerns lie in assessing the particular dangers of working with electronic equipment. Test for live voltage in wires before touching or wear insulative gloves if appropriate. Although there is often talk of booby-traps in computers, this usually refers to methods for destroying data, not physical traps; however, in this age of enhanced homeland security, actual traps may be an issue. If the investigation involves terrorism, then additional concern should be taken in the planning and execution of the search.

Securing the Scene

Procedures for securing a crime scene typically include removing suspects, witnesses, and bystanders from the area to be searched. Technical assistance provided by a computer owner or the owner's designated operator may require their presence, but they should be supervised by an officer trained in the rules of evidence. Many system administrators happily comply with law enforcement requests, but do not understand the legal requirements of collecting evidence. To prevent inadvertent alteration of evidence or inadmissible collection techniques, an investigator should be present and understand the operations of the system administrator. It is preferred to have a resident expert in the system execute the commands rather than on-site experts. This allows for efficient testimony at trial. Sometimes a suspect may be allowed to assist in the collection of ongoing data or the dismantling of evidence seized; this is not common and should come only after careful consideration.

Handling Ongoing Activity

For the last ten years, the question that seems to get the most attention is what to do about an active computer. The one certain rule is: If it is off, leave it off. Various procedures are used to deal with computers that are running. The knowledge and experience of the investigator will have a lot to do with the decision of how to proceed. A first responder may have to be trained with very few choices; an experienced investigator or a subject matter expert accompanying the investigator may be able to interpret the situation with more finesse. Generally it is safe to leave a running computer on, but excessive hard drive activity or network activity may require immediate action to preserve evidence. Table 11.1 provides a side-by-side comparison of pros and cons for the decision to turn off a running computer.

If the decision is made to turn off the computer, video or photographic documentation of activity should be attempted, if applicable, before shutting down a system abruptly. However, if there is enough reason to believe that it is necessary to shut it down, then it should be done at once. The best current practice is to remove the power cord from the rear of the computer and not use the power switch. Many switches activate a software command to power down. This command can be changed to alter data when the switch is used. Even old electrical switches can be modified to destroy evidence. It is also wise to make a note of the reasons leading to this decision as soon as possible after the computer is powered down. Many procedural questions that may arise later can be answered with a brief articulation of the facts leading to a good-faith decision.

Examining the Crime Scene

Safety is always the first concern, but a close second is the overriding concern of evidence collection: Do not alter the evidence. Any unavoidable alteration (e.g., packaging the evidence for transportation) should be documented so well that it can later be reassembled exactly as it was. After safety is assured, and the scene is secure, the

TABLE 11.1   Should a Running Computer Be Turned Off?

Pros	Cons
Systems in the process of deleting incriminating data are stopped.	Large computer systems, especially UNIX, may be damaged by abrupt power loss.
The system is protected from timed events or outside intrusion once it is turned off. In the world of wireless networking, simply removing a network cable is not sufficient to stop intrusion by an accomplice.	Network connections and potential evidence may be lost by severing a network connection; even on a single-scene search, such connections may allow investigators to develop probable cause to search other systems.
The system will have to be turned off for transportation anyway.	Windows 2000™ and Windows XP™ can use an encrypting file system that makes data recovery difficult if the password is lost by turning the computer off.

entire scene should be photographed before altering it. If possible, lists and diagrams should be included with notes of observations. Particular attention should be given to the monitor screen, front of the computer including indicator lights, wire connections, mouse and keyboard place, and screen saver status. An investigator should record in notes all actions taken and any changes observed on the monitor, computer, printer, or other peripherals that result from the search. The monitor is (1) on, (2) in sleep mode, or (3) off. The state of the monitor will decide which of the following situations applies.

1. If the monitor is on and a work product and/or the desktop is visible, photograph screen and record information displayed.

2. If the monitor is on and screen is blank (sleep mode) or shows a screen saver, move the mouse slightly (without pushing buttons). The screen should change and show work product or request a password. If mouse movement does not cause a change in the screen, DO NOT perform any other keystrokes or mouse operations. Photograph the screen and record the information displayed.

3. If the monitor is off, make a note that it is off. Turn the monitor on, then determine if the monitor status is as described in either situation 1 or 2 above and follow those steps.

Once the scene is documented in its entirety, the process of collecting and preserving evidence can begin.

Collection and Preservation of Evidence

All evidence collection activities may be later called into question by the defense. It is best to establish a written procedure and use it every time. It is good to initial each step completed or note, in writing, why departure from the procedure was necessary. The following procedure is suggested by the National Institute of Justice.[5] An officer should . . .

1. Photograph and diagram the connections of the computer and the corresponding cables. This step allows reconstruction of the system later if necessary.

2. Regardless of the power state of the computer (on, off, or sleep mode), remove the power source cable from the computer–NOT from the wall outlet. At this point, the question of whether to turn it off or not has been resolved; this procedure applies to collection, preservation, and transportation of evidence. If dealing with a laptop, in addition to removing the power cord, remove the battery pack. The battery is removed to prevent any power to the system. Some laptops have a second battery in the multipurpose bay instead of a floppy drive or CD drive. Check for this possibility and remove that battery as well. If dealing with a large multiuser system (e.g., a UNIX™ system), follow a safe shutdown procedure recommended by a subject matter expert.

3. Check for any outside data connection (e.g., telephone modem, cable, ISDN, DSL). If a telephone connection is present, attempt to identify the telephone

number. The easiest way to do this is to connect a telephone and ask the operator to identify the number being used.

4. To avoid damage to potential evidence, remove any floppy disks that are present, package the disk separately, and label the package. If available, insert either a seizure disk or a blank floppy disk. This procedure prevents the magnetic heads of the floppy drive from damaging the disk in transit. Since CDs and DVDs are read by a laser and not by a physical read/write head, it is not required to remove CDs. In fact, there is no reason even to touch the CD drive when preparing a computer for transport.

5. Place tape over all the drive slots and over the power connector. This prevents accidental insertion of a disk or power cord. It also preserves the integrity of evidence in the drives.

6. To provide an additional level of security against confusion at the crime lab or during the sometimes lengthy storage, record make, model, and serial numbers of the computer. This information is also required on a report generated from the seizure and on an inventory of seized items to be given to the owner.

7. Label all connectors and cable ends (including connections to peripheral devices) to allow for exact reassembly at a later time. Label unused connection ports as "unused."

8. Record or log evidence according to departmental procedures.

9. Recovery of nonelectronic evidence can be crucial in the investigation of electronic crime. Proper care should be taken to ensure that such evidence is recovered and preserved. Items relevant to subsequent examination of electronic evidence may exist in other forms (e.g., written passwords and other handwritten notes, blank pads of paper with indented writing, hardware and software manuals, calendars, literature, text or graphical computer printouts, and photographs) and should be secured and preserved for future analysis.

Packing and Transportation of Evidence

If transport is required, package the components as fragile cargo. Actions taken should not add, modify, or destroy data stored on a computer or other media. Computers are fragile electronic instruments that are sensitive to temperature, humidity, physical shock, static electricity, and magnetic sources. Therefore, special precautions should be taken when packaging, transporting, and storing electronic evidence. To maintain chain of custody for electronic evidence, document its packaging, transportation, and storage. An investigator should . . .

1. Ensure that all collected electronic evidence is properly documented, labeled, and inventoried before packaging.

2. Pay special attention to latent or trace physical evidence, like fingerprints or fiber samples, and take actions to preserve it. Testing for latent prints

involves chemicals and dust, which may be harmful to electronic devices or storage media. Electronic evidence should be extracted before physical forensic examination. Specifically marking the evidence needing physical forensic examination will allow forensic analysts to avoid altering latent or trace evidence.

3. Pack magnetic media in antistatic packaging (paper or antistatic plastic bags). Avoid using materials that can produce static electricity, such as standard plastic bags or styrofoam "packing peanuts."

4. Avoid folding, bending, or scratching computer media such as diskettes, CD-ROMs, and tapes.

5. Ensure that all containers used to hold evidence are properly labeled. If multiple computer systems are collected, label each system so that it can be reassembled as found (e.g., System A—mouse, keyboard, monitor, main base unit; System B—mouse, keyboard, monitor, main base unit).

6. Keep electronic evidence away from magnetic sources. Radio transmitters, speaker magnets, and even heated vehicle seats are examples of items that can damage electronic evidence.

7. Avoid storing electronic evidence in vehicles for prolonged periods of time. Conditions of excessive heat, cold, or humidity can damage electronic evidence.

8. Ensure that computers and other components that are not packaged in containers are secured in the vehicle to avoid shock and excessive vibration. For example, computers may be placed on the vehicle floor and monitors placed on the seat with the screen down and secured by a seat belt.

9. Maintain the chain of custody on all evidence transported.[6]

Storage of Seized Evidence

The storage of seized evidence is as exacting a task as seizure and transportation. Above all, the evidence must remain unaltered until it is analyzed and the continuity of the chain of custody must be maintained to prove it. Investigators in all but the smallest departments must turn evidence over to an evidence custodian. The evidence custodian is typically a ranking sworn officer. The custodian is then responsible for the evidence from that time until trial. When evidence is submitted for forensic analysis, the custodian delivers that evidence to the department's designated analyst (maybe another sworn officer; nonsworn employee; or off-site contract service). The evidence custodian obtains a receipt from the analyst. When the analysis is completed, the custodian receives the evidence and retains custody of the evidence until it is needed at trial. The evidence custodian maintains a secure area called an evidence locker to prevent general access to evidence stored therein. The custodian maintains logs of officers working shifts in the evidence locker. If officers are allowed to enter the locker, their entry is logged too;

however, typically the custodian will bring evidence requested by officers or investigators to a window. That transfer is noted in the chain of custody, as is the return of the evidence. The chain of custody can be introduced and affirmed by calling the investigator, the custodian, and the analyst who examined the evidence.

The following procedure is suggested by National Institute of Justice and annotated with standard practices for all evidence.[7] Investigators should . . .

1. Ensure that evidence is inventoried in accordance with departmental policies. This typically includes "marking" the evidence for later identification at trial. Without proper markings, one mass-produced computer is nearly indistinguishable from another. Investigators typically inscribe the metal case of the computer with their initials, the date, and case number—if possible. Containers can also be marked with indelible markers. Evidence tags can become separated from evidence, so actual marking is preferred.

2. Store digital evidence in a secure area away from temperature and humidity extremes. Protect it from magnetic sources, moisture, dust, and other harmful particles or contaminants.

3. Many electronic devices contain memory that requires continuous power to maintain the information, such as a battery or AC power. The most common example is the CMOS (complementary metallic-oxide semiconductor) battery that stores critical setup data for older computers. Data can be easily lost by unplugging the power source or allowing the battery to discharge. Collect and store the power supply adaptor or cable, if present, with the recovered device.

4. Potential evidence such as dates, times, and systems configurations may be lost as a result of prolonged storage. Since batteries have a limited life, data could be lost if they fail. Therefore, appropriate personnel (e.g., evidence custodian, lab chief, forensic examiner) should be informed that a device powered by batteries is in need of immediate attention.[8]

The basic police work involved in obtaining planning a search and obtaining a warrant are familiar tasks to investigators. Two key differences distinguish digital evidence from familiar physical evidence. First, electronic evidence must be contained in a physical medium. Since digital evidence can be copied flawlessly and frequently, there is no reason to limit a search to a single physical container. Anything capable of storing digital information may contain digital evidence. Second, digital evidence is fragile. A quick action by the suspect can erase digital information. Inadvertent mishandling of digital evidence can contaminate or destroy its evidentiary value. Specific procedures have been recommended by the National Institute of Justice to preserve the digital evidence for later analysis while maintaining its probative value. The ability properly to seek a warrant and execute a search forms the building blocks of more complex investigations.

Multiple-Location and Network Crime Scenes

Multiple-scene computer crimes are complicated by a number of factors beyond the standard single-scene seizure. Networked environments may contain evidence on multiple machines using multiple operating systems, in multiple physical and/or network locations, and in multiple jurisdictions. To further complicate search and seizure operations, current law enforcement practices, called minimization procedures, demand minimal intrusion to the operation of the network. Even the relatively few network experts in law enforcement may not be sufficiently familiar with a target network to extract evidence with sufficient legal integrity and not disrupt the operation of the target network. Officers skilled at single-scene seizures may feel overwhelmed at the thought of collecting network trace evidence. Fortunately, an investigator is not alone in attempting a multiple-scene or network investigation. Subject matter experts can be enlisted to guide investigators through unfamiliar networks. By concentrating on the purpose of investigation—the collection and preservation of evidence necessary to prove the elements of a crime and to connect the suspect to the crime—an investigator can coordinate the efforts of people with more technical knowledge. The investigator needs only the communication tools necessary to convey the purposes and precise needs of law enforcement to the local computer system administrators, who must often serve as guides in these unique environments.

Distinguishing Single-Scene, Multiple-Scene, and Network Crime Scenes

The distinction made is not based on technical differences, so much as functional differences for investigation. A single-scene crime involves only a single computer, for example, possession of child pornography or use of a computer to further a criminal enterprise. A multiple-scene crime involves more than one computer, with the possibility of an intervening network. Personal computers on a Local Area Network (LAN) can often be handled as several individual single-scene seizures. Additional complications include noting network connections and network identities for each machine. Data storage (i.e., network drives) can be spread across several machines on the network, but may be represented as a single unit to network users. In spite of the use of "network" technology, any geographically compact (same jurisdiction) crime scene under the administrative control of a single entity (one person, one corporation, etc.) is considered a multiple-scene crime. Network crime scenes would involve the Internet and any LAN or Wide Area Network (WAN) that makes extensive use of dedicated servers, network or multiple-user operating systems (Unix™, Windows 2000 Pro™, etc.), or switching equipment. The presence of affected computers in multiple jurisdictions may also make it a network crime. The skill-set required to investigate this type of scene may exceed even a veteran investigator's ability. Further, an investigator may need numerous warrants or other legal search instruments (see ECPA in Chapter 9) to follow criminal activities. Cooperation from the companies owning the network resources can be the key to success. The need for such cooperation, either with Internet Service Providers (ISPs) or law enforcement agencies in other jurisdictions, distinguishes a multiple-scene crime from a network crime.

Identifying Network Architectures

Although there are numerous technical distinctions between different network architectures, investigators are not charged with maintaining these systems or understanding their full complexities. An investigator needs to know how to trace a transaction through the network and identify any potential sources of network trace evidence: latent signs of the transaction being traced.

Internet versus Intranet Investigations

The primary distinction of interest to an investigator is between Internet and intranet. An intranet is a Wide Area Network that uses a common addressing and transfer protocol suite called TCP/IP (Transfer Control Protocol/Internet Protocol). The key difference to an investigator is that an intranet is often administered by one authority; thus, it may be possible to get to a system administrator or system administration team and get definitive answers. Seeking technical assistance involves identifying the network administrator. This can usually be accomplished by looking up the domain registrant on a service like "whois" (see below).

The Internet is a network of networks owned and maintained by various private, corporate, and governmental interests. The only feature truly common to all of these various component systems is the use of TCP/IP. Seeking technical assistance involves identifying the Internet Service Providers (ISPs) involved. Steps taken to preserve Internet evidence must be quick. Routine logs are often quickly purged due to the huge volume of Internet traffic. If the network can be traced to a corporation, the corporate information technology (IT) department may be of further assistance. Investigators may issue preservation letters (by fax, if speed is vital) to require service providers to retain relevant information. Preservation letters do not require a magistrate's signature; however, a warrant or lesser instrument may be required to obtain the evidence requested for preservation. In many cases, public Internet service providers cannot voluntarily release information to investigators.

Modeling Network Transactions

At the most fundamental level, all networks can be described with the Open Systems Interface model. It is a standard used world wide. By tracing the way each process of this model is completed, an investigator can slowly make sense of the most complex network environment. In general, the model proceeds from the most concrete, at layer 1 (e.g., a wire) to the most abstract, at layer 7. Abstraction makes a computer network more versatile because it can operate with many different purposes. Concreteness makes an operation easier to understand for exactly the opposite reason: It can only do one or a few simple tasks. For example, a wire can only carry electrical impulses from one end to the other. In a multiple-scene investigation, connected computers can often be identified by tracing the wire runs. At the other extreme, the applications (what we call programs, like MS Outlook™) can be used for a variety of purposes.

Beyond the traditional seven layers of the OSI model lies the even greater abstraction of human users (layer 8) and policies governing them (layer 9). Although the OSI model may seem very complex, it is actually a tool used by computer scientists simply to communicate about network functions. The seven layers of the model each serve a function in the transmission of data. The specific function of each layer is described in Table 11.2. An investigator familiar with the OSI model can communicate with system administrators using vastly different software. The investigator doesn't have to understand how each network component functions, only what happens to data in a network. This leaves the system administrator to sort out the details.

The addition of layers 8 and 9 emphasizes the role of human users and the policies which govern the network to investigators; they are not part of the worldwide standard. They originally stem from a joke about network breakdowns caused by user errors or corporate policies which inhibit network function, but investigators should keep in mind that all information transfer ultimately occurs because of a human operator or a policy that dictates it. Security flaws can also be examined with these additional layers. For example, insider crimes are the most common forms of computer crime. If an investigator suspects an insider, layer 8 reminds him or her to look into personal matters and backgrounds. Layer 9 reminds him or her to check company security policies to see who has access to the machines, both network and physical. It is easy to get stuck

TABLE 11.2   Layers of the Investigation

9. Policies	Human	The rules, policies, and management controls that govern the actions of users
8. User		The human being using the computer and network
7. Application	Application services	Provides direct interaction with the user (e.g., Netscape or Explorer)
6. Presentation		Standardizes data transmission formats (i.e., file types such as JPEG)
5. Session		Provides checkpoint, fall back, and encryption services (e.g., SSL)
4. Transport	Network services	Allows multiple simultaneous operations across a single network connection (e.g., TCP)
3. Network		Provides unique addressing for transmission across different networks (e.g., IP)
2. Data link		Assembles bits into packets, provides error correction, and flow control (e.g., Ethernet)
1. Physical		Provides a path for the transmission of bits (e.g., wires, fiber optic, and radio waves)

in the mode of assuming that a computer crime has a computer cause. The hacker trick of social engineering[9] recognizes that the most common weakness in computer security is the human operator, especially if the operator works in a large organization with complex policies (layers 8 and 9).

The application services are generally not retained in network trace evidence except for a few specific types of logs. These are the abstract services most directly under the control of the user—or in the case of a computer crime, the criminal. They can be encrypted and still function. However, key information, such as file names and sizes, might be retained and matched to a user.

The network services are most often tracked by system administrators because they are necessary for proper network maintenance and function, but do not reveal private information without further investigation. Routine logs contain a wealth of information (discussed below) about network service transactions.

Locating Evidence

Local system administrators are the best source of information about network logging. Routine business records are not considered hearsay and are therefore considered admissible to court (see discussion of hearsay later in the chapter). Various security systems, commonly used by business, have logging features that may help detect anomalous activities. For instance, intrusion detection systems (IDSs) are designed primarily to log network traffic and examine it for known patterns indicating attacks. If the crime in question uses such a signature, the presence of an IDS can be of tremendous assistance to an investigator. Similarly, many firewalls—systems that block network traffic based on rules established by an administrator—have logging systems. For other cases, such as intellectual property violations, large volumes of apparently legitimate traffic might be ignored by an IDS, but show up in an administrator's log as an unusually large amount of network traffic (i.e., a usage spike). Administrators must plan for network growth, and often track network usage statistics. They also manage network loads with a system of resource allowances reserved for each user (i.e., a user quota system). If a user exceeds his or her storage quota, even briefly, the administrator's log may note the event. In a final example, ISPs often keep logs of user activity to help predict demand and plan for growth as well as keeping logs for billing purposes. If a user dials into a "front" account under an assumed name, the dial-up record may record his or her actual telephone number.

All of this potential evidence is kept for various purposes on various machines on the network. It may be up to the investigator quickly to notify competent authorities to preserve the evidence. The great volume of log evidence generated in a typical business cannot be economically maintained for extended periods. Many logs purge after as little as 24 hours. Federal law (the Electronic Communications Privacy Act) allows a "preservation letter" to be sent to a company or individual with potential electronic evidence; it requires the responsible person to maintain the evidence pending further investigation.

Key Information for Locating Network Trace Evidence

The logs mentioned in the previous section use identifiers to match network transactions with the actual machines involved. These identifiers are often associated with a level of the OSI model. The identifiers are necessary for proper network function. With a few relatively rare exceptions, network communication is literally impossible without them; therefore they will be present as latent evidence in network crimes.

MAC Address

The Machine Access Control (MAC) address is a unique hardware address associated with each network card or other network device. The MAC is used at layer 2 of the OSI model. Layer 2 is the data link layer; it is the most concrete electronic layer. MAC addresses are only used at the local network level. Network transactions that use TCP/IP usually strip the MAC address away from data. Therefore, MAC addresses are most useful in multiple-scene investigations using a single local area network (LAN). They may also help prove that a criminal had access from inside the victim's network.

The MAC address is usually reported in hexadecimal couplets. Hexadecimal is a numbering system that uses base 16 instead of the familiar base 10^{10} that we use for counting. Although an investigator does not need to know all of the intricacies of network addressing, recognizing the pattern of network addresses is helpful. Hexadecimal uses pairs of the characters 0–9 and A–F to represent 8 bits (also called a byte) for example: 00-AF-03-05-0E-B9. Contrary to common wisdom, MAC addresses can be changed with software configuration, so failure to match a MAC is not definitive proof that the computer was not involved in an incident.[11]

IP Address

The Internet Protocol address is a unique address assigned to every computer on the Internet. Like all numbers used by computers, the IP address is a binary number made up of bits. Although an IP address can be found represented with hexadecimal couplets like the MAC address, the IP is almost always reported in the decimal-dot notation. "Decimal-dot" means four decimal elements (base 10, like we use to count) ranging from 0 to 255 separated by dots, for example: 192.168.0.0. Although many people recognize the decimal dot notation, they do not understand how it works. Because the decimal number represents 8 bits each, it cannot exceed 255. There are 2^8 (256) possible values for 8 bits. 255 is the maximum number that can be represented because computers start counting at 0, not 1. An investigator should know that any value over 255 cannot be part of a valid IP address. Thus, if a suspect reports an Internet address of 345.300.123.205, an investigator will know that it is false.

The IP is associated with transactions at layer 3, the network layer, of the OSI model. IP addresses are often dynamically assigned to computers when they start up. However, many, especially servers, use static IPs that do not change. The owner of a given IP can be determined through ARIN, the American Registry for Internet Numbers. Note: International investigations may require the use of the European and African authority RIPE[12] or the Asian authority APNIC.[13]

BOX 11.2   Understanding IP Addresses

Understanding how IPs work can help an investigation. In this hypothetical example, a Web-based fraud scheme manipulates the way browsers interpret Internet Addresses. The following URL will take a browser to eBay™, the leading Web-based auction site:

http://pages.ebay.com/index.html?ssPageName=h:h:home:US

The following URL will take a browser to the Web site of anyone with the $50 fee required to register a Web address:

http://www.ebay.com@homeshoppingforyou.com

Without even registering a Web domain, the following URLs can provide access to a criminal's page from anywhere on the Web. By using these URLs from a Web page on a legally owned Internet address (called a "front" in fraud investigations), the criminal can claim ignorance of where the links go. The links below can easily be altered to lead to anywhere on the Internet without changing anything in front of the "@" sign.

http://www.ebay.com@192.168.23.56

http://www.ebay.com@%C0%A8%17%38

These URLs go to the exact same place. The IP address 192.168.23.56 (in decimal dot notation) is the same as %C0%A8%17%38 (in hexadecimal notation). Neither of the addresses will get a potential fraud victim to the real e-Bay site. All of the security used at E-bay is useless if the customer never gets to the page. However, for the victim to reach the criminal, the address must point to a valid location on the Internet. The administrative details of that site may prove to be a rich source for search and seizure.

DNS

Domain Name Resolution is a protocol that allows users to enter meaningful words instead of IP addresses to identify a computer. DNS is a helper service for layer 3 of the OSI model in TCP/IP systems. The Internet does not work on English words. To find a particular computer on the Internet, a user must have the Internet address (IP); as we saw in the previous section, these can be very difficult to decipher in their native form. To make it easier to use the Internet, the DNS system was established to create a place to look up (also called resolving) the IP of a computer based on its human readable name. Thus, when you type in a Web address like www.eBay.com, your browser sends a request to a system of databases of domain names and matching IPs maintained by ICANN (the Internet Corporation for Assigned Names and Numbers) or its subset databases hosted throughout the Internet.[14] A reverse lookup is available to convert an IP to its human-readable equivalent.

PPP

Point-to-point Protocol is most commonly used by modems that dial in to an Internet service provider. PPP works at layer 2 of the OSI model, like Ethernet. Unfortunately, there is no equivalent of the MAC address used by Ethernet because PPP connections are point to point. When there are only two computers involved in the connection, they do not need identifiers. Although the protocol itself yields little information, the routers that handle such connections often log useful information such as the account accessed and authenticated with a password and the times at the beginning and end of the session.

Collecting Network Trace Evidence

Due to various historic and legal problems with digital evidence collection,[15] it is the best current practice to minimize the intrusion of network investigations. Seizing a business's critical IT assets could easily do more harm to that business than the worst denial of service attack. Even lengthy down time can cost the business substantial amounts. The seizure of evidence can be a significant deterrent to businesses reporting computer crime.

Minimization procedures have to be balanced against the needs of evidence integrity and the mission of law enforcement, but cannot be discounted automatically. Typically, if evidence is available from an existing backup tape or can be copied from an existing source without disrupting operations, it is acceptable. When a machine must be taken off line, on-the-spot imaging is often used to collect evidence with minimal intrusion.

PRESENTING DIGITAL EVIDENCE AT TRIAL

Any reasonably experienced law enforcement official knows that police work does not end when a suspect is arrested and transferred to a jail custodian. Paperwork, reports, and possibly interviews with a prosecutor are as important as the investigation itself. Consider that an investigation is like writing a lengthy paper. The paper can be a masterful, witty, comprehensive coverage of the topic, but if you never hand that paper in, it is worthless. An investigation, no matter how well conceived and executed, is worthless if the case does not end in a successful prosecution. In fact, the quality of the investigator's report, credibility, and willingness to participate fully often influence plea bargains. If a case does go to trial, an investigator will be required to present the facts represented in the report or explain the procedures used to discover and collect evidence. The testimony of the investigator is often the bedrock of a case. Competent presentation and procedure are as vital to investigators as any technical skills.

The rules of evidence require that the foundation for physical evidence be established with testimony; thus, evidence does not speak for itself.[16] The prosecution must establish when, where, and how the evidence was collected. The prosecution must also be able to establish that the evidence was not altered to prejudice the trial by either act (such as intentionally altering the evidence) or omission (such as allowing the evidence to be degraded or contaminated). Finally, the prosecution must also establish that the evidence collected conforms to the warrant or guidelines for commonly accepted warrantless searches. As the person responsible for these procedures, the investigator is the primary witness used to introduce evidence.

The Hearsay Rule

Black's Law Dictionary defines hearsay:

> Hearsay includes any statement made outside the present proceeding which is offered as evidence of the truth of matters asserted therein.[17]

It is fundamental to our system of justice that the accused be able to confront his or her accusers and offer evidence to rebut their statements. Witnesses must only testify to matters of which they have direct knowledge. This gives the accused a chance directly to confront and discredit statements made against him or her. According to the Federal Rules of Evidence (§§801–04), the hearsay rule excludes statements made outside of the ability of the accused to confront the person making the statement before the jury[18] unless such statements fit one of several well known exceptions.[19] The following section describes the most relevant applications of the hearsay rule to digital evidence-related testimony.

Using Notes on the Witness Stand

Investigators have large caseloads and must often wait months before testifying in a case. It is permissible to use case notes, journals, and logs created during the investigation to help the investigator recall fine details such as serial numbers, model numbers, and other minutia. The central question in the use of notes on the witness stand is whether the witness (i.e., the investigator) actually recalls the events or is relying on the notes entirely. If the witness uses notes to prompt memories of the events and recall details, it is known as "past recollection recalled."[20] Past recollection recalled does not violate the hearsay rule. The defense has a right to examine the notes and test the witness' memory before allowing the testimony. This test will establish the degree to which the witness has an independent recollection of the events.

If the investigator relies entirely upon the notes for any recollection of the events, it is known as "past recollection recorded."[21] Past recollection recorded does violate the hearsay rule. If the investigator does not recall the events of the case, the best the prosecutor can do is have the reports and notes read into evidence. If this is necessary, the entire contents of the notes become available. Many patrol officers use a spiral-bound notebook to record all kinds of information while at work and even at home. Investigators should avoid this and use loose-leaf sheets for a single case. There is a classic story about crime scene investigation where the defense noted missing pictures in a series. The officers were required to produce the negatives. Although the missing pictures did not provide evidence to clear the suspect, they did show one of the officers "posing" with the corpse. In a spiral-bound notebook with many cases and doodles, there are probably many such potentially embarrassing tidbits.

Business Records

It is an established exception to the hearsay rule that records or summaries created in the normal course of business (not specifically for law enforcement purposes) are not hearsay and are therefore admissible. "The courts generally have admitted computer records upon a showing that the records fall within the business records exception."[22] The Federal Rules of Evidence §803(6):

> Records of regularly conducted activity. A memorandum, report, record, [etc.] made at or near the time by, or from information transmitted by, a person with knowledge, if kept in the course of a regularly conducted business activity, and if it was the regular practice of that business activity to make the memorandum, report, record, or data compilation, all as shown by the testimony of the custodian or other qualified witness, unless the source of information or the method or circumstances of preparation indicate lack of trustworthiness. The term "business" as used in this paragraph includes business, institution, association, profession, occupation, and calling of every kind, whether or not conducted for profit.[23]

The key to this section is that the "business process" be regular or routinized in such a way that the accuracy of the product may be assessed by the court. Failure to meet this standard does not mean that creating logs for law enforcement purposes is illegal. It does not even mean that such logs will be inadmissible. Other techniques can be used to admit such logs, but these methods are not covered in this book.

Presenting Best Evidence

Black's Law Dictionary states that the principle of best evidence . . .

> requires that best evidence available be presented in lieu of less satisfactory evidence . . . This rule prohibits the introduction into evidence of secondary evidence unless it is shown that original document has been lost or destroyed or is beyond jurisdiction of court without fault of the offering party . . . [T]he basic rule [is] as follows: "To prove the content of a writing, recording, or photograph, the original writing, recording, or photograph is required."[24]

The best evidence rule simply states that the court requires the original copy of evidence. Courtroom presentation is the ultimate purpose of collecting evidence. It does not make sense to store the original safely in a vault while using a (possibly imperfect) copy in the courtroom. Although best evidence is often considered to be the original copy, with digital evidence the original copy is inaccessible to human beings because it is usually a series of magnetic zones on a hard disk. Courts have accepted printouts of the contents of a disk as best evidence. However, the contents of a disk are usually too large to print in their entirety. There is no technical basis to say that displaying information from the actual hard drive of the computer seized or the monitor seized along with it is any more likely to be best evidence than an exact digital copy displayed on a projector, paper, or other medium.[25] Subject to verification, a digital copy in a convenient form may be presented in court without violating the best evidence rule.

However, presenting a "live" demonstration of digital evidence on the accused's own computer with the accused's own monitor can have a powerful impact on the jury. Live demonstrations should be planned carefully and tested prior to presentation. Given the unpredictability of some technology, a video might be prudent and allowable under exceptions to the best evidence rule. For the convenience of the court, voluminous evidence may be presented in summary form. Federal Rules of Evidence §1006 states:

> The contents of voluminous writings, recordings, or photographs which cannot conveniently be examined in court may be presented in the form of a chart, summary, or calculation. The originals, or duplicates, shall be made available for examination or copying, or both, by other parties at reasonable time and place. The court may order that they be produced in court.

Similarly, if the process in question cannot be adequately represented in a printout, the court may allow alternate presentation.

Chain of Custody

Black's Law Dictionary defines chain of custody:

> In evidence, the one who offers real [physical] evidence . . . must account for the custody of the evidence from the moment in which it reaches his custody until the moment in which it is offered in evidence. [The] chain of custody is proven if an officer is able to testify that he or she took control of an item of physical evidence, identified it, placed it in a locked or protected area, and retrieved the item being offered [in evidence] on the day of the trial.[26]

The chain of custody is a legal document that records a history of who had the evidence and when. In the hypothetical example cited in *Black's Law Dictionary,* the chain is relatively simple. In a typical computer crime investigation, the chain of custody can be extensive. As more specialists (computer forensic technicians, subject matter experts, off-site laboratories, etc.) work on a piece of evidence, the chain of custody becomes more complex. Complexity is not necessarily bad, but it never helps establish evidence. For this and other reasons, departments and agencies have established evidence-handling procedures. At a minimum, these procedures include a list of anyone accessing the evidence with notations of time and place. They also include a notation of where the evidence was taken, if transported, and any changes, such as removing a piece for analysis. Digital information requires additional protection and even more elaborate protections have been devised for it.[27]

The investigator seizing the evidence may be required to testify to the provenance of the evidence. This foundational testimony describes how the evidence was collected, where it came from, and what has happened to it since it was seized. An investigator can provide more effective testimony by using established procedures every time. The plan for conducting a search should include a designated custodian of evidence who will document and transport the evidence to maintain the chain of custody.

Expert Testimony

This section has focused on the presentation of the fruits of an investigation. Although there has been mention of subject matter experts, their contributions have been limited to assisting the investigator to produce a case. Experts undoubtedly play a role in helping the investigator gather evidence of the elements of a crime and may have opinions that help establish probable cause.

SUMMARY

An investigator is charged with identifying that a crime has taken place, establishing the elements of that crime, and associating the crime with a suspect. The investigator must gather compelling evidence in a manner that allows it to be presented in court. If possible, an investigator should work with the prosecutor to understand the type of evidence specifically needed for the prosecutor's strategy. Even without direct input from the prosecutor (perhaps prior to the prosecutor's decision to take the case), an investigator must be able understand the events constituting the crime. Several tools and procedures exist to help the investigator in this process. Unless the investigator has an unusually high degree of experience with computers, subject matter experts will play an important role in assessing the details of the crime. However, the primary burden of presenting a case to the prosecutor and eventually to the court falls on the investigator. Proper procedure and documentation guided by an understanding of the "endgame" in court will increase the odds of a successful prosecution.

REVIEW QUESTIONS

1. Explain how labor is divided among professionals involved in the investigation of computer crime. Which role do you prefer and why?
2. Outline the process of preparing and executing a search warrant for electronic evidence. How does search and seizure of electronic evidence at a single scene differ from physical evidence search and seizure?
3. Explain the difference between single-scene, multiple-scene, and network investigations. In what ways do single- and multiple-scene investigations differ from network investigations?
4. Explain the procedures for securing digital evidence. After officer safety, what is the primary concern of the investigator during this whole process?

ENDNOTES

1. NEWBURGHER, E.C. *Home Computers and Internet Usage in United States: August 2000,* U.S. Census Bureau, 2001, p. 1.
2. STOLL, C. *The Cuckoo's Egg: Tracking a Spy Through the Maze of Computer Espionage.* New York: Doubleday, 1989.
3. STEPHENSON, P. *Investigating Computer-Related Crime.* Boca Raton: CRC Press, 2001.
4. U.S. Constitution, Amendment Four.

5. Technical Working Group for Electronic Crime Scene Investigation. *Electronic crime scene investigation: A guide for first responders.* National Institute of Justice (NIJ 187736). Washington, DC: National Institute of Justice, 2001.

6. *Ibid.*

7. *Ibid.*

8. *Ibid.*

9. Social engineering is basically lying to a person on the telephone or in person to get access to a desired resource (see Chapter 3 for a more extensive discussion).

10. This means that when we reach the highest individual digit (at the number 9), we then start to repeat digits (at 10). This is called base 10. Base 16 uses the following sequence before it repeats: 0, 1, 2, 3, 4, 5, 6, 7, 8, 9, A, B, C, D, E, F. The next number is 10 (think of it as 1 then 0, not 10). 10 in base-16 notation equals 16 in decimal.

11. STEVENS, W.R. *TCP/IP Illustrated Volume 1.* Addison Wesley, 1994.

12. RIPE (Réseaux IP Européens) is a collaborative forum open to all parties interested in wide area IP networks in Europe and beyond. The objective of RIPE is to ensure the administrative and technical coordination necessary to enable the operation of a pan-European IP network. (RIPE Web page: *http://www.ripe.net/ripe/index.html*)

13. APNIC is one of four Regional Internet Registries currently operating in the world. It provides allocation and registration services which support the operation of the Internet globally. It is a not-for-profit, membership-based organization whose members include Internet service providers, National internet registries, and similar organizations. APNIC represents the Asia Pacific region, comprising 62 economies. (APNIC Webpage: *http://www.apnic.net/info/about.html*)

14. This explanation greatly simplifies the DNS system, but accurately describes the general function. For an extensive discussion of DNS systems, see STEVENS, W.R. *TCP/IP Illustrated Voume 1.* Addison Wesley, 1994.

15. *Steve Jackson Games* v. *United States Secret Service,* 816 F.Supp. 432 (W.D.Tex, 1993).

16. The opposing side may waive the requirement of foundation by accepting the evidence without question of provenance (called stipulating).

17. BLACK, H.C., J.R., NOLAN, and J.M. NOLAN-HALEY. *Black's Law Dictionary* (6th ed.). St. Paul, MN: West Publishing, 1990.

18. It is part of the jury's job to assess the credibility of statements made. If a statement from an unreliable informant is repeated by an utterly reliable witness, the jury cannot properly assess the truth of the statement.

19. Federal Rules of Evidence §§801–04.

20. SWANSON, C.R., N.C. CHAMELIN, and L. TERRITO. *Criminal Investigation* (8th ed.). San Francisco: McGraw-Hill, 2003.

21. BLACK, NOLAN, and NOLAN-HALEY, *ibid.*

22. KERR, O. *Computer Records and the Federal Rules of Evidence* (USA Bulletin, *http://www.usdoj.gov/criminal/cybercrime/usamarch2001_4.htm*). United States Department of Justice, 2001.

23. The Federal Rules of Evidence §803(6).

24. BLACK, NOLAN, and NOLAN-HALEY, *ibid.*

25. I do not advise arguing with a judge as to what comprises best evidence. Most courts can be convinced through expert testimony and there is sufficient precedent to allow the broader interpretation of "best evidence."

26. BLACK, NOLAN, and NOLAN-HALEY, *ibid.*

27. SWANSON, CHAMELIN, and TERRITO, *ibid.*

Chapter 12

Digital Forensics

Chapter Objectives

After completing this chapter, you should be able to:

- Outline and explain the process used to preserve the verifiable integrity of digital evidence.
- Suggest probable locations for particular types of digital evidence needed for various types of investigations.
- Explain how the storage system works in the computer.
- Describe, in broad detail, how information is stored on hard disks.
- Identify and explain hidden sources of information on a hard disk.
- Identify common storage media.
- Outline a basic universal procedure for examining removable storage media.
- Explain the basic logical structures of the hard drive and related magnetic devices.

INTRODUCTION

Forensic: "[b]elonging to courts of justice."[1] Although this chapter will deal with the technical details of computers and data storage, it will always be guided by the understanding that technical knowledge is secondary to the forensic analyst's ability to present technical information to the court. The various forensic sciences all share the role of bridging technical expertise with the courtroom process. Digital forensics can encompass many areas of inquiry. Civil-court applications of digital forensics can include any aspect of computer science or information science. Information network analysis, source code analysis, and many other areas from civil litigation may eventually find their way into criminal investigations, but it is still fairly rare to see anything except storage forensics used in criminal court. However, recent trials involving virus writers indicate criminal investigations may soon include some of these other areas.

The field of storage forensics covers the examination of information stored on a physical medium. A physical medium is a real-world object that may be inside the computer (e.g., a seized hard drive) or outside the computer (e.g., a floppy disk or CD). When information is stored on a physical medium, it is said to be "static." The fact that the information is static, or not moving electronically, distinguishes it from information on an active or "live" network. The examination of stored data[2] is often referred to as *post mortem* analysis because it is not on a live network. There is no functional distinction between the quality of evidence derived from a live network and from storage media, but the laws surrounding the collection and the collection procedures differ greatly. However, once the live data is stored, the forensic process is virtually identical.

THE BASIC PROCESS OF STORAGE FORENSICS

As with any other forensic operation, maintaining the continuity of evidence from the source to the final analysis product is the most important task of the examiner. The forensic analyst must have the ability to demonstrate the link between the seized drive, hereafter called the evidence drive and the final analysis. Remember: The evidence exists on an unaltered original storage device (e.g., hard drive); analysis creates leads and summaries, not evidence. It may be necessary to demonstrate the process used to obtain the summaries and leads through documentation and, sometimes, even replication of the analysis. This section describes the best current practices to reduce uncertainty when presenting the results of an analysis in court. Unfortunately, the complex reality of investigations and forensic analysis does not always allow for the implementation of "best practices." For example, multiple scene and network crimes do not always allow the seizure of the evidence drive. Anything short of best practices presents uncertainty in court, but does not signal the end of the investigation or preclude prosecution. Whenever possible, commonly accepted exceptions will be noted, but this section is primarily concerned with the most common situation found in law enforcement: a hard drive seized and in the possession of the analyst.

Some symbols will be used in this section to demonstrate visually the processes explained. These symbols are the standard flow chart symbols used to describe computer processes.

FIGURE 12.1   Flow chart symbols and definitions used in this chapter

PREPARATION FOR FORENSIC ANALYSIS

Some preparations must be made before any lab analysis is attempted. An analyst must be able to ensure that the result of an analysis comes from the evidence, not from contamination or error. The gold standard is that an analyst must be able to reliably reproduce any result from procedure notes and a copy of the original data seized.[3] Thus, the steps of an analysis should be documented. A successful practice is to have a standard procedure for types of evidence and document any modifications to this procedure, noting the reasons why they are necessary. Such procedures are designed specifically to prevent challenges to the analysis in court. Many computer experts could quickly determine several more efficient ways to collect and analyze information, but these alternative methods would not be likely to meet the standards and common objections found in criminal court. Beware of helpful computer experts that do not understand the mission of forensics. That is, evidence could probably be obtained without going through these procedures, but it would be more vulnerable to challenge if not completely useless in a criminal court.

It is also necessary to prepare an appropriate environment for the analysis. Using "clean," or verified, software tools with valid software licenses is an important first step. It can be embarrassing and expensive to have to admit to using illegal software. Lab equipment should be in working order. When new equipment is introduced, its function should be verified and documented in case later questions arise. One important early step is to obtain a "hash" value (like an electronic fingerprint) of the hard drive used for analysis (also called a bench drive). A program implementing the Message Digest 5 (MD5) is the most commonly used method of creating a hash. The process of hashing will be further explained later in this section. A hash of the blank bench drive will be used to verify that it is clean after an analysis.

FIGURE 12.2   Before the first step of a new analysis, it is necessary to obtain a comparison value for the blank hard drive to be used in the analysis.

Note: These diagrams (steps 1 through 7) are explained throughout this section. Together, they describe, in order, a complete process. This process is easier to understand if you keep in mind that we need a way to verify that the drive analyzed has not been contaminated or altered since it was seized from the suspect (called the evidence drive).

A final preparation, often overlooked, is to verify the qualifications and skills necessary to explain the analysis in court. The information technology field is full of self-taught experts. While many of these "experts" are highly skilled, many are also frauds. Of those who are legitimate experts, many are incapable of a convincing (or in some cases comprehensible) courtroom presentation. The analyst conducting the analysis must be able to understand and explain the process of the analysis. It is dangerous for an analyst to be completely dependent on point-and-click tools combined with one-size-fits-all procedures.

Acquisition of Data

The forensic process described in this section assumes that the evidence drive is available to the examiner; however, an image can be obtained and authenticated in the field if circumstances require it. Field acquisition is not the preferred method, because failure to maintain control of the evidence drive can also lead to problems in establishing the authenticity of the evidence in court. It is possible to obtain a written stipulation as to the authenticity of the evidence acquired. This is often used if a suspect wants the evidence drive returned prior to the end of the trial. If it is impossible to obtain a stipulation, the evidence is not necessarily inadmissible; it simply requires a greater showing that the evidence is authentic.[4] For example: A computer owned by an on line publisher contains potential evidence. The magistrate signing the warrant places a special condition on the search that investigators use the absolute minimally intrusive search to avoid interfering with the First Amendment rights of the publisher. The suspect will not stipulate the contents of the search—having nothing to gain by doing so. The publisher's hard drive can be imaged and authenticated on the spot, but the seizure will be closely analyzed by the defense. Expert testimony as to the imaging process may be required.

Regardless of whether the image acquisition occurs in the field or in the forensic lab, different acquisition systems require different efforts to preserve the evidence drive. The acquisition usually runs from a specially designed forensic system. If the acquisition system uses the Windows™ operating system, acquisition can be performed against a hard drive with a write blocker installed (see Box 12.1). Other acquisition

---

BOX 12.1   Unintentionally Altering Digital Evidence

Almost any action taken on a computer, even the simple act of starting it, alters potential evidence and gives the defense an avenue to attack the credibility of the analysis. Kruse and Heiser cite a statement from the Federal Law Enforcement Training Center (FLETC) that 400 files are altered in the start-up process of a Windows™ 9x machine and 500 files are altered in the start-up process of a Windows NT™ machine.

Several hardware write blockers are available to investigators. Once installed, the device absolutely prevents a write operation to the original evidence hard drive. In the Windows™ operating environment, the hardware write blocker is the only way to be sure to prevent write operations. Unfortunately, if the seized hard drive requires specialized hardware device drivers, the hard drive may not work with a write blocker. Write block devices range in price from $70 to over $1,000.

Other operating systems, notably Unix™ or Linux™, allow hard disks to "mount" (i.e., be recognized by the computer) as "read only." This too absolutely prevents writing to the evidence drive. However, familiar Windows forensics packages may not be available for Unix™ systems.

Source: Kruse, W.G. and Heiser, J.G. (2002). *Computer Forensics: Incident Response Essentials.* San Francisco, CA: Addison-Wesley.

---

systems use a true read-only mount of the file system (often not possible in Windows) with analysis proceeding from a drive mounted for read-only operations.

Authentication of Data

The prosecutor must be able to prove that the evidence presented or summarized in court came unaltered from the defendant. The digital forensic analyst has an easier job. The product of forensic evidence must be shown to be an authentic product of the evidence seized. There is a unique quality to digital evidence that allows it to be more easily authenticated than physical evidence. When evidence is seized, it can be summarized mathematically in a process called hashing (see Box 12.2). A hash is a unique numerical value calculated from the data in a digital file. No other naturally occurring file can have the same hash value.[5] A hash value (or, simply, hash) is essentially the "fingerprint" of the digital file. By comparing this fingerprint with a new fingerprint taken at each step of the analysis process, we can verify that the digital file being examined is a true and authentic copy of the original evidence.

The forensic analyst should calculate an MD5 hash of the evidence drive. The real work is accomplished by the software. All the analyst has to do is issue the command and identify the file to be hashed. The analyst can then compare this hash to a hash of any subsequent copies. If the hash matches, the copies are authenticated to the value of a single bit within a known (infinitesimal) probability of error. This authentication procedure should be performed and noted whenever an image is copied or loaded

BOX 12.2   The MD5 Hash

An algorithm is a process or procedure used to produce a specific result. A hashing algorithm takes a large body of digital information and produces a mathematical value or "hash" that uniquely identifies the data, like a fingerprint identifies a person. A hash is quite small compared to the amount of data it represents. The most commonly used hashing algorithm is the Message Digest version 5 (MD5) hash created by Ron Rivest of RSA Inc. The odds of having two data sets, at random, that produce the same MD5 hash are calculated to be 10^{38} or a 10 followed by 37 more zeros. That is more time than the complete age of the universe, start to finish in seconds. An alternative algorithm called Secure Hash Algorithm (SHA) was developed by the National Institute of Standards and Technology. It provides greater security, but is slower.

onto an analysis machine. As always, the analyst should document the results of the procedure. Documentation can be as simple as cutting and pasting the hash value into a computer log and noting that it is the same. This provides a basis of comparison that the evidence cited in the analysis has not been altered by error or intentional act.

Imaging of the Evidence Drive

With any seized system, it is important to create a working copy for forensic analysis. The best method is to create a bit stream copy (also called a mirror or image). A bit stream copy reproduces every bit of information found on the evidence drive. This method reproduces both active files and latent data. Active files are those files available to the user or created by the user. Word processing documents, spreadsheets, text files, graphics, etc. are all considered active files. Unless the crime being investigated is fairly technical (e.g., hacking-related crimes) the bulk of evidence obtained will be from the active files. No special tools are required to access these files. A simple search for known keywords or fragments of file names (e.g. *.jpg, where * can be equal to any text) can provide positive results. Latent files are files that are not recognized by the operating system; thus, they do not show up on a list of files. The most common source of latent files is deletion. When most computers delete files they do not actually erase the bits in the file; they simply allow new files to be saved to that space when it is needed. Until then, the file is left virtually intact. Recovery of deleted files will be discussed later in this chapter. Another type of latent data, accessible without

FIGURE 12.3   Step 1 is to verify mathematically the contents of the evidence drive. This value will prove that any future copies match the original exactly.

extraordinary effort, is found in protected system files. These can be accessed by booting the computer from a floppy disk or boot CD. Most commonly, this includes that swap file or paging file used by Windows™ to simulate additional physical memory.

Logical copies, created with the copy command included with the operating system, do not reproduce latent data. Images can be created by readily available software with a hardware write blocker in place. Best current practices require the use of a write blocker because it simplifies courtroom presentation of the evidence. However, it is equally acceptable to boot from a CD or floppy and use an imaging program to produce a bit stream copy. Bootable floppies and CDs create a RAM drive (storage to active memory, not the hard drive) and can be used to load larger programs that do not fit on a single floppy disk; thus, they do not alter data on the hard drive. If possible, the image produced should be written to true, write-once media (e.g., DVD-R or CD-R), so that the copy cannot be altered; however, the size of modern hard drives makes even DVDs cumbersome to use.[6]

An image can be authenticated with an MD5 hash comparison and contains potential evidence that may be hidden from the operating system. The hash value of the Archival Image (#1) matches the hash of the Evidence Drive (#1). As always, document the results of the procedure. Documentation can be as simple as cutting and pasting the hash value into a computer log and noting that it is the same. This provides a verifiable record that the evidence has not been altered by error or intentional act.

The rule of best evidence requires that the original evidence, not a copy, be brought to court. However, the Federal Rule of Evidence 1001(3) allows unaltered digital evidence to be presented as a copy; thus the image of a disk is considered to be "best evidence." A comparison of MD5 hashes can verify that the data is unaltered. The data may even be mathematically compressed and retain its integrity. Compression simply reduces the size of a file for storage or transportation. There are many techniques used to compress data; one variety, called lossless compression, is not considered alteration. Lossless compression will produce the exact binary data as was compressed and can

Step 2 is to create an exact "image," or bit-stream copy, of the evidence drive.

FIGURE 12.4   Step 3 is to verify that the image of the evidence drive is a true copy of the evidence drive. Note that the hash value produced (#1) is the same as the hash from the evidence drive.

be mathematically and empirically verified to do so. The key is that the uncompressed version produces a hash value equal to the original.

Wiping the Analysis Drive

The analyst must ensure that the target area is free from contaminates of previous analyses. For example, analysis on a child pornography case may lead to loading pornographic images from the image of a suspect's drive. If this material is not thoroughly wiped, it may be detected in a later analysis of another suspect's drive in a fraud case. To avoid having to explain this in court, it is best to establish a procedure that wipes both data and the space between data called slack space. By wiping the analysis drive before restoring the image, the analyst will be able to refute any claim that the drive was contaminated. Most common implementations of a wiping program meet the standards of Department of Defense Directive 5220.22—the DoD wipe (see Box 12.3).

After performing a suitable wipe, the results can be verified by hashing the blank drive and comparing the resulting hash value to the value of the blank drive. As always, document the results of the procedure. Documentation can be as simple as cutting and pasting the hash value into a computer log and noting that it is the same. This provides a verifiable record that the bench drive is not contaminated with evidence from a previous case.

Restoring

While small-scale, 4.7GB or less, analysis can be performed from a DVD or other write-once medium, larger volumes of data can only be practically handled from a hard drive. Consider even a relatively small evidence drive at 20GB. If completely full, it would take five DVDs to hold the contents. Each step of an analysis protocol (see the next section) must be performed five times, with the operator switching disks as needed. In addition to raw size, an internal hard drive has a much faster data transfer rate than any of the current removable media. Consider that to search a hard drive for one key word,

---

BOX 12.3   The DoD Wipe

The United States Department of Defense issued Directive 5220.22-M as part of its National Industrial Security Program. The directive sets security standards for Department of Defense contractors. The process, popularly known as a DoD wipe, is actually the standard used to "sanitize" a hard drive that contained data less than top secret. Although it is not absolutely necessary to use a DoD wipe, it has become a de facto standard; that is, the use of another technique would require explanation.

The use of the DoD wipe recognizes the potential of latent data to exist even after a drive is deleted or even formatted. Once the DoD wipe is performed, the hard drive cannot recognize latent data. Without extraordinary measures, the use of a DoD wipe places evidence beyond the reach of current law enforcement techniques, but recent advances with magnetic force microscopes and electron tunneling microscopes may change this some day.

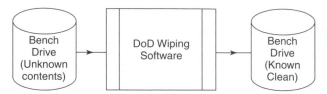

Step 4 is to wipe the bench drive to be used when analyzing the archival image.

FIGURE 12.5   Step 5 is to create a hash of the clean bench drive and compare the value to the value of the drive when it was last known to be blank. Note that the hash value produced (#0) is the same as the hash from the blank bench drive.

the entire contents of that hard drive must be read and brought into the computer's memory. Even a marginal speed advantage makes the restoration procedure necessary.

To perform forensic analysis of the data, it must be loaded onto a clean target drive or folder. When the image is loaded, it should be authenticated to verify that it is a true copy of the original.

Documentation can be as simple as cutting and pasting the hash value into a computer log and noting that it is the same. This provides a verifiable record that the evidence has not been altered by error or intentional act.

BOX 12.4   Size in Computers

Term	Value	Value in bytes	Volume in pages
Bit	1	1/8 byte	Less than 1 page
Byte	8 bits	1 byte	Less than 1 page
Kilobyte (KB)	1024 bytes	(2^{10}) bytes	About ½ page
Megabyte (MB)	1024 KB	(2^{20}) bytes	About 500 pages
Gigabyte (GB)	1024 MB	(2^{30}) bytes	160-foot stack of paper

Understanding the scale of data handled in digital forensics is difficult. In one of the defining cases in data storage, Kevin Mitnick, accused of criminal hacking, possessed 9GB of data when arrested. Prosecutors and the court refused to allow Mitnick access to a computer to view the evidence against him because of fears that he could cause damage or seek revenge.[7] Astronomical figures about the amount of paper needed to print that amount of potential evidence were used to justify not releasing it to Mitnick. To print all of the evidence would have required a stack of paper 1,440 feet tall.

Step 6 is to restore the archival copy (from Step 3) of the evidence drive to a blank bench drive (from Step 5).

FIGURE 12.6   Step 7 is to authenticate the restored image by calculating an MD5 hash and comparing that hash value to the hash of the evidence drive. Note that the hash value produced (#1) is the same as the hash from the evidence drive (#1).

The Complete Process

Step 1 is to verify mathematically the contents of the evidence drive. This value will prove that any future copies match the original exactly.

Step 2 is to create an exact "image," or bit-stream copy, of the evidence drive.

Step 3 is to verify that the image of the evidence drive is a true copy of the evidence drive. Note that the hash value produced (#1) is the same as the hash from the evidence drive.

FIGURE 12.7   Summary
(Before the first step of a new analysis) it is necessary to obtain a comparison value for the blank hard drive to be used in the analysis.

Step 4 is to wipe the bench drive to be used when analyzing the archival image.

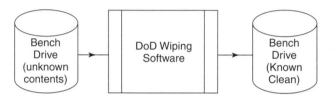

Step 5 is to create a hash of the clean bench drive and compare the value to the value of the drive when it was last known to be blank. Note that the hash value produced (#0) is the same as the hash from the blank bench drive.

Step 6 is to restore the archival copy (from Step 3) of the evidence drive to a blank bench drive (from Step 5).

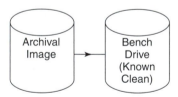

Step 7 is to authenticate the restored image by calculating an MD5 hash and comparing that hash value to the hash of the evidence drive. Note that the hash value produced (#1) is the same as the hash from the evidence drive (#1).

FIGURE 12.7   (*cont.*)

FORENSIC ANALYSIS

Computer forensics books often describe the identification of evidence in meticulous and exacting terms. In any given investigation, the variety of possible analyses is as broad as the evidence sought. Essentially, the analyst attempts to find information that is in itself incriminating (e.g., child pornography) or evidence that helps establish the elements of a crime (e.g., paper trail for a fraud case). When planning an analysis, the investigator and forensic analyst may wish to look for everything that might be incriminating. However, the fact is that over-analysis is as dangerous as under-analysis. Imagine an officer having to search every house and building in a neighborhood where a burglar has been reported. Ignoring the legal implications, it is too much work for an uncertain return. The officer might discover new crimes, but could become so busy with minutia that he or she would never complete the original investigation. The search warrant and original purpose of the investigating officer determine what type of evidence may be sought. This is not only a sensible strategy to limit a search, but exceeding the warrant may result in the evidence being ruled inadmissible in court. Further, a well planned analysis can even be used to justify a plain-sight exception to the requirements of the warrant or the inadvertent discovery of a new crime. The plan can be used to demonstrate how the plain-sight viewing occurred.

The National Institute of Justice produces a work entitled *Electronic Crime Scene Investigation: A Guide for First Responders*. The section covering "Forensic Examination by Crime Category" contains a listing of broad types of crime with descriptions of where to find evidence for that particular type of crime. This material indicates the most productive avenues for forensic examination as they relate to specific crime categories. These findings help define the permissible scope of an examination to be performed for a specific crime. Box 12.5 essentially contains a recipe for locating evidence for various crimes. For example, if you are investigating on line child exploitation, you could reasonably expect to find evidence in

- Chat logs
- Date and time stamps
- Digital camera software
- E-mail/notes/letters
- Games
- Graphic editing and viewing software
- Images
- Internet activity logs
- Movie files
- User-created directory and file names that classify images

Other crimes clearly have other evidence, but there is a significant overlap in the location of evidence for many of these crimes. This allows the opportunity for plain-sight

BOX 12.5   Common Evidence of Select Crime Types

Auction Fraud (Online)

1. Account data regarding on line auction sites
2. Accounting/bookkeeping software and associated data files
3. Address books
4. Calendar
5. Chat logs
6. Customer information/credit card data
7. Databases
8. Digital camera software
9. E-mail/notes/letters
10. Financial/asset records
11. Image files
12. Internet activity logs
13. Internet browser history/cache files
14. Online financial institution access software
15. Records/documents of "testimonials"
16. Telephone records

Child Exploitation/Abuse

1. Chat logs
2. Date and time stamps
3. Digital camera software
4. E-mail/notes/letters
5. Games
6. Graphic editing and viewing software
7. Images
8. Internet activity logs
9. Movie files

10. User-created directory and file names that classify images

Computer Intrusion

1. Address books
2. Configuration files
3. E-mail/notes/letters
4. Executable programs
5. Internet activity logs
6. Internet protocol (IP) address and user name
7. Internet relay chat (IRC) logs
8. Source code
9. Text files (user names and passwords)

Death Investigation

1. Address books
2. Diaries
3. E-mail/notes/letters
4. Financial/asset records
5. Images
6. Internet activity logs
7. Legal documents and wills
8. Medical records
9. Telephone records

Domestic Violence

1. Address books
2. Diaries
3. E-mail/notes/letters
4. Financial/asset records
5. Medical records
6. Telephone records

Economic Fraud, Online Fraud, and Counterfeiting

1. Address books
2. Calendar
3. Check, currency, and money order images
4. Credit card skimmers
5. Customer information/credit card data
6. Databases
7. E-mail/notes/letters
8. False financial transaction forms
9. False identification
10. Financial/asset records
11. Images of signatures
12. Internet activity logs
13. Online financial institution access software

e-Mail Threats/Harassment/Stalking

1. Address books
2. Diaries
3. E-mail/notes/letters
4. Financial/asset records
5. Images
6. Internet activity logs
7. Legal documents
8. Telephone records
9. Victim background research

Extortion

1. Date and time stamps
2. E-mail/notes/letters
3. History log
4. Internet activity logs
5. Temporary Internet files
6. User names

Gambling

1. Address books
2. Calendar
3. Customer database and player records
4. Customer information/credit card data
5. Electronic money
6. E-mail/notes/letters
7. Financial/asset records
8. Image players
9. Internet activity logs
10. Online financial institution access software
11. Sports betting statistics

Narcotics

1. Address books
2. Calendar
3. Databases
4. Drug recipes
5. E-mail/notes/letters
6. False identification
7. Financial/asset records
8. Internet activity logs
9. Prescription from images

Prostitution

1. Address books
2. Biographies and photographs
3. Calendar
4. Customer database/records
5. E-mail/notes/letters
6. False identification
7. Financial/asset records

(continued)

BOX 12.5   continued

8. Internet activity logs

9. Medical records

10. World Wide Web page advertising

Software Piracy

1. Chat logs

2. E-mail/notes/letters

3. Image files of software certificates

4. Internet activity logs

5. Serial numbers

6. Software cracking information and utilities

7. User-created directory and file names that classify copyrighted software

8. At a physical scene, look for duplication and packaging material

Telecommunications Fraud

1. Cloning software

2. Customer database/records

3. Electronic Serial Number (ESN)/ Mobile Identification Number (MIN) pair records

4. E-mail/notes/letters

5. Financial/asset records

6. "How to phreak" manuals

7. Internet activity

8. Telephone records

Source: Technical Working Group for Electronic Crime Scene Investigation. *Electronic crime scene investigation: A guide for first responders.* National Institute of Justice (NIJ 187736). Washington, DC: National Institute of Justice, 2001.

discovery. If evidence of another crime can be found, the analysis should stop immediately and the analyst should confer with the investigator and prosecutor to obtain a new warrant based on the plain-sight discovery.

Once an image is secured, that image can be loaded onto a new hard drive and placed in the seized machine (while storing the original hard drive in a safe place). A basic examination can quickly be accomplished using the tools of the operating system. If there is reason to suspect a highly sophisticated user, this technique may be insufficient, but the vast majority of digital evidence will not come from a master hacker. It is possible that there will be no competent effort to hide evidence on the computer—not even so much as deleting it. A quick result in this case is infinitely preferable to an extensive analysis six months in the future. Further, directory structure and file naming conventions can be used to associate a user with a particular piece of evidence discovered. A search of the active files through the operating system itself also produces the maximum chance of inadvertently discovering evidence of a new crime in plain view.

If simple techniques do not yield results, more extensive analysis techniques are available to the analyst. Regardless of the meaning of the information sought, all digital information is simply a pattern of bits. Discovering evidence becomes a process of matching a known pattern of bits, whether they form the first portion of a child pornography specimen (a picture previously known to law enforcement) or the name and social security number of an identity theft victim. By identifying the presence of the unique pattern of bits that corresponds to that decoded data, we can match the evidence drive with the illicit information.

THE FORENSIC ANALYST AS EXPERT WITNESS

After the completion of the analysis, the forensic analyst generates a report describing what evidence was identified, what elements of the crime it proposes to establish, how the evidence was identified, and finally, how and why any summaries of evidence were created. Depending on how the analyst was brought into the case, either the prosecutor or the investigator receives the report and decides to proceed with the case or not. Assuming that the analysis provides suitable evidence to proceed, the court process often takes a substantial amount of time and the analyst proceeds with new work. Depending on the credibility of the report or the convincing nature of testimony in a deposition, the analyst's simple presence may be used to assist in plea bargaining negotiations. This does not invalidate all the work and preparation put into preparing the analysis for trial; quite the contrary, it means the evidence is so compelling that the defense does not want to risk a trial. If the case comes to trial and the analyst is called, he or she will have two duties. First, the analyst must testify to his or her direct experience. That is, the analyst may testify about everything from receiving the initial evidence to the final report. Given the time lag between analysis and testimony, this is where a routine set of well documented procedures is most helpful. Second, the analysis may play the role of a technical expert, qualified to give summaries and opinions as to the meaning of evidence. The expert witness presents simplified explanations and abbreviations to the fact finder (judge or jury, depending on the trial). In essence, expert testimony allows the fact finder to make an informed decision without having to become an expert. In both roles, the forensic analyst should avoid partisan testimony. Independence and professional stature of the expert witness lend credibility that appearing to take sides would invalidate. It is typical for "opposing" expert witnesses to cooperate to determine facts and come to a satisfactory understanding of events and evidence.

To ensure the examiner's ability to demonstrate the link between the seized drive, hereafter the evidence drive, and the final analysis, the evidence drive itself must be maintained in the exact state it was in when it was seized. The best current practice in storage forensics usually involves creating an exact copy, hereafter image, of the seized drive. All analyses are performed on an image to avoid altering the original. The extra step of creating a copy for analysis is necessary because forensic analysis often changes the underlying data structures if performed on an active drive. While conducting the analysis, the forensic examiner must stay within the boundaries set by the original search warrant or consent of the evidence drive's owner/competent custodian.

COMPUTER STORAGE SYSTEMS

It surprises many people that we cannot simply identify where information is physically found on the evidence drive. Many forensic experts fall into the trap of explaining data structure with real-world analogies and are forced into explanations of the physical structures of computers. In recent years, the field of storage forensics has been complicated by the introduction of new hard drive technologies and rapidly growing storage capacities. These developments can be understood in the context of the two imperatives of hard drive manufacturers: storage density and speed (see Box 12.6).

Volatile Storage Systems

The structures of computer storage can be divided into two parts: volatile and nonvolatile storage. The primary difference between these types of storage is that volatile storage is lost when the computer loses power. Thus, the decision to unplug a computer may lose the volatile or active memory. Volatile memory is difficult to access without special software, and impossible to access without altering it. Such alteration can be explained in court, but does not come without risks.

Processor

Although not actually a storage system, the processor is the benchmark for speed and the organizing factor in nonvolatile storage. There has been a great deal of attention given to processor speeds ever since the first PCs. Today, the processor is by far the fastest part of the computer, completing operations over 4 billion times per second. To feed this incredibly rapid cycling of information, the storage system must bring large quantities of information at a relatively slower pace. Typical systems operate at 60 per-

---

BOX 12.6   Speed and Density

Storage density allows manufacturers to increase the storage capacity of hard drives. By packing more bits closer together, storage capacity has increased without the form factor (physical size) of the device increasing. Some of the physical differences in hard drives can be explained by the increasing density of information. For example, multiple platters allow more storage space. A denser magnetic medium means that individual bits can be written in smaller physical space and still resolved by new, more sensitive read heads. More precision means less space must be wasted between tracks of data arranged in concentric rings on the disk. Speed is a constant goal of storage manufacturers. The storage system of most computers is its slowest link. By increasing the speed of the hard drive, significant speed increases can be obtained for common tasks. The fastest part of the computer can only operate as quickly as the data and instructions can arrive. Computer architecture is designed to keep the most frequently used and most vital information in the fastest storage possible.

cent of possible throughput. Most systems spend substantial amounts of idle time; however, bursts of activity can use the full capacity of the processor's speed. Forensically, the processor is of little interest. Information in the processor is altered billions of times per second. Further, any information in the processor is completely inaccessible to human beings.

Cache

All cache systems are volatile, which means that when power is removed, information held in RAM disappears. The Level 1 cache operates at speeds approximating the processor. Level 1 (L1) cache is built into the processor to reduce delays in getting information to the processor. Level 2 (L2) cache is often built onto the processor's daughterboard along with the control chip set that feeds information and instructions in and carries out operations based on the results. L2 cache is slower than L1, but holds more information. L2 cache serves as a buffer between L1 and the system's main memory (RAM). Forensically, the cache holds little interest, as it is inaccessible to the user.

Main Memory (RAM)

Random access memory (RAM)[8] is the large reserve of information that supplies the processor through the cache systems. The bulk of the system's active data is held in RAM. Anything the user is doing, any open programs or files, will be in the RAM contents. Like cache, RAM is volatile storage. When the control systems predict the processor will need more data or must switch to a different task, the data is moved into the cache from RAM. When new processes are loaded or new data is requested by the user, the RAM draws information from the nonvolatile storage systems.

Forensically, RAM may be of some use. If software is already installed, RAM can be viewed by the user. All Unix™ systems provide a method to save RAM to a file with a process called a core dump. Windows™ systems require the use of special software called a hex editor to allow users to read RAM. Installing such software would undoubtedly alter the contents of the RAM and possibly purge them as well. If the computer uses virtual memory, a system that allows expansive, but slow, hard drive storage to substitute for RAM (see below), portions of the RAM contents may be saved on the hard disk in a file called a swap file or paging file. The swap file is normally inaccessible when the computer is running, making its contents latent data. Functionally, the swap file can be considered to be part of the RAM subsystem. In spite of the difficulties in accessing RAM, it can prove to be a treasure trove of useful data. Passwords, recently accessed files, and network settings may all be found in the contents of RAM.

Nonvolatile Storage Systems

Unlike previous components, the purpose of storage is not simply to convey data to the processor. Storage also maintains information when it is not needed or even when the power is removed from the system. Thus, storage systems are not volatile. Storage systems compromise between storing masses of information efficiently and allowing quick retrieval.

Hard Disk Drives

The hard disk is the primary storage device of most computers along with removable, peripheral systems such as CD-ROMs, floppy drives, and similar devices. Storage systems are far slower than RAM, cache, or the processor. Unlike the other systems, the hard drive relies on physical motion (usually a spinning disk and even slower read/write heads). All the other systems are solid state—no moving parts. All of their operations are electrical. Because hard disks must physically spin and physically seek locations to read and write, they will always be the slowest link in the information chain.

A few years ago, the lack of main computer memory (RAM) forced computers to crawl relative to today's computers. The biggest reason for this was that the lack of RAM forced computers to use the hard drive to trick the system into believing it had more memory through a system called virtual memory. More memory (even the slower, virtual memory) meant that larger files could be manipulated, more programs loaded, and more features could be built into programs. The trade-off was overall system speed.

Hard drive manufacturers have found many ways to improve the initial performance of their products. Data structures optimize "seek times," thereby reducing the delay between the call for data and the hard drive's ability to retrieve it. Multiple platters (disks) allow more than one read/write head to work at once. Faster spin speeds allow more data surface to pass under the read/write heads. The structures of the hard disk are the product of evolutionary search for speed and storage density. The rapid change in hard drive technology and competition between hard drive manufacturers make it exceedingly difficult accurately to describe the function of a given hard drive in all but the broadest terms. Forensic analysts should avoid using the physical and low-level structures of a hard drive to describe how data was obtained.

Removable Storage Media

There are two broad classes of removable storage media: direct access and sequential access. Disk drives allow direct access storage. That is, they do not have stored information in sequential order like a magnetic tape or other sequential access device. In direct access storage devices, the time required to access data is reduced, making retrieval faster. Tapes provide sequential access storage. Sequential access storage requires longer to fast forward through unneeded data to find the data requested. This is analogous to selecting a scene with a DVD player versus fast forwarding a VHS tape. Direct access devices need an index to locate information that may be scattered across the disk. The index holds a list of locations and the files currently residing in those locations. If portions of large files are scattered in many locations (fragmented), it takes longer to retrieve them, but still much faster than a sequential device. Sequential storage devices provide an attractive option for archival storage because of their low cost. Further, because tape drives are an older technology, they enjoy greater support in the proprietary systems of the non-Windows™ world.

Many different types of storage media are used today. An analyst must be able to identify correctly the equipment needed to acquire evidence from a seized storage device. Before any type of forensic operation can be completed, the analyst must be able to read the storage device. Fortunately, most modern drives have cross-compatibility (allowing them to read data written with other standards) and backward compatibility (allowing them to use older standards). Sometimes an analyst will be confronted with a storage device that is not standard. Fortunately, the device to read that storage device is often seized with the storage device. On occasions when it is not, the analyst might have to acquire a compatible device. An up-to-date knowledge of common storage devices and storage device readers will greatly benefit the analyst. One of the best ways to stay current with storage devices is simply to visit the local computer superstore.

Although there appears to be a bewildering array of storage media available, each contains essentially the same kind of information as contained by a hard drive. Procedures for examining this evidence are essentially the same, except for the acquisition.

FILE SYSTEMS

A file system is part of the computer's operating system. When a disk is formatted, it is imprinted with the structures used to control files. Several different systems have been developed to meet the growing needs of users for larger drives, greater efficiency, more speed, and security. This discussion focuses on the Windows™ family and its file systems. Although there are many arguments as to the superiority of operating systems, it is an indisputable fact that the Windows™ family of operating systems is by far the most common operating environment. It is almost certain that the majority of investigations will occur in the Windows™ environment.

The Windows™ family of operating systems can be divided into two groups. The Windows 9x series includes Windows 95 through Windows 98 and the follow-up Windows ME. All of these systems were designed to be consumer systems and do not seriously attempt to implement security. For example, the logon password can easily be circumvented by hitting a conveniently close and clearly labeled "cancel" button. The other group is the Windows NT™ series, which includes Windows 2000™ and Windows XP™. Although Microsoft was not always successful, the Windows NT™ series attempted to improve security. Later versions contain some meaningful protection. Of greatest forensic interest is the file system used. File Allocation Table (FAT) file systems provide the least security. The New Technology File System (NTFS) has progressed and may prove difficult to examine in its latest incarnation.

The easiest way to identify the version of Windows™ on a booted machine is to examine the system properties or by entering the "ver" command at the command prompt.

Windows 9x	File System	Windows New Technology (NT)	File System
Windows 95	FAT 16	Windows NT 3.5	NTFS 3.5
Windows 95 OSR2	FAT 16/FAT 32	Windows NT 4.0	NTFS 4.0
Windows 98	FAT 16/FAT 32	Windows 2000	NTFS 5.0
Windows 98 Second Edition (Win SE)	FAT 16/FAT 32	Windows XP	NTFS 5.0
Windows Millennium (Win ME)	FAT 16/FAT 32		

FIGURE 12.8   The Windows™ family of operating systems and associated file systems.

FAT: File Allocation Table

One of the characteristics of the FAT systems most useful to forensic analysts is that deleted files aren't wiped from the drive. Most people know that somehow deleted files can be recovered. The reason that works is the need for speed. To save time on unneeded operations, when a file is deleted, the file is not altered, except for a marker at the beginning. The only real change is that the file allocation table marks the clusters[9] used by the file as open or "unallocated." If no new data is stored to those clusters, the data can sit there intact for years. Even if new data is saved, it may not completely fill the unallocated space. This leaves fragments of the previous file in places that cannot normally be accessed. In the diagram below, full clusters of stored data are shown in grey. The red portion at the end of one of the clusters represents space not used by the new file occupying this cluster. The red cluster following it represents a currently unused cluster that may contain latent data from a previously deleted file. Both types of latent data are found in "slack space," disk storage space unused by active data, potentially containing latent data.

For forensic analysts, one problem with FAT32 systems is that MS-DOS cannot access FAT32. Newer versions of DOS have been modified to use FAT32. The DOS that underlies Windows 98 works well with the newer features of FAT32.

NTFS: New Technology File System

Windows NT™, 2000™, and XP™ systems use NTFS. NTFS has numerous advantages over the FAT system, especially in terms of security. To the forensic analyst, the only difference is that DOS-based tools do not work. Some utilities have been created that allow DOS to read NTFS, for example NTFS-DOS is freeware that allows DOS operations on an NTFS volume. Although NTFS implements a different method for dealing with files, it still has slack space and unallocated clusters that may contain old data. One of the primary advantages to users of NTFS is that it uses storage space more efficiently. This produces less wasted space between files. This wasted space has long

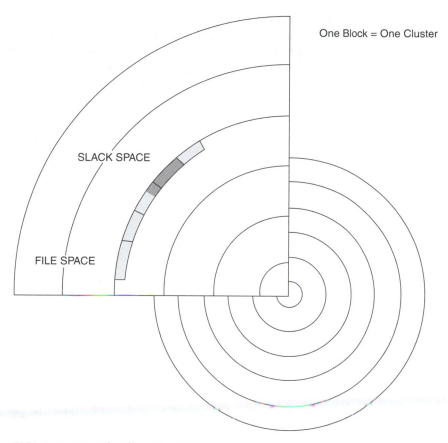

FIGURE 12.9   File Allocation Table

been a treasure trove of supposedly deleted material for forensic analysis. Two other features of NTFS pose specific problems to forensic analysts.

Dynamic Disks
Dynamic disks manage disk space without partitions and offer numerous advantages to administrators, but are not compatible with previous versions of NTFS or other operating systems (including DOS). These volumes can be imaged, but can only be read with a Windows 2000™ or other compatible boot disk.

Encrypting File System (EFS)
The encrypting file system presents a challenge to forensic analysis. If the machine is discovered in an operable condition (no screen saver and powered on), an investigator can use the Microsoft Management Console to create a key recovery certificate. It would also be possible to turn EFS off for each folder. Assuming that does not happen, there are other options. A centrally managed network using EFS will usually make the

domain administrator the key recovery agent. Thus, a key may be available from the domain administrator. The initial seizure at the crime scene may include a floppy disk with the recovery key. Experienced users of encryption know how important it can be to keep an extra key around. Losing the only copy of an encryption key can make stored data useless.

A standalone machine makes the administrator the default key recovery agent. Achieving administrator access by resetting the admin password or cracking the admin password would make EFS completely transparent. No passwords are needed; simply being the administrator opens all the protections. Removing the Windows™ password file (sam) resets the administrator password. EFS cannot protect system files like the sam. When restarting, the administrator password will be blank, but the administrator can still access the key to EFS.

APPLICATION: DEFRAGMENTING A DISK

When a disk is formatted for the first time, all of its clusters are open; there is no slack space. Reformatted disks can contain latent data, but it is not technically in slack space. When new data and programs are saved to the disk, they occupy clusters. Each cluster is represented by a number in the file allocation table.

0034	0035	0036	0037	0038	0039	0040	0041	0042	0043
used	used	used	used	used	used	used	used	used	used

When those files are moved or deleted, the FAT de-allocates the clusters and makes them available for new files.

0034	0035	0036	0037	0038	0039	0040	0041	0042	0043
used	open	open	open	used	used	used	open	used	used

Over time, clusters are allocated and de-allocated. Files fit wherever there is space or they are saved in several spaces. The file system tracks these fragmented pieces of file so the user has access to what appears to be a complete file. In this case, a new file needs three clusters to fit. It is placed in clusters 35–37.

0034	0035	0036	0037	0038	0039	0040	0041	0042	0043
used	new	new	new	used	used	used	open	used	used

When a file increases in size but there is no adjacent open cluster, the new cluster is saved in the nearest available cluster. In this case, the new file needs another cluster for newly saved material. It now occupies clusters 35–37 and 41.

0034	0035	0036	0037	0038	0039	0040	0041	0042	0043
used	new	new	new	used	used	used	new	used	used

This process goes on over time and slowly reduces the efficiency of the hard drive. To acquire all of the pieces of a file, the read/write heads must travel to several parts of the disk. Eventually, the delay becomes noticeable to the user and he or she defragments the drive. Using a utility program, the user frees up a large area of disk space and then saves fragmented files as continuous files. The process repeats until the disk is defragmented; however, as soon as new information is added to a file, the fragmentation process begins again. Some utilities track frequently changed files and give them a little buffer space during the defragmentation process.

EVIDENCE RECOVERY FROM SLACK SPACE

As noted above, the efficient operation of the computer's file system leaves both active data and latent data. Active data is available through the file system itself or through the methods described below. Latent data is not available through the file system; however, common tools can give analysts access to it. The box item, examining the bits, describes one such tool called a hex editor. The hex editor can be used to examine intact files (active data) or deleted and obscured data (latent data) from the hard disk without interference from the file system. Thus, incriminating bit patterns (e.g., a victim's credit card number or a specimen from a child pornography image) can be discovered.

In this hypothetical example, an analyst has to prove that a suspect accessed data critical to a company and downloaded it using a security hole in the company's Web server. Investigators found a supposedly anonymous user in a chat room claiming to have secrets from the victim company. This led to the suspect and the seizure of his computer. A quick review of likely places on the image of the seized disk found nothing. Apparently the suspect had deleted the information or might have had it elsewhere. The analyst suspects that there may be evidence in the slack space that the suspect forgot to clear.

The analyst wipes the hard drive of a lab bench machine (called an analysis drive) and verifies it with an MD5. The hash of the analysis drive matches the hash taken when it was brand new and empty. He notes that fact in a bench journal on a separate computer.

The analyst applies the image to the analysis drive and verifies it with another MD5. The hash of the analysis drive now matches the hash taken from the suspect's drive and the hash of the image (because they are the same). He notes that fact in a bench journal on a separate computer.

From a bootable CD, he opens a freeware utility called *Strings,* which searches for text words embedded in a program. He looks for the company's name anywhere on the disk. He finds one hit in cluster 0040. The company includes its name in executable programs at the end. He notes that fact in a bench journal on a separate computer.

From a bootable CD, he opens a hex editor (see Box 12.7). Using the hex editor, he searches for unique patterns of bits found at the beginning of the program believed stolen. He finds a match in cluster 0034. He notes that fact in a bench journal on a separate computer.

BOX 12.7 Examining the Bits

The interoperation of computers across networks and different operating systems has required the use of standard file systems. Typically, there are indicators at the beginning of a file (called a header) that inform the software of the file's characteristics. To read this information we need two things: (1) Software capable of accessing the raw data and (2) a codex to allow us to interpret the raw data. The illustration below (labeled wtc-photo.jpg) depicts the initial bit-by-bit values of a picture of the World Trade Center. The hex editor allows an analyst to view every detail of the file.

Hex editors report binary information in "hexadecimal couplets" (on the left in the illustration). Binary data, commonly understood as ones and zeroes (i.e., bits), is difficult for humans to interpret. Hexadecimal couplets are used to represent groups of eight bits—often called bytes. Two hexadecimal characters {0, 1, 2, 3, 4, 5, 6, 7, 8, 9, A, B, C, D, E, or F} can replace eight binary characters {0, or 1}. Once trained to do so, analysts find it much easier to make sense of this mind-numbing collection of 1–9 and A–F than an eight times larger collection of ones and zeroes. Fortunately, most hex editors also attempt to translate the bits into text (on the right in the illustration). The photograph of the World Trade Center was produced with Adobe Photoshop 3.0™.

wtc-photo.jpg

wtc-photo.jpg

Offset	0	1	2	3	4	5	6	7	8	9	A	B	C	D	E	F	
00000000	FF	D8	FF	E0	00	10	4A	46	49	46	00	01	02	01	03	F8	ÿØÿà..JFIF.....ø
00000010	03	F8	00	00	FF	ED	16	3A	50	68	6F	74	6F	73	68	6F	.ø..ÿí.:Photosho
00000020	70	20	33	2E	30	00	38	42	49	4D	03	ED	00	00	00	00	p 3.0.8BIM.í....
00000030	00	10	03	F7	FB	D6	00	02	00	01	03	F7	FB	D6	00	02	...÷ûÖ.....÷ûÖ..
00000040	00	01	38	42	49	4D	04	0D	00	00	00	00	00	04	00	00	..8BIM.........
00000050	00	78	38	42	49	4D	03	F3	00	00	00	00	00	08	00	00	.x8BIM.ó.......
00000060	00	00	00	00	00	00	38	42	49	4D	04	0A	00	00	00	00	......8BIM......
00000070	00	01	00	00	38	42	49	4D	27	10	00	00	00	00	00	0A	....8BIM'.......
00000080	00	01	00	00	00	00	00	00	00	02	38	42	49	4D	03	F5	..........8BIM.õ
00000090	00	00	00	00	00	48	00	2F	66	66	00	01	00	6C	66	66	.....H./ff...lff
000000A0	00	06	00	00	00	00	00	01	00	2F	66	66	00	01	00	A1	........./ff...¡
000000B0	99	9A	00	06	00	00	00	00	00	01	00	32	00	00	00	01	██.........2....
000000C0	00	5A	00	00	00	06	00	00	00	00	00	01	00	35	00	00	.Z...........5..
000000D0	00	01	00	2D	00	00	00	06	00	00	00	00	00	01	38	42	...-..........8B
000000E0	49	4D	03	F8	00	00	00	00	00	70	00	00	FF	FF	FF	FF	IM.ø.....p..ÿÿÿÿ
000000F0	FF	FF	FF	FF	FF	FF	FF	FF	FF	FF	FF	FF	FF	FF	FF	FF	ÿÿÿÿÿÿÿÿÿÿÿÿÿÿÿÿ
00000100	FF	FF	03	E8	00	00	00	00	FF	FF	FF	FF	FF	FF	FF	FF	ÿÿ.è....ÿÿÿÿÿÿÿÿ
00000110	FF	FF	FF	FF	FF	FF	FF	FF	FF	FF	FF	FF	FF	FF	03	E8	ÿÿÿÿÿÿÿÿÿÿÿÿÿÿ.è
00000120	00	00	00	00	FF	FF	FF	FF	FF	FF	FF	FF	FF	FF	FF	FF	....ÿÿÿÿÿÿÿÿÿÿÿÿ
00000130	FF	FF	FF	FF	FF	FF	FF	FF	FF	FF	03	E8	00	00	00	00	ÿÿÿÿÿÿÿÿÿÿ.è....
00000140	FF	FF	FF	FF	FF	FF	FF	FF	FF	FF	FF	FF	FF	FF	FF	FF	ÿÿÿÿÿÿÿÿÿÿÿÿÿÿÿÿ
00000150	FF	FF	FF	FF	FF	FF	03	E8	00	00	38	42	49	4D	04	08	ÿÿÿÿÿÿ.è..8BIM..
00000160	00	00	00	00	00	10	00	00	00	01	00	00	02	40	00	00	.............@..
00000170	02	40	00	00	00	00	38	42	49	4D	04	14	00	00	00	00	.@....8BIM......
00000180	00	04	00	00	00	01	38	42	49	4D	04	0C	00	00	00	00	......8BIM......
00000190	14	AA	00	00	00	01	00	00	00	70	00	00	00	70	00	00	.ª.......p...p..
000001A0	01	50	00	00	93	00	00	00	14	8E	00	18	00	01	FF	D8	.P..█...█.....ÿØ
000001B0	FF	E0	00	10	4A	46	49	46	00	01	02	01	00	48	00	48	ÿà..JFIF.....H.H
000001C0	00	00	FF	EE	00	0E	41	64	6F	62	65	00	64	80	00	00	..ÿî..Adobe.d█..
000001D0	00	01	FF	DB	00	84	00	0C	08	08	08	09	08	0C	09	09	..ÿÛ.█..........
000001E0	0C	11	0B	0A	0B	11	15	0F	0C	0C	0F	15	18	13	13	15	....

The analyst must now recover as much of the program as possible to provide statistical certainty of the match. Some of the clusters have been overwritten. He creates the chart below to show exactly where the evidence came from. Each box is one cluster. Each cluster is labeled with a number in the FAT. The original file was 112 kilobytes (112k). Unallocated clusters are marked in white; allocated clusters are marked in gray.

0034	0035	0036	0037	0038	0039	0040	0041	0042	0043

Cluster size = 16k

Cluster ID	Status	Used by file	Size of new file	Original file	Recoverable
0034	Empty		0k	16K	16k
0035	Used	M024MNFB.HTM	4k	16K	12k
0036	Used	M02505DE.CSS	2k	16K	14k
0037	Used	M1NSVN76.HTM	16k	16K	0
0038	Used	M1NSVN76.HTM	6k	16K	10k
0039	Empty		0k	16K	16k
0040	Empty		0k	16K	16k
					84,000

By subtracting the amount of the new file overwriting each cluster of the original, the analyst calculates that about 84,000 bytes survived and can be matched to the missing file. The odds that that combination of bits occurred by chance alone are one to a number greater than the age of the universe in seconds; the analyst has a match. The analysts can now prove that the missing proprietary file was on the suspect's computer—even though the suspect tried to delete it. The presence of the fruits of a crime, and motive, a disgruntled former employee, constitute the elements of a crime. Because his methods followed the best practices of the field, he will be able to present this summary of the evidence to the court in a convincing manner.

COMMERCIAL FORENSIC PACKAGES

Modern forensic packages offer numerous advantages to the investigator, but also present pitfalls to investigators unsure of the fundamentals. To use these tools to their maximum benefit, the investigator must understand the way information is stored. Perhaps more important, to convincingly testify as to the proper use of these tools, the forensic examiner cannot be a passive observer of the analysis; he or she must plan and adapt the analysis based on an understanding of the technology and the specific legal requirements of the case at hand. A good forensics package must cover each of the basic forensic functions described in this chapter: importing data, hashing, wiping, imaging, and search capabilities.

Extended Analysis and Searching

All digital data is stored as a pattern of bits, the pattern of bits tells the computer how to decode the patterns into pictures or text or other meaningful symbols. Computers cannot interpret symbols the way humans do. They can, however, match patterns of bits in storage to a sample provided by the analyst. In some cases, different encoding techniques are used. This means that the bit pattern used to represent the same symbol to the human user could be vastly different on different systems. For example, Unicode is used by Window NT/2000/XP™ and the IBM extended character set is used by DOS. This is another reason these two systems are incompatible. A forensic package must be versatile enough to recognize these common encoding schemes as well as the commonly used proprietary data storage formats. For example Microsoft Outlook™ uses a proprietary database (called a DBX file) to store all of its e-mail. Without a third-party utility program, an analyst would have to install Microsoft Outlook™ to simply read seized e-mail. However, modern forensic packages have plug-ins that can decode proprietary file formats. Although freeware utilities are available to read Outlook DBX files, exporting data to separate utilities can be cumbersome and is prone to creating errors. Further, broad search protocols do not work unless the search software is aware of various encoding schemes.

Speed is a primary concern in searches run by forensic packages. When huge volumes of data must be searched, simple, one-at-a-time pattern matching would take too long. Forensic packages have routines that search for all the desired patterns at once. If a suspect's drive has 80GB of data, that full amount of data must be run from the hard drive and into the processor for comparison. As previously noted, the hard drive is the slowest part of the storage system. Instead of bringing all of the information through the hard drive several times, forensic packages bring it through once and search for all of the terms indicated by the analyst programming the search.

The ability of a search to achieve results is called the power of the search. Beyond the recognition of encoding schemes, searches should be able to distinguish near misses caused by minor user errors. Simple search routines are very literal; if the searched data does not contain the exact phrase or combination of characters, the search will return negative results. Most people are familiar with the need for proper capitalization and spelling in some search programs. More powerful search engines can search from context, or with allowances for small errors. Powerful searches also allow the user to search for multiple terms, or small variations of those terms, at once. Modern forensic packages offer powerful and flexible search programs.

User Interface

Fatigue is a primary concern of forensic analysts. Huge backlogs of seized evidence are the rule, rather than an exception. Requiring an analyst to fight through uncomfortable menus to achieve simple tasks results is wasted time and repetitive, unproductive use of an analyst's time. Many forensic packages have pseudo-programmable features that allow an analyst to set up an analysis with a list of commands rather than requiring direct input at each step. Other interface features include common search term dictionaries. Thus, a standard search of threatening terms can provide the basic foundation for an analysis of a stalking case. These basic dictionaries can be enhanced with terms specific to the case from another list—names and addresses of suspects for example. Another key to a good forensic package is consistency of commands. Most of the features of a forensic package can be found in individual programs—many of which are freely available. However, starting numerous programs and keeping track of the analysis requires much more effort. Further, each programmer of the freeware has his or her own notion of how commands operate. A forensic package has one consistent set of commands and menus to perform various functions on the data.

Centralized Report Writing and Auditing

A forensic analyst should be able to replicate every action that led to the discovery of evidence. A good forensics package should have the capability to track the analyst's actions to a log, so that productive procedures can be saved without requiring excessive notes. This may also include cataloging of key files for easy reference later. This log can form the basis for a more extensive report or simply be used as lab bench notes from the witness stand.

Validation and Support

A primary advantage to using a forensics package is that it has generally been validated by an external expert and used in standard practice. This saves an analyst from having to defend every tool used from attacks by the defense. As new versions of the package are released, they receive similar expert validation.

Support goes beyond the basic help-desk function. Forensic software vendors usually offer training to validate an analyst's skill and knowledge with the product. The credential provided by the vendor, upon successful completion of the training, is often a key validation of the analyst's skill.

When available, forensic packages will greatly increase the productivity of an analyst. Although the packages cost several hundred dollars, the wasted, salaried time of an analyst is worth considerably more to most organizations. In addition, the training provided by forensic package vendors can increase the productivity of an analyst by keeping him or her abreast of recent developments. A good package covers all the basics and helps keep the analysis organized and documented.

SUMMARY

The basic process of digital forensic analysis is designed to present the elements of a crime in evidence from stored digital materials. In court, a forensic analyst will be asked to answer several questions about the evidence:

1. When restoring a backup to another machine, will it contain all of the files, no more and no less tha[n] were on the original?

2. Will the restored version's file be identical, faithful copies of the original?

3. Will [latent data] be faithfully reproduced?

4. Will the restored backup contain all the data, and only the data, on the original?

5. How do we know that our answers to these questions are accurate?[10]

By following the methods described in this chapter (especially the documentation), the analyst will be able to prove the answers to these questions. Other basic skills include a working knowledge of the devices used to store digital information and the tools required to analyze it. Computer forensics involve more that just computer knowledge, forensics also involves a detailed understanding of criminal law and the legal process.

REVIEW QUESTIONS

1. Explain the process used to preserve the verifiable integrity of digital evidence. How does this ensure that data is preserved unmodified? How can an analyst show that the original evidence is unmodified?

2. Trace and explain how the hardware of a computer organizes and stores information for later retrieval from an active file being processed in the processor chip to a mass storage device (hard disk or removable storage). What is the trend in terms of speed in this progression of components? What is the trend in terms of size and capacity in this progression of components?

3. Describe in broad terms how the software of a computer organizes information for storage and later retrieval. Does this process yield any potential locations for latent digital evidence? Is latent evidence always intact? Why or why not?

4. What advantages are offered by commercial forensic packages? Are there any disadvantages to using them? If so, what are they?

ENDNOTES

1. BLACK, H.C., J.R. NOLAN, and J.M. NOLAN-HALEY. *Black's Law Dictionary* (6th ed.). St. Paul, MN: West Publishing, 1990.

2. "Data" is the plural form of datum. A single datum is one piece of information. Common usage allows discussion of data as a single grouping of information (e.g., "data is easily obtained"). This chapter uses data in this latter, common form.

3. STEPHENSON, P. (2000). *Investigating Computer-Related Crime.* Boca Raton, FL: CRC Press.

4. ORTON, I. "The Investigation and Prosecution of a Cybercrime." From *Cybercrime: The Investigation, Prosecution and Defense of a Computer-Related Crime.* Durham, NC: Carolina Academic Press, 2001.

5. It is possible, although complex to forge a file to produce a certain hash value, but it is extremely unlikely that the forged file could be confused with the original.

6. A single DVD can hold about 4.7GB of data, but it would take more than 16 of them to hold the contents of a common consumer hard drive.

7. The underlying issue was that one GB of the data was encrypted and the prosecution did not want to release the data because they could not read it. Mitnick refused to supply a decryption key based on his Fifth Amendment privilege against self-incrimination.

8. Random access memory (RAM) carries its name forward from the earliest days of computers. "Random access" distinguishes it from sequential access memory like a tape; this means that the processor can call for information located at any address in the RAM. In the 1960s, this was a tremendous improvement. Today, there are no other schemes for managing memory in common use, but we still specify "Random Access Memory."

9. Clusters are storage units that can be of several different sizes depending on how the file system on the hard drive is configured. They are the most accurate way to describe storage space on a hard disk.

10. STEPHENSON, *ibid.*

Chapter 13

Information Security
and Infrastructure Protection

Chapter Objectives

After completing this chapter, you should be able to:

- Understand the concept of risk as applied to information security and infrastructure protection.
- Discuss the major principles of risk analysis.
- Identify and define the primary security technologies used to protect information.
- Discuss the various functions of firewalls and identify their limitations.
- Define encryption, and discuss its use in terms of authenticity, integrity, and confidentiality.
- Identify and explain some of the security vendor technologies used today to secure information.

INTRODUCTION

Risk analysis will always be an art informed by science. We cannot know all possible outcomes and weigh them rationally. Risk analysis involves projecting the most probable outcome and allocating available resources to address that outcome. At the same time, a risk analyst must remember that assets (computers, networks, etc.) were purchased to fulfill a mission. If risk management strategies substantially interfere with that mission, then the assets are no better off than if they had been compromised through a security-related risk.

This section introduces the concept of risk by discussing several epochs of computer development. Each era presents its own risk and at least somewhat functional responses to that risk. Early decisions weighing the risk of computers not providing a useful function against potential or unknowable future security threats produced results that we still live with today. It is easy to criticize early decisions based on our knowledge of the outcomes, but even with hindsight, we may fail to see that the benefit provided greatly outweighs the harm. In fact, some decisions that have produced security vulnerabilities were absolutely essential to the basic functioning of computers and networks for their intended purposes.

MASTERING THE TECHNOLOGY AND THE ENVIRONMENT

In the earliest days of computing, before extensive networking and multiple user systems, the primary problem faced by users was the technology itself. During these early days, programmers created the computer functions that we take for granted.[1] Early innovations included interactive operation (rather than batch processing and output), rudimentary networking, graphics, tools and utilities, and so on.[2] In many cases, the primary limitation was the capacity of the hardware. Limitations imposed by operating memory, storage, and processing speed each forced adaptations. The net effect was the absence of security. At the time, physical security (i.e., locked doors) was sufficient to protect computing resources. The primary concern of system architects was the expansion of useful function and overcoming hardware limitations. Although decisions made at this early point would later have negative effects on security, they were really unavoidable.

As technologies matured and found supporters in mainstream business, the computer moved from research platform to business tool. Complex software was created for business and essential functions were transferred from armies of clerks to computer systems. Such moves were always in one direction. It is impossible to re-employ clerical staff and re-implement paper-based procedures once the existing system is gone. Further, the cost savings of computers make such a backwards move unlikely. This placed new emphasis on availability of data and recovery from errors and disasters. Computer centers were created to concentrate technical expertise and provide a controlled environment in which to maximize the availability of computing resources. Innovations in fire suppression,[3] efficient environmental controls,[4] and administrative procedures (i.e., back-up schedules) gave reasonable assurance against disaster.

The user was undeniably part of the computing environment. During this era, legitimate users were the primary human threat to computers. More harm was caused by failure properly to maintain systems and back-up schedules than from intrusion or malicious intent. When malicious intent played a part, it was typically on the part of an insider.[5] Although there are documented cases of intrusion and loss, a much greater threat came from the relative scarcity of experts to operate and maintain systems. Once again, the operational need for availability was more pressing than security.

Personal Computers and Intruders

Although recreational system intrusion was not unknown in the previous era, it was largely restricted by access to computers. Few people had access, and fewer still had the skill to break through the rudimentary security on most systems. Those that did were often deeply invested in terms of time and resources spent to acquire that knowledge.[6] Recreational intrusion was a minor problem at best. The advent of the home computer in 1975 marked the beginning of the democratization of computing. It also marked the movement of hacking from the old school era to the bedroom hacker era (see Chapter 4).[7] By the end of the 1970s, the restraint of peers and the investment in knowledge no longer provided reasonable protection against malicious users.

In this era, intruders sought knowledge and resources to continue their use of computers. Much of the literature is devoted to detailing the social connections or lack thereof among intruders and hackers.[8] Most pundits resort to the myth of the hacker as loner and contentious in interaction with other hackers.[9] An often-overlooked facet of the hacker culture is the need for information and resources. In the early era of intrusion, access to other computers required a phone connection, usually to a long distance number. Thus, the search for access to resources and knowledge of how to exploit them dominated the vast majority of hacker interactions.

For the first time, intruders became a significant threat to routine computer use. Although efforts were made to secure computers, long-standing demands for the availability of computing resources and the expansion of computer capabilities simply eclipsed demands for security. Hollinger and Lanza-Kaduce provide one of the very few significant criminological works describing the efforts to supplement the computer industries' meager efforts toward security with law.[10] Various states and the federal government passed laws in the hopes of deterring would-be computer criminals and punishing those who were caught.

The Internet Explosion

The explosive growth of the Internet has been the subject of numerous books and articles in the popular press,[11] scholarly publications of general interest,[12] and works of technical research.[13] The dramatic influx of new users to computer networks has burdened both the technical infrastructure and the social cohesion of on line communities.[14] The loss of social cohesion of the computer underground gave rise to script kiddies, low-skilled network intruders with little desire to pursue the traditional goals of hackers (see Chapter 4). At the same time, the influx of new users, also with low levels of skill, gave script kiddies and other larval hackers a rich field of targets. Unless a computer system holds particular interest (politically—like the World Trade Organization; technologically; or as a trophy—like NASA or the Pentagon), the most likely threat comes from script kiddies. This fact will be important when considering security policies.

Another security consequence of the Internet's increased availability is the proliferation of hacker tools and "philez" (information files). Without tools, script kiddies would be unlikely to cause harm. Such tools existed in the previous era, but were not as widely distributed. When they were shared among hackers, they came with enculturation to the hacker ethic and other prosocial, if not legal, subcultural values.

The information contained in philez can transform a "newbie" hacker into an accomplished network intruder. The only limitation on the skill attainable is the ability to read and comprehend technical concepts. Given the potential of the Internet to find and retrieve information from almost any jurisdiction, it is unlikely that a single nation's efforts could remove these tools from wide circulation. It is also undesirable to remove technical information from our networks; technological advancement depends on the open exchange of ideas.[15]

PRINCIPLES OF RISK ANALYSIS

Risk analysis is performed at many levels and with many degrees of detail. Risk analysis services are provided by Fortune 500 consulting firms like Deloitte & Touche, Ernst & Young, KPMG, and many others. Reports from a major risk analysis can cover every aspect of business and run into the thousands of pages. Risk analysis may also be performed by small organizations or even individuals in the course of their business. Such informal decision making does not follow the comprehensive steps of the more elaborate analyses. Deciding where to draw the line on the depth of a risk analysis is an art with no clear standard. The principles of risk analysis presented here are broad, but examples are narrowly tailored to illustrate network security risks and remedies. Above all, this process shows that there is no single solution to security. The effort required to eliminate all risks (even if that is possible) would surely overwhelm an organization. All known factors relevant to an organization should be weighed so that a specific level of acceptable risk can be matched to a risk management strategy.

Assessment and Evaluation

The first step of risk analysis is correctly to assess and evaluate the existing information technology systems within an organization. Unfortunately, those who often conduct risk analysis studies tend to focus on external vulnerabilities and threats. Most losses of information come from inside the organization and through relatively simple security failures of existing information systems and networks. This assessment must include an evaluation of the organizational, managerial and administrative procedures directly relevant to information technology systems. Hopefully, the organization has and uses a well developed and well defined information technology plan. This plan should include information relating to the acquisition and purchase of future IT equipment and systems, as well as a strategy for expanding information security parameters as the system grows or changes. Interestingly, most organizations have plans that represent large "bibles" of procedures and policies that sit on bookshelves (get dusty) and are rarely read or followed. Most managers and directors outside of IT fail to comprehend the complexity of information security. It is not simply the purchase of a new device or the implementation of a new password procedure, but rather an ongoing culture within the organization that re-enforces security awareness and security protocols. Information and computer security must be a part of the everyday working culture of the organization. The information security plan is not just a written compendium of policies and procedures, but a living document that guides the organizational methodology for providing and improving information security. In this manner, the development of a specific risk analysis plan never really ends. New software and equipment acquisitions, new technologies, and new system requirements demand constant change and "tweaking" of the overall system, and hence, the security of the system as well. Similar to or part of an information resource management (IRM) plan, risk analysis highlights synergism and cooperativeness, as well as overall improvement in information exchange through the use of new and varied technology and work processes.[16] This cannot be a haphazard experiment; it most be a well thought out plan implemented through a series of phases on a timely basis. Without such objectives in mind, existing information technology resources flounder and security breaches proliferate. It should go without saying that constant training improves security knowledge and engenders security awareness within an organization. Training must accompany the development of any risk analysis or information security plan.

Executives must also be aware of a growing problem existing within information system security. Most executives are not highly information and computer technology literate. As such, they must rely on the technical advice and expertise of subordinates. This situation makes the executive vulnerable to "information security elites." Recognized and identified by a number of scholars during the technology boom of the 1980s, information security elites often gain control over others (influence) and resist control by supervisors.[17] This is often accomplished by occupying key positions whose competencies are essential to the overall success of the organization. In some cases, executives are almost held "hostage" by those who have the niche technical knowledge to understand specific information security systems. Information is critically important to an organization. Individual managers and personnel must have immediate access to secure and correct data as well as communication systems that link them to a global marketplace. This demand places the highest value on those who can assure both the quality and security of data and the information system. It also creates a potential environment for significant security loss and abuse. Who is monitoring those in charge of information security? For this reason, external reviews have significant advantages over internal assessments, particularly in the area of risk analysis.

Threats

The second important aspect of risk analysis is to identify the threats facing an organization. The single largest threat to an organization and its information security is from within. Many times, organizations suffer from key individuals intentionally stealing information or corrupting files. The vulnerability of the organization is extreme and as such, so is the loss. Additionally, in many instance of information security breaches from within, there is virtually no detection of an incident that has occurred. Many times, information is accessed, altered, stolen, or sabotaged without the organizational victim's knowledge—either the crime is covered up through the use of special programs, or simply not detected in an audit.

Other than routine personnel and employment checks, incorporating solid hiring practices, and constant monitoring, very little can be accomplished to eliminate totally this type of threat. The most pernicious part of this threat is that it invariably leads executives not to trust their subordinates. It takes just one relatively minor problem from within for an executive to realize just how vulnerable the organization really is from this type of attack. Paranoia can become a problem, the breakdown of trust between executives and managers causes other significant personnel problems. Once again, frank awareness and training can help to instill the type of organizational culture required in today's information society.

Formal risk analysis also categorizes external threats with great detail and elaborate terms, especially after the events of September 11, 2001. Terrorism, sabotage, espionage, and criminal theft are real, and comprise a bulk of the identified threats to an organization. Just as dangerous (and threatening) are the age-old issues presented by natural disasters, hurricanes, tornadoes, and earthquakes. Effective risk analysis should cover these types of standard threats as well. Interestingly, preparing for natural disasters often provides the type of secure information environment that thwarts insider problems and external attacks by people.

We are concerned primarily with risks and vulnerabilities to information systems, and as such will focus our discussion pertaining to problems associated with these types of systems. These are usually summarized in terms of threats to information: integrity, authenticity, confidentiality, and availability. Threats to integrity are threats that actually alter data. Adding, moving, and deleting all change the integrity of data. These actions are also legitimate uses of data. The risk is that an unauthorized or unintentional action will cause a threat to integrity. To make matters more difficult, threats to integrity are not limited to malicious actions. Unintentional alteration (e.g., deleting a useful file) is far more common that malicious activity. The recycling bin found in Microsoft™ systems is a risk management tool to avoid such unintentional deletions. It trades hard drive space and annoying pop-up dialogs, asking you to be sure before you delete for a second chance to recover a file.

Authenticity is a more subtle concept, but it is related to integrity. In these terms, authenticity is the ability to trust the integrity of data. In broader terms, authenticity is the justified ability to trust. Data that cannot be verified or trusted is less useful than authenticated data, if not completely useless. Further, if an intruder is detected in the network, data may have perfect integrity (i.e., be unaltered), but if authenticity cannot be established, the organization cannot verify that fact. It may as well be altered.

Confidentiality acknowledges that some information is more valuable if it is not publicly available. Confidentiality is treated more extensively in the section on encryption (below).

The final broad category of threat to information is availability. A denial of service attack can make information unavailable, but so can overly rigid security policies. What is the difference to the legitimate user who needs the information? Information systems exist to store, manipulate, and utilize data. When data is unavailable the

---

BOX 13.1   Complete Security Is Not the Complete Solution

Computer experts have long recognized that it is possible to make a computer completely secure. The steps are as follows: (1) unplug the network cable, (2) encrypt the data with strong encryption, (3) delete the encryption key and forget the password, (4) unplug the power, (5) lock the computer in a vault, and finally (6) cover the vault with concrete. This security procedure also makes the computer perfectly useless. For an asset to be worth protecting, it must have value. Most assets have value in the work they do for the business.

---

system's fundamental purpose is disturbed. Each of these categories of threat must be balanced against each other in an attempt to manage risk.

Cost-Effective Security

Risk management is predicated on the rational calculation of potential damage against certain damage of non–mission related expenditure. The concept of risk management acknowledges that while it may be possible virtually to eliminate all risks, the resources expended to do so would greatly outweigh the potential gains.

   With this in mind, computer security experts seek to optimize the balance between the intended function of the information asset (network, computer, etc.) and securing the asset from risk. Many strategies of risk management overlap. For example: Protecting a system from natural disaster by maintaining a decentralized network also protects the system from local network outages or denial of service attacks on a single point of failure.

SECURITY TECHNOLOGIES

The primary purposes of risk analysis are to identify threats and then to provide recommendations to address these threats. Concerning information systems and technologies, the focus has historically been on protecting individual components such as software, hardware, and connected devices. While a hard drive can be replaced, the information contained on the hard drive may be irreplaceable, and its loss may be catastrophic to an organization. Here, more than in almost any other area of risk analysis and information security, an ounce of prevention is truly worth a pound of cure! Coupled with solid personnel hiring practices and an aware organizational culture, the following security technologies provide a sound base for information systems and networks.[18]

Backups

Backups are the single most important security measure a company or individual can take. As noted above, most of the value of an information system lies in its information. In the event that threats to integrity, authenticity, or availability cannot be prevented, the information can survive risk actualization if a backup copy exists in a safe location.

BOX 13.2   Case Study in Risk Analysis—Backup Schedules

Although there is no rule as to how often backups should be created, a good rule of thumb is to consider how much of the data you can afford to reproduce. When you exceed that point, create a backup. For example, a company pays people to enter data. A backup system capable of handling their demands costs $12,000. They have 120 employees making $10 per hour. They create a backup every ten hours (120 × 10 × 10 = 12,000). The benefit is that they only pay for the backup system once, with small recurring costs for tape and a portion of an administrator's time. If they recover data from a ten-hour shift once, the system has paid for itself. If they suspect an intruder has tampered with the data, they can simply compare it to a backup and restore the good data if necessary.

A backup is a copy of data. If data is lost, destroyed, or altered, the backup may provide the only way to recover the data. If there is reason to suspect that the integrity of the data was compromised, a secure backup provides a basis of comparison. If the suspect data matches the backup (plus any expected changes), integrity has been restored. If alteration is evident, then the harm from compromised data has been isolated.

Mission-critical data (data that cannot be lost) is often protected with an instantaneous backup as it is stored. A device called a Redundant Array of Inexpensive Disks (RAID) saves the data to two hard drives at once, making failure of a single drive less damaging.[19] Since RAID only makes two copies of the hard drive, regular backups are also necessary to protect against alteration.

Firewalls

Another way individuals and organizations can protect their computer networks is by using firewalls. A firewall is a device or software that acts as a checkpoint between a network or standalone computer and the Internet. A firewall checks all data coming in and going out. If the data does not fit strict rules, it does not go through. In the past, firewalls were not widely used, since they could significantly reduce access from the protected network to the outside world. Firewalls have since improved greatly and are now relatively fast and easily configured by the user. Software development, combined with rapidly increasing computer-based crime occurring through interconnected networks, has led to the widespread use of firewalls.

A firewall is a tool to be used as part of a security strategy. It cannot protect a user from all threats. In fact, firewalls are a classic example of risk analysis. If the rules set in a firewall are too restrictive (i.e., more secure), then normal network functions may be impaired. Such impairment may make it impossible for users to conduct business—the whole reason for the network in the first place. If the firewall rule set is not restrictive enough, it may expose the network to an intruder. This critical balance is the primary problem with firewalls. A special administrator is often necessary for large corporate firewalls. This administrator constantly balances security versus business efficiency to configure the firewall rule set. New applications or new work zones force new rules for the firewall. For example, a sales force in the field may need access to the corporate network. The firewall must allow these users to penetrate the network while excluding unknown users. One solution (see below under Encryption) is to allow a virtual private network (VPN) using encrypted data. Many early VPNs had difficulty penetrating firewalls because the firewall could not read the data headers (directions on how to deliver the data).

Perimeter and Host-Based Firewalls: The standard, corporate Internet firewall places a single barrier between the internal network and potential attackers. Servers that require public access, (e.g., Web servers or mail servers), are placed outside the firewall to minimize penetration from the outside. Such servers, called "bastion" servers, have their own security measures. Like the curtain wall of a medieval castle, the firewall protects the interior while towers, or bastions, provide hard defense points for contact with a threatening environment. This configuration places all of the defenses at the perimeter. If a malicious user attacked the network from within the "secure" area, there are no defenses. On the other hand, a single dedicated firewall can be built to handle a large volume of traffic without slowing the network.

A second layer of security can be provided with host-resident firewalls installed on machines within the secure perimeter. Host-resident firewalls are software programs installed on a computer. Clearly, there is an additional burden on every computer running such a program. There is also an additional cost for software and burden in administering host-resident firewalls. There is no requirement that all computers within a perimeter have a host-resident firewall. Particular resources within the secure perimeter may require additional protection. Using both types of firewall allows fine-grained control over network security. This means greater flexibility to manage risks. For example, a perimeter firewall might have to allow traffic into the perimeter due to use needs, but a host-resident wall could restrict such traffic on all computers except those that need access.

Packet Filtering: One of the most basic functions of a firewall is to block certain traffic that may be harmful. One of the protocols that run the Internet, Transfer Control Protocol and Internet Protocol (TCP/IP), assigns numbers to computers called Internet Protocol Addresses (IP Addresses). TCP assigns "ports" to each computer that allow different programs to communicate.[20] Imagine that each computer on the Internet is a hotel. Each hotel has about 65,000 rooms. The IP portion of TCP/IP identifies each hotel with a street address so traffic can find it (IP address). The TCP portion of TCP/IP assigns room numbers so that traffic can go to the right place. Most of the higher rooms are not regularly used. Packet filtering allows a firewall to block traffic from a known bad location (a scruffy hotel in a bad neighborhood). It also allows the firewall to block traffic to a room that should be unused (which may indicate an unwanted "guest" in the hotel). The addressing information that is absolutely necessary for Internet communication is used to block potential threats. By using a firewall to block unused ports, many security threats can be eliminated. If the filtering rules are too aggressive, beneficial traffic may be blocked. Again, a security policy must carefully weigh the need for legitimate service versus security.

Stateful Inspection: Stateful inspection relies on another feature of TCP. To travel across the Internet, data is broken into smaller chunks called packets. IP addresses packets to find the right computer using the IP address of that computer. Each IP packet is an independent agent, finding its way across the Internet with the best guess of the shortest route. Sometimes packets take different routes and arrive out of order. These must be reassembled into the proper order before the computer can use them.

In addition to labeling ports, TCP reassembles packets by tracking sessions (a series of exchanges between computers). The TCP portion of each IP packet contains a sequence number that is based on a pseudo-random process negotiated between the two computers communicating in the session. Stateful inspection monitors these sequence numbers and other information to make sure that malicious data doesn't enter into a stream of legitimate data. This is most frequently done by denying an external attempt to open a session with a computer that is not a server. Packet filtering cannot block all traffic (or else the computer may as well not be connected to the Internet), but stateful inspection can be used to ensure that only information request from within the perimeter can enter.

Network Address Translation (NAT):   Although technically not a security function, many firewalls allow administrators to use special reserved Internet addresses. All the machines inside the perimeter have these special addresses. These special addresses are not allowed on the Internet. To use Internet services, the internal machines start a session with the firewall server. The firewall uses NAT to assign an IP to that session, not to the internal machine. Going back to the hotel analogy, imagine a desk clerk with mailboxes. Data traffic goes to the mailbox and is then delivered to the guest. That way, no junk mail gets through; in this case, junk mail would be specially crafted attacks against an internal computer designed to bypass firewalls. A firewall with NAT stops these attacks because it moderates all communication from inside to the outside.

Air Gaps: Air gaps are the ultimate in firewall network protection. An air gap is literally a separation between computers containing nothing but air. That is, the machine is not on the network. Data has to be carried back and forth through the air gap by a person. The benefit to this is that no outsider can ever access the air-gapped machine. The down side is that no one on the inside can reach the air-gapped machine through the network. Air gaps are typically only used with the most sensitive data. Data carried to the air-gapped machine may contain malicious code like a virus, but the air-gapped machine is 100 percent immune to network attacks. Unfortunately many security equipment vendors label devices as air gaps when they actually connect to the network; these are "virtual air gaps." Absolute protection only occurs when there is no electrical connection—virtual air gaps do not fulfill this requirement.

Limitations of Firewalls

Firewalls are powerful and increasingly versatile tools for managing risks on a computer network; however, they are not *the* single solution to network security. Firewalls have to be managed to allow for growth in network function while maintaining the highest level of protection. This requires interaction between the firewall administrator and other users of the network. In large organizations, this interaction is formalized in a security policy. A security policy requires updates as situations change, and it requires auditing to ensure that users and management are complying with the policy. The security policy tells the firewall administrator how to balance risks when configuring the firewall. It also allows the security administrator to plan other layers of security, if necessary, to cover the holes in the firewall made necessary by legitimate network functions.

Firewalls cannot stop improper use of legitimate services. This is why bastion servers are placed outside the secure perimeter of the network. Servers exist to provide interaction with people and systems outside the company; however, many network attacks exploit flaws in server software to gain unfettered access to the computer running the server software. If the server was inside the firewall, such malicious traffic could enter the secure perimeter. If the server is compromised, then the attacker would have a base of operations to explore the inside network.

Firewalls exist as part of an overall security strategy. They are not magical talismans that protect the network from all harm. Many users believe that the firewall will protect them; however, as we have seen in recent e-mail-based viruses and worms (see Chapter 4), this is not always so. Users surfing the Web from inside a firewall are still vulnerable to exploits written into the Web pages they access. There are remedies for these security risks not handled by firewalls, but they all exist as part of an overall security strategy.

Encryption

Bruce Schneier defines cryptography as "the art and science of securing messages."[21] Messages can be any data. Encryption is a technique of securing data by scrambling it into apparent nonsense, but doing so in such a way that the message can be recovered by a person possessing a secret code called a key. The requirements for a good encryption scheme include protecting the classic elements of computer security discussed above: authenticity, integrity, and confidentiality. Availability is generally not facilitated by encryption. Encrypting data has the inherent effect of confidentiality. This comes into play most often when confidential data must be sent through an insecure medium. An encrypted message (i.e., the scrambled message) can be stored or transmitted to another point with a reasonable expectation of security—even if the medium used to transmit it is not secure (e.g., the Internet). Integrity can be assured through a similar technique called hashing. Hashing produces a unique signature of the original data—like a fingerprint. At the other end of the transmission, a new hash is calculated on the data and compared to the old hash. If they match, the data has not been altered. A public key/private key system allows a user to authenticate data by matching a key— the only way to decode the data—with a well known and publicly available key. This form of security is only as good as the secrecy of the key, but it offers a way to authenticate without being physically present (more about public key/private key systems below). Using these three techniques together provides a reasonable expectation that the message is private and unaltered.

To illustrate this process, imagine a check being mailed to a creditor. You create a transaction by filling in an amount to a preformatted check with all of your bank information already on it. You also fill in the receiver's name. You authenticate the instructions to your bank by signing the check. If there is any question as to who wrote the check, your signature can be checked against a signature card you filed when you opened the account. You place the check in an envelope to protect the confidentiality of your transaction. You then turn it over to the U.S. Postal Service and they deliver it. Evidence of tampering should be noticeable by the condition of the envelope. The elements of this transaction are authenticity—signature; confidentiality—envelope; and integrity—envelope. To conduct the same transaction over the Internet, you face different risks, but you still have tools to assist you.

To illustrate the on line process, imagine that instead of writing and mailing a check, you log onto the bill payment section of your creditor's Web site. You enter your confidential bank information. Since you cannot sign a computer screen, you provide information that only you should know—a password. This password serves as your signature.[22] In the same way that your signature was verified by your presence in a bank with identification documents, your password is verified with identifying information when you start to do business with the on line entity. Since only information is being exchanged, not a physical object like a signature on paper, confidentiality of your identifying information is imperative. The authenticity of your password is directly related to its confidentiality because anyone with the password would appear to be you. Both this information and the transaction details are protected with encryption. Finally, the integrity of the transaction details are guaranteed with a hash that accompanies the encrypted message. It is possible, although usually pointless, to blindly alter an encrypted message—a process called bit-flipping. A hash calculates a unique mathematical value for a message. When the message reaches its destination and is decrypted, a new hash is calculated. Any alteration of the message contents will cause the hashes not to match. The elements of this transaction are authenticity—password; confidentiality—encryption; and integrity—hash value. The transaction can be carried by the insecure Internet and retain a reasonable expectation of security.

A "reasonable expectation of security" does not mean absolute security. All encryption can be broken. "If the cost required to break an [encryption technique] is greater than the value of the encrypted data, it is probably safe."[23] The most essential feature of encryption is that scrambled data can be returned to a useful form by its intended user and cannot easily be returned to a useful form by others. Again, the concept of risk analysis can be applied to this security technique. The more valuable the information transmitted or the more determined a third party is to intercept the information, the more resources must be devoted to protecting it.

Encryption is used to store passwords on your home computer system, credit card numbers in "on line wallets," and to secure e-commerce transactions. Modern encryption *can* be broken, but except for the most basic forms of encryption, like the encryption protecting Windows™ passwords, most criminals would find it immensely easier to look for other methods to get the data. While e-commerce may be protected as it crosses the Internet, credit information is often stored on unsecured computers at the merchant's site. It is important to remember that encrypted e-commerce data is decrypted at the other end. While e-commerce transactions are generally safe, few merchants have devoted the resources to securing their whole computer system.

Using Public Key/Private Key Encryption to Enhance Confidentiality: A public key and private key are parts of a matched pair of values. That is, they are mathematically related in such a way that no other value could be substituted for one of them. It is also impossible to predict the value of one based on the other. Thus, having access to a public key will not help an attacker (a person attempting to break the encryption). When a message is encrypted with one key, only the other can decrypt it. Thus, having access to a public key will not help an attacker decrypt a message encrypted with the public key. The idea of the key pair is that one key can be freely distributed while not compromising the other. When a key pair is generated, either one may become the public key. That does not need to be determined until it is actually distributed. Finally, having a document encrypted with either one of the keys does not necessarily help an attacker guess the key value used to encrypt it.

Public keys are often registered with a public key authority. Anyone wishing to send a confidential message to the key owner can use the public key to encrypt the message.

The resulting encrypted document can be sent across an insecure channel, like the Internet. The receiver simply uses the private key associated with the well known public key to decrypt the message.

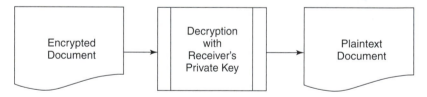

A malicious user intercepting the encrypted message cannot successfully decrypt the message with the public key.

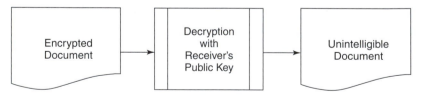

The process of encrypting a document simply assures the recipient of the confidentiality of the document's contents.[24]

Using Digital Signatures to Enhance Authenticity and Integrity: Another application of the public key/private key pair allows a user to authenticate a document with a "digital signature." Digital signatures use a hashing algorithm to create unique numeric value associated with the document. This value has two primary attributes. One, if the unaltered document is hashed again, it will produce the same hash value, and two, if the document is altered in any way, it will not produce the same value if hashed again. The problem with this method is that if the unencrypted original document is intercepted, it can be altered and a new hash value can be calculated based on the altered document and substituted for the old hash value. This means that the hash must be sent through a separate, secure mechanism or it must be cryptographically protected.

This is where the second step of the digital signature comes in. Once the hash value is calculated, it is encrypted with the sender's private key. Recall that having a document encrypted with the private key does not necessarily assist an attacker in

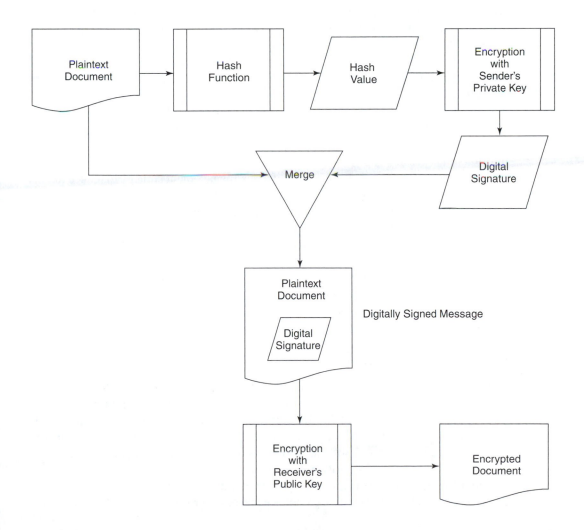

trying to break the encryption or guess the key. To authenticate that the person claiming to have sent the message actually sent it, the signature is decrypted with the sender's public key. The sender's public key is known to be associated with the private key supposedly used to encrypt the message. If the signature decrypts properly, then the receiver knows that someone in possession of the supposed sender's private key sent the message; this is assumed to be the supposed sender.[25]

Using Encryption in Daily Life: Most users do not directly use tools that provide public key/private key encryption. Pretty Good Privacy (PGP) is one example of a common encryption package. It is commonly used to encrypt e-mail messages. In spite of the relative rarity of such encryption packages, most computer users today use encryption without knowing it. Web browsers have built-in encryption functions. Secure Web pages, such as shop cart check-out pages in e-commerce sites, or any other secure information transfer page, use encryption to protect the transaction. This leads to an interesting problem with public key/private key encryption: It is very slow by computer standards. It is fine for small text files or very light graphics, but for wholesale secure transfer of information, it is simply inadequate. Symmetric key encryption is much faster, but it requires both parties to the transaction to have the same key; the key cannot be left unprotected to provide convenient authentication. The solution to this problem uses a hybrid of both symmetric key and public key/private key technology. A temporary symmetric key called a session key is generated for each data transfer "session." It is sent using a public key/private key exchange. The session key is simply information to be encrypted. Once both parties have the key, fast exchange of secure information is possible. As soon as the session is done, the session key can be discarded.

Encryption and hashing can be part of a risk management strategy to reduce threats to data authenticity, integrity, and confidentiality. The particular techniques discussed only indicate the possible uses of encryption. For example, a technology called IPsec (Secure Internet Protocol) utilizes cryptography to reduce threats to authenticity, integrity, and confidentiality of data as it travels on a network. IPsec is used to create secure cryptographic "tunnels" across the Internet so that eavesdroppers do not know where a packet is going after its next stop, nor do they know what it contains. Without IPsec or similar measures, information traversing the Internet is vulnerable to even relatively unsophisticated eavesdropping attempts.[26] This and many other uses of cryptographic technology provide options to manage threats.

Password Discipline

The single greatest problem in computer security is password protection. Although there are some basics do's and don'ts, there are also sophisticated software programs that address the issue. Several approaches have been taken, including password-creation software, one-time password generators, and user authentication systems—like biometric devices. There is a variety of software programs that system administrators can use to in order to improve password security. Some programs force users to change their passwords on a regular basis, perhaps every month or few months, or even every week. Other programs automatically create random pronounceable passwords for users, such as "jrk^wud" which is pronounced "jerk wood." The user remembers that the ^ character is between two words. Such pronounceable passwords are subject to dictionary attacks by hackers, are easily remembered by users, and do not relate to user information (such as a child's first name or user Social Security number) that might be easily determined by an intruder.

SECURITY VENDOR TECHNOLOGIES

SecurID, from Security Dynamics Technologies, Inc. is perhaps the most popular one-time password generator, with over 3 million users in 5,000 organizations worldwide. SecurID identifies and authenticates each individual user on the basis of two factors: (1) something secret that user knows—a memorized personal identification number (PIN); and (2) something unique that the user physically holds—the SecureID card. Under this system, a computer user logging on first types in his or her PIN. Then the user types in the number currently displayed on his or her SecureID card, which changes every 60 seconds. Each individual SecurID card is synchronized either with hardware or software on the computer system that the user is attempting to access. The result is a unique access code that is valid only for a particular user during a one-minute time period.

Kerberos is a program developed at MIT by the Athena Project. It is a leading network and data encryption system. Cygnus Support, a Mountain View, California company, has developed Kerberos-based user-authentication software—Cygnus Network Security (CNS)—that eliminates the need to use clear, unencrypted text passwords on a network. In this system, an individual user is given an encryption key to encrypt and decrypt Kereros passwords, log-ins, and other computer system transactions. When this individual wants to access the network, he or she will send a message to the Kerberos server. This computer sends back an encrypted package that can be read only with that user's secret key. This package also includes a temporary encryption key good for only that session on the computer. To prove his or her identity, the user then sends a message coded in the temporary encryption key back to the computer. The Kerberos computer then acknowledges the user's identity by sending a second encrypted message to the user, which can be decoded only by using the temporary encryption key previously sent to the user.

Kerberos is just one program that utilizes encryption and password technologies. Many other programs also create encrypted sessions between the user's computer and the destination computer, thus protecting passwords and other sensitive information from cybercriminals and -terrorists.

Symantec, the maker of Norton Utilities, is also a world leader in information security technologies. Focusing primarily on Internet security issues, Symantec offers a variety of security monitoring plans, management services, best practices, proactive protection methodologies, and educational services for enterprises and home users. In a recent white paper distributed by Symantec, the authors eloquently point out that the Internet was developed primarily as an unregulated, open architecture.[27] This is an ideal environment for crime and terrorism where simply developed passwords may not be enough.

New technologies are altering the face of user identification. The use of tools such as digital fingerprint identification, retinal identification, and voice recognition greatly increases the accuracy of user identification, sometimes replacing passwords. The future of computer security will continue to link a user's unique physical attributes (those that do not change or cannot be easily altered) to known passwords or stored encryption keys. Biometrics do not provide absolute security, but they make it increasingly difficult for intruders to guess passwords by adding another level of complexity to the password, but not making it harder for the user to remember the password. A retinal scan and a short password are effectively a 10,000–20,000 digit password. The longer the password is, the harder it is to guess.

Home Users

Cyber attacks have also focused on the home computer user. For instance, the latest "Blaster" attacks not only destroyed data on home computers, but also used a myriad of home computers as points of origination or servers of the destructive virus. By using exploits within the Microsoft™ operating system, these "bot" programs essentially infected a home PC and then turned it into a virus center by corrupting the e-mail address files within that computer. Thus each infected PC became an origination point that infected thousands of other computers through their own e-mail file.

Home users must also take computer security very seriously. Aside from the routine backups and use of antiviral software, home users must periodically conduct maintenance on their machines. Using the analogy of a car: A person buys a car and then performs routine maintenance such as oil changes, brake replacement, tune-ups and the like as the automobile is used. Similarly, people who purchase new personal computers need to conduct routine maintenance on their machines by updating their antiviral software on a regular basis, checking reports from their operating system Web site, and repairing software glitches through provided "patches" offered by a number of credible sources. The personal computer is much more like an automobile that needs constant care and upkeep, rather than an appliance like a refrigerator that is simply plugged into the wall and will continue to function without much maintenance. For the most part, this is a user awareness problem demanding a significant shift in attitude and philosophy on the part of literally millions of home users. Fortunately, all of the major operating system companies (e.g., Microsoft™, Linux™) provide well developed Web sites that offer the latest information on problems and remedies. Software fixes and patches often require simply a stroke of the key to download a specific file from the Web site. Then too, the Computer Emergency Response Team (CERT®) at Carnegie Mellon University maintains a well developed Web site that tracks and reports trends in computer viruses.[28] Established in 1988, the CERT® Coordination Center (CERT/CC) is a center of Internet security expertise, located at the Software Engineering Institute, a federally funded research and development center operated by Carnegie Mellon University. This site should be regularly visited by all computer users.

SUMMARY

We live in the "third wave" of the information society, and undoubtedly, abuses in information security resulting in computercrime and cyberterrorism will only grow in the future. Unfortunately, the losses suffered directly from these types of abuses may be only a part of overall economic devastation facing organizations. Indeed, the civil litigation resulting from loss of privacy, denial or loss of service from partner-type corporations, and loss of reputation and key executives may comprise a much more lasting and severe economic loss to victims of computer crime and cyberterrorism. In addition, the individual committing these attacks will no longer be the relatively uneducated "crook" of the past. He or she may well be a very sophisticated criminal, a greedy inside employee, or a highly motivated terrorist. To be sure, the attacker will be attuned to the intricacies of computer databases and the means to defeat information security systems within closed networks and open architecture systems like the Internet.

Risk analysis offers a continual strategy to assess and evaluate current systems and potential threats. The recommendations offered by risk analysis exercises often focus on the development of an aware organizational culture as well as the use of various security technologies: backup and redundant file systems, firewalls, encryption, and the use of passwords. There are no guarantees or immunities. Developing such programs only offers a first line of defense as the computer hacker, vandal, or cyberterrorist is just one step behind in his or her ability to defeat the latest security measure. Information system security must be flexible, dynamic and everimproving, characterized by an organizational culture that not only appreciates the issues associated with information security, but encourages and supports the types of work processes, upfront expenses, and awareness training consistent with change.

REVIEW QUESTIONS

1. What are the major principles of risk analysis? List the common steps in developing a risk analysis strategy.
2. Define the following terms in relation to information security: integrity, authenticity, confidentiality, and availability.
3. What is a firewall? Identify and explain some of the functions of a firewall.
4. What is TCP/IP?
5. What are the limitations of a firewall?
6. What is encryption and hashing, and how are they used to secure data and information?
7. How does a digital signature enhance authenticity and integrity of data?
8. How are new security technologies altering the face of user identification?

ENDNOTES

1. HOLLINGER, R.C. (1997). *Crime, deviance, and the computer.* Brookfield, VT: Dartmouth Publishing Company.
2. LEVY, S. (1984). *Hackers: Heroes of the computer revolution.* New York: Dell Publishing; and HAFNER, K. and M. LYON (1996). *Where wizards stay up late: The origins of the Internet.* New York: Touchstone.
3. A fire in the data center was the ultimate disaster. Spraying water onto running computers would destroy them as surely as fires. A "dry" chemical called Halon^{TM} and later CO^2 fire suppression systems were, and still are, used to protect data centers.

4. Computers generate large amounts of heat. Heat adversely affects the operation of computers when it builds up. Even the earliest computer required massive refrigeration systems and special floor-vent air conditioning systems. Failure of the air conditioner meant failure of the computer.

5. BLOOMBECKER, B. (1990). *Spectacular computer crimes: What they are and how they cost American business half a billion dollars a year.* Homewood, IL: Dow Jones-Irwin; and PARKER, D.B. (1976). *Crime by computer.* New York: Scribner.

6. LEVY, *ibid.*

7. LOPER, D.K. (2000). "The criminology of computer hackers: A qualitative and quantitative analysis." *Dissertation Abstracts International, 61* (08), AAT 9985422.

8. HAFNER, K. and J. MARKOFF (1991). *Cyberpunk: Outlaws and hackers on the computer frontier.* New York: Touchstone; SLATALLA, M. and J. QUITTNER (1995). *Masters of deception: The gang that ruled cyberspace.* New York: Harper Collins Publishers; LITTMAN, J. and R. DONALD (1997). *The watchman: The twisted life and crimes of serial hacker Kevin Poulsen.* Boston, MA: Little, Brown and Company; J. LITTMAN (1996). *The fugitive game: Online with Kevin Mitnick.* New York: Little, Brown and Company; MUNGO, J. and CLOUGH, S. (1992). *Approaching zero: The extraordinary underworld of hackers, phreakers, virus writers, and keyboard criminals.* New York: Random House.

9. SLATALLA and QUITTNER, *ibid.*

10. HOLLINGER, R.C. and L. LANZA-KADUCE (1988). "The process of criminalization: The case of computer crime laws." *Criminology, 26,* 101–126.

11. HAFNER and LYONS, *ibid.*

12. COMER, D.E. (1997). *The Internet book* (2nd ed.). Upper Saddle River, NJ: Prentice Hall Inc.; and S. BAASE (2003). *A gift of fire: Social, legal, and ethical issues in computing* (2nd ed.). Upper Saddle River, NJ: Prentice Hall Inc.

13. HOWARD, J.D. (1997). *An analysis of security incidents on the Internet 1989–1995* (Doctoral dissertation, Carnegie Mellon University, 1997). Retrieved July 13, 1999 from the World Wide Web: *http://www.cert.org/research/JHThesis/;* and M. LOTTOR (1992, January). *Internet growth (1981–1991)* (Request for Comments 1296). Menlo Park, CA: SRI. Retrieved July 13, 1999 from the World Wide Web: *http://www.nw.com/zone/rfc1296.txt*

14. HAFNER, K. (2001). *The well: A story of love, death and real life in the seminal on line community.* New York: Carroll & Graf.

15. Free Software Foundation (2001). *Why we exist.* Retrieved March 15, 2001 from the World Wide Web: *http://www.gnu.org/philosophy/philosophy.html*

16. The concept of an IRM plan was first introduced in the 1980s, as network systems first emerged. See D. CORBIN (1988) "Strategic IRM plan: User involvement spells success." *Journal of Systems Management* (May), pp. 12–16.

17. See KRAEMER, J. and K. DANZIGER (1984). "Computers and control in the work environment." *Public Administration Review* (January/February), pp. 32–42; and TAYLOR, ROBERT W. (1989) "Managing police information," *in* D.J. KENNEY, *Police and Policing: Contemporary Readings* (1989). New York: Praeger Press.

18. Much of this section has been adapted from R.W. TAYLOR and D.K. LOPER, "Computer crime" *in* C.R. SWANSON, N. CHAMELIN and L. TERRITO (2003). *Criminal Investigation,* 8th edition. New York: McGraw-Hill.

19. RAID comes in many schemes. For other RAID configurations, see *http://www.whatis.com*

20. STEVENS, W.R. (1994). *TCP/IP illustrated: The protocols* (vol. 1). New York: Addison-Wesley.

21. SCHNEIER, B. (1996). *Applied cryptography: Protocols, algorithms, and source code in C* (2nd ed.). New York: John Wiley & Sons.

22. There are many other methods of on line authentication, including third-party trust-based relationships, token-based authentication, and challenge hand-shake mechanisms, but simple passwords (preshared secrets) illustrate this point well enough.

23. SCHNEIER, B. (1996). *Applied cryptography: Protocols, algorithms, and source code in C* (2nd ed.). New York: John Wiley & Sons.

24. SCHNEIER, *ibid.*

25. SCHNEIER, *ibid.*

26. KAUFMAN, E. and A. NEWMAN (1999). *Implementing IPsec: Making security work on VPNs, intranets, and extranets.* New York: John Wiley & Sons Inc.

27. GORDON, S. and R. FORD (2003). "Cyberterrorism?" A white paper distributed by Symantec Corporation, Cupertino, California.

28. See: *www.cert.org*

Chapter 14

Digital Crime and Terrorism

A Forecast of Trends and Policy Implications*

Chapter Objectives

After completing this chapter, you should be able to:

- Identify the future trends and issues the criminal justice system will have to contend with regarding digital crime and digital terrorism.
- Be able to discuss the areas of computer crime victimization that are growing in both incidence and prevalence.
- Describe the impact that digital crimes and digital terrorism are likely to have in the future.
- Identify and understand the eight general forecasts that experts believe are likely to occur in the area of computer crime.
- Understand what response the criminal justice system and other governmental agencies should adopt to deal with future issues in digital crime and digital terrorism.

THE IMPACT OF COMPUTER CRIME: THE FUTURE IS NOW

Sikellis[1] extrapolated data from the FBI/CSI annual computer crime survey and estimated that annual "losses related to computer crimes in the U.S. alone now total over $10 billion a year".[2] That same survey[3] found that the average loss from theft of pro-

*Adapted from David L. Carter and Andra J. Katz-Bannister, "Computer Crime: A Forecast of Trends and Policy Implications." Paper presented at the 2003 meeting of the Academy of Criminal Justice Sciences.

prietary information is over $1.2 million and that the average loss from data or network sabotage is over $1.1 million. The reliability of such data is inherently questionable, not because of impropriety, but because of the lack of uniform definitions of behaviors and uniform methods of accountability. Assessing the economic impact of any crime is difficult, at best. Estimates are based on a wide range of variables: discovery of the loss; extrapolation of indirect losses; valid reporting of direct losses; operational definitions of where the offense occurred, and the time frame during which losses were incurred as a result of the crime. Currently, there is no system for documenting cyberoffenses.[4]

With a uniform computer crime reporting system, operational definitions can specify the types of incidents which can be classified as a "computer crime," regardless of a specific jurisdiction's statutes. For example, one jurisdiction may define the theft of a computer as a computer crime. Another jurisdiction may define an offense as a computer crime only when a computer is used to steal information from a network. Uniform definitions would resolve different interpretations so that agencies and consumers of the data understand the parameters of cybercrime data. Similarly, guidelines can be developed for the calculation of losses. While subjectivity is inevitable for estimating losses of indirect costs or loss of potential income, methodological guidelines will nonetheless introduce some controls as well as perspective.

All of these factors complicate the ability to articulate the impact of computer crime. The problem is further compounded by the tendency to view cybercrime one-dimensionally. The multidimensional nature of computer crime must be considered as individual categories for estimates of losses to be more meaningful (see Box 14.1).

Piracy and counterfeiting are areas where some of the best estimates exist on the impact of computer crime. The United States Customs Service predicted that copyright violations and counterfeiting on a global basis was going to dwarf every type of crime in the coming years. It is estimated that U.S. companies lose $200 billion a year to all types of piracy and counterfeiting of goods, although it is difficult to determine how much of this loss is directly or indirectly attributable to computers. Globally, software piracy alone is estimated to cost the industry $11 billion, with 38 percent of the 615 million new software installations being illegal copies. These data represent the proverbial tip of the iceberg. For appropriate allocation of resources and crime control strategies, a formal system to comprehensively and uniformly report and document cybercrime needs to be developed. The challenge is daunting.

Predicting the Future: Surveying the Experts

For the purposes of this chapter, a qualitative study was conducted including 26 interviews with law enforcement officials, intelligence analysts, government officials, investigators, and corporate security directors, all of whom deal with some aspect of computer-related criminality. The interviews, in most cases, followed a consistent protocol which documented the interviewees' experience and observations on current issues and trends. In addition, there were eight interviews which were done under incidental situations, typically at a conference where the interview time was limited. Even in these cases, the researchers were able to ask and record primary questions from the protocol.[5]

BOX 14.1   Estimating Computer Crime Losses

Factors in estimating computer crime losses must be able to differentiate between different behaviors, such as:

- Internet fraud
- Theft via computer
- Piracy of software
- Royalty losses from copyrighted materials placed on the Internet without permission for downloading (e.g., music, documents, video, software)
- Intellectual property losses by trying to:
  - Detect intellectual property which has been stolen, and
  - Placing an accurate and fair value on the loss of the intellectual property
  - Estimating losses of future income as a result of the theft
- Expenses, including time/labor, software maintenance, and/or equipment repairs associated with:
  - Hacked web pages
  - Server intrusions
  - Malicious software
- Telecommunications losses either as a theft of service or "piggybacking" a telecommunications system for remote or long-distance networking
- Theft of computer equipment
- Theft of information/data which has a dynamic value (such as a credit card or billing account number)

The original intent was to gather information on the different types of computer crime the interviewees' organizations experienced, including the frequency of incidents, losses, offender information, and resolution of the crime (e.g., Was the offender identified, arrested, and prosecuted? Were losses recovered?). After a very short period it became clear that the protocol had to be altered because the information was not available[6] or the organization would not authorize release of the data. Collectively, the information was compiled to identify trends and recurring issues related to computer crime and abuse. Using this information as a foundation, the authors integrated contemporary issues and trends in criminal justice and national security. Applying inductive logic, the forecasts were developed.

Limitations to Data Collection

Two important limitations to the forecasts are the lack of empirical data and the inability to be precise in anticipating incidents of computer crime. Forecasts of behavior—like weather forecasts—often lack pinpoint precision, but they can help prepare a response and minimize damage from a phenomenon. Based on the authors' previous research as well as interviews with those who work in this field, it has become evident that there is no database or currently available data source which can provide reliable information on computer crime or computer criminals. Similarly, there is limited knowledge about the incidence, methods, dispersion, character and trends of computer crime to collect data on these variables or their derivatives. While anecdotes exist on these factors, they have not been scientifically categorized using methodological controls or analyzed in detail to assess the validity of typological constructs. In essence, the literature contains logical speculation and assumptions, but virtually no data or information collected and analyzed under controlled methods. It should be noted that these limitations are recognized by the authors, as is the problem of poor data sources and the lack of a uniform reporting system for computer-related crimes.

Other important factors limit the ability to analyze or collect valid and reliable quantitative data. One significant factor is the difficulty—and sometimes impossibility—of determining when a computer crime has occurred, for example, the undetected incursion of a system by a cracker or the undetected theft of intellectual property by an employee who copies files to removable media. Another factor is the tendency of businesses to not report computer-related crimes which have been detected. There are several reasons for this: In some cases, businesses view this simply as a "loss" or even an expense, but not a crime. In other cases, businesses hold the perspective that offenders will not be caught due to the difficulty of investigation, thus reporting the crime would be "wasted effort." Perhaps, however, one of the more fundamental reasons is the fear that publicity of computer crime victimization would undermine the confidence of the company's clients.[7]

THE FUTURE OF DIGITAL CRIME AND DIGITAL TERRORISM: FORECASTS

Based on the analysis of information collected in this study, the authors have developed eight primary forecasts related to computer crime.

FORECAST 1: The number of offenses reported to the police involving computers and electronic storage media will increase substantially requiring changing priorities for resource allocation, new training for line officers and investigators, new police specialties, and new knowledge for prosecuting attorneys and judges.

Perhaps a key word in this forecast is "require." There is already an increasing number of police agencies which have a high tech or computer crime unit. In addition, more prosecutors and judges have taken an interest in computer crime and have learned the subtleties involved in dealing with the unique law and vagaries inherent in these cases. Indeed, these individuals are frequently blazing the trail into many undefined areas of law. Unfortunately, these are the exceptions, rather than the rule.

Interviews with police officials and investigators in a major, multijurisdictional area of the United States with over three million residents found only three computer forensic specialists in the entire region. All three stated they had a backlog of several *months* for computers which had been seized as evidence and needed to be analyzed forensically. All interviewees stated they increasingly had to turn people away who were requesting analytic assistance. An increasing number of computers were being seized just as police agencies were receiving more calls reporting all forms of computer-related crime. This same situation was found in other jurisdictions, yet comparatively little had been done by the police—in most cases nothing was done—to deal with the problem. It was essentially ignored. Further, in many agencies which had computer crime investigators and forensic specialists, it was common to find investigators using their own equipment and/or "scrounging" for equipment to use in their work.[8] While resources are always in demand, at present, computer crime units appear to suffer disproportionately (see Box 14.2).

A reasoned, analytic assessment documenting criminal incidents in a jurisdiction would give meaningful insight on which to make basic decisions. Ideally, a routinized data collection system—perhaps similar to the National Crime Survey—to include computer crimes would be a useful planning tool. More useful, however, would be a system of collecting data on reported cyber-offenses by jurisdiction. This would permit crime analysis for a better understanding of jurisdiction-specific offenses, offenders, and targets. As we have learned with predatory crime, deployment of personnel and resources is most effective when based on crime analysis.

Judicial, prosecutorial, and investigative officials as well as scholars and computer security specialists knowledgeable about cybercrime should perform a comprehensive review of criminal laws and procedure related to the unique character of computer crime. Additionally, hypothesized voids in a jurisdiction's penal code and anticipation of changes which may be needed in response to technological evolution need to be conducted continually. In all likelihood, even current computer crime laws will become dated as greater integration of computers, telecommunications and entertainment networks occurs. Similarly, with more databases, information systems, multimedia, and integration software—such as Motorola's Digital DNA and Sun Microsystems' Jini—the complexity of defining criminal offenses, and even distinguishing what is criminal and what is civil, will become more complex. Among other issues which may need to be reassessed are privacy issues, a redefinition of open records, changes in Freedom of Information law and processes, and new applications of liability law to law enforcement personnel.

New policies are needed to resolve questions of jurisdiction, the expenditure of resources in multijurisdictional investigations of network incursions, and multijurisdictional cooperation. Creative new policy areas must also be explored. For example, should a corporate computer crime victim be responsible for any costs of the investigation if the crime was due, in part, to inadequate computer security?[9] If so, how are these issues decided? Would the criminal justice system be better served if computer crime investigation and prosecution were privatized? Are state or regional computer crime units the best mechanism to deal with this problem? If so, how are they funded, and what are the boundaries of their jurisdiction? These and other policy issues must realistically be considered.

BOX 14.2   Responding to Computer Crime

A scenario will describe the current situation: A business owner arrives at the office and discovers locked filing cabinets have been broken into; some documents have been destroyed and others stolen. The owner, suffering losses from both the forced entry damage and theft, calls the police, reporting a burglary. A patrol officer responds to take an offense report; a crime scene technician may be called to search for and collect physical evidence. In all likelihood, a burglary detective will conduct a follow-up investigation by reviewing the evidence, interviewing the victim, checking leads from the burglary's *modus operandi* and perhaps checking with informants. The police have a defined response procedure with personnel fully trained to report and investigate the crime.

Now, assume the same business owner calls the police to report the office computer has been hacked and there were some files destroyed and others stolen. What would the police response be? The losses are essentially same, except that the first crime was physical, the second virtual. In the first case, the burglar may have used a crowbar on the door and the file cabinets; in the second case, the thief used only keystrokes.

When confronted with this scenario, one investigator said many departments would probably refer the victim to another agency. The investigator went on to say that he regularly received calls from victims outside of his jurisdiction saying they had been referred by another police department. These cases usually took a lower priority, which would anger the citizen. What has made police agencies willing to respond immediately to a burglary, yet show hesitation and less than a full response to a computer crime? This is clearly inconsistent with the contemporary "customer-oriented" philosophy of community policing. Why should a virtual community be different from a physical community? Several factors apparently exist: Uncertainty of jurisdiction, lack of knowledge about computer crimes generally, and having a perspective that this is not a "real problem" are clear issues. Others include the lack of trained personnel who know the questions to ask, how to process a computer-based crime scene, the lack of knowledge and skill to analyze the computer forensically, and the lack of follow-up resources (such as informants) to "work" the case. While police officials would not consider denying a response to a burglary, they will deny a response to a computer crime.

Training and expertise development obviously go hand in hand. At a basic level, during pre-service training related to criminal investigations, police officers need to be trained to regularly look for computers and removable storage media as evidence. They also need to know how to protect and collect cyber evidence as well as the elements of computer crimes and information needed in preparing reports of these offenses. At a more advanced level, training is needed for computer crime investigators—for example, understanding networks, tracing audit trails, dissecting telecommunications systems, tracing wireless transmissions, and associated other technical aspects which may be encountered. Similarly, if a police agency is large enough to have a crime laboratory, it is of sufficient size to warrant a trained computer forensic analyst.[10] Essentially, the model used to investigate and forensically analyze evidence for physical crimes should also be used for virtual crimes. Similarly, judges and prosecutors need to have training on the character and unique aspects of computer crime in order to handle these cases fairly and effectively.

With these aspects of training, necessary expertise will be developed. Police agencies might also consider some changes in personnel management. Is it better to take a trained investigator and teach him/her the technical aspects of computers and networking or to employ a computer expert and teach that person about law, investigation, and criminal case development? Maybe a hybrid model would be better wherein nonsworn computer specialists are hired as in-house technical consultants assigned to computer crime investigations. Another aspect of expertise may lead to computer crime prevention specialists. Since there are clear methods—both technical and behavioral—which can be used to prevent cybercrime, the investment of expertise in this arena may be a functional addition to other crime prevention initiatives. Each jurisdiction must evaluate its needs, and follow the avenue which best serves its goals.

Training, new personnel, and developing new expertise obviously leads to resource allocation issues. In all likelihood, most agencies are not going to be given generous new budget lines to address these issues. Where will the money come from? Realistically, resources will have to be redirected from other departmental programs. Difficult questions of resource redistribution must be undertaken with careful study. In any such redistribution, there are issues which go beyond finances, including "turf," vested interests, and other crime concerns. Changing and rapidly advancing technology results in the need to keep training up to date, which can be quite costly.

The need to share expertise and resources in computer crime investigations appears inevitable for most law enforcement agencies. This sharing will likely extend beyond the interaction of government agencies and includes the need to work with the private sector. This raises some complicated issues related to the payment of expenses, privacy, and the parameters describing the types of cases and/or circumstances where external agencies and private companies are used. All aspects of these issues need to be fully explored and articulated in Mutual Aid Pacts (where assistance between agencies is exchanged *quid pro quo*) and contracts (where financial reimbursement is provided.)

> **FORECAST 2:** The largest computer crime problem affecting local law enforcement representing the largest number of victims and the largest monetary loss will be Internet fraud, including fraud via identity theft.

This forecast should not be interpreted as diminishing other forms of computer crime. However, given the current experiences and trends with e-commerce, on line trading, and a virtual buffet of other financial schemes coupled with the growth of personal computing, it appears fraud is the offense most likely to touch the largest number of community members. One survey reports that 62 percent of surveyed on line business said that on line fraud was a "serious problem."[11] Increasingly, local police agencies will receive complaints on these offenses with the expectation that reporting and an investigation will occur, just as would be the case of a noncomputer crime. As noted previously, most local law enforcement agencies, at this point, would have difficulty comprehensively responding to and investigating an Internet fraud.

With home Internet access becoming more common and more people using e-commerce, the probability of Internet fraud has increased significantly. This had led to numerous, legitimate companies specializing in developing integrated databases which they then use to sell marketing and browsing information which may be used to further fraudulent activity. For example, if a database development company integrates information people provide when registering products they have purchased, this provides important insight about potential fraud targets. Coupled with the e-commerce movement of "mass customization," a fraudulent enterprise can tailor a business offer to a person which capitalizes on the potential victim's specific interests. As a result, the probability of a successful fraudulent transaction increases. This practice also increases spam.

Frauds—and other Internet crimes—will increase simply because the massive size of the Internet makes monitoring or spotting potential fraudulent schemes difficult. Even with technological monitoring techniques of keyword targeting, the size and dynamic character of the Internet presents major barriers. These barriers are aggravated by the difficulty of transjurisdictional investigations and communications. A fraud scheme targeting Americans, and operated by American criminals, may have a Web site based in a country such as Myanmar which has virtually no Internet monitoring and only casual relations with U.S. law enforcement authorities. This will hamper investigations, with little U.S. authorities can do except provide warnings to citizens.

Finally, it is relatively easy to create a fraudulent enterprise on the Internet with minimal cost. As a result, the range of people who can create a virtual fraud is quite broad. Moreover, the inability to readily determine the authenticity of claims or organizations helps further the fraud. This is particularly true when the scheme is related to alleged changes in technology-related businesses, such as Initial Public Offerings (IPOs), new mergers, or new products. Technology businesses and stocks have been so profitable in recent years, many people feel a sense of urgency to complete a transaction while the opportunity is "hot." As a result, they frequently do not take the time to verify the offer's legitimacy. To further the appearance of legitimacy, the Web site may include fallacious quotes from recognized authorities and untrue statements of affiliations with respected businesses to lend further credence to the scheme's legitimacy.

The inherent character of the Internet and the expansion of the global economy, particularly related to technology issues, are fueling the growth of Internet fraud. The most effective tool for dealing with Internet fraud is prevention. The need to inform consumers of the potential for and character of fraud, notification of newly emerging fraud schemes, and precautions before investing or purchasing over the Internet are among the proactive approaches a local law enforcement agency may pursue. Delivery of this information could be from the police agency's Web page, creation of a listserv which describes newly discovered fraud schemes, and public service announcements. The significant point to note is that investigating Internet fraud is extraordinarily difficult, with a comparatively low rate of clearance. A comprehensive prevention strategy is the most efficacious approach to the problem.[12]

FORECAST 3: Virtual crimes against persons will increase at a faster rate compared to past years as a result of the significant expansion in networking and personal computing. These hybrid crimes, which have coercive characteristics similar to those found in psychological warfare, will require new laws expressly to address the problem and new methodologies for investigation, prevention and education.

Virtual crimes against persons encompass diverse behaviors; however, the common factors of these behaviors is (1) use of networking and (2) a manifestation of social-psychological dynamics. Networking is a key factor because this is the medium through which the behavior is facilitated, most frequently by e-mail but also through bulletin board services (BBSs) and Web site postings (particularly hate and pedophilia). One survey by the Novell Corporation found that 50 percent of the respondents had received unwanted e-mail from a persistent sender. Thirty-five percent of the offending messages contained unsolicited pornography."[13]

The social-psychological factors take diverse forms. For example, cyberstalking and threats induce fear, while harassment can induce anger. Hate messages can produce discriminatory behavior and pedophilia can engender exploitation and intimidation. Interestingly, these behaviors are similar to the common law definition of assault. As a U.S. government report of the problem observed, "Make no mistake: This kind of harassment can be as frightening and as real as being followed and watched in your neighborhood or in your home."[14]

The manifestation of virtual crimes against persons is the product of several factors. First, virtual crimes against persons are easy and convenient. The offense may be committed immediately without leaving home and gratification is instantaneous. The offender may also take action without physically confronting the victim. In all likelihood there are people who have a propensity to commit a retaliatory act of some form, but do not because of reluctance to confront another physically. It is therefore probable that some of those people would act on that propensity through networking.

Just as the offense may be committed without confrontation, it may also be committed with relative anonymity. The anonymity is obviously sought to protect the identity of the offender, but anonymity can add to the victim's fear. There are various techniques which may be used to maintain one's anonymity in networked communications, the easiest of which is sending threatening or harassing e-mail through a Web site that obfuscates the SMTP audit trail.[15] Also contributing to the anonymity of these virtual offenses is the fact that there is no physical evidence of the crime, such as a fingerprint on the paper of a threatening letter or DNA from saliva on an envelope. Neither are there voice nor handwriting specimens from the offender which may be used as evidence. Consequently, developing a criminal case that can meet the burden of proof in court becomes challenging.

The authors hypothesize that a significant factor contributing to the growth of virtual crimes against persons is the increasing loss of privacy which is occurring through on line sources. When greater personal information is available about an individual, it is easier for an offender to locate them. Moreover, if an offender provides personal information about the victim in an harassing message—such as a description and license number of the victim's car; a Social Security number, or information about the victim's family—then a cyberassault can become even more frightening. As the prevalence of these crimes increase, they must be analyzed to determine the adequacy of existing law and policy to deal with them effectively. While they may not produce physical harm, the psychological damage, fear, and anxiety can be debilitating.

On a final note, the likelihood is strong that there will be an increase in "virtual workplace violence." A great deal of physical workplace violence appears to be retaliatory acts toward the organization and/or individuals who are perceived to have "wronged" the offender. It is clearly probable that employees with access to critical databases and/or information systems could vent their retaliation by the destruction of those files. Similarly, harassment and the creation of a hostile work environment can now be accomplished electronically.

> FORECAST 4: Some computer hacker groups, notably those characterized by the "offender" and "predator" categories, will evolve into networked criminal enterprises.

The basis of this forecast lies in the integrated characteristics of the hacker culture and the development of criminal enterprises. Many active computer crackers belong to groups which share common interests. That interest may be in using certain types of computers, cracking specific types of systems, supporting a specific cause—such as opposition to government controls on the Internet—or simply a self-selected group who feel their hacking skills are greater than others and who hack into challenging systems as a demonstration of their abilities. In furtherance of their common interest they share techniques, and may even agree on a specific plan to accomplish their hacking goals.

Generally, these groups are informal, with "membership" varying a great deal; a relative few appear to be more formally structured with an explicit goal. For example, the group Masters of Downloading hacked a number of U.S. government Web sites to demonstrate their skills as evidenced by the phrase on the hacked U.S. Senate Web page: "MAST3RZ 0F D0WNL0ADING, GL0B4L D0MIN8T10N '99!"[16] Another group known as United Loan Gunmen (ULG) has been credited with breaking into the Web sites of NASDAQ, the American Stock Exchange, C-SPAN, the American Broadcasting Company, and the Associated Press.[17] The FBI has also reported that for several months a number of hacker groups have been using coordinated scans and probes of Web sites.[18] Among those attacks were multiple government sites which were penetrated and changed in the same day. The salient point to note is that there is a wide range of these groups, some of which are operating with common purpose and success in penetrating security barriers.

The brazen nature of attacking systems and the practice of leaving condescending or insulting comments indicates both arrogance and elitism. The elitism is further demonstrated with egocentricity based on attitudes toward other people who do not have the same level of computer skills. The hacker ethic "all information should be free" suggests little or no self-responsibility for actions related to computer incursions.[19] Indeed, some comments of hackers suggest it is a system administrator's fault if their system is hacked because the administrator should have employed better security to prevent a successful incursion. Conversely, hackers appear to be hypocritical because they have little tolerance for those who criticize them. A tone of anarchy permeates the language and culture of hackers, with most of their contempt directed toward government attempts at regulating the Internet, at businesses capitalizing on the Internet for e-commerce, and at casual users or Internet "surfers." Hackers clearly have a great deal of patience and tenacity. Most successful system incursions are products of substantial time investments attacking a system to identify weaknesses and circumvent security barriers.

Finally, crackers are collectors of information. When a system is successfully penetrated, they tend to download information as evidence of their success and frequently share this information with friends and others in their hacking collective. Typically the information is used only as an electronic trophy of a successful incursion. Kevin Mitnik, an icon of the hacker culture, had hundreds of valid credit card numbers with documentation information, and assorted other forms of intellectual property, stored on his hard drive when finally arrested. Mr. Mitnik stated he did not convert this information for personal use or monetary gain, but maintained it as evidence of his successful incursions.[20]

These facets of the hacker culture, when integrated with our knowledge of criminality, are the basis of the authors' forecast that hacker groups will develop into criminal enterprises. Carter[21] documented the development of organized crime groups which, over time, evolved from loose social relationships to structured criminal enterprises (see Figure 14.1). The process occurred on a continuum wherein social relationships, fueled by the common willingness to participate jointly in criminal incidents, became increasingly structured to further the enterprise. Following this pattern of thought, it is forecast that hackers will increasingly recognize the value of the information they obtain and use the structure of the group to facilitate income from stolen information and explore other sources of information or data as income commodities.

Clearly, as forecast by futurist Alvin Toffler in both *The Third Wave*[22] and *PowerShift*,[23] information is a commodity of extraordinary and growing value. One simply needs to look at the growth of e-commerce, the emergence of "dot.com" businesses, the growth of data mining as a marketing tool, and other information-based businesses and interests to see that Toffler's forecasts are being borne out. This information is all too frequently stored on databases linked to networked servers from which it can be stolen by those with the skills to penetrate the system.

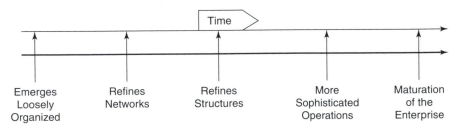

FIGURE 14.1   Development of Criminal Enterprises

The character of this problem is exacerbated because geography and national boundaries are completely irrelevant. This complicates investigation, prosecution, and communication between law enforcement and intelligence organizations. Moreover, "value" is difficult to attach to intellectual property or database information and it is frequently difficult to determine precisely what and how much information was taken.[24] It is clear that the process of investigation, evidence gathering, and case development is extraordinarily difficult, while economic losses can significantly surpass those of other crimes against property.

> **FORECAST 5:** Current organized crime groups, particularly those which are entrepreneurial, will increasingly adopt computerization as a criminal instrument.

Interpol defines organized crime as any enterprise or group of persons engaged in a continuing illegal activity which has as its primary purpose the generation of profits and continuance of the enterprise regardless of national boundaries.[25] Key factors in this definition with respect to the forecast is that organized crime groups are *entrepreneurial* and that they exist to make a profit. Just like legitimate businesses, organized crime groups have consistently used methods which will enhance efficiency and effectiveness to achieve profits. Many methods are illegal—such as use of violence, corruption or fraud—yet legal methods are also used, such as stock investments, purchase of real estate, and other principles common to legitimate businesses for distribution and marketing of a commodity. Globally, the character of organized crime is evolving into this entrepreneurial model. Traditional images of organized crime as a "Mafia-like" entity are dated, not reflecting the vast amount of organized criminal activity occurring around the world today. To neither recognize nor respond to this change is to perpetuate a myth. Law enforcement agencies must be proactive in devoting resources and attention to organized crime as entrepreneurial criminal enterprise. Based on information collected in this study, there is documented use of computerization by organized crime groups in several areas (see Figure 14.2). As in the past, opportunistic organized crime groups will exploit any possible illegal avenues for increased profit.

Record Keeping

Evidence by law enforcement and intelligence organizations have found crime groups keeping computerized records in a manner similar to businesses, using spreadsheets and databases. Records which have been discovered include contraband shipment schedules; income and expenses of contraband or commodities; databases of conspirators and "customers"; locations, account numbers, and status of monetary transactions (typically, money being laundered); records of monetary transfers and payments; databases and "status" of bribed or vulnerable officials; and database dossiers of officials, conspirators, and others in whom the crime group has an interest.[26]

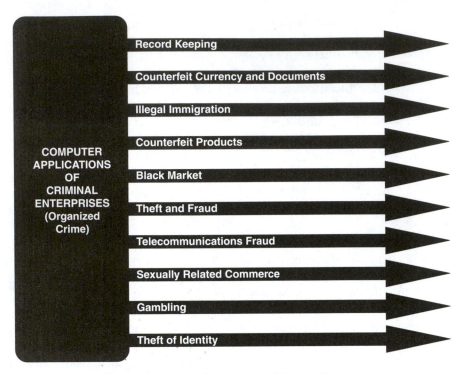

FIGURE 14.2   Uses of Computers by Organized Crime Groups

Counterfeit Currency and Documents

Computer technology has provided a revolution in the counterfeit currency and document business. Because of color scanners, color printers, sophisticated word processing and graphics software suites, and computer-driven color photocopiers, successful counterfeiting has not only significantly broadened, but also become much more difficult to detect. As an example, at one point the U.S. $100 bill the most frequently counterfeited currency in the world. With computerized counterfeiting, the global market was becoming flooded with counterfeit $100 bills (particularly Central and Eastern Europe). As a result, the U.S. Treasury changed the bill's design and incorporated a watermark (like most of the rest of the world's currency) and other security factors. It was announced by the Treasury Department that the new $100 bill was virtually impossible to counterfeit. Within a month of the new bill's introduction into circulation, good counterfeit copies surfaced in Eastern Europe. High resolution color scanning of an original can even pick up the watermark and colors of fibers in the paper which are, in turn, reproduced by high resolution printers.

The same scanning process and graphics software are used for counterfeit passports. Counterfeiters maintain scanned masters of various passports in computer files and are then able to readily enter appropriate names, photographs and identity information in the files to prepare a high quality counterfeit.[27] Because the counterfeits are near the quality of legitimate documents and the process of creating the counterfeits is fast, the enterprise yields high profits. In some cases, criminal enterprises offer a "package" to people who are illegally immigrating to Europe. One price includes the immigration documents, transportation, and an escort.

Another unique application of the technology has been found to make new certificates of origin and titles of stolen vehicles using the actual vehicle identification number (VIN) of the stolen auto. As with passports, master files of documents are scanned into a computer. They are then printed using the stolen vehicle's description and VIN along with the new "owner's" identification. Sophisticated auto theft rings operating from Poland to Morocco have used this method to ship luxury cars to the Mideast and Asia.

Illegal Immigration

Evidence has indicated that organized crime groups previously involved mostly in black market smuggling have created new processes to smuggle immigrants into Western countries with "appropriate" documentation, typically for a substantial fee. While computers play a comparatively smaller role in these enterprises, they nonetheless help expedite the scheme through the use of such processes as logistics and arrangements via e-mail; computer-forged immigration documents; and general record keeping related to this enterprise.

Black Market

Outside of its illegal commodities and avoidance of licensing and taxes, the black market operates much like any business. It is market-driven; requires suppliers, transportation and distribution networks; has a payroll; must remain competitive; and is obliged to keep its customers satisfied in order to maintain repeat clientele. Because of similarities to legitimate businesses, organized crime groups involved in the black market have increasingly begun to operate much like legitimate businesses.

Just as in any business, the black market needs to make its inventory descriptions known to both the "sales staff" and potential clients. Photographs, product descriptions, costs, inquiry processes, and related information for a wide variety of "commodities" have been found in computer files; in a few cases the files are accessible through a restricted server or Web site. Additionally, some black market merchandise is increasingly available for order through the Internet (under the guise of a legitimate business), vastly expanding the enterprises' market, hence profits. In addition, computerization via networking provides increased anonymity to specific individuals in the criminal group.

Counterfeit Products

The extent to which "traditional" organized crime is involved in this area is debatable; however, there is strong evidence that such groups are strongly involved in the "marketing" and distribution of these products in what is referred to by Her Majesty's Customs and Excise Service as the "fakes trade." While skilled craft workers have been quite successful in designing and manufacturing counterfeit products, one area which was frequently relied on by Customs and corporate security investigators was product logos and subtle design and coloration characteristics to distinguish licensed products from counterfeit ones. This too is changing because of computer technology.

As in the case of counterfeit currency and documents, criminal enterprises have been using color scanners and computer-driven color printers to scan legitimate logos, product tags, and such things as "jackets" and labels of videotapes, audio tapes, and software. Using the scanned images as masters, skilled printers are able to prepare these materials to legitimize the appearance of the counterfeit products. One corporate security director told the authors that while this process was an additional "wrinkle" for investigators to overcome, the intent of the counterfeiter was to make the product look more legitimate to the consumer. With packaging that makes the product appear authentic, the enterprise could sell more of their counterfeit products at higher prices and still undercut the legitimate manufacturer's sales.

Sexually Related Commerce

New criminal enterprises have emerged, largely consisting of intelligent young entrepreneurs who are familiar with the capabilities and potential of computers as a tool for sexual commerce. While these emerging groups may not fit neatly into traditional definitions of organized crime, they nonetheless are ongoing enterprises which are frequently violating the criminal law in order to gain a profit. A problem exists, however, because many activities of these groups fall into the gray area of law. Some of their activities may be lawful in their country of origin but unlawful in countries serving their clientele. Because of these legal ambiguities and the fact that sexual commerce is viewed as being less serious than other forms of crime, comparatively little attention is given to these groups.

Using the Internet to arrange for prostitution is one of the more common enterprises. This includes not only logistical arrangements (i.e., appointments) but even payment by credit card using e-commerce protocols. The process is discreet and safer for both the "service provider" and "customer." In one case, a criminal enterprise using a server based in Amsterdam was arranging for prostitutes in both London and Frankfurt. Although the enterprise has been closed, it was difficult because of limitations inherent in dealing with multinational jurisdictions. One investigator stated that if the enterprise had been based in a non–European Union country, it would probably still be in operation.

Gambling

It is only natural that entrepreneurial criminals would turn to computerization—particularly the Internet—in order to expand their gambling operations and their profits. The respected global marketing consulting firm Frost and Sullivan found that on line gambling yielded $834.5 million in 1999—a 100 percent increase over the previous year. Furthermore, they forecast that on line gaming could yield $10 billion by 2002 (see *www.frost.com/*). While these amounts reflect largely legitimate gaming, there are complicating factors. For example, the gaming may be lawful in the location where the gambling is based, but may be unlawful in the jurisdiction of some of its customers.

Moreover, one of the Asian police officials interviewed stated that virtually all of the licensed on line gaming operations based both in his city and in a neighboring country were clearly owned and operated by criminal enterprises. With the potential profits to be reaped combined with low overhead costs and comparative anonymity afforded by the Internet, the likelihood of criminal involvement will grow significantly, particularly in those locations where taxes and governmental regulation can be avoided through corruption or intimidation.

At this point it appears that most unlawful computerized gaming operations—notably in North America and Asia—are not on the Internet but accessible via modem directly into a server (albeit using Internet protocols). However, accessibility to such operations is increasingly available through the Internet using Virtual Private Network (VPN) access for security (largely from authorities) and to ensure payment for services. The expanded capacity for multimedia hardware and software is particularly fueling sites by enabling more effective simulation of video gaming machines.

Typically the user must "join a club" to be given access to the site for gambling. Part of the membership ruse is to pay "dues," which are used as bets. Most typically gamblers supply a credit card number wherein they can purchase "units" to wager—"units" are essentially electronic poker chips. In some cases, when a member joins and is given his/her personal identification number, they can then make a deposit—either by wire or money order—to a front company which serves as the "bank" for the gambling operation. All bets and communications are then conducted via the computer link. When the gambler wins, he/she is typically given credits which can be used for further wagers or they can request payment, typically through the front company which serves as a bank. Credit card "credits" are not used for two reasons: (1) The gamblers want their winnings quickly in a readily convertible form; and (2) it is feared that the issuance of too many credits to a given card number would raise questions leading to investigation. Interestingly, one investigator said that the financial transaction accounting procedures for unlawful gaming operations were typically quite accurate and reliable. The reason: The enterprise makes money from the "repeat business" of gamblers—if they cannot trust you, they will not bet their money.

Theft and Fraud

As computers are increasingly used to account for and make financial transactions, criminals are increasingly accessing them unlawfully to transfer funds, defraud, or steal information. Many anecdotes are available concerning employees or hackers who have committed such crimes. One of the most frequently cited is the case of a Russian organized crime group which stole $12 million from Citibank via computer (all but around $400,000 was recovered). This, however, is currently the exception rather than the rule for criminal enterprises.

Based on interviews with criminal intelligence professionals in Europe and Asia, the most common computer-assisted thefts by organized crime groups target intellectual property.[28] As noted previously, as information becomes an increasingly valuable commodity, organized criminals have learned how to market stolen information for high profits and substantially less risk than more traditional illicit commodity trafficking.

Theft of information such as trade secrets, new product specifications, product pricing plans, and customer lists have proven to be highly profitable. The cost to a business competitor to pay for this stolen information is far less than original research, development, and marketing. Increasingly active in this arena are criminal enterprises in Japan, the United States, France, and Germany. While these transactions typically do not have the violence and emotional daring associated with more traditional organized crime activities, the economic toll can be far higher.

The second area of computer-assisted theft by organized crime is fraud. The Florida Division of Insurance Fraud has discovered fraud through altered computer programs which underreport insurance agency incomes. Medical and pharmaceutical overpayments through Medicare/Medicaid have also been fraudulently made in many ways through the altering of computer records and, more commonly, the use of shell companies billing the government for medical services, equipment, and pharmaceuticals. While these forms of theft net significant amounts of money, they typically are not products of broad-based organized crime, although they frequently meet the technical definition of a criminal enterprise. Such offenses are difficult to detect, difficult to investigate, and difficult to prosecute. Moreover, they engender little emotional outcry from the public. As a result, they offer little risk and high profits—an appealing combination of factors for the entrepreneurial offender.

Telecommunications Fraud

Telecommunications fraud is a particularly profitable area of computer-related crime that has many variations. Previously, individual criminal entrepreneurs committed these crimes, but they are increasingly being pushed out by organized crime groups because the profits are so high and the risk is so low. There are four types of telecommunications fraud in which criminal enterprises appear to be most involved. First is the theft of telephone credit card numbers which can be gained by accessing computer records, some computerized voice mailboxes, and telephone billing files. Prime targets are large multinational corporations, because discovery of the fraudulent billings takes longer. The billing numbers are either sold "on the street" (using "pushers" in the same way as drug dealers) or, as is increasingly the case, sold to other crime groups for their use. In one case, stolen corporate telephone billing numbers from a U.S.-based multinational company were being sold to various drug trafficking groups, which in turn used the stolen numbers to make arrangements for drug transactions and shipments. Payment for the stolen numbers was cheaper than paying for numerous international, calls and it was more difficult for investigators to link the calls to their principal investigative targets.

The second type of telecommunications fraud, which has actually decreased, involves hacking into telecommunications "switches" (which are computers) for the purpose of routing calls and changing billing numbers. While individual hackers still break into switches, organized efforts to do this have largely stopped as a result of more aggressive security precautions by telecommunications carriers and comparatively little profit to be made.

The third area is the largest and fastest growing: wireless phone theft and fraud. This too was started by individuals and small groups but is increasingly involving organized crime groups. The process originally involved the capture of wireless electronic identification numbers (EINs) being transmitted from users' telephones. Using a device which detects and records the number, it could then be sold and programmed into a person's wireless phone. The number is typically usable for about one month before being detected as stolen. The fraudulent user would then need to purchase a new number.

Interviewees stated that because of the large number of wireless telephones in use and the ease in which a large number of EINs could be captured, the process became one of "assembly line theft."[29] Essentially, a "client" pays a flat fee and receives a new billing number each month, or whenever the number they are using is canceled.[30] The "service provider" typically also has the computer equipment to readily reprogram the client's cell phone. Averaging about $30 a month ($60 if a "new" telephone is also obtained) with several hundred clients in a "territory" and several territories within a given geographic area, the profits can add up quickly and, again, with minimal risk.

The fourth type—which has increased significantly—is where organized crime groups have compromised private automatic branch exchanges (PABX) of companies to use telecommunications services for their own benefit.[31] A PABX is the heart of a digital telecommunications system that can include a company's internal phone system, its wireless network, voicemail, e-mail, and internal data network. A criminal enterprise using this system can call anywhere in the world without costs. Moreover, using a compromised system makes it more difficult for investigators to gain a wiretap order or to follow a trail of telephone calls. The growth of phreaking tools available on the Internet and the digital integration of voice and text on servers make this form of telecommunications increasingly accessible. Thus, unlawful use of a PABX not only constitutes a real monetary loss to the victim, it makes investigations of organized crime groups more difficult.

Theft of Identity

A rapidly growing type of crime is the theft of identity.[32] While there are numerous variations, essentially it occurs when someone uses personal information about an individual—usually a Social Security number, a credit card number, address and phone number—to represent him- or herself as that person for fraudulent purposes. Examples include obtaining credit cards and loans in someone else's name and then not paying the bills; opening utility accounts; renting an apartment; obtaining a wireless telephone; and so forth. In some instances, cars have also been purchased with false identities. Another type of identity theft—a worst-case scenario—is when the perpetrator commits a crime in the victim's name and gives that person a criminal record.[33] Stolen identities have also been used by people for flight to avoid prosecution as well as to hide in order to avoid such things as the civil process or creditors.

Because this information has become easily attainable and fraud is so easily committed using a stolen identity, the crime is profitable. Since law enforcement agencies have comparatively little experience investigating identity theft and because most identity theft involves fraudulent purchases for which there is insurance, the risk of being caught and prosecuted is low. Collectively, these factors are appealing to criminal enterprises.

> FORECAST 6: Terrorist groups will increasingly use global networking as a tool to accomplish their goals. This includes use of the Internet for surreptitious communications and coordination purposes as well as attempting to use network access to critical infrastructure systems to strike for their cause via the creation of chaos, disinformation, and file destruction—cyberterrorism.

The work of the National Infrastructure Protection Center (NIPC) clearly demonstrates the vulnerabilities of critical services in a modern society (see *www.fbi.gov/ nipc/index.htm*). Indeed, most countries studied in this research project had explored some aspect of concern for infrastructure protection from terrorists. Generally, critical infrastructure components include (1) the continuity of government services; (2) information and communications; (3) banking and finance; (4) electrical power, oil, and gas production/storage; (5) water supply; (6) public health services; (7) emergency services; and (8) transportation. Not surprisingly, most of these services in developed countries rely, in varying degrees, on computerization.

A recent intelligence assessment by the Central Intelligence Agency (CIA) noted that al Qaeda and other Sunni extremists are improving their ability to conduct cyber attacks. The report goes on to note that the Japanese terrorist group[34] that released sarin gas in a Tokyo subway, killing 12 people in 1995, appears to be aggressively developing computer skills that could be applied to cyber attacks.[35]

Beyond unlawful intrusions designed to disrupt computer systems, virtually all types of extremist groups—international and domestic—are relying on computers for everything from communicating to spreading propaganda to fundraising. It is reasonable to conclude that increasing numbers of these groups will, as computer skills and opportunities develop, become involved in some aspect of cyberterrorism or terroristic support. In light of these facts, what are the implications for state and local law enforcement with respect to cyberterrorism? The challenge seems daunting for a local police agency, yet given the omnipresence of computer networking and the ease with which one may digitally traverse the global in nanoseconds, local police must accept this as a part of the challenge they face.

As a consequence, examples of cyberterrorist activity may include use of information technology to organize and carry out attacks, support groups activities and perception-management campaigns. Experts agree that many terrorist groups such as al Qaeda and the Islamic militant group Hamas have adopted new information technology as a means to conduct operations without being detected by counterterrorist officials.[36] While not as inherently destructive, it may be argued that if networked communications are used to plan, organize, and execute a terrorist attack, the computer is as much of an instrumentality of terrorism as the bomb. If so, does that mean that anyone involved in these communications is equally liable (from a pure criminal law perspective) for a terrorist attack? Probably not—a lesser offense, such as conspiracy, would be more likely. As a result, the simple communications may not constitute cyberterrorism.

Clearly, the human tragedy of cyberterrorism does not approach that of traditional (physical) terror attacks. Yet the damage to assets, resources, and the fundamental principles of life in an open society for those who rely on such systems is significant. Indeed, *a successful cyber-attack can make people begin to question the sanctity, security and reliability of critical institutions on which we have daily reliance:* The proper functioning of our government and our banking systems are two important examples. If trust is lost in banks as a result of cyberterrorism, wherein bank balances are incorrectly reported, there is likely to be mass withdrawal of cash from the banks. Should this occur, the banking system could collapse. ATMs, credit cards, and checks could become worthless. Uncertainty about loans and investments would create chaos and people would be pushed into a "survival mode." This would clearly lead to a growth in fear and possibly violence as people attempt to protect their assets.

A cyberattack would not need to be nationwide to generate such fear and lack of confidence in public institutions—the attack would only need to be publicized. Fear is irrational—a factor which terrorists rely on. If a cyberattack is successful, it can create chaos, which will translate to fear and eventual destruction, or at least damage to, our critical infrastructure through distrust and failure to rely on institutions. Table 14.1 depicts different levels of seriousness of perpetrators committing similar types of Web intrusions. The legal implications based upon motive,[37] as manifest by the character of the attacker, vary significantly.

The growth of networked systems and ability of crackers to penetrate such systems are ingredients in a terroristic recipe which may lead to increasing levels of cyberterrorism. In all likelihood, this will also lead to an evolution of terroristic practice to include holding information or processes of a system hostage until a ransom is paid. Thus, the growth of this form of terrorism may include the growth of cyber

TABLE 14.1   Characterizations of a Cyberattack

Perpetrator	Intrusive Act	Legal Interpretation
Computer cracker	Defaces Web page of Internet service provider to protest increased fees	Criminal mischief or destruction of property
Racist group	Defaces Web page of a minority organization with racial epithets	Hate crime; possibly ethnic intimidation
Organized crime group	Changes address and contact information on Web page of a charitable organization so that contributions are sent to the crime group	Theft by a continuing criminal enterprise; possibly RICO violation
al Qaeda	Changes Web page of FBI, threatening future attacks against Americans similar to 9/11	Terrorism/terroristic threat

kidnapping. Indeed, the Strategic Intelligence section of the Criminal Intelligence Service Ontario, Canada (CISO) has documented that organized crime and terrorist groups are involved in cybercrime. The CISO notes that these groups had collected over £200 million UK Sterling ($330 million USD) internationally by holding computer networks hostage.[38] The diversity of terrorism by computer will no doubt continue to grow.

FORECAST 7: The character of espionage will continue to broaden into the arenas of information warfare, economic espionage, and theft of intellectual property.

A U.S. Department of Defense study on emerging threats to national security observed that the field of battle is increasingly moving away from political ideology and geographic control and toward economic issues.[39] The essence of national security is to maintain the homeostasis of a country's sovereign principles and socioeconomic health. In a global economy punctuated by multinational corporations and international dependence, that homeostasis is inextricably related to economic stability.

In making a link between cyber-criminality and national security, the Director of the U.S. Defense Intelligence Agency (DIA) observed:

> I am increasingly concerned about . . . international criminal activity, for instance "cyber-criminals" who attempt to exploit the electronic underpinnings of the global financial, commercial, and capital market systems, and nationally based "Mafia" groups who seek to undermine legitimate governments in states like Russia and Nigeria. Globally, criminal cartels are becoming more sophisticated at exploiting technology, developing or taking control of legitimate commercial activities, and seeking to directly influence—through infiltration, manipulation, and bribery—local, state, and national governments, legitimate transnational organizations, and businesses. Increased cooperation between independent criminal elements, including terrorist organizations, is likely (Hughes, 1999: Senate testimony).

Global networking adds an important dimension to this problem. John Chambers, President and CEO of Cisco Systems, a leader in producing networking hardware and software, stated, "The Internet levels the playing field between countries . . . regardless of size or political form of government, in a way that has never occurred before." Thus, the threat to national security is significantly increased as we move toward digital economies. Government policy in Malaysia, Thailand, and Singapore are expressly developing technology centers to become major economic sectors of the global e-economy. A number of countries—notably Japan, China, and France—provide government support to businesses based in their countries through assistance with the surreptitious acquisition of intellectual property. Clearly, with the emergence of global networking and the digital economy, the greatest target threat for economic espionage is through cyber attacks on business networks rather than on government installations.

FORECAST 8: Criminals, terrorists, and anarchists will increasingly use technology-based instruments and methodologies which can surreptitiously capture data/information or destroy technological communications, information processing and/or storage appliances.

Part of the forecasting process is applying inductive logic to known facts. That logic is based on evidence and the reasonable extension of that evidence to a future state. The authors emphasize this point in the current forecast in light of three important factors. First, all of the technologies discussed in this forecast currently exist—in some cases, for at least two decades or more—yet they were not readily (or even feasibly) usable by criminals or terrorists because of technological complexities and/or limitations. Second, the exceptionally rapid evolution of computer-related technology and miniaturization of hardware and components in the past few years is making these offensive weapons more accessible and easier to use. These factors, coupled with the fiscal resources of criminal enterprises and "wealthy" terrorists,[40] make the development and use of these offensive weapons more probable. Finally, the wide adoption of computers for communications, commerce, information distribution, information management, and the integration of computer technology into everything from wireless telephones to automobiles, magnifies the potential impact electronic weapons can have on a business, government, or individuals.

As reported to the authors, experiences of both investigators who target sophisticated criminals and intelligence professionals (both national security and corporate) demonstrate the willingness of criminals to gain an advantage over legitimate businesses and processes in any manner possible. For example, drug cartels have been found to use sophisticated weapons, surveillance devices, and intelligence techniques in order to maintain their competitive advantage in the drug trade, whether by undermining competition or attempting to corrupt officials. Since, as discussed previously, criminals are already taking advantage of computers and high-technology communications, it is reasonable to assume they will also adopt technologies which can surreptitiously capture information and/or incapacitate communications, surveillance, and information systems of government entities and businesses.

Electromagnetic Impulse and High Energy Radio Frequency[41]

The phenomenon known as an electromagnetic impulse (EMP) was discovered in the 1940s during the testing of nuclear weapons. Essentially, the EMP disabled electrical devices as a result of the massive electromagnetic field created by the nuclear blast. Research on this phenomenon led to the discovery that an EMP could also be produced by generating a High Energy Radio Frequency (HERF), typically by using a truck-sized device. The impact of a HERF electromagnetic emission is that any electronic "equipment can be irreversibly damaged or in effect electronically destroyed . . . and may require complete replacement of the equipment."[42] Not only are computers and peripherals subject to destruction by HERF, but so are ". . . radios, satellites, microwave equipment, UHF, VHF, HF, and low band communications and television equipment."[43]

The HERF effect is real, with substantial research on its development as an electronic warfare tool in the United States, England and Russia and speculated research on HERF as a weapon in China. The research is not focusing on creating an EMP, per se, but on accurate targeting and miniaturization.[44] Indeed, there has been research in the law enforcement community on the use of HERF as a less-than-lethal weapon which could be used to disable fleeing vehicles. There has also been a wide range of experimentation—typically unsuccessful—by hobbyists in developing homemade, handheld HERF devices. The probability is high that functional and portable HERF devices will be developed in the short term. Just as weapons ranging from machine guns to surface-to-air missiles have found their way to organized crime groups and terrorists, so will HERF technologies. The destructive impact such weapons could have is evident, from disabling communications systems and computers in police cars to disrupting the computers of the New York Stock Exchange: The systems do not need to be hacked, nor does physical entry have to be gained—simply the transmission of a High Energy Radio Frequency which will not harm people, but will destroy or disable every electrical device in its range from coffee pots to computers.

In addition to HERF, there is development of Low Energy Radio Frequency (LERF) devices which are less damaging, but can disrupt communications and data systems through "jamming" the signals. Whether used by a criminal to disrupt communications during a surveillance, by a terrorist to disrupt air traffic control communications at a busy airport, or by a speeder trying to disrupt radar, these devices could also have a significant impact.

Fortunately, research has also explored promising ways to minimize the effects of HERF and LERF attacks (such as encasing computers in a wire mesh shroud to absorb the RF signal). The point to note is that EMP weapons are on the horizon and will eventually be in the hands of criminals. Plans for protecting assets, preventing attacks, recovering from attacks, and investigating offenders must be developed.

Compromising Electronic Emanations and TEMPEST/Emissions Security (EMSEC)[45]

The capture of Compromising Electronic Emanations (CEE), which has been fully classified by the National Security Agency (NSA) for roughly ten years, permits the surreptitious capture of electromagnetic signals emanating from computers. Also known as Van Eck phreaking in the hacking/phreaking community, the system works by capturing the computer's keystrokes, which are transmitted to the display (monitor). Each character (or keystroke) emits a unique characteristic which can be received with the proper equipment. By capturing these emanations, whatever was displayed on the target computer can also be read on the equipment of the CEE user.

The use of such devices for surveillance and espionage are obvious. A person with CEE equipment may be sitting outside a building surreptitiously capturing information from a target's computer. Just as there are privacy concerns with this technology, there are also concerns when CEE technology reaches the hands of criminals. Beyond gathering confidential information—such as intellectual property—information could be used for blackmail, the basis for corruption, to undermine investigations, and to identify confidential informants or undercover personnel.

The implications for abuse of this technology are pervasive. What is the potential for this technology to become available for criminals? According to intelligence and law enforcement personnel interviewed in both Europe and Asia, the potential is quite high. One high-ranking police official in Asia told the authors that his organization has learned that wealthy drug traffickers in a neighboring country of the Golden Triangle had gained access to CEE equipment. While being used by criminals, the police official stated that his agency did *not* have this technology.

Electronic filters and interference devices can be defenses to Van Eck phreaking. However, at present the CEE threat is not sufficiently severe to warrant widespread adoption of these defenses. Technological development of the systems and defenses are ongoing. Suffice it to note there is a "dark side" to every technological development, that will be exploited by criminals.

Malicious Software

Malicious software (or code) refers to viruses, worms, Trojan horses, logic bombs, and other "uninvited" software designed to disrupt a computer's operations or destroy files.[46] Information—frequently hoaxes[47]—about malicious software traverses the Internet pervasively. News stories about viruses such as Melissa, Explore.zip, and potential millenium viruses are found frequently in the popular media. The effect of a virus can range from being an inconvenience to the destruction of data, as evidenced by the wide range of documentation about the thousands of computer viruses and their effects.[48] The point to note is that malicious software is widespread and widely available on the Internet, with new viruses being created regularly.[49] While it appears most viruses are developed or introduced as a bent sense of entertainment, evidence reported to the authors indicated that malicious software had been used in espionage cases—either to destroy information or conceal evidence of information theft—and was being examined as a tool of information warfare.

Concerns about viruses should be particularly focused on those which are based in "mobile code." This code travels a network and is automatically executed on client machines, enabling users to download highly useful applets.[50] One computer security expert in Hong Kong expressed his concern about this software to the authors by noting that "Java is an active virus code with a marketing budget." The concern is that using mobile code, malicious software could be introduced into a system more passively; it would be more difficult to detect; and would be capable of causing greater damage. If active code can be used to develop and introduce viruses, it will clearly happen.

According to Brandt,[51] viruses will become a pervasive threat. As an illustration, he reports,

> . . . a virus that works through a screen saver called Pretty-Park.exe. Click on the application which comes as an e-mail attachment and, if you are an mIRC user, the virus enters your computer to steal network passwords and other data, then attaches itself to out going e-mail.[52]

For the purposes of this discussion, the significant point to note is that malicious software may become a tool of criminal offenders and terrorists, particularly if the capacity of mobile code is exploited for virus creation. When used as a weapon, the viruses and their effects will be more purposive, more destructive, and more widespread. Going beyond being an irritant, as malicious software is currently viewed, as an electronic weapon, malicious software could conceivably create a virtual epidemic in a system which would result in disruption of operations, likely data loss, chaos, and expenses required for repair. All of these effects would serve the goals of terrorists and criminals alike.

OVERARCHING FACTORS CONTRIBUTING TO THESE FORECASTS

The hyper-evolution of technology and networking are fueling not only e-commerce and communications, but the technological parameters of these trends. For example, growth of wireless local area networks (WLANs) has not only increased mobile computing, it has made networks easier to penetrate by outsiders. One example is "war driving," where persons drive through a community with a wireless network card in a laptop computer activated in order to detect the presence of a wireless network.[53] The "war drivers" then attempt to access the network—often successfully—and use this as a portal to the Internet. Less scrupulous users will also attempt to penetrate the network's computers—essentially a "drive-by hacking." Interestingly, wireless networks are fairly easy to penetrate because they are frequently "open" with no security, apparently to make it easier for the network's users; of course, this makes it easier for the intruder also.

Another technological trend is the increased availability of wireless micro-integrated and multifunction devices that have increased storage and networking capacity. The most common illustration of this is the integrated wireless telephone and personal digital assistant (PDA). Given the types of information often kept in PDAs—ranging from credit card numbers to passwords to Social Security numbers and various types of account and financial information—the ability to access this information using a combination of "phreaking tools" and PDA operating system exploits by intruders is a threat to be reckoned with. The presence of these devices, integrated with WLANs, and combined with the growth of e-commerce and e-government, make the probability of technological criminality even more pervasive.

Finally, there is a significant growth in the number of home computers using broadband access to the Internet. Generally speaking, whenever these computers are booted, they are connected to the Web, whether being used or not by the owner. Moreover, home computers are less likely to have security (such as a firewall), or if they have security, it is usually a form that is easier to penetrate. Hackers, using port scanners, can identify computers connected to the Web and can conceivably access personal and financial information. If, for example, a person manages their banking account and pays bills using a program such as QuickBooks, then the intruder could easily access those files and obtain a significant amount of information that could be used in frauds or other forms of identity theft. Essentially, the growth in capacity, speed, and ease of computerization and networking will also contribute to the speed of exploitation by offenders. The brief history of computer crime has shown that offenders are faster and more adaptable than law enforcement in using the technology.

SUMMARY

Organizations—public and private alike—must be made aware of the real threat posed by technology-related abuses and its impact on both crime and national security. One of the greatest challenges in this process is the willingness of organizations and people to be alert to changing criminal trends and devote resources to address emerging problems. As part of this change process, there must be development of new law and policy where voids exist. Policy should include regular development of both strategic and tactical intelligence as related to the integrated criminal and national security threats posed through computer crime and its evolution. Similarly, there must be a body of both civil and criminal law developed which expressly addresses the unique elements of cybercrime. This includes attending to the issues of transnational criminality and the ambiguities of attaching value to information and intellectual property. In addition, effective policy must address security, prevention, investigation, prosecution, and damage recovery of electronic property. There must also be a new standard of personnel development to ensure employees have skills necessary to deal with computer and technology-related crime. These include knowledge of security issues, processes, and practices; investigative techniques; and the capacity to perform forensic analysis of electronic evidence.

Global crime issues require global strategies. In this regard, it would be advisable to have a transnational working group of police; national security; and relevant commerce, security and regulatory groups to help guide efforts in the prevention, investigation, and prosecution of computer-related crime. With the furious pace of technological development coupled with the global growth of e-commerce, networked computers are increasingly becoming as commonly used as the telephone. Dogmatism and traditional beliefs that "this is not a problem" must be set aside and replaced with an aggressive policy to address these trends. To help remedy this dogmatism, there needs to be empirical data collection and analysis on computer criminality to define the problem more accurately, map trends, and fully understand the character of the offenses and offenders. While exploration of hardware and software system protection is important, as is operational security of computers, research must go beyond this. Defining behaviorally based prevention, exploring the cybercrime equivalent of crime "hot spots," developing a catalog of best practices for investigation and prosecution of computer crime, and researching crime control methodologies in a fashion similar to predatory crime are all strategies where emerging research must focus. As with any forecast, neither a timetable nor certitude can be provided. A forecast is probabilistic; however, there is strong evidence supporting the evolution of cybercrime as described in here. A willingness by public officials to openly explore the feasibility of these forecasts is warranted.

REVIEW QUESTIONS

1. What are the biggest problems facing the criminal justice system in the area of computer crime?
2. What are the reasons why cyber victimization is likely to increase in the future?
3. What types of computer crimes are going to become more prevalent in the future?

4. Describe the mechanisms and tactics terrorist organizations are likely to use in the future.
5. Which of the forecasts described in this chapter is most likely to come to pass? Which of the forecasts is least likely to come true? Why?

ENDNOTES

1. SIKELLIS, R. (1999). *Guarding Against High Technology Crimes.* DSFX, International. Posted on the corporate Web site at *www.dsfx.com/html/hi_tech.html*
2. This estimate is likely skewed by single incidents involving large values, reported in statistical means. Reporting the data using the median would probably provide a more accurate measure of central tendency of these losses.
3. Computer Security Institute (1999). *Issues and Trends: 1999 CSI/FBI Computer Crime and Security Survey.* San Francisco: Computer Security Institute.
4. The *National Center for Computer Crime Data* (1222-17th Avenue; Santa Cruz, CA 95062; 408.475.4457) is a private entity which seeks to document cybercrime. Reports are voluntary and there appear to be no controls for validity and reliability. While the center can provide anecdotal evidence, there are significant methodological problems to permit any form of meaningful analysis or generalization of trends.
5. Those persons interviewed were primarily from North America, Europe, and Asia as well as five from Africa. Persons were selected for the interviews based on their knowledge and experience in light of the positions they hold with their organizations. The researchers were given access to a wide range of investigative reports and documents. A content analysis was completed with these materials to the extent possible. In a few cases the authors were permitted to read and take notes from the documents, but not copy them. "Electronic interviews" were also conducted with three self-described hackers. This was essentially an exchange of e-mail of persons who were identified through their own hacker Web sites. A content analysis of hacked Web sites was conducted to identify trends or characteristics which reinforced information gathered through the interviews and e-mail exchanges. A content analysis was also done of hacker "prophiles" (sic) and hacker articles contained in Phrack, the on-line hacker electronic magazine (*see www.phrack.com*). With respect to reporting results, because of regulations for the protection of human subjects and the critical nature of information involved in this study—frequently of a "classified" or "confidential" nature—interviewees were guaranteed confidentiality in their specific responses to questions. In some cases, the persons interviewed permitted use of their comments and in other cases comments were stated in an open forum. In these instances, the comments were attributed by position and affiliation.
6. More likely than not having the data available, was that the data was not readily accessible without research and compilation by the organization.
7. CARTER, D.L. and A.J. KATZ (1999). "Computer applications by international organized crime groups." In L. MORIARITY and D.L. CARTER, *Criminal Justice Technology in the 21st Century.* Springfield, IL: Charles C Thomas, Publisher.
8. One investigator stated that he worked closely with the department's narcotics officers and urged them to seize computers as part of asset forfeitures. He would help the narcotics officers and in turn "maintain custody" of the computer equipment for use in forensic analysis. (N.B.: Hard drives are required in forensic computer analysis in order to "mirror" a seized system. This way, analysis of the memory's contents can be made without jeopardizing the integrity of the originally seized system.)

9. There is precedence for charging fees and placing responsibility on citizens. For example, many jurisdictions charge fines or service fees for police responses to false burglar alarms. In another illustration, the Arlington, Texas Police Department does not dispatch officers to "gas drive-offs" at convenience stores because a prepay policy can prevent that crime.

10. The Tampa Division of the Florida Department of Law Enforcement (FDLE) has organized the computer forensic analyst in the Crime Laboratory section, treating it the same as other forensic evidence analysis.

11. Information Security (2000). *By the Numbers.* (January)12.

12. A good source of information on Internet fraud schemes can be found at the National Fraud Information Center: *www.fraud.org/welcome.htm.* Information is also available through searching the U.S. Federal Trade Commission Web site: *www.ftc.gov*

13. National Criminal Intelligence Service (1999). *Project Trawler: Crime on the Information Highways.* An NCIS project report. London.

14. U.S. Department of Justice (1999). *Cyberstalking: A New Challenge for Law Enforcement and Industry.* A report to the Vice-President. *www.usdoj.gov/ag/cyberstalkingreport.htm*

15. The Simple Mail Transfer Protocol (SMTP) audit trail can give a wide range of information about the sender of e-mail: the sender's name, e-mail address, Internet service provider, e-mail client software, date, time, etc. There are Web sites which offer the service of hiding this information and sending an audit trail with e-mail which "can't be traced." For example, see *The Anonymizer, www.anonymizer.com*; *Hushmail, www.hushmail.com*; or *Disappearing Inc., www.disappearing.com*

16. Note the alphanumeric combinations in the text; a characteristic commonly seen in hacker written communications. Instead of using their names, hackers tend to use "handles"such as Coolio, KnightLightning, Doom Prophet, Lex Luthor, Dr. Cypher, The Mentor, or Doc Holiday.

17. *Security Wire Digest* (1999). Vol. 1, No. 6 (on line at *www.infosecuritymag.com/newsletter*)

18. Federal Bureau of Investigation (1999). *CyberNotes.* Vol. 3, pp. 1–13.

19. The frequently cited hacker ethic was written by Stephen Levy in *Hackers: Heroes of the Computer Revolution,* Bantam Books, 1984. Commonly found on hacker Web sites today, the ethical "canons" state (*project.cyberpunk.ru/idb/hacker_ethics.html*):
    - Access to computers should be unlimited and total.
    - Always yield to the hands-on imperative.
    - All information should be free.
    - Mistrust authority—promote decentralization.
    - Hackers should be judged by their hacking.
    - You can create art and beauty on a computer.
    - Computers can change your life for the better.

20. The statement was made in an interview on *CNN Talk Back Live,* February 9, 2000.

21. CARTER, D.L. (1994). "International organized crime: Emerging trends in entrepreneurial crime." *Journal of Contemporary Criminal Justice* (10)4, pp. 239–266.

22. TOFFLER, A. (1980). *The Third Wave.* New York: Bantam Press.

23. TOFFLER, A. (1990). *PowerShift.* New York: Bantam Press.

24. In the vernacular of Fourth Amendment search and seizure law, precise descriptions are needed to meet the constitutional standard showing the accused possessed "particularly described property" which is contraband.

25. CARTER, D.L. (1994). "International organized crime: Emerging trends in entrepreneurial crime." *Journal of Contemporary Criminal Justice* (10)4, pp. 239–266.

26. SANDHU, H. (1999). "Underground banking and alternative remittance systems." *INTERPOL and Technology in Partnership.* London: Kensington Publications Limited.

27. The new European Union passport is particularly popular for counterfeiters.
28. While this was clearly the perception of interviewees in Europe and Asia, interviews with U.S. officials and security professionals were not as specific. It is unclear if this means that in the United States there is less organized crime targeting of intellectual property or whether criminal enterprises target intellectual property in the United States and it has either not been discovered or not reported.
29. A telephone does not have to be in use, but simply turned on, in order to emit the EIN.
30. Traffickers in stolen wireless telephones and number recommend that a stolen number not be used over one month in case it is being traced by investigators.
31. Federal Bureau of Investigation (1999). *CyberNotes* (3) pp. 1–13.
32. Information related to protection and responses to identity theft can be found at *www.consumer.gov/idtheft*
33. Public Interest Research Group (1999). *Identity Theft II: Return to the Consumer X-Files.* PIRG Report on line at *www.igc.org/pirg/consumer/xfiles/index.htm*
34. Formerly known as Aum Shirinikyo, and now known as Aleph.
35. TENET, G. (2002). Testimony of Intelligence Threats. Senate Intelligence Committee, U.S. Congress. *http://www.odci.gov/press*
36. *Ibid.*
37. Motive is typically not an element (i.e., part of the *corpus delecti*) of a crime; hence, while it can be presented in court, it is not required. Nonetheless, demonstrating the motive can aggravate or mitigate the actual crime charged as well as the severity of the penalty.
38. HAGERMAN, C. (1998). *Introduction to Technology Crime.* Toronto: Criminal Intelligence Service Ontario.
39. When NATO began bombing Serbia in March 1999, Serbian hackers began a low-level campaign of harassment directed at the U.S. government and military groups involved in the NATO actions. The "Black Hand" hacker group and the "Serbian Angels" hacker group threatened to damage NATO computers in retaliation for the war against the Serbs. On March 29, the White House Web site was defaced by red letters reading "Hackerz wuz Here." It was speculated that anti-NATO activists were involved. On March 30, hackers damaged a NATO Web server, forcing it off line for a short time. *Information Security* (December, 1999), p. 26.
40. The wealth amassed by drug dealers has purchased a wide array of sophisticated technology and the services of people—frequently intelligence personnel from the security services of the former Soviet bloc countries—to use these technologies to further their enterprises and avoid prosecution. Similar wealth has purportedly furthered terroristic acts, such as terrorism networks supported from Afghanistan by Osama Bin Laden.
41. The authors reinforce the point that our focus is on *behavioral applications* of the weapons discussed in this section. Details on the development and mechanics of the technologies are available from a wide range of sources.
42. KOPP, C. (1999). *The E-Bomb: A Weapon of Electrical Mass Destruction.* A paper posted on the Web site of the Department of Computer Science, Monash University, Australia. *www.cs.monash.edu.au/~carlo/*
43. *Ibid.*
44. Miniaturization of a HERF weapon to a handheld size appears probable. As a comparison: A laptop computer that can be purchased by mail order today has more processing speed, more memory, and more diverse capacity (such as audio and video) than a state-of-the-art mainframe computer of 1980 which required an entire room with strict environmental controls to be housed.

45. Much of the information in this section is based on a confidential interview with two intelligence specialists—one from the United States and one overseas—familiar with this technology. The reader is also referred to the *TEMPEST Information Page* on the Internet at *www.eskimo.com/~joelm/tempest.html*, which contains a great deal of information released from the U.S. National Security Agency (NSA) through Freedom of Information Act requests.

46. Computer Systems Laboratory Bulletin (1994). *Malicious Software Information Bulletin*. Washington: Computer Security Resource Clearinghouse, National Institute of Standards and Technology. *csrc.nist.gov/nistbul/csl94-03.txt*

47. SYMANTEC corporation operates a comprehensive and easy-to-use Web site for checking information about a virus to determine if it is a hoax. See *www.sarc.com/avcenter/hoax.html*

48. The European Institute for Computer Anti-Virus Research is an excellent source for ongoing information about computer viruses. See *www.eicar.org/*. See also the U.S. Computer Security Research Center Web site for virus information at *csrc.ncsl.nist.gov/virus/* and the Computer Emergency Response Center at *www.cert.org*

49. Web sites where a virus may be downloaded are typically accompanied with a disclaimer that the code is available for educational and security purposes only. See, for example: *www2.spidernet.net/web/~cvrl/*

    Hacker Web sites will also frequently have viruses for downloading. See *www2.netdoor.com/~rickn/haax.html*

50. CLARK, E. (1999). "Mobile code safety." *Network Magazine* (14)12, p. 37.

51. BRANDT, A. (2000). "Tomorrow's digital diseases." *PC World.* (January)130.

52. *Ibid.*

53. See *http://www.wardriving.com/* for a good understanding of the practice and the culture.

Index